Business Calculator Operations

Joan Elizabeth Warner
The University of Akron

Reston Publishing Company, Inc.
A Prentice-Hall Company
Reston, Virginia

Library of Congress Cataloging in Publication Data

Warner, Joan Elizabeth
  Business calculator operations.

  Includes index.
  1. Calculating-machines—Problems, exercises, etc. I. Title.
HF5688.W37   651.8'2   77-20664
ISBN 0-87909-097-9

© 1978 by Reston Publishing Company, Inc.
A Prentice-Hall Company
Reston, Virginia 22090

No part of this book may be reproduced in any way, or by any means, without permission in writing from the publisher.

10 9 8 7 6 5 4 3 2 1

Printed in the United States of America

Contents

PREFACE vii

INTRODUCTION 1

Importance of Office Machines and Data Entry, **1** Techniques for Successful Machine Operation, **1** Basic Mathematics Pretest, **2** Basic Mathematics Review, **4** Fractions, **17** Percent, **27** Sample Unit Examinations, **30**

Unit 1 THE TOUCH SYSTEM FOR TEN-KEY OFFICE MACHINES 93

Proficiency Test, **95** The Home Row, **98** Fingering Drills—Home Row, **98** Timed Stroking Drill 1, **99** Fingering Drills—First Row, **101** Fingering Drills—Third Row, **103** Fingering Drills—First Column, **104** Fingering Drills—Second Column, **105** Fingering Drills—Third Column, **106** Fingering Drills—Diagonals, **108** Timed Stroking Drill 2, **109** Fingering Drills—1-9 Keys, **110** Fingering Drills—Zeros, **112** Fingering Drills—Three Figures, **114** The Touch Method—Decimals, **115** The Touch System—Dollars and Cents Practice, **117** Timed Stroking Drill 3, **118** Review Quiz 1, **119**

Unit 2 ELECTRONIC CALCULATOR BASIC OPERATIONS 120

Touch System Review, **120** Decimal Settings and Round-Off, **122** Credit Balances, **126** Addition and Subtraction, **128** Repeated Addition, **130** Repeated Subtraction, **132** Addition and Subtraction of Fractions, **133** Subtotals, **136** Non-Add Function, **138** Multiplication, **139** Three-Factor Multiplication, **140** Division, **141** Mixed Problems, **142** Decision Problem, **146** Review Quiz 2, **147**

Unit 3 ELECTRONIC CALCULATOR PERCENT APPLICATIONS 148

Touch System Review, **148** Finding the Percentage of a Number, **150** Finding the Number if the Percent is Known, **152** Finding What Percent One

Number is of Another, **154** Percent of the Whole, **156** Proration, **159** Percent of Increase or Decrease, **164** Chain Discount, **166** Cash Discounts, **168** Sales Taxes, **171** City Taxes, **174** Simple Interest, **177** Decision Problem, **179** Review Quiz 3, **180**

Unit 4 BUSINESS PROBLEMS 182

Touch System Review, **182** Cost of Items, **184** Extensions and Crossfooting, **185** Finding the Amount of Simple Interest, **191** Interest—Finding the Interest Period in Days, **191** Interest—Finding the Rate of Interest, **192** Compound Interest, **193** Figuring Compound Interest With the Table, **194** Amount of Markon and Total Cost, **195** Percent of Markon, **198** Percent of Selling Price, **200** Finding the Selling Price, **200** Markup, **201** Markdown, **202** Sales Commission, **203** Payroll—Wages With Overtime, **204** Payroll—Piecework Rates, **206** Salary and Hourly Wages After Taxes and Other Deductions, **206** FICA, **207** Salary Increases, **210** Insurance—Percent Insured, **210** Insurance—Cost of Premium, **211** Long-Term Premiums, **212** Promissory Notes—Maturity Date and Maturity Value, **213** Promissory Notes—Discounting and Proceeds, **214** Banking—Checking Accounts, **215** Deposit Slips, **216** Reconciling Bank Balances, **218** Decision Problem, **220** Review Quiz 4, **221**

Unit 5 PRACTICAL PROBLEMS 223

Touch System Review, **223** Installment Buying, **225** Installment Loans, **227** Real Estate—Taxes, **229** Real Estate—Total Price, **229** Profit Margin on Services, **230** Stocks—Dividend Yield per Share, **231** Stocks—Purchases, **231** Stocks—Earnings per Share, **232** Stocks—Current Ratio, **233** Bonds—Market Value, **233** Bonds—Interest, **234** Depreciation—Straight-Line Method, **235** Depreciation—Sum-of-the-Digits Method, **235** Depreciation—Declining Balance Method, **236** Unit Prices, **239** Basic Statistics, **240** Grouped Data, **242** Travel—Miles per Gallon and Miles per Hour, **246** Travel—Air, **247** Monetary Exchange, **247** Measure and Cost, **248** Inventory Valuation, **249** Income Statements, **250** Decision Problem, **252** Review Quiz 5, **253**

Unit 6 THE INTERNATIONAL SYSTEM OF UNITS (SI) 254

Touch System Review, **254** Prefixes, **256** Abbreviations, **257** Metric Weight, **257** Metric Length, **266** Metric Area, **271** Metric Volume, **275** English-Metric Conversions, **277** The Celsius Thermometer, **282** Review Quiz 6, **286**

CONTENTS v

Unit 7 THE PROGRAMMABLE ELECTRONIC CALCULATOR **289**

Touch System Review, **289** Basic Operations, **291** Using Prerecorded Programs, **306**

Unit 8 TEN-KEY ADDING AND LISTING MACHINES **312**

Decimals, **312** Addition, **313** Subtraction, **315** Credit Balances, **317** Non-Add Feature, **317** Subtotals, **318** Multiplication, **319** Multiplication With Zeros, **321** Multiplication with Decimals, **321** Short-Cut Multiplication, **322** Amount of Markon, **324** Division, **325**

Unit 9 TEN-KEY PRINTING CALCULATORS **327**

Addition, **327** Subtotals, **329** Subtraction, **330** Credit Balances, **331** Non-Add Feature, **332** Multiplication, **333** Division, **334** Multiplication of a Percent, **335** Finding What Percent One Number is of Another, **336** Constant Multiplication, **337** Payroll, **339** Markon, **340** Markup, **341** Markdown, **342**

Unit 10 FULL-BANK ADDING MACHINE **344**

Entering Amounts, **344** Error Correction, **344** Decimals, **344** Addition, **345** Double Addition, **347** Subtraction, **348** Credit Balances, **349** Non-Add Feature, **351** Subtotals, **351** Multiplication, **353** Division, **355**

Appendix A DECIMAL EQUIVALENTS OF COMMON FRACTIONS **357**
Appendix B TABLE OF RECIPROCALS **359**
Appendix C COMPOUND INTEREST TABLE **362**
Appendix D CHAIN DISCOUNT EQUIVALENTS **365**
Appendix E METRIC CONVERSIONS **367**
Appendix F ANSWERS TO EVEN-NUMBERED PROBLEMS **370**

GLOSSARY **422**

Preface

Today inquiry-response and data entry systems on standard ten-key entry devices are widespread. The importance of handling numerical data quickly and accurately cannot be overemphasized. Proficiency in office machines is an invaluable aid in achieving success in a business career and in managing your own personal finances.

Business Calculator Operations will enable you to learn how to solve problems on electronic calculators, both desk-top and hand-held models; on ten-key adding machines and printing calculators; on full-keyboard adding machines; and on programmable electronic calculators. In addition you will become familiar with many business procedures, learn how to solve a variety of business problems, and strengthen your general mathematical ability. Since simple, detailed step-by-step directions are given for learning the basic processes, this book is nearly self-teaching. The learner can make progress by working on his own as well as in a class. The instructor is saved from the trying-to-be-everywhere-at-once syndrome, and each learner can work and progress at his own pace.

The book lends itself to battery, rotation, and lecture-laboratory methods of teaching office machines. Because the problem-solving units involve a rather thorough review of basic mathematics and business mathematics procedures, the text correlates with and strengthens the student's understanding of topics covered in business mathematics courses.

The Introduction includes illustrations of typical tape, display, and combination tape-display calculators used in business; it also presents overall techniques for successful machine operation, a thorough review of basic mathematics, and sample examinations. Unit 1 makes possible job-level proficiency in the touch system for ten-key calculators. Touch operation is purposefully reviewed throughout the text. Units 2, 8, 9, and 10 clearly present basic operations and include a large number of practice problems so that the learner can make these processes automatic and build speed.

The reasoning problems in Units 3, 4, and 5 challenge the student by presenting actual business and practical problems as well as the use of business forms. The learner solves problems of percent, simple and compound interest, markon, markup, markdown, payroll, taxes, insurance, banking, installment buying, real estate, stocks and bonds, depreciation, proration, chain discounts, basic statistics, and monetary exchange.

In the lifetime of today's students, the metric system will become standard.

After completing Unit 6 on SI (the metric system), the reader will be able to work comfortably in the commonly used measurements in this system.

Unit 7 introduces the student to the programmable calculator, which is used extensively for such applications as banking, installment buying, and engineering problems.

Appendixes include a table of decimal equivalents of common fractions, table of reciprocals, compound interest table, table of chain discount net equivalents, metric conversion tables, and the answers to the even-numbered problems in the text. A teacher's manual, which includes examinations, is provided separately.

The author is indebted to Professor James Bell of The University of Akron; Mr. John DiSabato of the Office Equipment Company; representatives of Marchant, Victor, Texas Instruments, and Monroe for their help in the preparation of this book; and to the students who helped her test it.

The author would also like to thank the following reviewers, whose comments were helpful in the development of the manuscript: Jane H. Adams, Essex Community College; Sallie Branscom, Virginia Western Community College; Adele Jones, St. Louis Community College at Florissant Valley; and Sheldon Somerstein, Queensborough Community College.

Introduction

IMPORTANCE OF OFFICE MACHINES AND DATA ENTRY

In our world, where man communicates with computers and computers transmit to each other, data entry and the ability to handle numerical data quickly and accurately make proficiency in office machines more important and necessary than ever before.

Inquiry-response and data entry systems on standard ten-key entry devices are common in business. Today's ten-key calculators are being tied in with data communications systems. Optical font characters from ten-key calculator tapes are optically scanned and fed into the computer with no intermediate encapsulating or capturing of the data being necessary.

When companies spend over a billion and a half dollars a year in order to transmit data at speeds as high as 56,000 bits per second, rapid data entry and rapid handling of numerical data on the part of office workers are needed and expected. Today, when one error entered into a complex data communications system can multiply itself a hundred times in a hundred places, office workers more than ever need to be able to handle ten-key and other office equipment with a high degree of accuracy and expertise.

A learner who uses this text properly will become proficient in the touch system for all types of ten-key machines, will learn to operate ten-key calculators (including hand-held ones) and full-keyboard adding machines, will become familiar with the programmable calculator, will learn how to solve many types of business problems, will gain a better understanding of business procedures, and will improve his general mathematical ability.

TECHNIQUES FOR SUCCESSFUL MACHINE OPERATION

To become a skilled office machines operator,

1. Remember that your attitude, as much as your ability, will determine your success in acquiring skill.
2. Read and follow instructions carefully. Study Figures 1 through 7. These illustrations of typical calculators define for you the function keys.

3. Cover as much material as you can each time you sit down to practice.
4. Begin immediately to learn ten-key machines by touch. *Never* use incorrect fingering, since this will keep you from acquiring speed.
5. Develop speed and accuracy in entering numbers and adding on ten-key machines. The majority of the figure work in offices today is addition and multiplication.
6. Realize that there is no substitute for deliberate, repetitive practice to develop speed and accuracy in touch operation.
7. Train yourself to look at the entire number in groups rather than as individual digits within the number; for example, read and record $861.73 as 861/73, not as 8, 6, 1, 7, 3.
8. Decide if your answers are reasonable ones. For example, if your problem is to discount a $90 item by 10% and 5%, it is clear that an answer of $769.50 is incorrect. You couldn't be expected to pay *more* than the original cost!
9. Realize that the decimal point is the most important part of your answer. There is a world of difference between $55.34 and $5,534.
10. Try for 100 percent accuracy all the time. Never sacrifice accuracy for speed.
11. Sit up straight with both feet on the floor to improve performance and reduce fatigue. Place the calculator at a height and angle comfortable for you.
12. Be sure to write down all your answers quickly and neatly, with the figures and decimals properly aligned. There is a correlation between careless writing and careless thinking when working with numerical data.
13. Remember to indicate credit balances by including a minus sign in your answer or the abbreviation *Cr* for credit balance. It certainly makes a big difference whether you have $49.69 in the bank or are overdrawn at the bank by $49.69.
14. Strive for speed with *accuracy*. However, at times it is desirable to check the figures against the tape. Remove the tape and check each amount against the original data.
15. Care for your machine. Always turn off your electronic calculator when you are finished working. Protect all machines by keeping them covered when not in use. Help prevent *your* calculator from malfunctioning!

BASIC MATHEMATICS PRETEST

A thorough knowledge of basic mathematics is essential for solving the business problems you encounter in both your personal and your professional life. An understanding of basic mathematical concepts and number relationships will enable you to handle your own finances wisely.

In order to assess your fundamental mathematical skill, do the following basic mathematics test by longhand. Round off decimal answers to four places. Check your results with the answers given in Appendix F in the back of this book.

Addition

1. 931.26
   18.75
   3.05
   817.63
   34.90

2. 230.66
   19.09
   132.24
   7.78
   69.75

3. 54-1/5
   6-2/9

4. 3-2/3
   17-1/4

Subtraction

5. 23,907
   −20,869

6. $43.66
   −35.99

7. 18-1/4 − 12-7/8 =

8. 40-1/3 − 9-5/6 =

Credit Balances

9. 40.82
   −58.43

10. 106.65
    −199.47

Multiplication

11. 359.2 × 18.67 =

12. 40.6 × 90.5 =

13. 39,500 × 1,000 =

14. 869.45 × 100 =

15. 3-1/2 × 5-2/3 =

16. 12-5/8 × 3-1/7 =

Division

17. 26.983 ÷ 4.64 =

18. 4,093.1 ÷ 23.7 =

19. 3-1/2 ÷ 2-3/4 =

20. 16-2/3 ÷ 8-1/4 =

21. 29,432.6 ÷ 100 =

22. 97,347.08 ÷ 10 =

23. .3687 ÷ 100 =

24. 1.3857 ÷ 1,000 =

Complements

Give the complements for the following numbers:

25. 27   26. 4   27. 41%

Convert the following decimals to fractions:

28. .349   29. .6   30. .81

Convert the following fractions to decimals. (Round to four decimal places.)

31. 3/4   32. 7/8   33. 19/37

Rounding Off

Round off to tenths: **34.** 97.86

Round off to thousands: **35.** 54,790

Percent

Convert the following decimal to percent: **36.** 1.384

Convert the following percent to decimal: **37.** 86.3%

Convert the following fraction to percent: **38.** 6/7

Thought Problems

39. Your new car averages 14-1/2 miles per gallon of gasoline. How many miles can you travel on 20-1/3 gallons?

40. James Jackson earns $5.95 per hour. If he works 3-1/2 hours overtime at time and a half, how much does he earn for his overtime work?

BASIC MATHEMATICS REVIEW

In order to be successful in performing mathematical processes on calculators, you must first understand how to do each process in longhand. The calculator will enable you to perform complex mathematical operations quickly and easily. However, understanding basic mathematical operations and problem solutions is necessary before you can use the calculator to advantage. Solve the problems in the basic mathematics review *without* using a calculator.

Decimal System

Our number system is based on 10s; we have ten digits—1 through 9 and 0. Also, on the left side of the decimal, 10 ones equal 10, 10 tens equal 100, etc. On the right side of the decimal, it takes ten .1s to equal 1, 100 .1s to equal 10, etc. Our number system is also positional; in other words, the value of a digit changes depending upon its position. The digit 3 has a different value in each of the following positions:

3	
30	(ten 3s)
300	(one hundred 3s)
3,000	(one thousand 3s)
30,000	(ten thousand 3s)
300,000	(one hundred thousand 3s)
3,000,000	(one million 3s)
30,000,000	(ten million 3s)
300,000,000	(one hundred million 3s)
3,000,000,000	(one billion 3s)

and

.3	(3 tenths)
.03	(3 hundredths)
.003	(3 thousandths)
.0003	(3 ten-thousandths)
.00003	(3 hundred-thousandths)
.000003	(3 millionths)
.0000003	(3 ten-millionths)
.00000003	(3 hundred-millionths)
.000000003	(3 billionths)

Reading Numbers

A *number* contains one or more *digits*. For example, 1,394 is a four-digit number. The 4 is in the *units* position; the 9 is in the *tens* position; the 3 is in the *hundreds* position; the 1 is in the *thousands* position. This number should be read: *one thousand three hundred ninety-four*. The word *and* should not be used. The word *and* should be read *only* before a decimal. The number 426.97 should be read *four hundred twenty-six and ninety-seven hundredths,* or *four hundred twenty-six point nine seven*. To write a check for $5,629.18, we should write *Five thousand six hundred twenty-nine and 18/100* dollars.

Addition

$$\left.\begin{array}{r}7\\6\\4\\3\end{array}\right\} \text{addends}$$
20 sum or total

Example 1. 27 + 309 + 4 + 1,306 =

Remember to align your numbers so that units are added to units, tens are added to tens, hundreds are added to hundreds, etc.

$$\begin{array}{r}27\\309\\4\\\underline{1,306}\\1,646\end{array}$$

Example 2. 3.6 + 1.97 + 4 + 31.063 =

Remember to align your decimals so that you add digits of equal positional value.

$$\begin{array}{r}3.6\\1.97\\4\\\underline{31.063}\\40.633\end{array}$$

A quicker and easier way to add is to use combinations of tens. Look for digits in the column which add up to ten, add these first, and then add the remaining digits.

Example 3. Add by using combinations of tens:

(a) $\begin{array}{c} 1 \\ 46 \\ 12 \\ 34 \\ 73 \\ \hline 165 \end{array}$ (b) $\begin{array}{c} 2 \\ 8.7 \\ 1.9 \\ 4.2 \\ 2.1 \\ 9.3 \\ \hline 26.2 \end{array}$

In (a) add 6 and 4 first (10), then 2 (12), then 3 (15). In the second column, add 3 and 7 (10) first, then 1 (11), then 4 (15), then 1 (16).

In (b) add 7, 2, and 1 first (10), then 9 (19), then 3 (22). In the second column, add 2 and 8 (10), then add 1 and 9 (20), then 4 (24), then 2 (26).

Checking Sums

The simplest way to check your answers in addition is to add the columns in reverse order. That is, if you added the figures from top to bottom, add them again from bottom to top.

Another method of checking addition is to add each column separately.

Example 4. Add: 2,414   Check: 2,414
　　　　　　　　　　3,219　　　　　　3,219
　　　　　　　　　　　576　　　　　　　576
　　　　　　　　　　6,781　　　　　　6,781
　　　　　　　　　　9,432　　　　　　9,432
　　　　　　　　　　1,987　　　　　　1,987
　　　　　　　　　　3,204　　　　　　3,204
　　　　　　　　　　27,613
　　　　　　　　　　　　　　　　33　(4 + 9 + 6 + 1 + 2 + 7 + 4)
　　　　　　　　　　　　　　　　28　(1 + 1 + 7 + 8 + 3 + 8 + 0)
　　　　　　　　　　　　　　　　33　(4 + 2 + 5 + 7 + 4 + 9 + 2)
　　　　　　　　　　　　　　　　24　(2 + 3 + 6 + 9 + 1 + 3)
　　　　　　　　　　　　　　　27,613

Note: Be sure to indent one column for each sum.

Transpositions

It is a common error to transpose digits when copying numerical data; that is, to copy 7,3<u>41</u> instead of 7,3<u>14</u>. When a transposition has been made, the *difference* in the sum arrived at and the *correct* sum is divisible by 9.

BASIC MATHEMATICS REVIEW 7

Example 5. Correct Figures: Figures with Transposition:

           3,941   3,491
             298   298
             617   617
           4,856 Correct sum   4,406
           4,856
          −4,406
             450 Difference

Since 450 is divisible by 9 (450 ÷ 9 = 50), we know that we should check our figures for a possible transposition.

Addition by Using Subtotals

It is often simpler to break up long columns of large figures by adding parts of the problem and then adding the subtotals.

Example 6.   19,432
                  5,066
                  7,988   32,486
                  8,977
                 23,014
                 31,018   63,009
                  6,101
                    569
                  7,707   14,377
                        109,872 Total

Crossfooting

Some business forms require addition to be done both horizontally and vertically. These forms are arranged so that totals for more than one type of information can be provided. Also, since horizontal and vertical grand totals must be the same, an automatic check for accuracy exists.

Example 7.

PRODUCTION UNITS

Day	Employee A	Employee B	Employee C	Employee D	Total
Monday	39	38	35	34	146
Tuesday	41	42	45	40	168
Wednesday	35	28	30	36	129
Thursday	51	49	48	50	198
Friday	46	39	47	48	180
Total	212	196	205	208	821

INTRODUCTION

From this form you will be able to see at a glance the total units produced by each employee for the week, as well as the total units produced by the four employees for each day of the week.

Practice Problems 1. Do the following addition problems, using combinations of tens when possible. Check each problem by adding in reverse order.

1. 304	2. 1,043	3. 18,614	4. 81,643	5. 294
91	29,691	2,294	2,919	3,012
65	8,326	239	104,811	1,136
4,928	44	672	6,204	84
5,388				
6. 8.413	7. .071	8. 91.46	9. 321.01	10. 8.047
.09	.038	817.071	678.27	6.315
29.6	.042	25.53	144.23	9.142
11.24	1.373	46.62	291.64	.301
11. 9,321	12. 230,119	13. 41,614	14. 700,421	15. 2.914
10,867	4,576	8,755	35,689	86.357
4,321	107,234	932	10,132	.078
5,560	19,312	1,342	4,675	9.01
7,689	79,780	6,587	9,890	18
9,877	9,876	90,021	124	2.43
21,391	6,056	344	33,466	5.06
104,327	1,234	576	150,579	.7
6,754	17,860	401,235	43,821	1.89
91,302	1,932	6,897	1,762	.73

16. Add the columns and rows. The horizontal total and the vertical total should be the same.

SALES

Month	Dept. A	Dept. B	Dept. C	Dept. D	Total
Jan.	3,914	543	817	1,004	_____ (a)
Feb.	1,218	275	234	2,915	_____ (b)
March	2,755	861	569	1,367	_____ (c)
Total	_____ (e)	_____ (f)	_____ (g)	_____ (h)	_____ (d)

Subtraction

Example. 29.6 minuend
         −21.4 subtrahend
          8.2 difference

Check the answer by mentally adding the difference and the subtrahend. This sum should equal the minuend.

Add: 8.2 (difference)
       21.4 (subtrahend)
       29.6 (minuend)

Practice Problems 2. Do the following subtraction problems and check each one.

1. 91,432
   -85,670
   ──────
    5,762

2. 104,691
    -38,372

3. 6,147,891
     -398,576

4. 917,643
   -742,880

5. 1,394,675
     -298,097

6. 38,691 - 27,823 =

7. 13,254 - 7,899 =

8. 6,049 - 3,275 =

9. 977 - 862 =

10. 78,492 - 387 =

11. 1,395.18
     -964.72

12. 8,391.44
   -7,074.57

13. 871.99
    -594.07

14. 2,395.79
      -64.73

15. 791.22
    -643.98

16. 28.617
    -9.32

17. 14.6154
   -12.9878

18. .07364
   -.05918

19. .13947
   -.06852

20. .765
   -.3178

Note: You may add ending zeros to decimal numbers without altering the value; for example, .765<u>0</u> in problem **20**.

Negative Difference (Credit Balance)

If the subtrahend is larger than the minuend, the difference is a negative, or deficit.

Example.   914.32
            -1,061.81
            ────────
             -147.49

Subtract the smaller amount from the larger amount. If the larger amount is negative, the difference will be negative. Be sure to place a minus sign before your answer (difference).

Multiplication

Multiplication is a shortened form of repeated addition. That is, 6 times 3 is 18, the same as 6 added 3 times. If you don't know your multiplication tables by heart, review them before you proceed.

Example 1.
```
    764 multiplicand
     28 multiplier
   ----
   6112
  1528
  ------
  21,392 product
```

Multiplication answers may be checked by dividing the product by one of the multipliers to obtain the other multiplier.

$$21{,}392 \div 764 = 28$$

Multiplication answers may also be checked by reversing the multiplicand and the multiplier:

```
      28
     764
   ----
     112
     168
     196
   ------
  21,392
```

Example 2.
```
    61.031
      2.72
   -------
    122062
    427217
    122062
   --------
   166.00432
```

Decimals need not be aligned in multiplication. The number of decimals in the product equals the number of decimals in the multiplicand added to the number of decimals in the multiplier (3 + 2 = 5). Point off from right to left the total number of decimals.

Multiplying by 10, 100, 1,000, etc.

When multiplying by 10, 100, 1,000, etc., move the decimal point one place to the right for every zero in the multiplier:

$$29 \times 10 = 290 \ (29\smile)$$
$$37 \times 100 = 3{,}700 \ (37\smile\smile)$$
$$46 \times 1{,}000 = 46{,}000 \ (46\smile\smile\smile)$$
$$8.74 \times 10 = 87.4 \ (8.\overset{\frown}{7}4)$$
$$39.8 \times 100 = 3{,}980 \ (39.8\smile)$$
$$.046 \times 1{,}000 = 46 \ (.046\smile)$$

Multiplying Numbers with Ending Zeros

Example 3. (a) 170 (b) 432 (c) 2,100
 34   90   60
 680   38,880   126,000
 51
5,780

It is unnecessary to multiply by ending zeros. Merely bring down the ending zero(s) and multiply only by the remaining digits.

Practice Problems 3. Do the following multiplication problems, using shortcuts when possible. Check your answers.

1. 294 × 375 = 110,250
2. 8,194 × 865 =
3. 17,932 × 7,491 =
4. 875 × 431 =
5. 21,695 × 14,328 =
6. 6.97 × 5.38 =
7. 3.71 × .6579 =
8. 14.36 × 2.817 =
9. .453 × .291 =
10. 36.1495 × 2.865 =
11. 36.5 × 10 =
12. 2,704 × 100 =
13. 419 × 1,000 =
14. .00476 × 1,000 =
15. 29.4341 × 100 =
16. .0314 × 10 =
17. 870 × 260 =
18. 1,600 × 300 =
19. 197.4 × 110 =
20. 200 × 43 =

Division

Division is a shortened form of repeated subtraction. Thus, $32 - 8 - 8 - 8 - 8 = 0$ can be expressed as $32 \div 8 = 4$, or $32/8$, or $8\overline{)32}$.

Example 1.
$$\text{divisor } 6\overline{)742}\begin{array}{l}123 \text{ quotient}\\ \text{dividend}\end{array}$$
$$\underline{6}$$
$$14$$
$$\underline{12}$$
$$22$$
$$\underline{18}$$
$$4 \text{ remainder}$$

1. Since 6 will go into 7 once, write a 1 over the 7.
2. Multiply 1 times 6 and place the answer, 6, under the 7.

3. Subtract 6 from 7 and place the answer, 1, under the 6. The number arrived at here *must* be smaller than the divisor.
4. Bring down the 4, making 14 the next number to be divided into.
5. Since 6 goes into 14 twice, place a 2 in the quotient position over the 4.
6. Multiply 2 times 6 and place the answer, 12, under the 14.
7. Subtract. Place the 2 under the 2. Since this number is smaller than our divisor, we may proceed.
8. Bring down the 2, making 22 the next number to be divided into.
9. Since 6 goes into 22 three times, place a 3 in the quotient over the 2.
10. Multiply 3 times 6 and place the 18 under the 22.
11. Subtract 18 from 22. The problem has a remainder of 4, which can be expressed as 4/6 (the 6 is the divisor) and then reduced to 2/3.

Example 2.

(a) $4.33\overline{)897.66}$ (b) $3.6\overline{)947.}$

$3.6\overline{)947.0}$

1. When working with a divisor that has a decimal, move the decimal in the dividend to the right as many places as there are decimals in the divisor. Since a division problem can be expressed as a fraction (4.33/897.66), we can multiply the numerator and the denominator by the same number (100) without changing the relationship of the two numbers.
2. After the decimal has been placed, divide just as you did with whole numbers.

Dividing by 10, 100, 1,000, etc. To divide by a power of 10, simply move the decimal in the dividend as many places to the left as there are zeros in the divisor.

Example 3. (a) $139 \div 10 = 13.9$ (b) $43.71 \div 100 = .4371$

Checking Division To check the accuracy of your quotient, multiply the quotient by the divisor. Your answer should equal your dividend.

Example 4. 1. $18 \div 3 = 6$
2. $6 \times 3 = 18$

Example 5. $19 \div 3 = 6\text{-}1/3$
$6 \times 3 = 18 + 1 = 19$

1. Multiply the quotient (6) by the denominator of the remainder (3).
2. $6 \times 3 = 18$
3. Add the numerator of the remainder (1) to your answer in step 2.
4. $18 + 1 = 19$
5. The division problem checks.

Practice Problems 4. Perform the following division problems. Carry out the quotients to five decimal places. Check each problem by multiplication.

1. 397 ÷ 43 = 9.23255
2. 3,071 ÷ 84 =
3. 876 ÷ 4.5 =
4. 449 ÷ .864 =
5. 28.7 ÷ 3.6 =
6. 124.9 ÷ 4.18 =
7. 79.4 ÷ .076 =
8. .0941 ÷ .91 =
9. 7.6 ÷ .39 =
10. 4.5 ÷ 9.1 =
11. .874 ÷ 1.5 =
12. 27 ÷ .09 =
13. 307 ÷ 18 =
14. 41.7 ÷ 206 =
15. 1,694 ÷ 10 =
16. 29.71 ÷ 100 =
17. 8,509 ÷ 1,000 =
18. 24.6 ÷ 10,000 =
19. 8,070 ÷ 10 =
20. .9374 ÷ 100 =

Complements

A complement of a number is the difference between the number and the next power of 10. For example, the complement of 4 is 6 (4 + 6 = 10); the complement of 21 is 79 (21 + 79 = 100); the complement of 5% is 95% (5% + 95% = 100%); the complement of 743 is 257 (743 + 257 = 1,000); etc.

Practice Problems 5. Give the complements for the following:

	No.	Complement
1.	3	7
2.	7	
3.	56	
4.	31	
5.	642	
6.	309	
7.	7-1/2% (100.0% - 7.5%)	
8.	2-1/4% (100.00% - 2.25%)	
9.	25%	
10.	40%	
11.	10%	
12.	8-1/2%	
13.	7-3/4% (100.00% - 7.75%)	
14.	12%	
15.	12-1/2%	
16.	12-3/4%	
17.	15%	
18.	33-1/3% (100.0% - 33.3%)	
19.	60%	
20.	5-1/2% (100.0% - 5.5%)	

Decimals

Decimal to Fraction

Any decimal may be expressed as a fraction:

.5 = 5/10
.33 = 33/100
.753 = 753/1,000
.3958 = 3958/10,000
.81246 = 81246/100,000

1.04 = 104/100
3.2 = 32/10
41.75 = 4175/100
2.6 = 26/10
2.64 = 264/100

Practice Problems 6. Convert the following decimals to fractions, and reduce the fractions to their lowest terms:

1. .4 = 2/5
2. .57 =
3. .842 =
4. .9568 =
5. .74395 =

6. 1.64 =
7. 3.1 =
8. 5.84 =
9. 6.917 =
10. 4.04 =

Fraction to Decimal

Any fraction may be converted to a decimal by dividing the numerator by the denominator.

Example 1. $1/2 = 1 \div 2 = .5$

Example 2. $3/7 = 3 \div 7 = $

```
       .4285
    7)3.0000
      2 8
      ‾‾‾
        20
        14
        ‾‾
         60
         56
         ‾‾
          40
          35
          ‾‾
           5
```

3/7 = .4285

Practice Problems 7. Change the following fractions to decimals. Carry out to four decimal places.

1. 81/97 = .8350
2. 97/81 =
3. 100/94 =

4. 3/8 =
5. 14/19 =
6. 2/5 =

7. 800/796 =
8. 41/89 =
9. 2/9 =
10. 5/6 =
11. 724/999 =
12. 17/18 =
13. 10/19 =
14. 4/9 =
15. 66/94 =
16. 5/12 =
17. 29/35 =
18. 34/21 =
19. 3/2 =
20. 2/3 =

Rounding Off Numbers If the digit after the desired number of decimal places (or the desired number of whole numbers) is 5 or more, round up one number. If the digit is 4 or less, leave the last desired place the same as it is.

Example 1. Round off 29.765 to two decimal places.

1. Since the digit after the desired two decimal places is 5, round up one number.
2. The rounded answer is 29.77.

Example 2. Round off 1,395.8742 to three decimal places.

1. Since the digit after the desired three decimal places is 2, leave the last decimal as is.
2. The rounded answer is 1,395.874.

Example 3. Round off $29.698 to the nearest cent.

1. Since the digit after the desired two decimal places is 8, round up one number.
2. Round up the 9 to a 10.
3. Carry the 1, which will change the 6 to a 7.
4. The answer is $29.70.

Example 4. Round off 748,617 to the nearest thousand.

1. Ignore all the digits after the hundreds place (6).
2. Since 6 is more than 5, round up one number.
3. The answer to the nearest thousand is 749,000.

Practice Problems 8. Round the following decimals to the nearest tenth (one decimal place):

1. 16.741 = 16.7
2. 29.368 =
3. 34.349 =
4. 104.21 =

5. 4,197.005 =
6. 11.4999 =
7. 566.059 =
8. 7.174 =
9. 875.33 =
10. 50,914.6607 =

Round the following decimals to the nearest hundredth (two decimal places):

11. 94.8774 = 94.88
12. 109.8439 =
13. 20,046.21157 =
14. 39.871 =
15. 10.39102 =
16. 1.86914 =
17. 15.0043 =
18. 77.3333 =
19. 81.66666 =
20. .095972 =

Round the following decimals to the nearest thousandth (three decimal places):

21. 11.4965 = 11.497
22. 27.00374 =
23. 18.09121 =
24. 3.649104 =
25. .00712 =
26. 1,698.0486 =
27. 54.28141 =
28. 1.00643 =
29. 71.20607 =
30. .327149 =

Round the following numbers to units:

31. 42.8 = 43
32. 78.39 =
33. 1.7 =
34. 1.0749 =
35. 997.6 =
36. 239.71 =
37. 42,389.41 =
38. 58.3 =
39. 6.09 =
40. 804.643 =

Round the following numbers to thousands:

41. 24,900 = 25,000
42. 6,492 =
43. 104,609 =
44. 18,291 =
45. 296,400 =
46. 39,674 =
47. 2,046 =
48. 500,600 =
49. 1,794,369 =
50. 869,294 =

Round the following numbers to tenths of a million:

51. 3.41 million = 3.4 million
52. 17.745 million =
53. 200.87 million =
54. 5.664 million =

55. 14.031 million =

56. 75.178 million =

57. 8.29 million =

58. 999.99 million =

59. 48.36 million =

60. 2.554 million =

FRACTIONS

Definitions

A *fraction* is one or more parts of a whole number. For example, in the fraction $\frac{2}{3}$, the *denominator* shows the number of parts into which the whole is divided (3). The *numerator* shows the number of parts (2). Any fraction can be expressed as a division problem; for example, 2 ÷ 3. Any fraction can also be expressed as a decimal; for example, 2 ÷ 3 = .6667.

A *proper fraction* is one in which the numerator is smaller than the denominator; for example, 1/2, 2/3, 3/4, 871/964. An *improper fraction* is one in which the numerator is larger than the denominator; for example, 5/4, 3/2, 97/68, 104/75.

Reducing Fractions

In most instances we want to reduce fractions to their lowest terms. An important concept to remember in working with fractions is that the numerator and the denominator can be either multiplied or divided by the same number without changing the value of the fraction.

Example 1. Reduce the fraction 8/12 to its lowest terms.

1. What number can be evenly divided into both the numerator and the denominator?
2. The number 4 will divide evenly into both.
3. 8 ÷ 4 = 2
4. 12 ÷ 4 = 3
5. Therefore, 8/12 = 2/3.
6. Since there is no number which can be divided evenly into both 2 and 3, the fraction has been reduced to its lowest terms.

Example 2. Reduce 270/450 to its lowest terms.

1. If the largest possible divisor is not readily apparent, reduce in steps. The final result will be the same.
2. Divide by 10 (270/450 ÷ 10/10 = 27/45).
3. Divide by 9.
4. 27 ÷ 9 = 3
5. 45 ÷ 9 = 5

INTRODUCTION

6. Since 3/5 cannot be reduced further, the fraction has been reduced to its lowest terms.

Example 3. Reduce 378/702 to its lowest terms.

1. Any number ending in an even digit can be divided by 2.
2. $378 \div 2 = 189$
3. $702 \div 2 = 351$
4. Divide by 9.
5. $189 \div 9 = 21$
6. $351 \div 9 = 39$
7. Divide by 3.
8. $21 \div 3 = 7$
9. $39 \div 3 = 13$
10. The fraction reduced to its lowest terms is 7/13.

These guidelines will help you in reducing fractions:

1. All numbers ending in an even digit (0, 2, 4, 6, 8) can be divided by 2.
2. Add the digits in the number. If the total can be divided by 3, the number itself can be divided by 3. For example, in the number 2,883, $2 + 8 + 8 + 3 = 21$. Since 21 can be divided by 3, 2,883 can be divided by 3.
3. Numbers ending in 5 or 0 can be divided by 5.

Practice Problems 9. Reduce the following fractions to their lowest terms:

1. 18/46 = 9/23
2. 147/225 =
3. 210/405 =
4. 36/94 =
5. 132/372 =
6. 289/415 =
7. 247/448 =
8. 18/90 =
9. 499/699 =
10. 104/648 =

Raising Fractions

The value of a fraction does not change if we multiply both the numerator and the denominator by the same number; for example, to raise 2/3 to ninths, multiply the 2 and the 3 by 3.

$$2 \times 3 = 6$$
$$3 \times 3 = 9$$
$$2/3 = 6/9$$

Example. Raise 5/12 to forty-eighths.

1. Divide the raised denominator (48) by the lower denominator (12).
2. $48 \div 12 = 4$
3. We now see that both factors must be multiplied by 4 to raise the fraction to forty-eighths.
4. $4 \times 5 = 20$
5. $4 \times 12 = 48$
6. Therefore, 5/12 = 20/48.

Improper Fractions

An *improper fraction* is one in which the denominator is smaller than the numerator; for example, 9/5, 4/3, 5/4. An improper fraction has a value greater than 1.

A *mixed number* contains a whole number and a fraction; for example, 2-5/8, 13-1/2.

Converting Mixed Numbers to Improper Fractions

Example. Convert 3-4/5 to an improper fraction.

1. Multiply the denominator (5) by the whole number (3).
2. $5 \times 3 = 15$
   Note: The whole number 1 = 5/5; thus, 3 = 15/5.
3. Add the numerator (4) to this product (15).
4. $15 + 4 = 19$
5. Place this number (19) over the denominator (5).
6. 3-4/5 = 19/5

Converting Improper Fractions to Mixed Numbers

Example. Convert 19/5 to a mixed number.

1. Any fraction in which the numerator is larger than the denominator is an improper fraction and has a value greater than 1.
2. To find the whole number, divide the denominator into the numerator.
3. $19 \div 5 = 3\text{-}4/5$
4. Since 5 goes into 19 three whole times, our whole number is 3; the remaining amount (4) is a fraction with 5 as the denominator.
5. 19/5 = 3-4/5

Addition of Fractions

In order to add or subtract fractions, the fractions must have a common denominator. In solving an addition or a subtraction of fractions, we need to find the lowest common denominator for the fractions in the problem. The *lowest common denomi-*

nator (*LCD*) is the smallest denominator into which all the denominators in the problem can be divided evenly.

Example 1. 2/3 + 1/4 + 5/8 =

1. Find the LCD.
2. We can see that the lowest denominator into which all the denominators can be divided evenly is 24.
3. Change each fraction to twenty-fourths.
4. 2/3 = ?/24
   24 ÷ 3 = 8
   8 × 2 = 16
   2/3 = 16/24
5. 1/4 = ?/24
   24 ÷ 4 = 6
   6 × 1 = 6
   1/4 = 6/24
6. 5/8 = ?/24
   24 ÷ 8 = 3
   3 × 5 = 15
   5/8 = 15/24
7. 16/24 + 6/24 + 15/24 = 37/24
8. Reduce the answer (37/24) to lowest terms.
9. Since the numerator (37) is larger than the denominator (24), 37/24 is an improper fraction and should be converted to a mixed number.
10. 37 ÷ 24 = 1-13/24
11. Since 13 cannot be divided by any number except 1 or 13, the fraction is in its lowest terms.
12. The sum of 2/3 + 1/4 + 5/8 = 1-13/24.
    Note: The number 13 is what is known as a prime number. A *prime number* is one that can be divided evenly only by itself or by 1; for example, 3, 5, 7, 11, 13.

Example 2. Add: 1/5 + 3/8 + 2/9 + 5/12 =

1. Find the LCD. Since the LCD is difficult to find here except by trial and error, the following method is helpful: arrange the denominators in a row horizontally.
2. Divide by the smallest number that can be divided into one or more of these denominators (2 in the first row).

	5	8	9	12
2	5	4	9	6
2	5	2	9	3
3	5	2	3	1

FRACTIONS   21

3. Divide this number (2) into as many denominators as possible: 8 and 12.
4. Bring down the quotients (4 and 6) to the second row. Also bring down the undivided denominators (5 and 9).
5. Continue this process until there are no more possible denominators.
6. Multiply all the divisors (2, 2, and 3) and all the numbers in the last row (5, 2, 3, and 1).

$$2 \times 2 \times 3 \times 5 \times 2 \times 3 \times 1 = 360$$

7. We now have 360 as the LCD. Convert each fraction in this addition problem to 360ths.
8. $360 \div 5 = 72$
   $1/5 = 72/360$
9. $360 \div 8 = 45$
   $3 \times 45 = 135$
   $3/8 = 135/360$
10. $360 \div 9 = 40$
    $2 \times 40 = 80$
    $2/9 = 80/360$
11. $360 \div 12 = 30$
    $5 \times 30 = 150$
    $5/12 = 150/360$
12. $72/360 + 135/360 + 80/360 + 150/360 = 437/360$
13. Convert to a mixed number by dividing 437 by 360. Then reduce the fraction to its lowest terms.
14. $437 \div 360 = 1\text{-}77/360$

Example 3. Add: $1\text{-}2/3 + 2\text{-}3/4 + 11/12 =$

1. Find the LCD for the fractions (12).
2. Change each fraction to twelfths.
3. $2/3 = 8/12$
4. $3/4 = 9/12$
5. $1\text{-}8/12 + 2\text{-}9/12 + 11/12 = 3\text{-}28/12$
6. Convert 28/12 to a mixed number.
   $28 \div 12 = 2\text{-}4/12$
7. Add this to the whole number 3.
   $3 + 2\text{-}4/12 = 5\text{-}4/12$
8. Reduce the fraction to its lowest terms.
9. $4/12 = 1/3$
10. Your answer is $5\text{-}1/3$.

Practice Problems 10. Add the following fractions:

1. 1-3/4 + 2/3 + 5/16 = 2-35/48
2. 2/7 + 9/49 + 13/14 =
3. 2-1/3 + 1-3/4 + 13/16 =
4. 5/6 + 7/8 + 5/12 =
5. 4-11/12 + 5-9/60 + 1-3/5 =
6. 2-5/8 + 4-1/2 + 1-7/8 =
7. 34-1/4 + 2-2/3 + 1-7/9 =
8. 31/6 + 14/11 + 59/66 =
9. 2-1/8 + 3-7/36 + 5-5/9 =
10. 4-5/16 + 2-1/15 + 14-7/30 =
11. 9-1/2 + 16-4/5 + 9/10 =
12. 40-5/8 + 8-2/5 + 1/6 =
13. 2-1/9 + 1-5/12 + 8-1/5 =
14. 6-3/8 + 10-3/4 + 2-5/12 =
15. 7-5/16 + 1-5/8 + 4/21 =
16. 14-2/7 + 43/45 + 19/6 =
17. 3-1/2 + 2-11/16 + 1/6 =
18. 14-2/9 + 1-4/5 + 8-2/3 =
19. 4-3/7 + 15-5/8 + 1-3/4 =
20. 5-7/12 + 1/25 + 3/50 =

Subtraction of Fractions

Example. 3-1/8 − 1-57/64 =

1. Find the LCD (64).
2. Convert 1/8 to 64ths.
3. 64 ÷ 8 = 8
4. 8 × 1 = 8
5. 1/8 = 8/64
6.   3-8/64
    −1-57/64

Since we cannot subtract 57 from 8, we must borrow 1 from the whole number 3. The 1 is equal to 64/64.

7. Add 64/64 to 8/64 (64/64 + 8/64 = 72/64).
8.   2-72/64   Subtract 57 from 72.
    −1-57/64   Subtract 1 from 2.
9. After subtracting, you have 1-15/64.
   Since the fraction is proper and is in its lowest terms, your final answer is 1-15/64.

Practice Problems 11. Complete the following subtraction problems:

1. 2-2/3 − 1-3/4 = 11/12
2. 14-5/6 − 12-11/12 =
3. 41-1/10 − 15-7/12 =
4. 20-7/15 − 16-16/27 =
5. 4-3/11 − 3-2/3 =
6. 7-7/30 − 5-7/10 =

7. 1-15/16 − 1/2 =
8. 10-3/14 − 6-10/21 =
9. 5-2/3 − 2-4/5 =
10. 11-2/9 − 8-2/3 =
11. 9-3/7 − 4-3/4 =
12. 5-4/15 − 3-1/5 =
13. 2-3/8 − 1-5/6 =
14. 19/36 − 11/24 =
15. 9/16 − 2/9 =
16. 5-7/8 − 3-5/12 =
17. 25-9/8 − 11-11/6 =
18. 12-1/5 − 7-5/16 =
19. 29-3/13 − 15-8/21 =
20. 4-1/4 − 2-5/6 =

Multiplication of Fractions

Example 1.   2/15 × 3/4 =

1. It is not necessary to have a common denominator to multiply or divide fractions.
2. Multiply the numerators. Then multiply the denominators.

$$\frac{2 \times 3}{15 \times 4} = \frac{6}{60}$$

3. Reduce the fraction to lowest terms.
4. 6/60 = 1/10

Example 2.   2/3 × 5/6 × 1/4 × 3/8 =

1. $$\frac{2 \times 5 \times 1 \times 3}{3 \times 6 \times 4 \times 8} =$$

2. We know that the value of a fraction does not change if we multiply or divide the numerator and the denominator by the same number. We can also cancel before multiplying. *Canceling* means to divide into groups of fractions that are to be multiplied. We must divide the *same* number into *one* of the numerators and *one* of the denominators.

3. $$\frac{\overset{1}{\cancel{2}} \times 5 \times 1 \times \overset{1}{\cancel{3}}}{3 \times \underset{2}{\cancel{6}} \times \underset{2}{\cancel{4}} \times 8} = \frac{5}{96}$$

   (a) Divide by 3 the 3 in the numerator and the 6 in the denominator, leaving 1 and 2.
   (b) Divide by 2 the 2 in the numerator and the 4 in the denominator, leaving 1 and 2.

4. Now multiply the numerators. Then multiply the denominators.
5. The answer in lowest terms is 5/96.

Example 3. 3-4/20 × 4-1/32 × 2-9/18 =

1. Convert the mixed numbers to improper fractions.
2. (20 × 3) + 4 = 60 + 4 = 64/20
3. (32 × 4) + 1 = 128 + 1 = 129/32
4. (18 × 2) + 9 = 36 + 9 = 45/18
5. Cancel where possible.

$$\frac{\cancel{64} \times 129 \times \cancel{45}}{\cancel{20} \times \cancel{32} \times \cancel{18}} =$$

(a) Divide 64 and 32 by 32, leaving 2 and 1.
(b) Divide 45 and 18 by 3, leaving 15 and 6.
(c) Divide 15 and 20 by 5, leaving 3 and 4.
(d) Divide 2 and 4 by 2, leaving 1 and 2.
(e) Divide 3 and 6 by 3, leaving 1 and 2.

6. Multiply the numerators. Then multiply the denominators.
$$\frac{1 \times 129 \times 1}{2 \times 1 \times 2} = \frac{129}{4}$$

7. Change the improper fraction to a mixed number and reduce to lowest terms.
129 ÷ 4 = 32-1/4

Practice Problems 12. Complete the following multiplication of fractions:

1. 1/2 × 4/5 = 2/5
2. 2/3 × 18/73 =
3. 5/6 × 21/27 =
4. 6/2 × 16/15 =
5. 9/8 × 24/19 =
6. 9-1/4 × 14-2/7 =
7. 3 × 3-1/4 =
8. 4-1/3 × 2 =
9. 3-1/5 × 6-2/3 =
10. 11-2/9 × 5-7/8 =
11. 1-2/3 × 4-5/8 =
12. 14-1/5 × 12-1/4 =
13. 7-1/9 × 13-3/4 =
14. 6-1/4 × 10-1/2 =
15. 3-5/8 × 6-5/6 =
16. 8-6/7 × 16-3/5 =
17. 20-1/4 × 2-7/10 =
18. 4-9/10 × 5-3/7 =
19. 5-5/9 × 3-2/3 =
20. 2-5/8 × 5-7/8 =

FRACTIONS 25

Division of Fractions

Example 1. $1/2 \div 2/3 =$

1. *Invert* your divisor by making the numerator (2) the denominator and the denominator (3) the numerator. Change the *divided by* sign to the *multiply* sign.

$$1/2 \times 3/2 =$$

2. *Multiply* by your inverted divisor.
3. $\dfrac{1 \times 3}{2 \times 2} = \dfrac{3}{4}$

Example 2. $4\text{-}3/8 \div 2\text{-}7/64 =$

1. Change these mixed numbers to improper fractions.
2. $(8 \times 4) + 3 = 35/8$
3. $(64 \times 2) + 7 = 135/64$
4. *Invert* your divisor and change the divided-by sign to the multiply sign.

$$35/8 \times 64/135 =$$

5. Cancel where possible.

$$\dfrac{\overset{7}{\cancel{35}} \times \overset{8}{\cancel{64}}}{\underset{1}{\cancel{8}} \times \underset{27}{\cancel{135}}} =$$

6. Multiply the numerators. Then multiply the denominators.

$$\dfrac{7 \times 8}{1 \times 27} = \dfrac{56}{27}$$

7. Convert to a mixed number.

$$56 \div 27 = 2\text{-}2/27$$

8. Your answer in lowest terms is 2-2/27.

Example 3. $5\text{-}1/4 \div 7\text{-}5/24 =$

1. Convert these mixed numbers to improper fractions.
2. $(4 \times 5) + 1 = 21/4$
3. $(24 \times 7) + 5 = 173/24$
4. $21/4 \div 173/24 =$
5. Invert the divisor and change the divided-by sign to the multiply sign.

6. Cancel where possible.

$$\frac{21 \times \overset{6}{\cancel{24}}}{\underset{1}{\cancel{4}} \times 173} =$$

7. Multiply the numerators. Then multiply the denominators.

$$\frac{21 \times 6}{1 \times 173} = \frac{126}{173}$$

8. The answer in lowest terms is 126/173.

Practice Problems 13. Complete the following division problems:

1. 1/3 ÷ 1/2 = 2/3
2. 7/8 ÷ 4/5 =
3. 3/4 ÷ 2/3 =
4. 3-1/3 ÷ 2-2/3 =
5. 7-1/2 ÷ 3-1/4 =
6. 12-1/2 ÷ 16-2/3 =
7. 18 ÷ 2/7 =
8. 30-1/2 ÷ 10-2/5 =
9. 8-1/9 ÷ 3-5/8 =
10. 2-1/7 ÷ 1-7/8 =
11. 8-1/5 ÷ 2-3/4 =
12. 11/12 ÷ 1-1/4 =
13. 9-10/11 ÷ 4-7/8 =
14. 42/2 ÷ 7/6 =
15. 5/4 ÷ 17/3 =
16. 2-9/10 ÷ 3-9/10 =
17. 5-11/13 ÷ 4-1/2 =
18. 33-1/3 ÷ 2/3 =
19. 1-4/7 ÷ 2-7/8 =
20. 5-2/5 ÷ 3-1/3 =

Aliquot Parts

An *aliquot part* is any number that can be divided evenly into another number; for example, 5 is an aliquot part of 100. Using aliquot parts can often simplify some of the mathematical problems in business and in your personal finances.

Example. 424 × .25 =

1. Since .25 equals 1/4, we can multiply by 1/4 instead of .25, which is a simpler operation.
2. 424 × 1/4 = 424/4
3. 424 ÷ 4 = 106

Practice Problems 14. (On money problems, round answers to the penny.)

1. Leslie Smith, Mary Allen, and Sylvia Jones are starting a secretarial service. They spent $6,320 on equipment and supplies. Leslie will pay one-half of the cost;

Mary will pay one-third; and Sylvia will pay one-sixth. How much will each woman pay? (*Ans.* Leslie, $3,160.00; Mary, $2,106.67; Sylvia, $1,053.33)

2. Mrs. Jamieson had a two-thirds interest in a tailoring store. She sold two-fifths of her interest to Miss Brown for $12,000. What was the total dollar amount of Mrs. Jamieson's interest in the store before the sale? What was the total dollar value of the tailoring store?

3. Joe, Ralph, Al, and David were hired to repaint some offices. The men will share the pay according to the fractional part of the work that each one did. Joe did one-fifth of the painting; Ralph did one-third of the painting; Al did one-sixth of the painting. What fractional part of the total painting job did David do?

4. Alicia McKinney is a member of a stock club and has a two-sevenths interest in the stock the club owns. Alicia sells one-fourth of her interest in the club to Jack Alexander for $9,000. What is the total value of the stock owned by the stock club?

5. Your new car averages 13-1/2 miles per gallon of gasoline. How many miles can you travel on 22-3/4 gallons?

6. One tire builder can build 6-2/3 tires in an hour. Another tire builder can build 7-1/5 tires per hour. How many tires can the two men build in an 8-hour work day?

7. Mrs. Patterson is planning to make matching draperies, a valance, and slip covers. She needs 12-1/2 yards of fabric for the draperies, 3-3/16 yards for the valance, and 7-5/8 yards for the slip covers. How many total yards does she need?

8. The Sweet Shop, a wholesale candy manufacturer, had 159-1/4 pounds of coconut creams in stock at the beginning of the week. On Monday they sold 24-3/4 pounds; on Tuesday, 12-1/8 pounds; on Wednesday, 17-1/2 pounds; on Thursday, 48-1/16 pounds; on Friday, 39-5/8 pounds; on Saturday, 15-7/8 pounds. The Sweet Shop likes to begin each week with 150 pounds of coconut creams in stock. How many pounds do they need to make for next Monday?

9. Tom Korns owns a tractor–trailer truck. He leaves for Chicago with his truck loaded to nine-sixteenths of its allowable weight. In Chicago Tom adds cargo which amounts to one-fourth of his allowable weight. In Evanston he delivers cargo amounting to five-eighths of his allowable weight. What fraction of the allowable weight is now remaining on the truck?

10. Marguerite Winston invested $4,306.50 in stock selling at 37-1/8 per share. How many shares did she buy? (37-1/8 = $37.125)

PERCENT

Converting Decimals to Percent

To convert a decimal number to a percent, move the decimal point two places to the right.

28 INTRODUCTION

Example 1. .2935 = 29.35%

Example 2. 1.0497 = 104.97%

Practice Problems 15. Convert the following decimals to percent:

1. 1.00 = 100%
2. .50 =
3. 2.00 =
4. 1.45 =
5. .78 =
6. .35 =
7. .05 =
8. .90 =
9. .97 =
10. .63 =
11. 3.098 =
12. .4 =
13. .8375 =
14. .832 =
15. .013 =
16. .0032 =
17. .9683 =
18. .00037 =
19. .3857 =
20. .5555 =
21. 2.3857 =
22. .0857 =
23. 10.3857 =
24. .2679 =
25. .5465 =
26. .3856 =
27. .2435709 =
28. .3 =
29. 3.385 =
30. 30.385 =

Converting Fractions to Percent

For any fraction for which you do not know the decimal conversion by heart, look in Appendix A, which gives decimal equivalents of commonly used fractions. To find any not given, you can convert any fraction to a decimal by dividing the numerator by the denominator. After the fraction is in decimal form, move the decimal point two places to the right to change the decimal to a percent.

Example 1. Convert 5/9 to a percent.

1. 5/9 = 5 ÷ 9
2. 5 ÷ 9 = .5556 (rounded to four decimal places)
3. .5556 = 55.56%

Example 2. Convert 1/4 to a percent.

1. 1/4 = .25
2. .25 = 25%

Practice Problems 16. Convert the following fractions to a percent. (Round your percent answers to two decimal places.)

31. 1/6 = 16.67%
32. 1/5 =
33. 1/4 =
34. 1/3 =
35. 1/2 =
36. 1/8 =
37. 3/8 =
38. 5/8 =
39. 7/8 =
40. 1/12 =
41. 2-1/2 =
42. 1-1/4 =
43. 3-1/3 =
44. 3-2/3 =
45. 34/67 =

46. 67/34 =
47. 238/857 =
48. 3/98 =
49. 253/476 =
50. 25/477 =
51. 3/7 =
52. 13/79 =
53. 2/9 =
54. 8/9 =
55. 2/7 =
56. 35/43 =
57. 4/5 =
58. 19/21 =
59. 2/5 =
60. 3/16 =

Converting Percents to Decimals

To convert a percent to a decimal number, move the decimal point two places to the left and drop the percent sign.

Example 1. 38.476% = .38476

Example 2. 204.877% = 2.04877

Practice Problems 17. Convert the following percents to decimal numbers:

61. 267.3% = 2.673
62. 28.4% =
63. 2.5% =
64. 160.7% =
65. 38% =
66. 90% =
67. 75% =

68. 38.28% =
69. 25.897% =
70. 14.3378% =
71. .8% =
72. .08% =
73. .008% =
74. 8% =

INTRODUCTION

75. 8.08% =   78. .055% =
76. .888% =   79. .945% =
77. .0975% =   80. .025% =

Rounding Off Percents

Example 1. Round off 39.64<u>5</u>% to two decimal places.

1. If the figure after the desired number of decimals is <u>5</u> or more, round up one number.
2. 39.64<u>5</u>% = 39.65%

Example 2. Round off 29.57<u>2</u>% to two decimal places.

1. If the figure after the desired number of decimals is <u>4</u> or less, leave the last decimal number as is.
2. 29.57<u>2</u>% = 29.57%

Practice Problems 18. Round off the following to hundredths:

81. 88.678% = 88.68%   84. 2.006% =
82. 103.463% =   85. 45.0003% =
83. 19.6666% =   86. 75.606% =

Round off the following to tenths:

87. 96.877% = 96.9%   89. 72.5783% =
88. 46.999% =   90. 15.3288% =

Round off the following to units:

91. 266.98% = 267%   96. 67.34% =
92. 100.04% =   97. 80.09% =
93. 74.5% =   98. 39.1% =
94. 86.23% =   99. 160.33% =
95. 25.5% =   100. 40.00999% =

SAMPLE UNIT EXAMINATIONS

The following pages contain a sample examination for each of the ten units in the text. As you complete each unit, turn back to the sample examination for that unit. Time yourself as you take the sample examination. Ask your instructor for the time limit and the standards used in your course.

UNIT 1 SAMPLE EXAMINATION

Your instructor may wish to use the stroking test shown in Unit 1, page 97.

UNIT 2 SAMPLE EXAMINATION
ELECTRONIC CALCULATOR BASIC OPERATIONS

Addition

1.	82.83	2.	.278	3.	3.902	4.	357	5.	23,100.20
	8.27		.285		2.389		283		15,328.39
	29.56		.188		1.385		938		9,382.35
	4.56		.093		8.382		385		10,375.39
	43.72		.205		1.564		667		236,385.66
	38.28		.114		9.392		874		88,926.34
	5.72		.432		8.275		910		4,355.68
	90.09		.932		6.627		208		21,305.47
	1.22		.478		3.333		136		8,900.06
	54.32		.555		5.273		379		1,562.37

6. 34.27 + 378.28 + 213.87 + 1,389.26 + 9,899.76 + 2.37 =

7. 1.027 + 1.573 + 9.930 + 8.375 + 4.365 + 2.358 =

8. .0923 + .9305 + .3562 + .5789 + .3852 + .9820 + .9283 =

9. 23,488 + 3,475 + 8,938 + 4,375 + 6,666 + 8,392 + 3,464 =

10. $23.48 + 3.87 + 5.67 + 23.88 + 73.82 + 89.80 + 3.48 =

Subtraction

11.	3,571	12.	10,273.82	13.	11.3807	14.	.28900
	−807		−9,297.86		−10.2738		−.12879

15.	100,379	16.	$138.28	17.	3,278.38	18.	1,859.2
	−92,366		−109.28		−127.76		−938.3

19.	1,372.38	20.	10,382.86
	−902.37		−8,390.55

Credit Balances

21.	48.11	22.	.9074	23.	66.26	24.	1.3151	25.	.9
	−50.38		−.9772		−9.56		−5.4132		−.8
	8.56		.1074		−99.93		.9025		−.6
	−4.22		−.8882		101.36		−7.3858		−.4
	−10.11		.0003		−503.77		−1.3095		.3
	−9.99		−.6743		34.25		.0004		.3

INTRODUCTION

26. 44,399	27. $103.28	28. 2.13	29. -483	30. 12.34
-8,378	-110.56	-9.28	139	-56.33
-2,314	4.76	1.46	-886	9.90
-4,444	48.91	-8.88	176	-8.36
-1,909	-98.98	3.32	29	-5.52
-50,392	-4.56	-5.34	-6	1.39

Addition and Subtraction

31. 27.63	32. 28.3857	33. 290.37	34. 1.48
-2.86	-3.8287	-129.66	-.38
8.34	40.0021	35.78	7.75
-5.55	-.9927	11.09	9.80
34.86	8.3568	-72.38	-.99
-18.64	-.2937	302.10	-.37

35. 20,398	36. 103	37. -583	38. 10,372.88
-356	-26	-290	-287.55
8,278	213	1,382	9,837.26
1,909	-56	6,372	562.01
-2,386	879	829	-76.33
457	28	-382	-89.32

39. 234,920	40. 1,382,390.87
-156,379	-876,324.33
56,238	1,978,455.67
-197,283	-4,456.78
983,566	3,421.09
-224,390	-34,669.90

Repeated Addition and Subtraction

41. 89.37	42. 34.22	43. 209.378	44. 2,388.80	45. .837
5.32	34.22	110.211	876.66	.222
5.32	34.22	110.211	876.66	.222
5.32	8.76	90.287	876.66	.285

46. 6,378.288	47. 126.83	48. $31.90	49. .0707	50. 37.28
-12.365	-2.30	31.90	.0707	-14.86
-12.365	-2.30	31.90	-.3838	-14.86
-12.365	-2.30	-20.15	-.3838	-14.86
-12.365	15.76	-20.15	.9072	382.38
-12.365	15.76	8.56	.3957	43.76

Addition and Subtraction of Fractions (Round to four decimals.)

51. 13-2/3	52. 5-2/3	53. 2-5/8	54. 1-12/16	55. 7-7/16
89-1/2	8-9/16	1-9/16	2-5/8	1-1/2
9-3/4	4-1/4	2-3/4	7-7/8	3-2/7
6-5/8	8-1/8	5-7/16	9-5/6	4-1/3

56. 12-3/4 − 8-5/7 =   57. 19-1/8 − 5-7/9 =   58. 2-15/16 − 2-1/4 =

59. 18-7/8 − 9-4/5 =   60. 40-1/5 − 30-11/12 =

Subtotals

61. 27,946
    4,266
    _____ Subtotal
    5,362
    1,377
    _____ Total

62. 2.372
    1.388
    _____ Subtotal
    6.672
    1.876
    _____ Total

63. 22,375.38
    1,213.65
    _____ Subtotal
    2,364
    890
    _____ Total

64. 5,380.28
    9,387.97
    1,762.01
    _____ Subtotal
    362.98
    _____ Subtotal
    131.22
    _____ Total

65. 90,397.26
    6,824.44
    550.01
    _____ Subtotal
    921.91
    _____ Subtotal
    3,309.76
    _____ Total

Multiplication (Round to four decimal places.)

66. .382 × 389.9 =   74. 1,027 × 378 =

67. 3,907.20 × 13.22 =   75. 1,937 × 1.970 =

68. 80.26 × 49.34 =   76. 999.9 × 382.8 =

69. .2837 × .38 =   77. .07403 × 13.1 =

70. 383 × 707 =   78. 5.388 × 32 =

71. 128 × 3.3872 =   79. .382 × 43.1 =

72. 10.2853 × 1.3827 =   80. 43 × 8.8275 =

73. 2,453 × 8.38 =

Three-Factor Multiplication (Round to four decimal places.)

81. 26 × 56 × 31 =   83. 1,590 × 2 × 1,902 =

82. .067 × 3.1 × 88.36 =   84. 61 × 88 × 30 =

INTRODUCTION

85. 18,279 × 3.1 × 24.66 =
86. 11.3 × 3.77 × .973 =
87. 34 × 22.66 × 5.53 =

88. 273 × 4.33 × 13.11 =
89. 4,071 × 31.1 × .377 =
90. 3.878 × 1.378 × 311.1 =

Division (Round to four decimal places.)

91. 34,311 ÷ 111.38 =
92. 27.36 ÷ 20.387 =
93. 68.37 ÷ 4.333 =
94. 2,831.1 ÷ 2,070.11 =
95. 109.375 ÷ 200.38 =

96. 87.36 ÷ 107.211 =
97. 3.888 ÷ 2.138 =
98. 127,709 ÷ 25,379 =
99. 35.50 ÷ 38.58 =
100. .4758 ÷ 38 =

Mixed Problems (Round to four decimal places.)

101. 2.35 × (86 ÷ 33.2) =
102. (23 × 3.4) ÷ 18.22 =
103. (27 ÷ 14) + 8.28 =
104. (8 - 2.6) × 3.288 =
105. (30.1 - 23.11) × 7.6 =
106. (5.3 - 4.3) × 2.2 =
107. (500.3 ÷ 3.17) ÷ 39.9 =
108. (1,375 - 972) × 7.77 =
109. (24.3 × 66.6) ÷ 80.8 =
110. (55.5 ÷ 3.2) + (16.1 - 2) =

111. (2.34 + 3.47 + 9.88) × 5.3 =
112. (30 × 2.7 × 8.9) ÷ 18.8 =
113. (9.9 - 3.45) ÷ (3.890 × 1.33) =
114. (24.44 × 8.8903) ÷ (54.5 ÷ 3.2) =
115. 81.7 × (39.79 ÷ 3.477) =
116. (81.1 × 4.2) + (53.88 ÷ 35.88) =
117. 88 × (567.7 ÷ 89.99) =
118. (14,390 - 12,370) ÷ 1,009.76 =
119. (2.6 + 3.8) ÷ (1.7 - .9706) =
120. (5.4 - 3.66) × 49.36 =

UNIT 3 SAMPLE EXAMINATION
ELECTRONIC CALCULATOR PERCENT APPLICATIONS

Finding the Percentage of a Number (Round your answers to the nearest whole number.)

1. In a group of 1,360 graduate students, 25% of them are majoring in law. How many students is this?
2. Forty-six percent of the 2,850 employees of Wrights, Inc., work in the factory. How many employees is this?
3. What is 37.83% of 2,913?
4. What is 46.3% of 41?
5. What is 86% of 3.9?

UNIT 3 SAMPLE EXAMINATION ELECTRONIC CALCULATOR PERCENT APPLICATIONS   35

6. What is 5.4% of 86?
7. What is 103% of 196.1?
8. What is 4.2% of 665?
9. What is 26.8% of 10.9?
10. What is 104% of 220?

Finding the Number if the Percent is Known (Round your answers to two decimal places.)

11. Ralph received a dividend check for $26.80, which represents a 6% return on the price of the stock. What is the price of the stock?
12. Alder's Department Store reduced the price of a coffee table by $40, which was 35% of the original price. What was the original price?
13. Alice received a commission check for $1,290, which is 26% of her total sales. What were her total sales?
14. Twenty-eight people, or 12.5% of the work force of Carpenter Windows Company, were laid off. What was their total work force before the layoff?
15. Thirty is 18.4% of what number?
16. Eighty-two is 48.1% of what number?
17. Seventy-four is 98.3% of what number?
18. Two hundred one is 103% of what number?
19. Sixty-four is 26.3% of what number?
20. Five is 8.9% of what number?

Finding What Percent One Number is of Another (Round your answers to two decimal places.)

21. On a recent psychology examination, you answered 78 questions correctly out of 90 questions. What percent is 78 of 90?
22. At one testing center for the CPS examination, 29 of the 35 examinees passed one or more sections of the examination. What percent is 29 of 35?
23. On his first stop, a trucker delivered 4,210 lb. of his total load of 18,900 lb. What percent is 4,210 of 18,900?
24. What percent is 82.3 of 91.7?
25. What percent is 104.6 of 102.1?
26. What percent is 221,300 of 321,600?
27. What percent is 3 of 7.3?
28. What percent is 84 of 75?
29. What percent is 121 of 980?
30. What percent is 50 of 61.5?

Percent of the Whole (Round your answers to the tenth of a percent.)

31.–40. John and Mary Smith have a monthly net income of $1,057.25. What percent of their net income is each of the following expenses?

			Percent of Net Income
31.	Food	$105.20	_____
32.	Rent	225.00	_____
33.	Car payment	110.50	_____
34.	Insurance	21.55	_____
35.	Medical	45.00	_____
36.	Gasoline	41.06	_____
37.	Savings	416.14	_____
38.	Clothing	40.00	_____
39.	Utilities	27.80	_____
40.	Recreation	25.00	_____

Proration

41.–50. Last year the total sales of the Textile Marketing staff were $70,500,000. The five salesmen made sales as follows:

Andrews	$15,400,000
Cory	10,100,000
Miller	23,000,000
Harper	12,400,000
McConnell	9,600,000
	$70,500,000

Bonus money of $50,000 is to be divided among these five people according to their prorated share of the annual sales total. Find the percent of sales for each person and each person's prorated share of the bonus money.

Name	Percent of Sales (to the tenth of a %)	$ Amount of Bonus (rounded to the penny)
Andrews	41. _____	42. _____
Cory	43. _____	44. _____
Miller	45. _____	46. _____
Harper	47. _____	48. _____
McConnell	49. _____	50. _____

UNIT 3 SAMPLE EXAMINATION ELECTRONIC CALCULATOR PERCENT APPLICATIONS

Percent of Increase or Decrease

51.–60. Below are shown the enrollments for five majors at the Willowville Community and Technical College for this quarter and last quarter. Find the amount of change and the percent of increase or decrease (to the tenth of a percent) for each major.

Major	Enrollment This Quarter	Enrollment Last Quarter	Amount of Change	Percent of Increase or Decrease
Secretarial	421	435	51. _____	52. _____
Transportation	206	200	53. _____	54. _____
Fire science	19	18	55. _____	56. _____
Electronics	167	165	57. _____	58. _____
Food service	129	134	59. _____	60. _____

Chain Discount

61.–70. What will a buyer pay for the following items after taking the allowed chain discount? (Round your answers to the penny.)

	Item	Price ($)	Discount (%)	Net Price ($)
61.	Corduroy pants	$14.00	10-10-5	_____
62.	T-shirt	12.95	15-5-1/2	_____
63.	Jeans	14.95	10-5-2-1/2	_____
64.	Blouse	18.99	25-10-5	_____
65.	Poncho	29.98	10-5-1/2-2	_____
66.	Boots	30.00	10-10-2-1/2	_____
67.	Overalls	21.00	15-5-5	_____
68.	Ski jacket	40.00	33-1/3-5	_____
69.	Raincoat	55.00	15-10-2-1/2	_____
70.	Scarf	8.00	15-5-2	_____

Cash and Quantity Discounts

71.–80. Calculate the amount due (rounded to the penny) on the following invoices. All of these invoices were paid within the discount period.

38   INTRODUCTION

	Amount of Invoice ($)	Quantity Discount (%)	Cash Discount Terms	Amount Due ($)
71.	194.61	10	2/10	_____
72.	24.18	5	3/5	_____
73.	671.94	15	—	_____
74.	4,691.55	—	2/30	_____
75.	302.00	20	2/60	_____
76.	2,115.05	25	2/10	_____
77.	15,490.18	12	1/90	_____
78.	740.10	5	2½/30	_____
79.	8,695.11	—	2/10	_____
80.	2,232.08	20	—	_____

Sales Taxes

81.–90. Find the amount of sales tax and the total price for each of the following sales. (Round your answers to the penny.)

Amount of Sale ($)	Sales Tax (%)	Amount of Sales Tax ($)	Total Amount of Sale ($)
32.89	5	81. _____	82. _____
446.23	4	83. _____	84. _____
1,533.01	6	85. _____	86. _____
125.86	5-1/2	87. _____	88. _____
71.15	7	89. _____	90. _____

City Taxes

91.–100. Compute the amount of city tax to be deducted from each of the following weekly paychecks. The city tax rate is 1/2 percent. (Round your answers to the penny.)

	Name	Weekly Pay ($)	Amount of Tax ($)
91.	Alder, J.	287.35	_____
92.	Benson, D.	194.30	_____
93.	Cartwright, A.	300.60	_____

UNIT 4 SAMPLE EXAMINATION ELECTRONIC CALCULATOR BUSINESS PROBLEMS

Name	Weekly Pay ($)	Amount of Tax ($)
94. Danville, P.	251.30	_____
95. Jochum, T.	187.56	_____
96. Kilroy, R.	231.90	_____
97. Lewis, L.	312.32	_____
98. McCann, J.	186.32	_____
99. Sanchez, P.	247.65	_____
100. Topouski, A.	289.54	_____

Simple Interest

101.–110. Calculate the amount of interest that must be paid for each of the following amounts of principal. Use 360 days as one year. (Round your answers to the penny.)

	Principal ($)	Rate (%)	Time (days)	Interest ($)
101.	1,031.45	6	300	_____
102.	548.22	7-1/2	90	_____
103.	25,000.00	9	360	_____
104.	412.90	6-1/2	720	_____
105.	5,600.00	8	180	_____
106.	30,850.00	9-1/4	172	_____
107.	58.29	10	113	_____
108.	788.91	9-1/2	60	_____
109.	543.20	10-1/2	320	_____
110.	6,921.35	8-1/2	15	_____

UNIT 4 SAMPLE EXAMINATION ELECTRONIC CALCULATOR BUSINESS PROBLEMS

Extensions

1.–8. Extend the amounts on the following invoice; then find the total. (Round your answers to the penny.)

INVOICE

February 3, 19--

To: Abra Cadabra Candle Company
    1800 N. Parkway
    Milan, USA

Item	No. of Items	Unit Price ($)	Total	
Pink wax	24 lb.	1.50 per lb.	_____	1.
Wicks	150	4.50 per C	_____	2.
Rabbit molds	2	8.75 ea.	_____	3.
		Total	_____	4.
		Deduct 2% cash discount	_____	5.
		Total	_____	6.
		Add 5% sales tax	_____	7.
		Net Amount of Invoice	_____	8.

Simple Interest—Amount

9. If you have $1,395.20 in your savings account, how much interest will you get at the end of the quarter if your bank pays 1-1/4 percent per quarter? (Round your answer to the penny.)

10. Jerry borrowed $600 at 7 percent interest to be repaid in 180 days. How much interest will he pay (rounded to the penny)?

Interest—Finding the Interest Period in Days

11.–20. Given the following information, determine how many days are needed to produce each amount of interest. (Round your answers to the day.)

	Interest ($)	Principal ($)	Rate (%)	Time (days)
11.	6	200.50	6-1/2	_____
12.	12	304.25	6	_____
13.	100	1,895.40	7	_____
14.	6.50	100.00	5-1/2	_____

UNIT 4 SAMPLE EXAMINATION ELECTRONIC CALCULATOR BUSINESS PROBLEMS

	Interest ($)	Principal ($)	Rate (%)	Time (days)
15.	15.40	2,914.00	5	_____
16.	1,000	54,691.20	7-1/2	_____
17.	21.55	3,915.80	12	_____
18.	3.40	75.00	9	_____
19.	56.45	1,491.56	9-1/4	_____
20.	10.75	654.89	7-1/4	_____

Interest—Finding the Rate

21.–30. Find the rate of interest that produces each of the following amounts of interest. (Round your answers to the tenth of a percent.)

	Interest ($)	Principal ($)	Rate (%)	Time (days)
21.	16.50	1,500.00	_____	58
22.	48.65	3,216.40	_____	60
23.	4.20	400.75	_____	50
24.	26.15	261.00	_____	300
25.	1.30	57.60	_____	180
26.	2.36	104.30	_____	68
27.	6.50	161.12	_____	121
28.	1.25	298.61	_____	30
29.	415.80	3,006.40	_____	415
30.	46.50	44,619.50	_____	5

Compound Interest (Figure without the Table. Round your answers to the penny.)

31.–38. If you deposit $200 in a savings account on January 1 in a bank which pays 5% computed quarterly, how much will you have in your account after two years?

31. Total in account after first quarter   _____

32. Total in account after second quarter _____

33. Total in account after third quarter   _____

34. Total in account after fourth quarter _____

35. Total in account after fifth quarter _____

36. Total in account after sixth quarter _____

37. Total in account after seventh quarter _____

38. Total in account after eighth quarter _____

Compound Interest (Figure with the Table in Appendix C. Round your answers to the penny.)

39.–40. Determine the amount of interest on $400 at 6% compounded quarterly for two years. _____ **39.**

What is the *total* amount in the account? _____ **40.**

Markon (on Cost)

41.–50. Find the amount of markon based on *cost price* and the selling price for each of the following items. (Round your answers to the penny.)

Item	Cost ($)	Markon on Cost (%)	Amount of Markon ($)	Selling Price ($)
Diamond ring	1,200.00	40	41. ____	42. ____
Class ring	48.50	20	43. ____	44. ____
Diamond earrings	125.00	35	45. ____	46. ____
12 mm pearls	924.50	30	47. ____	48. ____
Man's wrist watch	95.46	36	49. ____	50. ____

Markon (on Selling Price)

51.–60. Calculate the amount of markon (based on selling price) and the cost price for the following items. (Round your answers to the penny.)

Item	Selling Price ($)	Markon (%)	Amount of Markon ($)	Cost Price ($)
Record	6.90	18	51. ____	52. ____
Tape	8.95	20	53. ____	54. ____
Tape player	69.98	15	55. ____	56. ____
Speaker	59.99	15	57. ____	58. ____
Turntable	129.00	25	59. ____	60. ____

UNIT 4 SAMPLE EXAMINATION ELECTRONIC CALCULATOR BUSINESS PROBLEMS   43

Markon Rate (Percent) Based on Cost

61.–66. What is the rate of markon based on cost and the amount of markon for the following items? (Round your answers to two decimal places.)

Item	Cost Price ($)	Selling Price ($)	Amount of Markon ($)	Rate of Markon (%)
Coat	91.40	106.80	61. _____	62. _____
Lipstick	3.91	4.50	63. _____	64. _____
Piano	1,000.00	1,254.00	65. _____	66. _____

Markon Rate (Percent) Based on Selling Price

67.–72. What is the rate of markon based on selling price and the amount of markon for the following items? (Round your answers to two decimal places.)

Item	Cost Price ($)	Selling Price ($)	Amount of Markon ($)	Rate of Markon (%)
Sport coat	36.90	46.99	67. _____	68. _____
Raincoat	51.45	110.91	69. _____	70. _____
Dress	46.40	55.98	71. _____	72. _____

Percent of Selling Price (Round to two decimal places.)

73.–74. Allen Andrews sold one of his pieces of sculpture to Dan's Art Shop for $125. Dan's Art Shop marked it up 45% over the cost price. What was the dollar amount of markon? What percent of Dan's selling price did Allen Andrews receive?

75.–76. Appalachia Crafts, Inc., bought a hand-tied canopy from Mrs. Smithers for $130. Appalachia Crafts marked up the canopy 40% of the cost price. What was the dollar amount of markon? What percent of Appalachia's selling price did Mrs. Smithers receive?

Markup (Based on Selling Price)

77.–82. Find the amount of markup on selling price and the new selling price for the following items. (Round your answers to the penny.)

44 INTRODUCTION

Item	Selling Price ($)	Percent of Markup	Amount of Markup ($)	New Selling Price ($)
Coffee	3.50	20	77. _____	78. _____
Milk	.69	10	79. _____	80. _____
Cigarettes	.58	12	81. _____	82. _____

Markdown

83.-85. Calculate the percent of markdown based on selling price for the following items. (Round your answers to the whole percent.)

	Item	Original Selling Price ($)	Sale Price ($)	Percent of Markdown
83.	Lawnmower	179.90	159.00	_____
84.	Pillow	21.00	18.88	_____
85.	Hair dryer	29.99	24.99	_____

Sales Commission

86.-90. Each of the following people earns 2-1/2% commission on his first $12,000 in sales and 5% on sales over $12,000. How much commission did each earn? (Round your answers to the penny.)

	Name	Sales ($)	Commission ($)
86.	Bittiger, A.	26,000	_____
87.	Carlton, T.	29,500	_____
88.	Randolph, P.	23,200	_____
89.	Stern, I.	30,100	_____
90.	Tomoski, J.	20,500	_____

Payroll

91.-92. Calculate the weekly *net* wages for the following people. Overtime is paid at 1-1/2 times the hourly rate for hours over 40.

UNIT 4 SAMPLE EXAMINATION ELECTRONIC CALCULATOR BUSINESS PROBLEMS   45

Employee	Hours Worked	Hourly Rate ($)	Gross Pay ($)	FICA 5.85%	Other Deductions ($)	Net Pay ($)
91. Hanson, P.	42	5.91	——	——	38.60	——
92. Miletti, A.	48	6.25	——	——	41.20	——

Piecework Rates

93. José Mendoza works in rim finishing. He earns $9.203 for every 100 rims he processes. Last week he finished 1,850 rims. He works the night shift and receives $.138 per hour for night shift differential in addition to his piecework earnings. He worked 40 hours last week. What were his gross wages (rounded to the penny)?

Salary Increases

94. Margaret Schmidt earns $821.00 per month as a data processing assistant. She is scheduled to receive a cost-of-living increase of 3.8% of her present salary plus a $45 monthly merit raise. What will be the amount of her new salary (rounded to the dollar)?

Insurance–Percent Insured

95. Your company's office building is insured for $485,000 but is valued at $515,400. What percent of the building is insured? (Round your answer to the percent.)

Insurance–Cost of Premiums

96. Mr. and Mrs. Lentini's home is insured for $32,600. Their insurance premium costs 42 cents per $100 per year. The cost for three years is 2.7 times the annual premium. How much is their three-year premium?

Discounting Promissory Notes

97. Calculate the amount of proceeds received after the following promissory note is discounted. Use 360 days as one year.

Maturity Value	Discount Rate (%)	No. of Days	Proceeds of the Note ($)
97. $573.80	7-1/2	90	——

Banking

98. You want to open a checking account and have received the following information from the bank: The service charge is $1.50 a month. You may write 10

checks per month at no extra charge. However, after the first 10 checks, you must pay 10 cents for each additional check. There is no charge for deposits. If you write an average of 14 checks per month, how much will your checking account cost you for a year?

99. Determine the total for the following deposit slip:

```
LESTER NATIONAL BANK
Lester, USA
Endorse all checks and list separately.
Coin                              $    29.43
Currency                              65.00
Checks                                 9.41
                                      31.67
                                   1,004.81
                                     575.03
                                      10.91
                                   5,679.88
                                     421.14
                                      28.60
                                       4.81
            TOTAL    $_____
No. of Checks 9    Date 12-4
Account Number 3391-42-0087
```

100. Your company's bank statement, received on June 10, shows a balance of $25,258.14. Your check register shows a balance of $24,220.29. The following checks are outstanding:

#3041	$ 104.90
#3043	1,200.00
#3047	88.70

The bank service charge was $5.75. A deposit of $350.00, which was made on June 9, was not shown on the bank statement. What is the adjusted balance?

UNIT 5 SAMPLE EXAMINATION
ELECTRONIC CALCULATOR PRACTICAL PROBLEMS

Installment Buying

1. You buy a stereo which cost $400. You paid $75 down and made six monthly payments of $59 each. What percent of the list price is interest (rounded to two decimal places)?

UNIT 5 SAMPLE EXAMINATION ELECTRONIC CALCULATOR PRACTICAL PROBLEMS

2. Carl bought a used car for $1,000. He paid $50 down and will pay 18 monthly payments of $60.15. What percent is the installment charge of the list price?

3. Mrs. Allison wants to buy a new dining room set for $350.00 in cash, or $30.08 a month for 12 months. If she pays cash, she will lose 5% interest by removing the $350.00 from a savings account. Should she pay cash?

4. Mr. and Mrs. Phillips want to buy an antique armoire for $1,500 cash. If they pay cash, they will have to borrow the money at 7-1/2% interest. If they buy the armoire on time, the payments will be $182 a month for 12 months. Which would be cheaper?

True Annual Interest Rate

5.–10. In the following problems find the installment charge (rounded to the penny) and the true annual interest rate (rounded to the tenth of a percent):

Item	Cash Price ($)	Down Payment ($)	No. of Monthly Payments	Amt. of Monthly Payment ($)	Installment Charge ($)	True Annual Interest Rate
Sewing machine	229.99	25.00	6	36.10	5. _____	6. _____
Lawn mower	175.00	20.00	6	26.90	7. _____	8. _____
Wrist watch	189.00	–	12	16.80	9. _____	10. _____

Monthly Payments

11.–16. In the following problems, find the total interest based on the unpaid balance (rounded to the penny) and the amount of the monthly payments (rounded to the penny):

Creditor	Monthly Interest Rate (%)	Amt. of Acct. ($)	No. of Monthly Payments	Total Interest ($)	Amt. of Monthly Payments ($)
Loan company	1	500	12	11. _____	12. _____
Department store	1-1/2	240	6	13. _____	14. _____
Credit card account	1-1/4	380	12	15. _____	16. _____

Real Estate Taxes

17.–20. Calculate the amount of real estate taxes for each of the following properties. (Round your answers to the penny.)

Property	Real Value ($)	Assessed Value (%)	Tax Rate per C ($)	Tax Due ($)
17. Residence	35,400	60	5.20	_____
18. Farm	150,000	50	9.80	_____
19. Factory	2,000,000	45	10.20	_____
20. Office building	500,000	55	8.45	_____

Real Estate Prices

21. Allen Wolfe has $74,000 for the 20% down payment on an apartment house. What is the price of the apartment house?
22. Alice Smith has the 40% down payment of $9,500 to buy a condominium. What is the price of the condominium?
23. You have the one-third down payment of $11,500 needed to buy a duplex. What is the price of the duplex?

Profit Margin

In the following problems find the rate of profit (rounded to the tenth of a percent):

24. The Toski Construction Company added a room to the Millers' home for $3,850. If the cost to Toski for adding the room was $3,050, what was Toski's rate of profit?
25. The Appliance Repair Shop repaired a washing machine for $52.58. If the total cost of the repair was $41.00, what was the rate of profit?
26. The city of Midale had a new library built at a cost of $96,500. If the cost of building the library was $87,000, what rate of profit did the contractor realize?

Stocks—Dividend Yield per Share

27.-30. Find the dividend yield per share for the following stocks. (Round your answers to the tenth of a percent.)

Stock	Dividend per Share ($)	Price per Share of Stock ($)	Dividend Yield per Share (%)
27. Anfeld	1.85	28-1/8	_____
28. Skyway	3.05	40-1/2	_____
29. Startell	1.04	14-3/8	_____
30. A, B, & C	1.30	18-1/4	_____

UNIT 5 SAMPLE EXAMINATION ELECTRONIC CALCULATOR PRACTICAL PROBLEMS

Stocks—Purchases

31. Jean Jackson wants to buy 24 shares of Mountain, Inc., stock which sells for 50-7/8 per share. The broker's fee is $34.25. Add 1 cent for every $300 for the SEC fee. How much will the transaction cost Jean?

32. You want to buy 48 shares of Kalper Co. stock which is selling for 14-5/8 per share. The brokerage fee is $30. The SEC fee is 1 cent for every $300. How much will you pay altogether?

Stocks—Earnings per Share

33.-35. Find the earnings per share (rounded to the penny) for the following companies:

Company	Net Income ($)	Shares of Stock	Earnings per Share ($)
33. Lauren Co.	10,241,000	4,650,000	————
34. National Books	2,458,000	1,040,000	————
35. Bittners, Inc.	1,005,000	396,000	————

Stocks—Current Ratio

36.-38. Find the current ratio of the following companies. (Round your answers to two decimal places.)

Company	Current Assets ($)	Current Liabilities ($)	Current Ratio
36. Brent Co.	191,000,000	44,000,000	————
37. Robinson's, Inc.	3,115,000	2,005,000	————
38. Proffer Corp.	8,465,000	5,250,000	————

Bonds—Market Value

39.-42. What is the market value of the following bonds?

Number of Bonds	Face Value ($)	Current Quotation (per $100)	Market Value ($)
39. 2	10,000	93-1/8	————
40. 50	5,000	96-1/2	————
41. 100	1,000	98-5/8	————
42. 5	100,000	97-1/4	————

Bonds—Interest

43.–46. What is the amount of semiannual interest on the following bonds? (Round your answers to the penny.)

No. of Bonds	Face Value ($)	Annual Interest Rate (%)	Amt. of Semiannual Interest ($)
43. 2	1,000	5	_____
44. 25	5,000	5-1/4	_____
45. 10	25,000	5-1/2	_____
46. 1	50,000	6	_____

Depreciation—Straight-Line Method

47.–50. Calculate the annual depreciation for the following items using the straight-line method. (Round your answers to the penny.)

Item	Cost ($)	Salvage Value ($)	Estimated Life (yrs.)	Annual Depreciation ($)
47. Crane	45,800	5,700	25	_____
48. Automobile	5,750	1,500	5	_____
49. Truck	21,500	4,500	6	_____
50. Fork lift	15,000	2,000	20	_____

Depreciation—Sum-of-the-Digits Method

51.–54. Calculate the annual depreciation for the following item using the sum-of-the-digits method. (Round your answers to the penny.)

Grennen, Inc., purchased a truck for $7,300. The estimated useful life is four years, and the salvage value is $1,500.

51. depreciation first year   _____

52. depreciation second year _____

53. depreciation third year   _____

54. depreciation fourth year _____

UNIT 5 SAMPLE EXAMINATION ELECTRONIC CALCULATOR PRACTICAL PROBLEMS

Depreciation–Declining Balance Method

55.–59. Compute the amount of depreciation (at two times the rate) for each year on the following item. (Round your answers to the penny.)

The Jensen Accounting Service bought an electronic accounting machine for $1,899. The estimated useful life is five years, and the salvage value is $150.

55. depreciation first year _____   58. depreciation fourth year _____

56. depreciation second year _____   59. depreciation fifth year _____

57. depreciation third year _____

Unit Prices

60. How much will it cost to carpet a room 18.5 ft. × 13.5 ft. if the carpeting sells for $9.75 per square yard?
61. How much will you pay for 206 stencils if they sell for $17.85 per quire?
62. A 12-ounce box of petit fours sells for $4.99. How much are these confections per pound?
63. How much will you pay for 74 feet of nylon rope if the rope costs 89 cents a yard?

Basic Statistics

64.–66. Give the mean, the median, and the mode for the following array of salaries:

Employee	Annual Salary ($)
Manager	42,000
Assistant Manager	26,200
Technical Service Representative A	18,200
Technical Service Representative B	18,200
Technical Service Representative C	16,900
Technical Service Representative D	16,400
Technical Lab Trainee	13,500
Secretary	9,100
Stenographer	8,600
Typist	7,500
Clerk	7,400
Telephone Operator	7,200

INTRODUCTION

64. mean _____

65. median _____

66. mode _____

67.-68. Give the mean and the median in the following array:

Employee	Expense Report ($)
Chessar	925.36
DiDonato	914.20
Faith	905.10
Gomez	885.20
Hayes	875.60
Jacobs	840.18
Pietro	838.91
Schmitt	182.75

67. mean _____

68. median _____

69.-78. The Order Department of the Joy Toy Company received the following monthly orders (in dollars):

	Dolls	Games	Sports Equipment	Doll Furniture	Total
Jan.	3,212	5,717	6,811	4,320	_____
Feb.	3,419	6,810	8,715	5,100	_____
March	2,500	6,950	7,525	3,800	_____
April	3,200	5,900	6,900	4,520	_____
May	2,900	6,750	7,850	5,250	_____
June	4,650	5,850	6,950	4,600	_____
Total	_____	_____	_____	_____	

Find the mean for each month's orders and the mean for each type of toy.

69. Jan. _____

70. Feb. _____

71. March _____

72. April _____

73. May _____

74. June _____

UNIT 5 SAMPLE EXAMINATION ELECTRONIC CALCULATOR PRACTICAL PROBLEMS

75. Dolls   _____
76. Games   _____
77. Sports equipment _____
78. Doll furniture   _____

Travel and Monetary Problems

79.-80. On a round trip from Chicago to Jacksonville, Florida (1,040 miles one way), your car consumed 158 gallons of gasoline at 58.6 cents per gallon.

79. How much did you spend for gasoline (rounded to the penny)?
80. How many miles per gallon did you average (rounded to one decimal)?
81. On a one-way drive from Detroit to Birmingham, Alabama, you were on the road for 17 hours. The distance is 762 miles. How many miles per hour did you average? (Round to one decimal point.)
82. On a recent trip your odometer reading was 36,421.7 when you left New Orleans and was 37,372.8 when you reached Davenport, Iowa. You bought the following gallons of gasoline: 18.4, 15.1, 14.6, 15.4. How many miles per gallon did you average? (Round your answer to one decimal place.)
83. It is approximately 2,132 miles from El Paso, Texas, to Philadelphia, Pennsylvania, one way. If a round-trip first-class airline ticket costs $508, how much does this flight cost per mile? (Round your answer to the penny.)
84. On a recent visit to London you spent £91. How much is this in U.S. dollars?
85. You wish to exchange $200 for British pounds. How many pounds will you receive rounded to the pound?
86. If you buy a sweater that costs 71 Swiss francs, how much is this in U.S. dollars?
87. If you exchange $150 for Swiss francs, how many will you receive rounded to the franc?
88. If you buy a grandfather's clock in Germany for 850 marks, how much is this in U.S. dollars?
89. You want to buy $320 worth of German marks; how many will you receive rounded to the mark?
90. You buy a hand-woven basket in Mexico for 210 pesos. How much is this in U.S. dollars?
91. How many U.S. dollars will you receive for 805 pesos?

Measure and Cost

92. Your TWX transmits at 100 words per minute. (Five characters are counted as one word.) Yesterday your TWX transmitted 85,205 characters to your plant. It costs your company 28 cents per minute to transmit to your plant. How much did this transmission cost? (Round to the penny.)

93. Alice wants to make some draperies for her den. She needs 15-1/4 yards of fabric at $8.50 per yard, 15-1/4 yards of lining at $1.99 per yard, 2 spools of thread at 30 cents each, and 48 drapery hooks at 79 cents a dozen. How much will these items cost?

Inventory Valuation

94.–112. The following information is part of an inventory of the Shop-Well Super Market. Figure the value of the inventory based on unit price. Multiply the number of cases times the number of items in a case times the price per unit.

	Item	Cases in Stock	No. Items per Case	Price per Unit ($)	Inventory Valuation ($)
94.	Apple juice, 40 oz. bottle	9	12	.89	_____
95.	Apricot–apple juice, 32 oz. bottle	5	18	.77	_____
96.	Apricot nectar, 46 oz. can	3	12	1.19	_____
97.	Beefamato juice, 32 oz. can	4	24	.89	_____
98.	Clamato juice, 32 oz. bottle	3	12	.79	_____
99.	Cranapple juice, 32 oz. bottle	5	12	.79	_____
100.	Cranberry juice, 32 oz. bottle	6	24	.69	_____
101.	Cranberry juice, 48 oz. jar	4	12	1.09	_____
102.	Grape juice, 24 oz. bottle	18	24	.75	_____
103.	Grape juice, 40 oz. jar	10	12	1.15	_____
104.	White grape juice, 24 oz. bottle	8	24	.75	_____

UNIT 5 SAMPLE EXAMINATION ELECTRONIC CALCULATOR PRACTICAL PROBLEMS

Item	Cases in Stock	No. Items per Case	Price per Unit ($)	Inventory Valuation ($)
105. Grapefruit juice, 46 oz. can	15	8	.69	_____
106. Peach nectar, 12 oz. can	4	36	.43	_____
107. Pineapple juice, 46 oz. can	8	8	.79	_____
108. Prune juice, 32 oz. jar	5	24	.69	_____
109. Prune juice, 40 oz. jar	7	12	.79	_____
110. Tomato juice, 32 oz. can	18	24	.59	_____
111. Tomato juice, 46 oz. can	14	8	.69	_____
112. V-8 juice, 46 oz. can	9	8	.75	_____

Net Profit

113. Find the net profit based on the following information:

WALTER LELAND, M.D.
INCOME STATEMENT
FOR THE YEAR ENDED DECEMBER 31, 19—

Income:

Fees $78,390

Expenses:

Salaries and benefits	$16,300
Rent	8,490
Utilities	1,500
Insurance	2,400
Office & medical supplies	2,100
Other expense	2,030
Net Profit	_____

114.–115. Find the gross profit and the net profit based on the following information:

U-BELTS, INC.
INCOME STATEMENT
For the Month Ended April 30, 19--

Sales		$84,651
Less sales returns		2,486
Net sales		
Cost of goods sold		50,040
Gross Profit		
Operating Expenses:		
Salaries and benefits	$9,200	
Real estate taxes	340	
Utilities	4,850	
Selling expense	3,020	
Advertising	1,350	
Other expense	841	
114. **Gross Profit**		_____
115. **Net Profit**		_____

UNIT 6 SAMPLE EXAMINATION
THE INTERNATIONAL SYSTEM OF UNITS

Note: Metric conversions are given in Appendix E.

Prefixes

1. How many centigrams are in a gram?
2. How many milligrams are in a gram?
3. How many grams are in a kilogram?
4. How many milliliters are in a liter?
5. How many centimeters are in a meter?

Metric Weight

Convert the following grams to kilograms:

6. 384 g =   kg   9. 41 g =   kg

7. 2,311 g =   kg   10. 25,200 g =   kg

8. 904 g =   kg

UNIT 6 SAMPLE EXAMINATION THE INTERNATIONAL SYSTEM OF UNITS

Convert the following kilograms to grams:

11. 1.12 kg =   g
12. 2.81 kg =   g
13. 13 kg =   g

14. 64.7 kg =   g
15. 19 kg =   g

Convert the following centigrams to grams:

16. 97 cg =   g
17. 5,000 cg =   g
18. 189 cg =   g

19. 50,000 cg =   g
20. 25 cg =   g

Convert the following grams to centigrams:

21. .4 g =   cg
22. 41 g =   cg
23. 2,500 g =   cg

24. .052 g =   cg
25. 6.6 g =   cg

Convert the following milligrams to grams:

26. 2,000 mg =   g
27. 19,400 mg =   g
28. 420 mg =   g

29. .8 mg =   g
30. 24,000,500 mg =   g

Convert the following milligrams to centigrams:

31. 3,491 mg =   cg
32. 572 mg =   cg
33. 90,400 mg =   cg

34. 14 mg =   cg
35. 1,000,000 mg =   cg

Convert the following kilograms to metric tons:

36. 14,500 kg =   t
37. 1,300 kg =   t
38. 37,000 kg =   t

39. 37,000,000 kg =   t
40. 89.1 kg =   t

Convert the following metric tons to kilograms:

41. 146 t =   kg
42. 51 t =   kg
43. 6.1 t =   kg

44. .056 t =   kg
45. 18.4 t =   kg

Problems in Metric Weight

In the following calculations, give the answers in *grams:*

46. 2.82 kg + 394 g =
47. 18.1 kg + 28 g =
48. 904.1 kg + 680 g =
49. 81.34 kg - 586 g =
50. 21.38 kg - 46.9 g =

In the following problems give the answers in metric tons:

51. 254 kg + 2.6 t =
52. 18,000 kg + 18.9 t =
53. 340,000 kg - 2.4 t =
54. 85,390 kg - 3.5 t =
55. 100,500 kg - 98.1 t =
56. A box of crackers weighs 250 g and sells for 89 cents. A smaller box weighs 180 g and sells for 69 cents. How much does each cost per gram?
57. A can of chocolate syrup weighs 456 g and costs 49 cents. How much is this per gram?

In the following problems give the answers in kilograms:

58. 14.9 kg - 769 g =
59. 1,430 g - .46 kg =
60. 2.4 kg - 18.4 g =
61. 241,391 g - 96.3 kg =
62. 1.56 kg - 17.4 g =

Metric Length

Convert the following centimeters to meters:

63. 382 cm =   m
64. 14.4 cm =   m
65. 91,000.46 cm =   m

Convert the following meters to centimeters:

66. 23 m = _____ cm
67. .034 m = _____ cm
68. 5.8 m = _____ cm
69. 26.9 m = _____ cm
70. .02197 m = _____ cm

Problems in Metric Length

Express your answers to the following problems in meters:

71. 6 m 24 cm + 2 m 91 cm =
72. 8.4 m 20 cm + 2.4 m 18 cm =
73. 2.6 m 14 cm + 5.31 m 92.5 cm =
74. .6 m 84 cm + .4814 cm =
75. 18.1 m 41.6 cm + 5.4 m 7.6 cm =
76. 192 m 80 cm - 90 m 48 cm =
77. 2,804 m 75.3 cm - 1,291 m 89 cm =
78. 7.5 m 21 cm - 5.3 m 26 cm =
79. 203 m 86 cm - 146 m 91 cm =
80. 29.3 m 24.2 cm - 18 m 51.8 cm =

Convert the following meters to kilometers:

81. 1,462.1 m = _____ km
82. 14,871 m = _____ km
83. 832.5 m = _____ km
84. 57.6 m = _____ km
85. 4.1 m = _____ km

Express your answers to the following problems in kilometers:

86. 3.1 km 18 m + 5 km 32 m =
87. 9.05 km 106 m + 3.15 km 20 m =
88. 39 km 907 m + 203 km 609 m =
89. .86 km 12 m + 2.91 km 346 m =

INTRODUCTION

90. 8,110 km 196 m + 594 km 23.4 m =

91. 910.2 km 18.4 m - 806 km 4.3 m =

92. 4 km 945 m - 3 km 1,041 m =

93. 25.1 km 806 m - 20.9 km 902 m =

94. 1.3 km 224 m - 1 km 18 m =

95. 85 km 109.6 m - 70 km 29.1 m =

Express your answers to the following problems in centimeters. (Round your answers to four decimals.)

96. 34 m 18 cm ÷ 2.1 =

97. 5 m 49 cm ÷ 4.8 =

98. .6 m 8 cm ÷ 3.6 =

99. 18 m 29 cm ÷ 5.82 =

100. 104 m 99 cm ÷ 25.14 =

Area

Find the square centimeters for the following areas. (Round your answers to four decimal places.)

101. 18.6 cm X 11.3 cm =

102. 52 cm X 16.2 cm =

103. 391 cm X 12.3 cm =

104. 1.044 cm X 3.06 cm =

105. .386 cm X 1.491 cm =

Convert the following to meters; then determine the square meters. (Round your answers to four decimal places.)

106. 21 m 31 cm X 12 m 20 cm =

107. 1.3 m 90 cm X 2.3 m 18 cm =

108. 1 m 93 cm X 7.7 m 13 cm =

109. 204 m 14 cm X 11.4 m 14.1 cm =

110. 40 m 40 cm X 18 m 5.2 cm =

UNIT 6 SAMPLE EXAMINATION THE INTERNATIONAL SYSTEM OF UNITS

Convert the following square centimeters to square meters:

111. 9,000 cm² =   m²
112. 34,000 cm² =   m²
113. 3,046,291 cm² =   m²
114. 401,299 cm² =   m²
115. 208 cm² =   m²

Convert the following square meters to hectares:

116. 10,000 m² =   hectare(s)
117. 4,309 m² =   hectare(s)
118. 1,391,465 m² =   hectare(s)
119. 41,698 m² =   hectare(s)
120. 471,653.9 m² =   hectare(s)

Area Problems

121. A piece of land is 750 m × 1,158 m. What is the area in hectares?
122. A living room floor measures 18.5 m × 13.5 m. What is the area in m²?
123. How much will it cost to carpet a room 18 m × 14.2 m if the floor covering costs $11.99 per m²?

Volume

Convert the following milliliters to liters:

124. 31,561 ml =   ℓ
125. 46.89 ml =   ℓ

Convert the following liters to kiloliters:

126. 29.1 ℓ =   kl
127. 2,392 ℓ =   kl
128. 4,211,040 ℓ =   kl
129. 391.4 ℓ =   kl
130. .61 ℓ =   kl

131. A container is 22 cm long, 10 cm wide, and 12 cm high. Find the volume in milliliters.
132. A large drum holds 82,750 liters. Give the volume in m³.

133. A large water tank holds 21,309,421 liters. How much is this in kiloliters?

English–Metric Weight Conversions

134.–142. Convert the following English weights to metric weights (rounded to two decimal places):

Item	English Weight	Metric Weight
134. Tomato paste	6 oz.	_____
135. Coffee	16 oz.	_____
136. Jam	12 oz.	_____
137. Grated cheese	3 oz.	_____
138. Apples	3 lb.	_____
139. Peanut butter	1 lb. 2 oz.	_____
140. Pork roast	5.6 lb.	_____
141. Coal	3.5 tn. (T)	_____
142. Steel	18.6 tn. (T)	_____

143.–145. Convert the following metric weights to English weights:

Item	Metric Weight	English Weight
143. Rubber stock	2 t	_____
144. Canned pears	940 g	_____
145. Silver	25 g	_____

English–Metric Length Conversions

146.–150. Convert the following English units of length to metric units:

Item	English Measure	Metric Measure
146. Gold chain	18 in.	_____
147. Rope	40 ft.	_____
148. Ladder	24 ft.	_____
149. Sofa	90 in.	_____
150. Flagpole	150 ft.	_____

UNIT 6 SAMPLE EXAMINATION THE INTERNATIONAL SYSTEM OF UNITS

151. Your lot measures 55 ft. × 160 ft. What is your lot in m^2?

152. If you are traveling 50 miles per hour, how many kilometers per hour are you traveling?

153.–155. Convert the following English units of measure to metric units of measure:

Item	English Measure	Metric Measure
153. Airplane speed	920 mph	_____
154. Bridle path	3.7 mi.	_____
155. Ruler	6 in.	_____

English–Metric Volume Conversions

156.–164. Convert the following English volume to metric volume:

Item	English Volume	Metric Volume
156. Fruit juice	1.5 qt.	_____
157. Perfume	1/2 fl. oz.	_____
158. Gasoline	15.7 gal.	_____
159. Soft drink	36 fl. oz.	_____
160. Milk	1/2 gal.	_____
161. Shampoo	1 pt. 2 fl. oz.	_____
162. Grape juice	1 qt. 6 fl. oz.	_____
163. Cider	5.5 gal.	_____
164. Vinegar	3 qt. 1.5 pt.	_____

Fahrenheit–Celsius Conversions

Convert the following Fahrenheit temperatures to Celsius. (Round your answers to one decimal.)

165. 86° F. =   C.

166. 39° F. =   C.

167. 98.6° F. =   C.

168. 200° F. =   C.

169. 51° F. =   C.

170. 19° F. =   C.

Convert the following Celsius temperatures to Fahrenheit:

171. 90° C. =   F.

172. 39° C. =   F.

173. 25° C. =   F.

174. 10° C. =   F.

175. –10° C. =   F.

UNIT 7 SAMPLE EXAMINATION
THE PROGRAMMABLE ELECTRONIC CALCULATOR

Addition

1. 21.866
    8.2053
    9.05
    2.101
    5.0304
    29.245

2. $59.87
    87.46
    51.23
    86.78
    30.24
    109.74

3. .5604
    .7234
    .9881
    .4638
    .2474
    .6521

4. 81.39 + 27.046 + 38.99176 + 211.3 + 1.4241 =

5. 9,121 + 3,614 + 29,029 + 1,004 + 13,629 =

Subtraction

6. 96.14 − 87.321 =

7. 1,485.20 − 977.66 =

8. 121,461
    −87,577

9. $2,941,860
    −1,999,075

10. 21,416.75
    −19,787.04

Addition and Subtraction

11. 10.3
    27.9
    −3.86
    −2.11
    18.051
    −3.26

12. 9.74
    −41.22
    76.38
    −.47
    −8.27
    80.04

13. 0.21
    3.18
    −1.11
    −2.54
    7.10
    −1.29

14. 121.88
    774.61
    −613.09
    27.13
    −384.12
    75.70

15. 801.37
    −21.08
    −25.65
    −371.21
    488.47
    12.08

UNIT 7 SAMPLE EXAMINATION THE PROGRAMMABLE ELECTRONIC CALCULATOR

Repeated Addition and Subtraction

16. 81.146
    3.991
    3.991
    3.991
    3.991
    74.568

17. 28.84
    31.60
    7.27
    7.27
    7.27
    18.61

18. 2.61
    -.22
    -.22
    .88
    .88
    .88

19. 27,391.15
    27,391.15
    27,391.15
    -8,006.09
    -8,006.09
    -8,006.09

20. 120.1
    -3.2
    -3.2
    -3.2
    -3.2
    6.1

Multiplication (Round your answers to four decimal places.)

21. 715 × 324 =
22. 667 × 261 =
23. 13.1 × .69 =
24. 710.44 × 2.0697 =
25. 81.4439 × 12.765 =

Division (Round your answers to four decimal places.)

26. 17,411.25 ÷ 6.22 =
27. 5.114 ÷ 12.6 =
28. 60 ÷ 70 =
29. 99.143 ÷ 2.99 =
30. 104,691.86 ÷ 28,314.21 =

Addition of Constants

31. 63 + 12.1 =
32. 63 + 191.4 =
33. 63 + 26.18 =
34. 63 + 1.477 =
35. 63 + 2,095.43 =

Subtraction of Constants

36. 14.6 - 7.9 =
37. 297.55 - 7.9 =
38. 181.4 - 7.9 =
39. 2,230 - 7.9 =
40. 18,677.2 - 7.9 =

Multiplication of Constants

41. 5.9 × 316.7 =
42. 5.9 × 2,045.81 =
43. 5.9 × 74.55 =
44. 5.9 × 339,888 =
45. 5.9 × 3.068 =

Constant Divisors (Round your answers to four decimal places.)

46. 131 ÷ 4.6 =
47. 2,911 ÷ 4.6 =
48. 3.89 ÷ 4.6 =
49. 101,699.74 ÷ 4.6 =
50. .0439 ÷ 4.6 =

Percentage Problems Adding Percentage to Amount (In the percentage problems, round your answers to *two* decimal places.)

51. Add 7% to the amount of $41.
52. Add 6.1% to the amount of $20.41.
53. Add 26% to the amount of $504.20.
54. Add 9.6% to the amount of $47.
55. Add 30% to the amount of $86.

Discount and Sales Tax (Round your answers to the penny.)

56. What is the price of a $14.79 item that is discounted 24% and must include a sales tax of 4%?
57. What is the price of an $18.95 item that is discounted 15% and must include a sales tax of 5%?

58. What is the price of a $21.00 item that is discounted 40% and must include a sales tax of 6%?
59. What is the price of a $100.00 item that is discounted 18% and must include a sales tax of 5.5%?
60. What is the price of an $81.44 item that is discounted 35% and must include a sales tax of 5%?

Finding Percentage of a Number (Round your answers to the penny.)

61. What is 3.5% of $12?
62. What is 21.7% of $96.75?
63. What is 87.4% of $2.39?
64. What is 104.1% of $58.67?
65. What is 40% of $1,391.44?

Finding the Whole if Percent is Given (Round your answers to one decimal place.)

66. Twelve dollars is 21% of what amount?
67. Three hundred six is 18.9% of what amount?
68. Forty-eight is 46.3% of what amount?
69. One hundred seventy-five is 100.6% of what amount?
70. Seventy-seven is 96% of what amount?

Markdown Percent (Round your answers to one decimal place.)

71. A $20 item is marked down to $16. What is the discount percent?
72. A $100.50 item is marked down to $89.95. What is the discount percent?
73. A $45.99 item is marked down to $39.00. What is the discount percent?
74. A $55.99 item is marked down to $50. What is the discount percent?
75. A $999.95 item is marked down to $739. What is the discount percent?

Markup Percent (Round your answers to one decimal place.)

76. A $4.50 item is marked up to $5.50. What is the percent of markup?
77. A $1,200 item is marked up to $1,495. What is the percent of markup?
78. A $40.95 item is marked up to $44.95. What is the percent of markup?
79. A $9.95 item is marked up to $12.99. What is the percent of markup?
80. A $295 item is marked up to $309. What is the percent of markup?

Mixed Problems (Round your answers to three decimal places.)

81. $\dfrac{(41.3 + 6.9) \times (19.4 - 3.8)}{(71 + 20.8) \div (2.5 \times 5)} =$

82. $\dfrac{(12.3 - 2.6) + (204 \times 3.5)}{(41.2 + 5) \div (5.2 \times 3)} =$

83. $\dfrac{(61.8 + 2.84) \div (2.1 \times 2.6)}{(6.3 - 3.41) \times (17 \div 3)} =$

84. $\dfrac{(41.6 - 30.8) + (13.4 \times 3.8)}{(23 + 1.7) \times (18 \div 4.4)} =$

85. $\dfrac{(5.4 + 29) \times (19.3 - 5.9)}{(30 \div 5.4) + (9.4 - 6.8)} =$

Prerecorded Program—Compound Interest

86.-95. Solve the following problems on compound interest, using the program card:

	Present Value ($)	No. of Periods	Future Value ($)	Interest Rate (%)
86.	6,000	2	————	5.5
87.	4,500	36	————	7
88.	10,000	6	————	5.25
89.	5,050	24	————	6.5
90.	400	12	————	6
91.	2,525	————	9,281.41	7.5
92.	204	————	279.19	4
93.	100	————	164.78	4.25
94.	10,000	————	20,000	4.5
95.	16,000	————	51,314.17	6

Prerecorded Program—Add-On Rate Installment Loan

96.-100. Solve the following problems on add-on rate installment loans, using the program card:

No. Months	Odd Days	Add-On Rate (%)	Loan Amount ($)	Monthly Payment ($)	Total Interest	Annual Rate (%)
96. 18	2	7.5	1,500	————	————	————
97. 24	0	6.5	545	————	————	————
98. 28	15	7.75	1,275	————	————	————
99. 6	27	5	1,485	————	————	————
100. 10	3	5.5	690	————	————	————

UNIT 8 SAMPLE EXAMINATION
TEN-KEY ADDING AND LISTING MACHINES

Addition

1.	2.	3.	4.	5.
6.91	13.6134	0.391	139,600	$39.85
84.38	18.191	0.466	94,291	4.06
55.60	134.852	0.815	25,887	57.89
109.70	607.9988	0.615	1,223	9.87
3,211.49	11.75	0.089	9,087	2.02
86.57	2.6	1.311	16,654	18.61

6. 8,314 + 9,611 + 41,204 + 879 + 2,046 =

7. 0.394 + 0.865 + 0.21 + 0.391 + .86 =

8. 1.6 + 3.9 + 8.1 + 9.0 + 7.7 =

9. $29.36 + 18.77 + 291.50 + 12.44 + 3.89 =

10. 6,142.85 + 5,299.02 + 875.77 + 28.67 =

11.–12. Find the totals for the following deposit slips:

Coin	$ 9.47		Coin	$ 86.24
Currency	25.00		Currency	105.00
Checks	18.79		Checks	19.87
	34.68			46.77
	1.29			10.30
	4,811.80			294.81
	567.05			14,611.03
	333.98			50.00
11. Total	$_____		12. Total	$_____

13. Find the total units produced for the week:

Mon.	Tues.	Wed.	Thurs.	Fri.	Total
1,297	2,416	991	1,404	3,356	_____

14.–21. Total the monthly sales expense (in dollars) by department (add horizontally) and the monthly sales expense by item (add vertically) for the following:

Department	Magazine Advertising	TV Advertising	Expense Reports	Total
Fashion fabrics	3,400	50,300	14,930	_____ 14.
Industrial fabrics	15,069	20,755	21,614	_____ 15.
Home fabrics	2,455	10,914	5,398	_____ 16.
Auto fabrics	7,884	3,685	7,706	_____ 17.
	19. _____	20. _____	21. _____	_____ 18.

Subtraction

22.–30. Perform the subtractions indicated, and complete the following petty cash record for the current week:

	Balance $188.95			Balance
Envelopes	−1.49	27.		
22.	_____	Notebook paper	−1.91	
Paper plates	−3.61	28.	_____	
23.	_____	Picture hooks	−.78	
Parking fees	−10.38	29.	_____	
24.	_____	Taxi fare	−3.61	
Parchment paper	−4.73	30. Balance	_____	
25.	_____			
Stamps	−13.00			
26.	_____			
Coffee	−5.75			

UNIT 8 SAMPLE EXAMINATION TEN-KEY ADDING AND LISTING MACHINES

Credit Balances

31. 27.43
     -86.91
     17.85
      5.49
    -10.07
     -4.33

32. 1.334
    -2.117
     8.004
    -9.118
    -1.073
     2.765

33.   871,914
   -1,720,566

34. -19,614.30
    15,057.88

35.   11,791.89
   - 20,654.32

36. 71.65 - 88.42 =

37. 3.98 - 4.75 =

38. 18.70 - 29.32 =

39. 3,617.18 - 15,175.02 =

40. 86,921 - 140,367 =

Non-Add

41.–45. Use the Non-add key to enter the department number for each of the following inventory records:

Dept. 3096
   $1.38
   4.61
   4.61
   2.88
   3.16

41. _____ Total

Dept. 3098
   $2.74
   8.10
   2.30
   6.49

43. _____ Total

Dept. 3097
   $18.66
   14.29
    7.60
    8.87

42. _____ Total

Dept. 3099
   $1.40
    .69
    .85
    .39
    .18

44. _____ Total

45. _____ Grand Total for all departments

Multiplication

46. 39.1
   ×4.7

47. 1,041
   ×396

48. 21.04
   ×18.66

49. 67.1
   ×4.7

50. 138
   ×26

INTRODUCTION

51. 236.30 × 5 =

52. 18.79 × .29 =

53. 1,304 × 187 =

54. 538.2 × 10.4 =

55. 6.87 × 9.54 =

56. 18.91 × 46 =

57. 3,111 × 48 =

58. 7.114 × .3 =

59. 28.1 × 18 =

60. 34.66 × 11.04 =

Markon

61.–80. Calculate the amount of markon for the following items. (Round your answers to the penny.)

	Cost of Item ($)	Percent of Markon	Amount of Markon ($)
61.	24.79	21	_____
62.	245.21	17	_____
63.	10.49	13	_____
64.	2,040.88	6	_____
65.	74.93	15	_____
66.	3.80	10.5	_____
67.	37.90	50	_____
68.	560.34	40	_____
69.	9,114.86	25	_____
70.	98.02	12.5	_____
71.	1.18	44	_____
72.	5.79	30	_____
73.	10.41	20	_____
74.	2,643.80	15	_____
75.	769.75	22	_____
76.	2.99	15	_____
77.	.38	29	_____
78.	50.00	30	_____
79.	17.75	60	_____
80.	40.00	65	_____

Division

81.–90. Do the following division problems by the reciprocal method. (Round your answers to whole numbers.)

81. 36.4 ÷ 21 = _____
82. 15.3 ÷ 7 = _____
83. 128 ÷ 64 = _____
84. 18.78 ÷ 16 = _____
85. 294.7 ÷ 105 = _____

86. 125,042 ÷ 914 = _____
87. 41,075 ÷ 194 = _____
88. 6,732 ÷ 591 = _____
89. 54.91 ÷ 26 = _____
90. 919 ÷ 57 = _____

Cost of Individual Items   (Round your answers to the penny.)

91. What is the cost of an apple if six cost $1.19?
92. What is the cost of a typewriter ribbon if a dozen ribbons costs $35.90?
93. What is the cost of a small can of tomato juice if six cans cost 99 cents?
94. What is the cost of one pencil if a gross costs $11.90?
95. A fish bowl contains 158 ounces of water. How many quarts is this? (Round your answer to one decimal place.)
96. What is the cost of a pound of potatoes if 50 pounds cost $2.69?
97. You bought a box of black cherries for $9.00. When you canned these cherries, you had 26 pints. How much did each pint cost?
98. You bought a dozen cupcakes for $1.69. How much was each cupcake?
99. You bought a case of canned grapefruit juice (24 in a case) for $13.00. How much was each can?
100. A ream of bond paper costs $11.69. How much is this per sheet?

UNIT 9 SAMPLE EXAMINATION
TEN-KEY PRINTING CALCULATORS

Addition

	1.	2.	3.	4.
	3.61	.861	7,391	4.678
	6.45	.475	4,820	.249
	100.82	.890	2,566	10.369
	50.21	.121	988	.762
	32.68	.353	1,471	7.956
	217.46	.766	1,021	48.739

5. 994 + 347 + 1,095 + 45,610 + 524,510 =

6. 19.83 + 4.087 + 43,499 + .9152 + 2.0098 =

7. .45 + 5.67 + 6.59 + 11.72 + 11.40 =

8. 57.11 + 89.76 + 5.48 + 22.51 + 20.59 =

Subtotals

9.–12. Add the following weekly calls by salesmen. Subtotal after each salesman's calls, and total at the end.

Salesman	Calls	
A	29	
	16	
	15	
	30	
	18	
	9. ___	Subtotal
B	18	
	17	
	15	
	28	
	15	
	10. ___	Subtotal
C	24	
	30	
	31	
	8	
	16	
	11. ___	Subtotal
	12. ___	Total

Subtraction

13.–22. Perform the subtractions indicated and complete the following check register. Use the Subtotal key.

	Check No.	Date	Amount	Balance $1,542.95
13.	150	4/2	$ 84.71	_____
14.	151	4/2	211.00	_____
15.	152	4/5	110.40	_____

Check No.	Date	Amount	Balance
16. 153	4/7	100.00	_____
17. 154	4/7	15.95	_____
18. 155	4/15	25.00	_____
19. 156	4/21	160.00	_____
20. 157	4/22	15.00	_____
21. 158	4/28	24.16	_____
22. 159	4/29	46.10	_____

Credit Balances

23.–25. The following figures show deposits and check withdrawals from checking accounts. Add the deposits and subtract the withdrawals. *Some* of these accounts are overdrawn. Be sure to indicate *credit balance* for the overdrawn accounts.

23. Beginning Balance $942.60
    Check #202   373.49
    Check #203   507.75
    Check #204   54.90
    Deposit   100.00
    Check #205   175.00

    Balance   _____

24. Beginning Balance $1,043.80
    Check #671   1,064.25
    Check #672   486.75
    Deposit   119.79
    Check #673   2.50
    Check #674   31.67

    Balance   _____

25. Beginning Balance $491.20
    Check #888   26.00
    Check #889   128.75
    Deposit   25.30
    Check #890   221.00
    Check #891   95.28

    Balance   _____

Multiplication (Round your answers to four decimal places.)

26. 232 × 855 =
27. 78.5 × 44.3 =
28. 40.1 × 2.21 =
29. 9,022 × .512 =
30. .887 × .614 =

31. 300,211 × 50,361 =
32. 98.4 × .23 =
33. 771.4 × .866 =
34. 1.3344 × 2.6175 =
35. 1,014 × 25.6 =

Division

Add four zeros to each dividend to provide more places in the quotient. (Round your answers to four decimal places.)

36. 4,119.6 ÷ 2.6 =
37. 1,041.1 ÷ .56 =
38. 730.44 ÷ 3.76 =
39. 25.767 ÷ 44 =
40. 18.1711 ÷ 40 =

41. 698 ÷ 429 =
42. 5,215 ÷ 1,321 =
43. 8,611.7 ÷ 109.2 =
44. .7477 ÷ .86 =
45. 240 ÷ 13.6 =

Multiplication of a Percent (Round your answers to two decimal places.)

46. What is 18.24% of 8,640.21?
47. What is 5% of 216?
48. What is 25% of 8,216?
49. What is 66% of 21.304?
50. What is 11.2% of 50?
51. If 15% of the freshmen class of 791 are science majors, how many are science majors?
52. Twenty-six percent of the 4,211 students are over 21 years old. How many are over 21?
53. Fifty-six percent of the 1,391 students work part time. How many students work part time?

Finding What Percent One Number Is of Another

Add four zeros to your dividend. (Round your answers to two decimal places.)

54. What percent is 26 of 30.1?
55. What percent of 31.4 is 64.6?

56. What percent of 4.46 is 3.1?
57. What percent of 111 is 113.6?
58. What percent is 97 of 104?
59. What percent is 441 of 871?
60. What percent is 7,991 of 8,992?
61. Seventy-five of the 81 graduates in data processing are already employed. What percent is 75 of 81?
62. Thirty-six of the 42 members have an automobile. What percent is 36 of 42?
63. Of the 29 people who were laid off, 25 have been recalled. What percent is 25 of 29?
64. One hundred twelve of the 326 students carry their lunch. What percent is 112 of 326?

Constant Multiplication

65.–77. Calculate the FICA (5.85%) deduction for each of the following employees. (Round your answers to the penny.)

Employee	Weekly Gross Pay ($)	FICA Deduction ($)
65. Rodriguez	207.59	_____
66. Lance	300.46	_____
67. Beeson	220.91	_____
68. Johnson	271.47	_____
69. Solley	210.21	_____
70. De Rita	215.30	_____
71. Murphy	380.64	_____
72. Bertson	392.79	_____
73. Allen	376.19	_____
74. Shoal	170.61	_____
75. Zimmerman	87.92	_____
76. Littell	224.11	_____
77. Milo	161.94	_____

Markon

78.-89. Calculate the percent of markon based on *cost price*. (Round your percent answers to one decimal place.)

	Cost Price ($)	Selling Price ($)	Percent of Markon
78.	79.05	88.60	_____
79.	200.10	229.00	_____
80.	3.79	4.49	_____
81.	16.41	19.80	_____
82.	3,600.00	3,999.99	_____
83.	1,411.00	1,500.00	_____
84.	1.50	1.75	_____
85.	.69	.79	_____
86.	6.00	6.59	_____
87.	79.00	85.00	_____
88.	2.19	2.25	_____
89.	4,700.00	4,900.00	_____

Markup

90.-101. Calculate the percent of markup based on old *selling price* for the following problems. (Round your percent answers to one decimal place.)

	Old Selling Price ($)	New Selling Price ($)	Percent of Markup
90.	63.30	75.00	_____
91.	2.00	2.50	_____
92.	808.00	1,000.00	_____
93.	4,500.00	4,700.00	_____
94.	86.99	95.99	_____
95.	46.98	52.00	_____
96.	5.99	6.99	_____
97.	12.95	14.95	_____

	Old Selling Price ($)	New Selling Price ($)	Percent of Markup
98.	7.99	8.59	_____
99.	206.00	215.00	_____
100.	49.98	55.99	_____
101.	1,200.00	1,600.00	_____

Markdown

102.-111. Calculate the percent of markdown based on original selling price for the following problems. (Round your percent answer to one decimal place.)

	Original Selling Price ($)	Sale Price ($)	Percent of Markdown
102.	79.99	69.98	_____
103.	5.99	4.98	_____
104.	1,000.00	888.88	_____
105.	17.00	15.00	_____
106.	79.00	50.00	_____
107.	2,800.00	1,400.00	_____
108.	850.00	599.00	_____
109.	15.99	12.00	_____
110.	98.00	70.00	_____
111.	54.95	26.99	_____

UNIT 10 SAMPLE EXAMINATION FULL-BANK ADDING MACHINE

Addition

1.	2.	3.	4.	5.
9.27	981	3.925	25,699	$181.20
10.57	1,021	.467	18,471	93.67
98.91	2,224	9.923	15,303	250.00
103.17	367	.340	2,202	79.81
20.91	482	6.473	4,459	367.03
216.49	981	67.383	6,600	121.11

INTRODUCTION

6. 437 + 369 + 6,082 + 75,403 + 261,031 =

7. 72.8 + 5.73 + 6.4078 + 28 + 199.6 + .0703 =

8. 59 + .87 + 8,113.21 + .58 + 9.41 =

9. 24.81 + 6.717 + 26,409 + .6187 + 83.121 =

10. 81,091 + 4,217 + 8,630 + 4,620 + 3,791 =

11.–23. Add horizontally the number of V-belts produced by each employee for the week. Then add vertically the number of V-belts built each day.

Employee	M	T	W	T	F	S	Totals
Carr	130	127	120	140	123	–	11. _____
Jenkins	124	118	126	129	115	80	12. _____
Prizakolis	96	101	114	105	111	–	13. _____
Reber	140	136	137	135	135	90	14. _____
Sanderson	136	130	134	135	134	75	15. _____
Vulleman	118	126	130	127	125	87	16. _____
Totals	17. ___	18. ___	19. ___	20. ___	21. ___	22. ___	23. _____

24.–25. Find the total for the following deposit slips:

Currency	$259.00
Coin	26.81
Checks	121.30
	25.19
	73.63
	57.85
	356.39
	87.86
Total	_____ 24.
Date 11-3	

Currency	$819.00
Coin	34.79
Checks	106.85
	31.35
	44.60
	3.89
	271.00
	110.40
Total	_____ 25.
Date 11-4	

Double Addition

26.–34. In your answers, convert 16 ounces or over to pounds; convert 12 inches or over to feet; convert 3 feet or over to yards.

26. 6 lb., 4 oz.
    10 lb., 15 oz.
    21 lb., 18 oz.
     4 lb., 2 oz.
    15 lb., 11 oz.
     2 lb., 10 oz.
    ─────────────

27. 6 lb., 3 oz.
    11 lb., 14 oz.
    23 lb., 19 oz.
     3 lb., 4 oz.
    14 lb., 4 oz.
     5 lb., 2 oz.
    ─────────────

28. 6 ft., 11 in.
     2 ft., 5 in.
     9 ft., 7 in.
    24 ft., 3 in.
     7 ft., 9 in.
            8 in.
    ─────────────

29. 4 ft., 7 in.
     2 ft., 6 in.
    17 ft., 5 in.
     2 ft., 9 in.
    18 ft., 4 in.
     5 ft., 8 in.
    ─────────────

30. 3 yd., 9 ft.
     2 yd., 5 ft.
    16 yd., 3 ft.
     5 yd., 2 ft.
    19 yd., 4 ft.
    12 yd., 7 ft.
    ─────────────

31. 4 yd., 6 in.
     3 yd., 9 in.
    15 yd., 20 in.
     6 yd., 7 in.
    18 yd., 9-1/2 in.
     2 yd., 3 in.
    ─────────────

32. 7 yd., 2 ft., 1 in.
    10 yd., 3 ft., 7 in.
            1 ft., 9 in.
     4 yd., 2 ft.
     6 yd.,   3 in.
                 4-1/2 in.
    ─────────────

33. *Value*   *Shipping Weight*
     ($)   *(lb.)*
     ─────────────────────────────
      34.90   2.4
       8.75   1.2
     304.00   26.0
      16.35   5.5
      39.64   8.3
     181.32   34.8
     ─────────────────────────────

34. 17 yd.,   1 ft.,   1/2 in.
     7 yd., 2-1/2 ft.,   2 in.
     3 yd.,   2 ft.,   7 in.
    12 yd.,   4-1/2 in.
            2-1/2 ft.,   5 in.
     6 yd.,   3 in.
    ─────────────────────────────

Subtraction

35.–44. Perform the subtractions and subtotals indicated and complete the following check register:

	Balance	
	$14,719.33	
Check 77	− 27.14	
	_____	35.
Check 78	− 136.87	
	_____	36.
Check 79	−1,872.00	
	_____	37.
Check 80	− 591.26	
	_____	38.
Check 81	− 999.97	
	_____	39.
Check 82	− 50.71	
	_____	40.
Check 83	− 400.29	
	_____	41.
Check 84	−1,211.01	
	_____	42.
Check 85	− 36.20	
	_____	43.
Check 86	− 1.98	
Balance	_____	44.

Credit Balances

45.–52. The following problems represent checking account records. The positive numbers are deposits, and the negative amounts are checks drawn on the account. *Some* of these accounts are overdrawn. Be sure to indicate *credit balance* on the overdrawn accounts.

UNIT 10 SAMPLE EXAMINATION FULL-BANK ADDING MACHINE 83

Balance	$1,294.36		Balance	$540.29	
check	-380.24		check	-480.30	
check	-120.20		deposit	200.00	
check	- 14.87		check	- 24.30	
deposit	202.47		check	- 19.87	
check	-580.29		check	- 5.81	
	————	45.		————	46.

Balance	$139.64		Balance	$3,028.41	
check	-180.19		check	-1,211.87	
check	- 25.00		deposit	500.00	
deposit	50.00		check	-1,000.91	
check	- 26.18		check	- 479.00	
check	- 8.94		check	- 221.46	
	————	47.		————	48.

Balance	$ 6,291.44		Balance	$754.00	
deposit	30,811.06		check	-500.00	
check	-21,294.83		check	- 27.82	
check	-18,166.07		check	-220.01	
check	-13,961.67		deposit	13.85	
check	-10,000.30		check	- 46.73	
	————	49.		————	50.

Balance	$2,300.74		Balance	$492.00	
check	-1,299.40		check	- 37.40	
check	- 46.82		check	-110.40	
check	-1,000.00		check	-400.12	
deposit	550.00		deposit	25.00	
check	- 750.00		deposit	15.00	
	————	51.		————	52.

Non-Add and Subtotals

53.–63. The following are sales orders by customer for the month. Use the Non-add key to indicate the customer code. Take a subtotal after each customer and then take a grand total for all customers.

84 INTRODUCTION

Customer	Sales Orders ($)		Customer	Sales Orders ($)	
#3904	1,390		#4129	767	
	2,100			594	
	390			627	
	560				
	53. _____	Subtotal	58.	_____	Subtotal
#3918	2,149		#4151	1,299	
	575			947	
	860		59.	_____	Subtotal
	54. _____	Subtotal	#4172	2,390	
#3929	1,491			3,100	
	2,261			2,100	
	870			946	
	55. _____	Subtotal	60.	_____	Subtotal
#3986	561		#4191	541	
	324			322	
	756			129	
	29		61.	_____	Subtotal
	56. _____	Subtotal	#4206	4,105	
#4104	1,299			2,999	
	875			3,260	
	2,054		62.	_____	Subtotal
	57. _____	Subtotal	63.	_____	Total

Multiplication

Perform the following multiplications. (Round your answers to four decimal places.)

64. 736 × 291 =

65. 42.3 × 21.9 =

66. 60.49 × .416 =

67. .464 × .921 =

68. 666 × 2.54 =

69. 91.66 × 8.9113 =

70. .224 × 1.667 =

71. 9,002 × 24.1 =

72. 15.77 × 14.683 =

73. 38.1 × 4.16 =

74. 42.96 × 9.85 =

Markdown

75.-87. Calculate the amount of markdown for the following items. (Round your answers to the penny.)

	Regular Selling Price ($)	Percent of Markdown	Amount of Markdown ($)
75.	88.37	13	_____
76.	359.76	22	_____
77.	9.52	21	_____
78.	55.20	5	_____
79.	3,208.60	12	_____
80.	274.86	10	_____
81.	2.98	15	_____
82.	672.50	12.5	_____
83.	888.88	30	_____
84.	90.59	18	_____
85.	24.99	33	_____
86.	6.50	50	_____
87.	9.95	25	_____

Division

Perform the following division problems. (Round your answers to one decimal place. For money problems, round to the penny.)

88. $4.619 \div 4 =$

89. $352.14 \div 18 =$

90. $328.6 \div 54 =$

91. $6,919 \div 989 =$

92. $17.123 \div 25 =$

93. $2,129 \div 85 =$

94. $28,901 \div 671 =$

95. How many pounds are in 56 ounces?

96. What is the cost of one marking crayon if a dozen crayons costs $7.50?

86 INTRODUCTION

97. A room measures 191 square feet. How much is this in square yards?

98. A restaurant coffee server holds 1,000 ounces of coffee. How many gallons is this? How many 6-ounce coffee cups does the server hold?

99. What is the cost of an envelope if 40 cost 69 cents?

100. A thermos holds 22 ounces of liquid. How many pints is this?

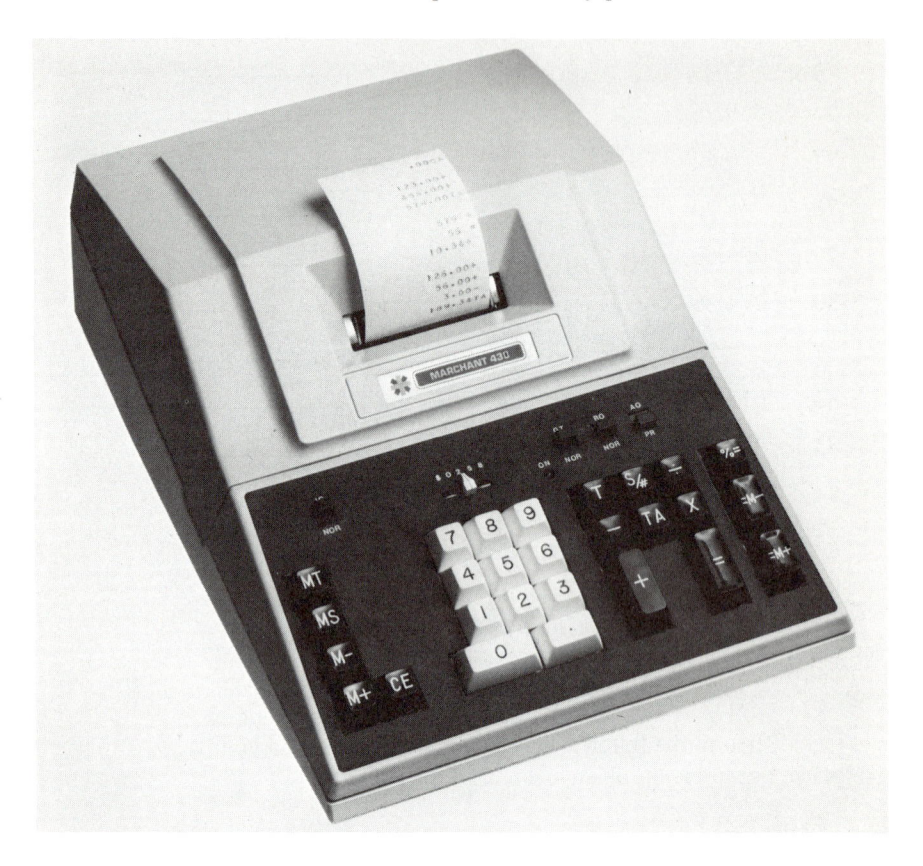

Marchant 430 (*Courtesy of Marchant, a division of Addmaster Corporation*)

IT	Item Count	T	Total
MT	Memory Total	S/#	Subtotal/Non-Add
MS	Memory Subtotal	÷	Dividend Key
M−	Memory Minus	−	Minus Key
M+	Memory Plus	TA	Tape Advance
CE	Clear Entry	X	Multiplication Key
$	Add Mode	+	Plus Key
0, 2, 5, 8	Decimal Selector	=	Equals Key
GT	Grand Total	%=	Percent Equals
RO	Round-Off Switch	=M−	Total Memory Minus Key
AO	Answer Only	=M+	Total Memory Plus Key

UNIT 10 SAMPLE EXAMINATION FULL-BANK ADDING MACHINE

Marchant 294D (*Courtesy of Marchant, a division of Addmaster Corporation*)

RO	Round-Off Switch	1F/2F	First Factor/Second Factor (Constant)
Cut	Cut Off		
$	Add Mode	AO	Answer Only
0, 2, 5	Decimal Selector	Disp	Display Only
MT	Memory Total	T	Total
MS	Memory Subtotal	–	Minus Key
M–	Memory Minus	+	Plus Key
M+	Memory Plus	S/#	Subtotal/Non-Add Key
TA	Tape Advance	%=	Percent Equals
IC	Item Count	=M–	Total Memory Minus Key
CA	Clear All	=M+	Total Memory Plus Key
CE	Clear Entry	÷	Dividend Key
0	Single Cipher	X	Multiplication Key
00	Double Cipher	=	Equals Key

INTRODUCTION

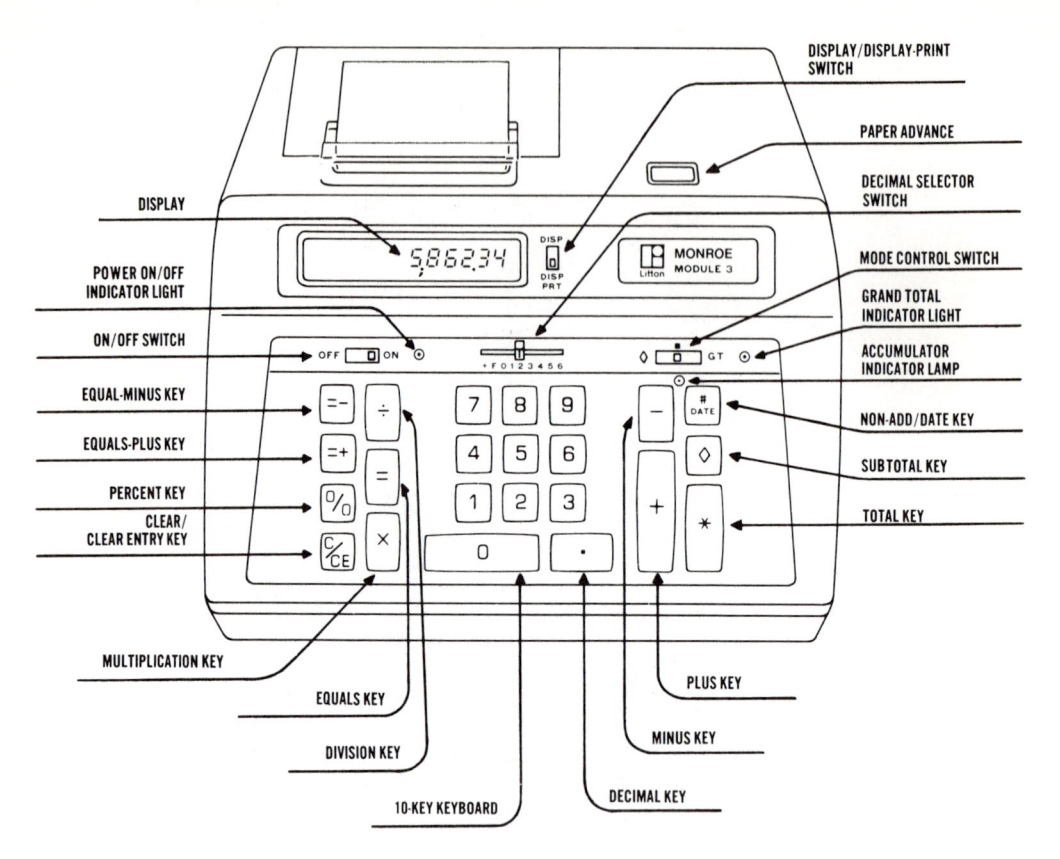

Monroe 1430 (*Courtesy of Monroe, The Calculator Company*)

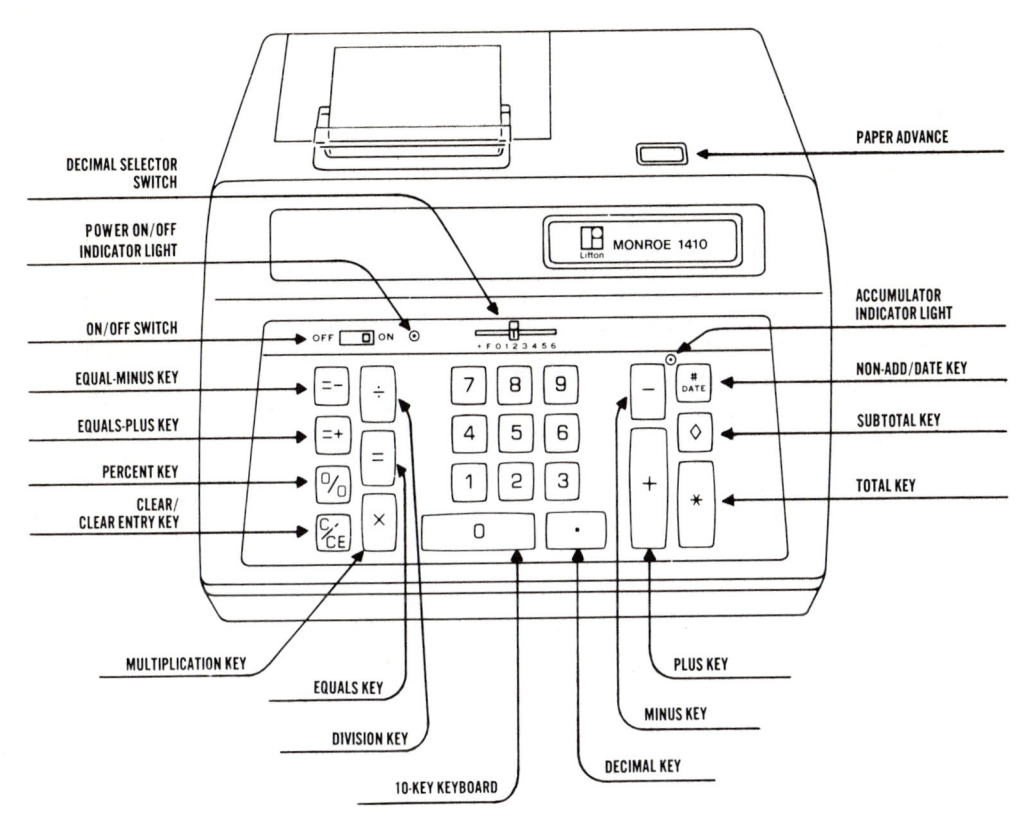

UNIT 10 SAMPLE EXAMINATION FULL-BANK ADDING MACHINE

Monroe 1410 (*Courtesy of Monroe, The Calculator Company*)

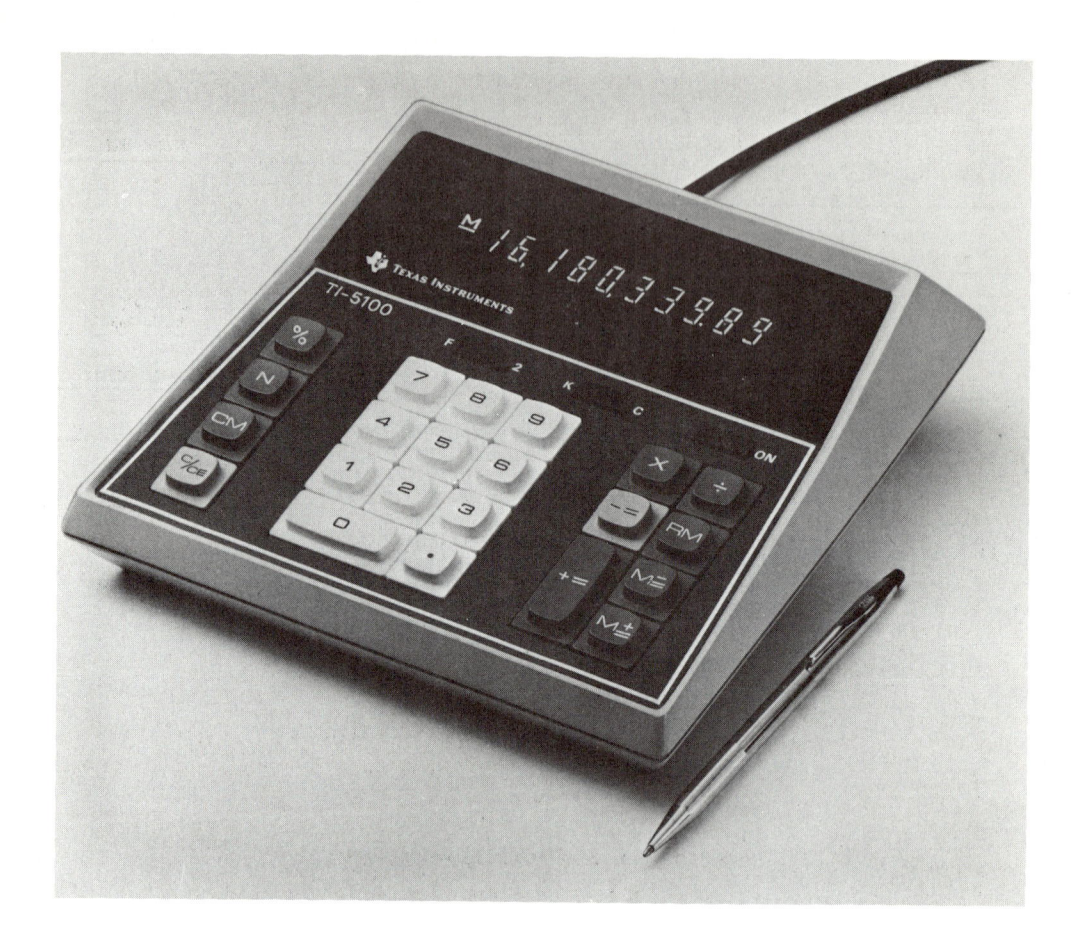

Texas Instruments T1-5100 (*Courtesy of Texas Instruments, Incorporated*)

%	Percent Key	−=	Minus Equals Key
N	Item Count	+=	Plus Equals Key
CM	Clear Memory	÷	Dividend Key
C/CE	Clear/Clear Entry	RM	Recall Memory
F	Floating Decimal	M≡	Memory Minus Equals
K	Chain or Constant Mode	M±	Memory Plus Equals
X	Multiplication Key		

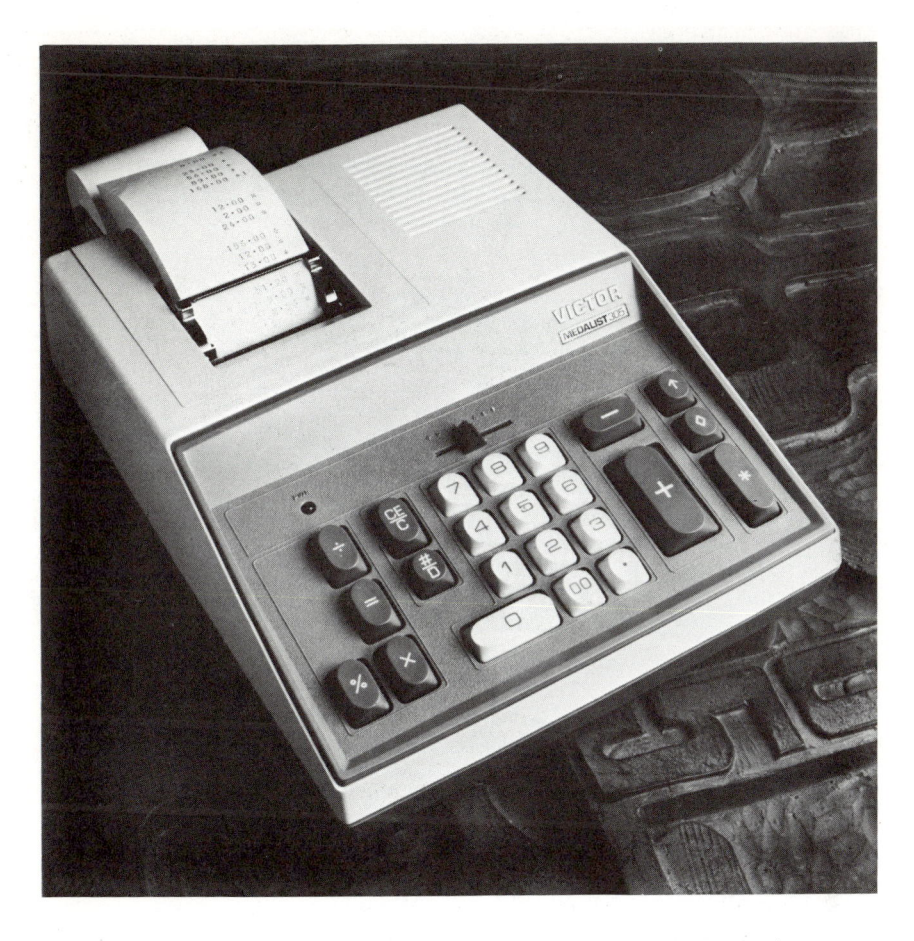

UNIT 10 SAMPLE EXAMINATION FULL-BANK ADDING MACHINE

Victor Medalist 305 (*Courtesy of Victor Comptometer Corporation*)

%	Percent Key	00	Double Cipher
÷	Dividend Key	−	Minus Key
=	Equals Key	+	Plus Key
×	Multiplication Key	↑	Tape Advance
CE	Clear Entry	◊	Subtotal Key
#/D	Non-Add/Date Print Key	*	Total Key
0	Single Cipher		

Victor Medalist 332 (*Courtesy of Victor Comptometer Corporation*)

CA	Clear All	−	Minus Key
=−	Equals Minus Key	+	Plus Key
=+	Equals Plus Key	↑	Tape Advance Key
%	Percent Key	N	Item Count Key
÷	Dividend Key	◊	Subtotal Key
=	Equals Key	*	Total Key
×	Multiplication Key	M*	Memory Total
CE	Clear Entry	M−	Memory Minus
#/D	Date Print Key	M+	Memory Plus
0	Single Cipher	M◊	Memory Subtotal
00	Double Cipher		

Unit 1

The Touch System for Ten-Key Office Machines

It is extremely important that you begin your skill development on ten-key office machines by learning the touch system. In the touch system, you always enter the same digit with the same finger, and you enter figures on the keyboard by touch—without looking at the keys. Begin using the correct fingering on your very first problem. If you use incorrect fingering, you will never be able to attain the speed and accuracy that is expected of a ten-key machine operator. *Never* enter a figure on the keyboard with the incorrect finger, because this habit is a difficult one to break and one which will impede your progress.

Keeping your eyes on your copy instead of turning your head or shifting your eyes back and forth between your copy and the keyboard will enable you to perform calculations in less than half the time and with less fatigue. Since only one hand is required to operate a ten-key machine, the other hand is left free for handling papers or for keeping your place as you go down a column of figures.

The touch method of operating calculators has been so successful and popular that now nearly all business machines, as well as data entry equipment, are designed with the standardized ten-key keyboard operated by the touch system. Therefore, your skill will be transferable to other machines. The touch system is used on all desk-top ten-key printing calculators, adding machines, and electronic calculators. Only the hand-held electronic calculator does not lend itself to the touch system because of its small-sized keyboard.

Study the illustrations which show the correct fingering and hand positions for ten-key machine operators. Cup your hand and rest your fingers lightly on the home row (4, 5, and 6). Right-handed operators use the index finger for the 4, the middle finger for the 5, and the ring finger for the 6. Many left-handed people are much more efficient using their right hand on ten-key calculators. However, if you *must* use your left hand, use the ring finger for the 4, the middle finger for the 5, and the index finger for the 6. Right-handed operators use the thumb for the zero and the little finger for the add bar. Left-handed operators use the thumb for the add bar, and either the little finger or the thumb for the zero.

The hand is kept hovering over the home row, and all keys are depressed from

THE TOUCH SYSTEM FOR TEN-KEY OFFICE MACHINES

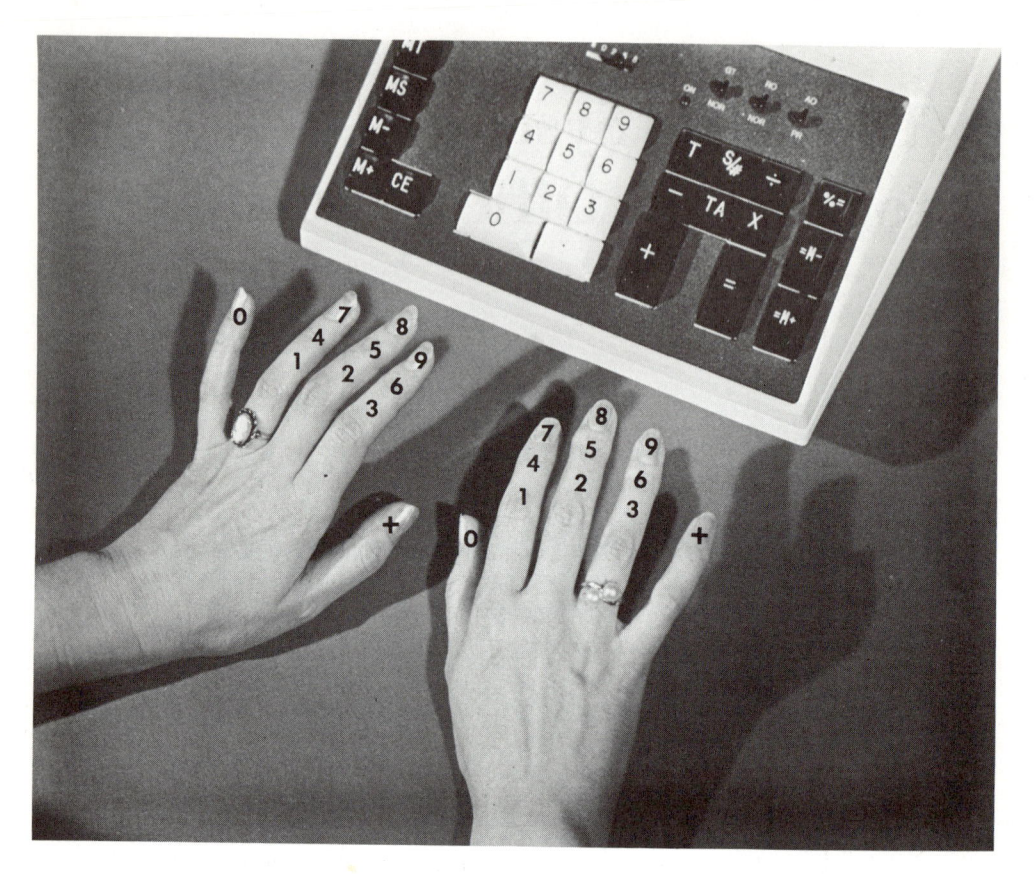

Touch System Fingering

this home-row position. Numbers are entered as read, from left to right. Your fingers will soon become sensitive to the feel of the home row. In fact, many calculators have a different curvature to the home row so that you can "feel" that you are on the correct row. Also, some calculators have a raised dot on the 5 key, which you can feel on your middle finger.

    Mastering the correct fingering and the touch system is a vital part of your learning. It will be needed in every operation you do on any ten-key equipment.

    Because addition represents one of the most frequently used processes performed in industry, and because proficiency in the touch system is expected, the mastering of the touch system is an integral part of your learning in this book. When you develop proficiency in the touch system, you should be able to enter over 200 strokes per minute on the ten-key keyboard.

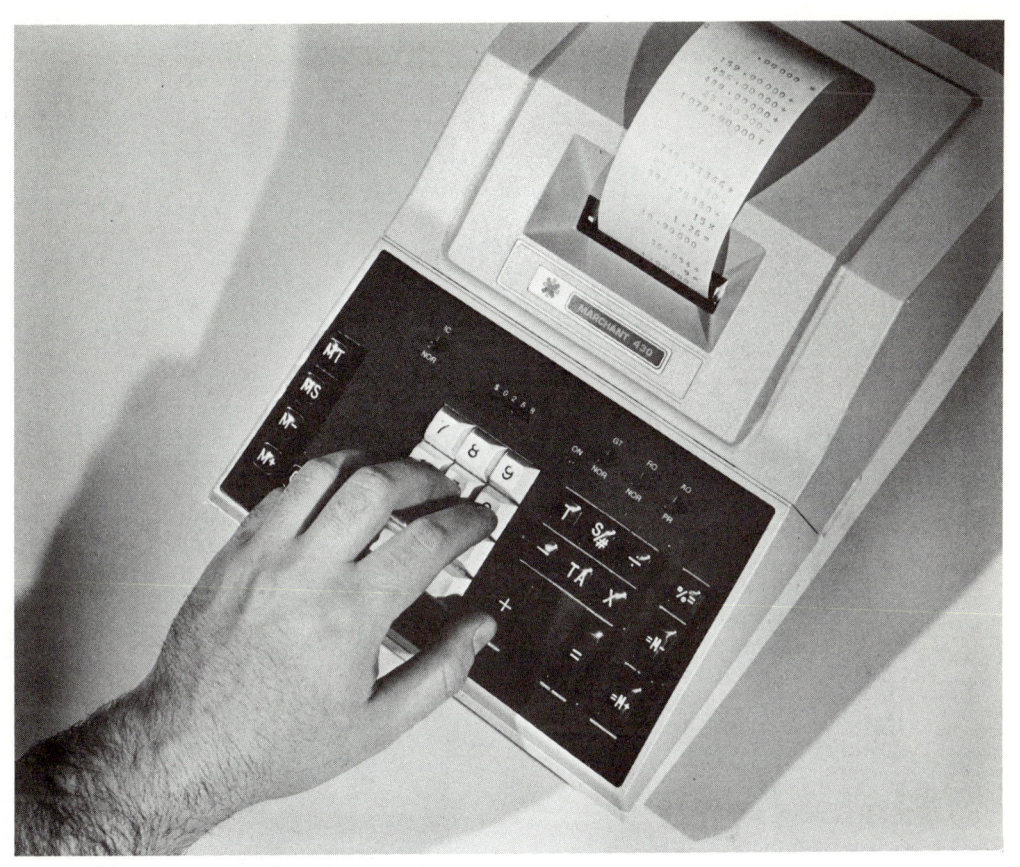

Home Row Position, Left Hand

PROFICIENCY TEST

Dr. Herbert S. Madaus and Mrs. Augusta C. Yrle, of the University of New Orleans, believe that a proficiency test can aid learners in achieving the skills of speed and accuracy in touch operation with a minimum of fatigue.[1] The test can be taken on *any* ten-key machine with a tape.

Their proficiency test, which is shown here, must be added correctly within a certain period of time. The grade is based on how quickly the student can correctly

---

[1] Herbert S. Madaus and Augusta C. Yrle, "Developing Proficiency in Ten-Key Touch Operation," *Business Education Forum* 30, no. 7 (April 1976):10–11.

Reprinted by permission of the National Business Education Association and the authors.

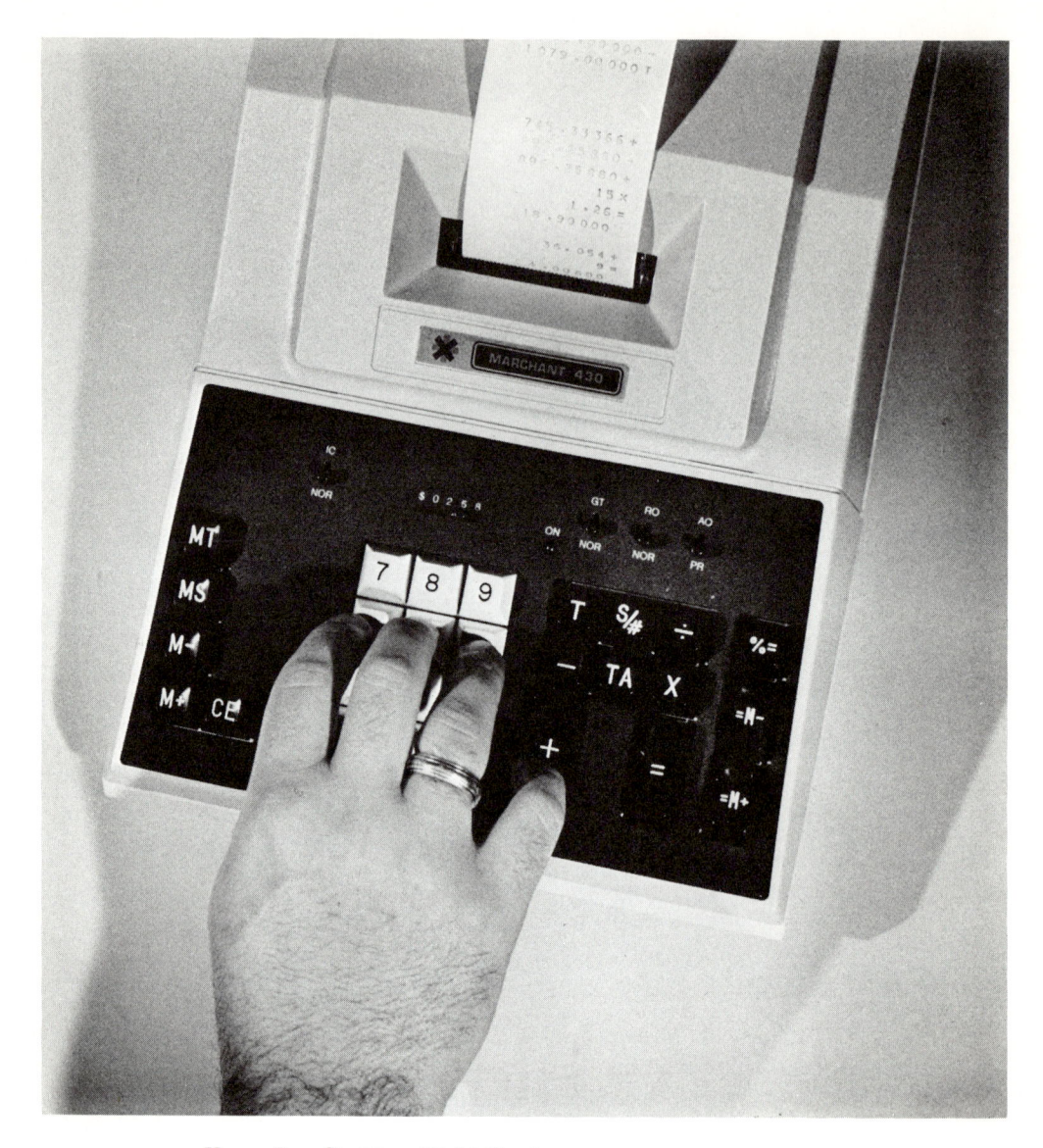

Home Row Position, Right Hand

add the two columns of figures on a ten-key machine. The student may practice ahead of time and may be retested. His best effort counts.

4,849	6,521
424	235,489
3,951	30,000
5,867	1,470
10,736	852
559	481,562
4,070	7,700
4,515	6,355
13,670	11,220
79,281	1,364
4	45
4,235,860	125
200	500
84,136	8,529
70,903	9
367,420	8,175
41,876	4,325
61	759
637	4,868
188	13,726
3,734	75
3,852	61,547
1,245	275,846
2,169	3,827
75	13,463
100	998
10,483	5,847
12,663	963
1,057	6,282
1,367	84,620
5,843	7,500
30,076	7,832
951	70
78,652	52,648
357	100
8,815	9,393
4,625	1,545
5,095,271*	1,356,150*

Standards

In order to qualify, both lists of numbers must be added correctly by touch. Grades are based on time, as follows:

120 seconds or less   A
121–140 seconds   B
141–160 seconds   C
161–200 seconds   D
over 200 seconds   F

After you have completed Unit 1 on touch operation, return to this test and practice it frequently in order to increase your speed and accuracy in touch operation. Then try the test under timed conditions until you are able to meet the standards. Your instructor may wish to use this test grade as a bonus grade or as one of the regular test grades in the course, using your best effort as the one that counts.

THE HOME ROW

Perform the following drills for developing touch addition on the home row. Be *sure* to use the correct finger for each key.

FINGERING DRILLS—HOME ROW

When working with whole numbers, set your decimal at 0. If you are operating the calculator with your right hand, use your index finger for 4, your middle finger for 5, and your ring finger for 6. If you are operating the calculator with your left hand, use your ring finger for 4, your middle finger for 5, and your index finger for 6. After you enter each number on the keyboard with the correct finger, depress the Add bar with the little finger (right hand) or the thumb (left hand). At the end of the column, depress the Total bar with the little finger (right hand) or the thumb (left hand).

45	45	64	55	66	64	64	54	66	46
45	56	64	44	44	46	64	44	66	46
44	65	46	66	55	65	56	45	55	64
55	54	46	56	64	56	56	46	55	64
45	44	65	65	65	66	55	45	44	65
54	55	65	46	46	56	55	46	44	65
55	66	56	64	56	46	54	46	45	56
56	64	56	44	46	65	45	64	45	56
65	46	46	45	64	66	56	64	54	64
66	65	46	54	45	65	66	46	54	46
530	560	554	539	551	595	571	500	528	572

Keep your pencil between your thumb and forefinger across your palm while operating the calculator. The point of the pencil will face out beyond your little finger. Merely pivot the pencil down with your thumb to record answers. This procedure will increase your speed and efficiency.

TIMED STROKING DRILL 1

45	65	46	64	64	55	64	45	44	45
56	64	45	66	64	56	64	45	55	56
65	66	46	45	45	54	46	55	66	65
54	65	45	45	54	45	46	55	55	54
45	64	56	54	45	65	45	66	44	46
56	65	65	46	46	56	45	66	45	64
66	56	56	64	64	46	54	65	46	56
65	56	65	46	65	65	45	65	64	65
64	46	44	64	64	64	56	56	64	66
64	46	45	56	66	45	65	56	56	64
580	593	513	550	577	551	530	574	539	581

Are you getting the right answers? If you get an incorrect total, redo the problem before going on to the next one. Sit up straight. Keep your feet flat on the floor.

54	46	56	65	64	54	45	66	65	64
54	55	64	64	65	54	56	55	64	64
45	56	46	46	46	45	65	44	64	46
46	65	55	56	56	45	54	55	46	46
64	56	66	54	55	54	45	55	46	45
54	45	55	45	66	54	56	46	54	65
45	46	44	54	44	45	65	65	56	64
56	65	46	45	45	56	54	65	65	46
65	64	64	46	45	56	45	64	64	64
54	66	54	64	46	65	55	64	56	46
537	564	550	539	532	528	540	579	580	550

TIMED STROKING DRILL 1

Have yourself timed for *four* minutes. Answers must be correct! If you do not complete the 500 strokes within four minutes, continue practicing the fingering drills. If you *do* complete the drill successfully, try the Proficiency Test on page 97.

1.	52,983		2.	1,487		3.	67,034	
	33,984			37,009			34,934	
	99			23,487			20,134	
	14,983			839,348			7,932	
	489,039	(23)		3,290	(74)		54,694	(124)
	40,115			187,347			87,349	
	398,583			21,319			98,347	
	394,384			9,003			80,765	
	11,349			14,834			52,870	
	78,302	(50)		432,984	(100)		984,232	(150)
	1,513,821			1,570,108			1,488,291	

4.
5,903
13,924
47,923
34,934
54,905 (174)
329,598
4,132
44,985
31,842
158,849 (200)
726,995

5.
934,219
32,837
1,982
239,933
42,985 (226)
5,534
193,925
8,988
28,629
19,414 (250)
1,508,446

6.
345,192
124,098
385
51,934 (270)
921,938
385,834
234,987
384
13,524
8,114 (300)
2,086,390

7.
984,993
158,286
35,402
1,348
3,209 (325)
325
3,987
213,514
115,398
394,938 (350)
1,911,400

8.
2,028
4,230
394
44,309
3,942
8,398 (374)
98,344,235
834,985
445,938
219,129 (400)
99,907,588

9.
49,003
8,345
543,625
8,355
934,984 (425)
449,934
385
584,913
952,395
6,385 (450)
3,538,324

10.
1,853
37,540
115,248
3,385
10,831 (474)
143,023
3,875
34,938
78,385
211,509 (500)
640,587

Is your calculator turned to a comfortable angle?

FINGERING DRILLS—FIRST ROW

64	45	66	44	56	45	55	55	46	56
65	55	65	45	55	54	66	56	64	54
66	66	56	46	54	56	55	65	45	55
65	65	46	45	45	45	45	64	46	66
64	55	64	44	55	66	54	66	45	64
46	54	65	55	56	46	65	45	44	65
45	44	56	54	65	64	56	56	54	56
56	45	46	56	64	55	64	65	56	46
65	46	64	55	46	44	46	66	55	54
64	64	44	66	54	55	64	64	54	45
600	539	572	510	550	530	570	602	509	561

Keep your fingers curved. Keep your eyes on the copy.

44	46	65	55	46	46	44	54	46	56
46	44	55	44	45	65	66	65	55	46
54	65	45	66	46	56	65	56	54	64
56	64	46	64	66	64	56	55	66	54
66	46	64	56	65	54	54	54	65	55
54	54	65	55	64	65	66	46	64	56
56	55	66	54	55	64	56	64	46	64
65	56	54	64	65	46	54	65	45	66
66	65	55	46	56	56	46	44	55	44
44	54	46	56	45	44	44	46	65	55
551	549	561	560	553	560	551	549	561	560

FINGERING DRILLS—FIRST ROW

For the right hand, use your index finger for 1, your middle finger for 2, and your ring finger for 3. For the left, use your ring finger for 1, your middle finger for 2, and your index finger for 3.

11	33	13	22	33	22	23	21	31	32
22	22	23	21	11	21	32	32	13	21
12	32	31	12	22	11	33	12	23	13
21	32	32	23	12	12	31	21	33	23
12	23	11	32	23	33	32	23	32	21
33	23	31	21	31	12	21	22	13	32
23	13	33	12	32	32	12	13	31	13
32	31	13	33	33	23	31	33	33	33
31	12	22	31	13	13	13	31	12	32
13	21	31	13	32	31	23	11	21	31
210	242	240	220	242	210	251	219	242	251

Keep your fingers hovering over the home row. Are you keeping your eyes on your copy? Soon you will be able to enter digits with accuracy, speed, and confidence.

12	31	12	23	21	23	32	12	22	23
22	12	23	21	23	32	23	23	21	32
22	12	32	12	13	32	12	33	11	33
11	31	31	32	21	22	21	12	12	31
13	12	13	21	32	33	22	22	33	32
32	23	32	32	23	32	23	21	12	21
23	32	31	23	12	31	12	32	32	12
31	13	33	33	31	23	22	31	23	31
13	31	32	12	13	31	11	21	12	13
21	12	23	31	32	13	33	21	31	23
200	209	262	240	221	272	211	228	209	251

Never enter a digit with the incorrect finger. You may be slow at first, but your skill will develop rapidly. Work quickly and carefully. Do not look at your machine except to check the total.

21	31	32	23	32	23	12	31	13	11
32	13	21	12	31	12	22	12	32	11
12	23	13	31	23	22	22	12	12	22
21	33	23	13	31	11	11	31	31	22
23	32	21	32	13	33	13	12	22	33
22	13	32	23	32	12	32	23	31	33
13	31	13	32	23	23	23	32	13	12
33	33	33	32	12	33	31	13	32	12
31	12	32	22	21	12	13	31	23	13
11	21	31	33	22	22	21	12	31	13
219	242	251	253	240	203	200	209	240	182

Are you becoming more accurate? Do *not* turn your head from your copy to your machine. You'll be able to do twice the work with half the effort.

21	21	23	11	31	12	13	22	31	11
12	32	23	12	32	21	12	13	31	12
21	31	31	22	33	12	11	21	13	13
12	21	31	23	13	21	33	22	13	32
12	21	13	33	12	13	22	33	31	33
12	13	32	33	11	21	11	31	31	21
21	21	13	32	13	23	23	32	13	22
23	23	31	23	31	32	32	33	31	23
23	31	13	23	21	33	13	11	31	32
32	32	31	32	12	22	31	12	23	31
189	246	241	244	209	210	201	230	248	230

FINGERING DRILLS—THIRD ROW

For the right hand, use your index finger for 7, your middle finger for 8, and your ring finger for 9. For the left, use your ring finger for 7, your middle finger for 8, and your index finger for 9. Use your little finger for the Total key (right). Use the thumb for the Total key (left).

77	77	79	87	78	98	98	77	78	97
88	98	98	89	79	89	78	99	87	98
99	89	79	89	79	89	89	98	89	89
99	79	98	97	97	78	98	89	98	98
99	89	87	89	87	79	87	89	88	98
99	99	89	98	89	77	79	78	87	78
89	77	79	78	87	98	97	87	89	87
98	78	97	77	89	88	89	88	79	78
97	89	98	78	78	89	87	89	78	88
98	89	89	79	89	89	88	98	79	89
943	864	893	861	852	874	890	892	852	900

Keep your fingers curved and hovering over the home row.

87	79	79	78	77	78	88	87	98	89
78	87	78	89	79	87	77	98	89	97
87	88	88	79	78	97	99	89	88	79
88	77	99	89	87	89	98	87	88	97
89	78	87	79	77	88	89	79	78	77
98	77	89	88	89	89	98	88	87	78
78	79	79	87	89	98	89	98	77	79
87	88	78	79	97	97	99	78	87	89
98	89	77	89	79	79	77	99	97	89
89	98	89	98	79	97	78	97	87	97
879	840	843	855	831	899	892	900	876	871

Sit up straight to avoid fatigue. Keep your feet flat on the floor.

99	97	88	88	89	77	98	97	88	87
99	79	89	79	99	79	78	98	98	98
79	89	99	97	97	87	99	99	87	87
89	87	97	98	78	98	77	98	87	89
98	78	79	97	89	78	79	89	89	98
78	89	87	87	78	79	97	87	97	87
79	97	87	77	89	77	88	79	98	88
97	88	97	78	98	99	89	98	88	78
87	99	77	78	97	78	98	87	87	98
89	87	98	87	79	89	87	79	79	79
894	890	898	866	893	841	890	911	898	889

Is your calculator turned to a comfortable angle for you? If you get an incorrect total, redo the problem before going on to the next one.

89	79	79	97	89	98	99	88	77	79
87	89	98	79	98	89	87	97	98	78
99	88	98	89	78	77	98	88	79	98
88	99	99	88	77	88	98	88	99	79
77	78	98	78	87	79	77	99	88	79
79	87	77	98	89	77	89	97	88	77
89	79	79	97	87	98	97	79	89	98
88	97	98	78	97	78	88	79	78	87
78	87	88	79	88	97	79	97	87	89
99	78	77	99	87	77	77	88	77	88
873	861	891	882	877	858	889	900	860	852

FINGERING DRILLS—FIRST COLUMN

For the right hand, use your index finger for 1, 4, and 7. For the left, use your ring finger for 1, 4, and 7. Don't raise your hand away from the keyboard.

14	47	74	47	14	47	71	47	74	47
47	17	71	44	74	41	17	41	17	74
47	74	14	41	47	44	14	44	41	14
74	71	41	47	71	11	11	74	14	14
71	11	71	74	74	77	44	41	47	71
17	74	17	71	47	74	47	77	74	74
74	41	47	17	71	71	74	44	47	71
71	74	47	41	17	14	71	11	44	11
41	47	74	14	47	17	17	14	41	14
14	17	41	74	71	41	47	17	74	47
470	473	497	470	533	437	413	410	473	437

Keep your fingers hovering over the home row!

71	74	47	71	17	47	71	14	41	11
41	71	74	71	14	74	47	41	14	14
14	71	14	74	14	71	41	77	17	44
14	17	77	47	17	77	44	71	47	41
41	47	44	74	11	71	47	17	74	74
11	71	11	44	14	74	41	11	17	77
14	17	17	41	17	71	14	14	77	14
17	47	17	14	47	74	17	44	71	74
17	74	74	14	44	77	47	41	17	74
74	47	71	14	41	74	74	74	14	47
314	536	446	464	236	710	443	404	389	470

Keep your hand cupped and your fingers curved.

44	74	71	47	47	14	41	14	74	41
77	47	74	47	17	41	44	17	71	14
47	44	17	71	71	77	47	74	11	17
17	41	14	71	11	71	41	71	14	74
71	11	11	17	14	74	74	41	41	41
41	17	74	17	47	71	47	47	14	74
11	77	71	77	17	44	14	74	14	41
41	44	77	71	47	47	17	71	41	74
14	47	47	74	71	41	41	77	47	44
17	41	74	74	74	44	41	44	74	77
380	443	530	566	416	524	407	530	401	497

Sit up straight. Keep your feet flat on the floor.

11	44	17	11	14	41	47	44	74	74
17	11	74	47	74	47	71	74	17	71
14	14	14	44	14	71	77	77	47	47
17	41	71	41	77	17	74	47	44	77
74	47	14	14	44	47	71	14	74	41
71	74	17	17	47	74	17	71	71	14
47	14	74	71	77	77	14	17	47	17
41	14	47	74	41	41	17	71	74	47
74	47	44	44	71	44	17	74	71	77
77	41	77	41	74	11	71	14	14	17
443	347	449	404	533	470	476	503	533	482

FINGERING DRILLS—SECOND COLUMN

Right-handed and left-handed operators use the middle finger for 2, 5, and 8.

28	58	28	85	25	82	58	25	52	28
82	25	82	25	22	28	85	28	58	85
88	52	25	58	82	88	88	25	85	25
22	88	52	88	28	58	58	58	52	88
55	82	22	28	58	52	85	88	25	25
52	58	55	85	85	82	28	52	25	58
58	25	88	88	52	52	82	25	58	85
85	58	82	52	85	88	58	85	85	52
82	85	85	25	88	22	85	28	28	22
85	52	58	28	82	55	25	82	85	55
637	583	577	562	607	607	652	496	553	523

Don't turn your head except to check your totals. This will relieve you of wasted motion and effort.

88	88	25	85	58	52	52	28	88	22
82	58	25	52	85	85	55	85	85	25
28	82	58	52	88	52	58	28	58	85
58	58	85	25	55	28	82	25	28	25
85	85	85	58	22	88	28	58	28	85
28	82	85	52	28	82	85	82	25	52
85	28	88	58	25	85	52	58	22	85
88	85	85	52	85	88	82	85	28	58
55	58	82	25	82	85	58	55	82	25
55	22	58	25	85	58	55	22	52	88
652	646	676	484	613	703	607	526	496	550

Are you becoming more confident?

85	25	52	88	88	85	82	55	55	25
28	52	82	28	85	25	25	52	88	52
58	88	28	82	55	25	28	82	82	25
25	85	52	58	52	88	58	58	28	28
85	58	25	85	58	55	28	85	85	22
58	82	58	88	55	52	52	25	82	25
82	52	85	58	88	25	82	58	85	52
22	28	82	52	22	58	55	52	88	55
58	58	58	85	82	82	52	85	28	25
28	25	28	25	52	82	82	85	82	22
529	553	550	649	637	577	544	637	703	331

Never enter a digit with the incorrect finger.

22	55	88	55	22	88	28	22	85	88
28	82	82	58	85	82	58	55	82	85
82	28	52	58	28	85	82	58	28	82
25	58	85	52	28	58	25	85	28	28
28	82	52	25	85	28	28	82	22	25
58	82	28	58	58	85	85	25	55	22
25	85	28	58	85	25	25	52	58	58
88	52	58	22	25	28	88	82	22	55
85	52	25	22	88	58	28	28	25	52
25	28	58	85	85	28	25	58	28	82
466	604	556	493	589	565	472	547	433	577

FINGERING DRILLS—THIRD COLUMN

Use the ring finger of the right hand for 3, 6, and 9. Use the index finger of the left hand for 3, 6, and 9.

FINGERING DRILLS—THIRD COLUMN

33	36	36	96	69	93	66	93	39	36
36	69	96	99	63	63	63	66	63	66
39	96	93	96	66	39	96	36	93	96
66	93	96	93	96	66	99	99	39	33
63	93	66	36	36	69	63	69	93	63
69	39	63	69	96	63	69	39	96	39
99	66	36	66	69	66	93	69	63	66
96	69	96	69	66	96	96	96	36	63
96	96	99	63	93	39	93	63	99	96
93	63	93	66	36	93	36	96	33	69
690	720	774	753	690	687	774	726	654	627

Keep your fingers curved and close to the home row. Don't raise your hand away from the keyboard.

93	33	66	93	36	39	66	99	39	69
39	36	69	96	63	36	63	96	63	99
96	69	63	99	96	33	69	93	69	66
69	69	36	39	63	93	96	39	96	93
66	66	96	69	66	66	63	96	33	36
63	63	99	66	63	69	69	69	99	39
69	36	93	69	69	96	93	36	96	66
96	96	96	69	99	39	96	66	69	36
36	66	93	93	96	93	96	96	39	96
96	39	39	96	66	63	66	69	66	63
723	573	750	789	717	627	777	759	669	663

Can you find the home row?

93	39	36	93	36	63	96	39	96	96
36	63	96	96	33	96	33	93	93	36
69	33	69	69	93	69	63	36	69	63
69	93	96	39	63	66	96	63	36	93
63	96	63	69	66	36	69	33	96	99
36	99	69	96	36	99	66	39	39	33
66	63	66	33	69	96	36	96	99	39
39	36	96	63	96	93	63	69	93	93
69	63	39	66	69	96	69	66	93	63
93	69	66	96	63	63	66	96	69	69
633	654	696	720	624	777	657	630	783	684

Don't look at the keyboard. Keep your eyes on your copy.

69	99	36	93	39	66	33	93	33	96
63	93	66	33	36	69	63	36	69	66
66	96	96	69	33	63	69	63	96	33
39	39	33	96	63	36	39	39	66	63
69	69	39	96	93	69	36	69	69	93
36	69	99	69	66	96	66	33	63	99
99	66	93	36	36	69	63	39	96	69
39	36	99	93	63	63	96	93	39	39
69	63	36	99	66	39	69	69	63	63
36	69	96	36	96	66	36	36	69	33
585	699	693	720	591	636	570	570	663	654

FINGERING DRILLS—DIAGONALS

15	91	55	95	11	95	51	15	91	51
91	19	95	91	55	51	59	59	19	15
59	95	19	15	99	19	55	15	15	59
95	51	19	15	95	51	95	91	51	91
19	95	51	95	91	55	91	59	95	19
91	55	15	19	19	95	11	91	51	51
51	15	59	59	15	51	19	19	15	95
15	91	59	95	59	59	91	59	55	59
15	15	91	55	51	19	59	95	95	59
59	59	95	99	19	95	51	51	99	19
510	586	558	638	514	590	582	554	586	518

Keep your fingers curved over the home row.

15	95	33	53	59	55	19	35	75	53
55	19	53	57	51	95	95	75	73	57
59	91	73	37	19	19	55	73	35	53
19	51	75	57	55	59	95	55	53	57
91	15	77	33	59	59	11	33	37	37
51	95	33	57	59	55	11	57	33	73
95	19	35	73	95	95	15	73	57	73
15	51	53	75	59	51	19	37	75	37
91	15	73	37	99	99	91	55	37	53
59	59	37	53	55	19	51	77	77	75
550	510	542	532	610	606	462	570	552	568

To build speed and reduce fatigue, keep your head turned toward your copy.

37	73	75	37	53	75	37	53	37	35
73	35	35	53	35	73	57	75	33	55
53	53	75	53	73	75	57	73	37	75
35	77	37	73	37	57	37	75	73	35
55	57	57	75	75	35	73	37	75	57
53	57	35	53	35	57	73	53	75	53
33	75	53	35	53	75	73	37	37	75
55	53	75	35	55	33	77	55	37	53
35	35	33	73	57	73	35	37	53	37
53	73	57	73	75	75	73	35	77	55
482	588	532	560	548	628	592	530	534	530

TIMED STROKING DRILL 2

Have yourself timed for *four* minutes. Answers must be correct! If you do not complete the 500 strokes within four minutes, continue practicing the fingering drills. If you *do* complete the drill successfully, try the Proficiency Test on page 97.

```
1.    52,790              2.      1,486            3.     76,043
      23,776                     37,009                   55,902
          22                     23,487                   20,139
      15,389                    830,345                    1,673
     439,037   (23)               3,290   (74)            45,639   (124)
      40,114                    187,347                   33,892
     390,582                     21,319                   21,424
     497,635                      9,001                   32,984
      31,497                     14,782                   11,924
      78,203   (50)             234,348  (100)           340,982   (150)
   1,569,045                  1,362,414                  640,602


4.     5,901              5.    431,219            6.    432,190
      31,492                     32,472                  124,907
      74,892                      1,856                      398
      38,983                    219,911                   51,358   (270)
      45,098  (174)              42,379  (226)           621,907
     321,589                      5,324                  377,754
       4,123                    180,905                  785,927
      34,387                      4,600                      257
      31,783                     27,609                   12,524
     187,750  (200)              19,414  (250)            8,112   (300)
     775,998                    965,689                2,415,334
```

7. 145,231   8.   2,027   9.   30,009
    158,286   4,687   8,345
     35,401   927   345,987
      1,287   77,430   6,344
      3,203 (325)   5,743   943,568 (425)
        922   8,397 (374)   443,934
      3,479   34,466,421   387
    213,513   721,578   430,612
    113,573   882,645   959,520
    934,275 (350)   219,921 (400)   6,348 (450)
  1,609,170   36,389,776   3,175,054

10.   1,485
     27,540
    141,495
      2,854
     10,812 (474)
    143,988
      2,854
     34,938
     76,834
    211,509 (500)
    654,309

FINGERING DRILLS—1-9 KEYS

Remember: If you are operating the calculator with your right hand, use your index finger for 1, 4, and 7. Use the middle finger for 2, 5, and 8. Use your ring finger for 3, 6, and 9. For the left hand, use your ring finger for 1, 4, and 7, the middle finger for 2, 5, and 8, and the index finger for 3, 6, and 9.

13	22	33	44	57	76	34	53	19	98
12	33	32	56	59	77	54	45	18	76
23	44	39	67	71	78	65	62	17	54
79	55	37	87	95	79	76	47	16	18
87	66	17	19	34	81	86	36	15	17
71	77	27	71	21	33	21	81	14	51
72	88	47	43	29	44	73	43	13	41
73	99	57	56	43	55	93	23	12	23
74	11	89	29	79	66	74	72	11	18
75	22	12	54	86	77	73	48	76	84
579	517	390	526	574	666	649	510	211	480

Is your calculator turned to a comfortable angle?

FINGERING DRILLS—1-9 KEYS

91	24	16	61	91	83	14	19	18	91
82	35	25	15	46	24	51	67	82	82
73	46	78	46	62	74	86	25	37	37
64	57	49	72	13	67	64	74	64	46
56	68	33	38	44	24	19	31	56	55
55	79	24	39	56	28	87	88	85	46
98	91	11	21	35	92	76	46	74	74
16	82	92	24	27	37	61	95	38	82
84	73	53	13	19	91	58	54	92	19
52	65	64	54	98	45	46	97	11	93
671	620	445	383	491	565	562	596	557	625

Keep your hand cupped over the home row.

49	28	56	16	57	69	46	56	69	26
32	38	76	27	82	75	75	81	14	73
64	47	28	16	72	69	69	53	22	45
16	65	79	27	38	73	73	97	43	47
29	65	38	38	27	83	83	13	69	79
23	85	31	49	38	94	94	69	43	15
53	67	35	91	94	83	83	24	56	62
47	78	57	24	51	49	49	79	25	37
95	87	13	18	27	15	15	15	38	84
68	99	82	21	83	62	62	26	68	13
476	659	495	327	569	672	649	513	447	481

Sit up straight to avoid fatigue.

57	34	41	64	27	37	51	81	42	53
51	92	24	94	89	18	36	92	71	58
72	69	98	68	56	92	58	34	29	37
95	61	69	69	78	28	66	76	16	58
41	16	89	58	52	87	31	45	14	32
22	13	51	99	64	28	96	32	52	76
63	75	25	15	87	72	54	19	37	16
27	93	61	25	24	76	14	87	68	84
87	81	11	61	93	37	45	66	93	92
86	17	27	11	25	95	52	75	41	69
601	551	496	564	595	570	503	607	463	575

Keep your fingers curved.

THE TOUCH SYSTEM FOR TEN-KEY OFFICE MACHINES

48	86	47	16	57	87	92	35	73	89
31	92	23	75	24	97	19	24	88	15
22	36	45	88	76	36	51	35	21	93
13	58	93	71	38	64	43	62	29	35
59	87	21	26	91	39	76	54	21	98
27	39	94	57	45	59	78	11	68	72
83	24	51	64	15	23	98	29	16	43
43	31	24	83	62	23	68	18	47	79
45	75	33	52	65	67	21	87	65	74
67	44	46	13	41	97	35	23	41	86
438	572	477	545	514	592	581	378	469	684

Never enter a digit with the incorrect finger.

14	25	32	47	25	58	57	98	78	96
63	74	61	88	91	25	12	37	21	39
69	57	38	19	32	96	22	29	47	23
48	31	24	73	48	31	95	47	58	67
92	51	52	66	79	42	61	46	89	75
25	93	31	24	45	48	61	73	77	13
85	89	15	63	57	99	21	62	12	18
67	68	15	68	96	86	78	61	66	56
79	16	23	43	45	13	12	87	93	76
74	33	27	68	94	57	89	13	23	18
616	537	318	559	612	555	508	553	564	481

FINGERING DRILLS—ZEROS

Use your thumb for the zero. For the left hand, use your little finger or thumb, whichever is easier for you.

10	90	10	60	50	80	50	20	20	50
70	80	30	40	30	10	10	70	40	10
50	20	40	20	90	30	30	80	50	20
10	60	80	40	70	60	70	50	80	10
30	20	70	70	90	70	20	90	10	70
50	40	90	50	40	40	90	80	30	40
80	60	30	80	30	90	30	90	30	10
10	20	10	30	80	20	60	70	80	70
20	70	40	60	50	60	40	40	90	10
90	20	80	50	10	10	80	60	30	60
420	480	480	500	540	470	480	650	460	350

FINGERING DRILLS—ZEROS

60	10	80	60	70	40	60	40	60	20
70	50	90	30	20	10	50	60	50	70
30	70	60	40	30	90	30	90	90	50
10	90	80	20	80	20	20	80	60	80
90	60	10	80	40	40	10	70	50	90
70	10	40	90	10	30	90	70	50	30
40	20	80	80	50	70	50	20	70	40
60	70	10	10	90	80	30	30	20	20
90	80	30	50	10	60	20	60	80	90
20	40	70	10	50	70	30	40	20	90
540	500	550	470	450	510	390	560	550	580

Return your hand to the home row between entries.

40	70	80	10	80	20	10	40	70	10
60	30	20	90	30	10	20	50	30	70
40	30	10	10	40	60	50	20	40	80
60	20	50	30	30	50	90	80	70	60
70	50	80	40	10	60	10	60	30	40
10	20	40	60	40	10	40	50	70	40
90	80	60	50	90	30	80	90	90	60
30	50	10	70	40	40	10	10	80	40
20	80	60	70	70	50	20	60	90	30
30	10	60	90	80	70	60	80	50	30
450	440	470	520	510	400	390	540	620	460

Can you find the home row by touch?

40	30	70	60	40	70	80	10	80	20
90	10	20	30	60	30	20	90	30	10
50	70	60	80	40	30	10	10	40	60
20	30	40	50	60	20	50	30	30	50
80	90	10	20	70	50	80	40	10	60
50	60	70	80	10	20	40	60	40	10
20	30	40	50	90	80	60	50	90	30
80	90	10	20	30	50	10	70	40	40
50	70	60	80	20	80	60	70	70	50
10	30	20	40	30	10	60	90	90	70
490	510	400	510	450	440	470	520	520	400

FINGERING DRILLS—THREE FIGURES

101	428	529	769	196	597	525	698	981	118
735	200	901	800	614	436	746	107	746	789
317	243	456	193	372	780	900	683	400	224
612	945	100	258	783	868	276	546	545	607
234	800	732	752	996	958	489	815	580	100
901	691	336	235	513	175	851	276	197	205
698	847	845	845	200	902	162	298	190	850
179	982	176	302	154	213	904	100	200	506
572	609	523	117	376	229	777	309	483	667
318	334	448	408	416	534	362	193	859	602
4,667	6,079	5,046	4,679	4,620	5,692	5,992	4,025	5,181	4,668

How is your accuracy?

770	382	525	230	363	193	752	950	793	928
819	846	132	359	502	257	184	663	332	579
100	707	540	684	446	681	953	244	384	176
698	198	377	280	202	109	265	674	928	216
577	162	700	968	130	465	703	724	865	970
493	100	769	701	435	869	944	610	704	157
154	782	109	346	344	599	190	613	130	578
535	290	389	476	765	450	475	849	375	295
600	413	894	800	251	355	200	154	678	753
298	564	230	254	763	100	743	815	439	732
5,044	4,444	4,665	5,098	4,201	4,078	5,409	6,296	5,628	5,384

Keep your eyes on your copy.

262	837	398	336	950	835	362	200	264	665
286	468	410	571	152	901	958	175	553	901
316	264	763	109	159	749	342	724	918	197
524	143	536	470	950	516	424	269	475	204
732	601	407	700	894	739	756	768	801	317
123	719	458	210	527	190	968	269	284	181
928	142	790	291	186	364	980	768	765	107
219	574	837	440	313	830	678	485	119	200
192	656	201	201	352	651	578	600	870	916
837	508	870	638	852	345	408	709	234	700
4,419	4,912	5,670	3,966	5,335	6,120	6,454	4,967	5,283	4,388

354	300	187	407	796	535	213	361	167	809
947	829	138	829	190	100	573	150	237	760
228	380	475	905	778	120	446	462	145	450
635	354	678	902	854	453	261	256	899	231
198	296	385	135	385	220	180	829	900	100
532	639	900	346	904	405	948	723	808	708
824	398	303	678	492	847	627	601	405	450
379	604	450	972	697	393	180	230	708	343
674	846	302	895	753	100	537	532	120	402
812	796	307	562	672	401	179	456	300	135
5,583	5,442	4,125	6,631	6,521	3,574	4,144	4,600	4,689	4,388

Save wasted motion to avoid fatigue.

280	370	209	397	262	837	398	336	950	835
856	564	408	780	286	468	410	571	152	901
453	217	345	453	316	264	763	109	159	749
789	675	607	630	524	143	536	470	950	516
200	436	560	821	732	601	407	700	894	739
160	935	880	144	123	719	458	210	527	190
102	663	707	805	928	142	790	291	186	364
305	887	505	800	219	574	837	440	313	830
503	909	234	546	192	656	201	201	352	651
239	808	300	542	837	508	870	638	852	245
3,887	6,464	4,755	5,918	4,419	4,912	5,670	3,966	5,335	6,020

THE TOUCH METHOD–DECIMALS

With most electronic calculators, it is necessary to enter decimal points manually. To enter 47.3912, enter [4] [7] [.] [3] [9] [1] and [2] . Students using the right hand usually use the little finger for entering the decimal. Students using the left hand usually use the thumb.

To enter a whole number, for example, 921, it is unnecessary to enter the decimal. The electronic calculator will treat any number entered without a decimal as a whole number. Also, if you have an ending zero *after* the decimal, you need not enter the zero. For example, to enter 33.70, enter [3] [3] [.] and [7] . Your calculator will print the ending zero.

If you are using a ten-key printing calculator or ten-key adding machine, you cannot enter a decimal. However, be sure to "line up" your imaginary decimal place in order to get the correct answer. For example, to add

39.1
69.346

you must enter [3] [9] [1] [0] [0] in order to line up your digits in the correct decimal position. You would then point off three places from the right to left in your answer for your correct decimal position.

Note: Be sure to enter and read your numbers in groups of two or three digits. For example, read and enter 69./346, *not* 6, 9, decimal, 3, 4, 6.

Add the following:

92.38	3.79	1.20	17.66	9.13	171.01
123.18	14.81	607.01	610.70	100.67	293.04
16.76	13.90	9.48	96.70	143.81	866.00
7.90	811.01	67.00	188.29	20.01	99.08
30.21	26.99	2.02	91.39	4.17	5.55
1.03	99.26	21.03	29.83	389.30	188.96
86.00	801.12	9.70	9.74	48.55	4.10
4.98	19.03	76.61	20.31	459.00	8.00
107.06	18.14	481.31	8.00	390.32	657.76
21.00	9.73	92.83	16.30	155.66	14.39
490.50	1,817.78	1,368.19	1,088.92	1,720.62	2,307.89

Some calculators have an Add Mode, which automatically prints two decimal places without your having to enter the decimal. You will, however, have to enter ending zeros while you are in the Add Mode; for example, 34.00 will have to be entered 3 4 0 0.

Set your decimal at four for the following additions:

296.1	3.917	119.1	2.4	56.76	5.3
18.04	14.81	26.304	5.00	51.00	17.87
3.669	5.6	18.1819	1.677	8.7143	2.611
1.00	65.71	6.063	4.0008	28.6	84.3
28.64	66.6778	12.00	19.942	1.91	203.00
18.79	4.1	417.01	10.15	18.03	2.10
2.006	8.00	11.2	9.0707	156.1	45.05
11.77	91.03	4.97	120.00	9.0704	76.7
88.5666	2.043	28.88	4.3	19.00	8.91
119.003	8.6	4.5	18.61	219.06	41.0723
587.5846	270.4878	648.2089	195.1505	568.2447	486.9133

Keep your feet flat on the floor.

32.611	7.21	97.54	129.06	26.4	916.45
4.7	45.56	30.04	13.4222	18.915	45.84
181.19	12.94	776.09	79.61	209.007	333.90
24.00	101.00	222.34	80.00	18.78	60.42
3.0764	100.00	85.85	490.03	3.43	.9415
8.2	86.543	904.32	7.58	47.99	.67
193.4	2.9	66.75	89.77	197.216	1.82
18.67	117.85	1.21	2.074	8.14	22.99
74.573	52.92	3.7	14.0006	99.75	148.75
3.202	7.89	49.04	197.88	909.55	.687
543.6224	534.813	2,236.88	1,103.4268	1,539.178	1,532.4685

THE TOUCH SYSTEM—
DOLLARS AND CENTS PRACTICE

On the electronic calculator set your decimal at 2, or use the Add Mode. In the Add Mode decimals at two places are entered for you automatically.

$ 13.13	$ 26.19	$ 814.56	$ 29.15	$ 8.12	$ 4.30
1,124.00	7.60	8.73	3.40	12.40	14.30
87.53	41.18	2.10	118.66	114.67	81.76
44.02	21.67	15.29	2.00	29.29	100.00
300.00	60.45	4.30	29.42	8.75	8.74
2.03	160.44	2.30	81.56	88.98	3.88
4.24	1,291.00	4.90	7.12	91,340.16	441.43
90.25	4.67	66.50	3.34	29.74	32.91
701.46	18.81	91.74	185.56	33.04	42,864.04
20.99	37.04	114.82	3.04	141.11	33.74
$2,387.65	$1,669.05	$1,125.24	$463.25	$91,806.26	$43,585.10

Be sure to keep your fingers curved and hovering over the home row.

$ 8.64	$ 443.66	$ 18.19	$ 12.90	$3,041.88	$ 2.00
9.29	38.42	2.91	71.06	366.02	43.41
301.41	29.00	3.82	864.41	47.38	887.56
98.92	5,931.77	69.80	7.07	89.47	65.18
12.34	68.99	67.01	18.16	3.00	4,100.03
2,193.47	684.24	14.34	9.20	9.21	2.34
96.88	16.71	646.20	89.79	187.44	77.84
466.04	34.14	41.00	778.65	64.29	2.46
39.87	776.85	79.89	3.27	5,000.41	9.20
76.11	3.28	77.86	6,070.01	87.93	83.24
$3,302.97	$8,027.06	$1,021.02	$7,924.52	$8,897.03	$5,273.26

Don't lift your hand away from the keyboard.

THE TOUCH SYSTEM FOR TEN-KEY OFFICE MACHINES

$ 4.62	$ 29.28	$ 84.24	$ 74.27	$2,110.47	$ 2.93
2.91	403.04	2.86	72.51	31.91	12,070.04
8.00	78.66	7.44	2,472.11	76.55	89.36
643.40	931.74	331.29	30.14	45.20	7.65
7.83	34.04	27.15	8.27	2.86	5.76
3,291.17	80.08	868.29	72.51	43.41	92.62
88.74	2.94	74.65	1,104.13	4.78	31.21
9.37	43.53	7.81	867.94	29.26	6.82
222.04	464.18	8,014.20	8.26	68.57	2.78
140.30	671.22	77.42	29.01	12.13	100.18
$4,418.38	$2,738.71	$9,495.35	$4,739.15	$2,425.14	$12,409.35

Are you gaining speed and accuracy?

$ 28.14	$ 3.41	$ 6.54	$ 23.13	$ 36.19	$ 714.56
19.47	51.92	29.87	2,124.00	6.60	7.73
5.56	20.10	1,311.06	96.53	31.18	3.10
9.04	7.83	21.44	54.02	11.67	25.29
32.00	418.65	5.67	400.00	50.45	5.30
8.74	6.62	840.00	1.03	260.44	1.30
22.13	999.30	91.04	3.24	2,291.00	3.90
5.67	6.75	31.22	80.25	3.67	56.50
99.03	23.12	4.32	601.46	28.81	81.74
6.25	4.78	11.88	30.99	47.04	214.82
$236.03	$1,542.48	$2,353.04	$3,414.65	$2,767.05	$1,114.24

TIMED STROKING DRILL 3

Have yourself timed for *four* minutes. Answers must be correct! If you do not complete the 500 strokes within four minutes, continue practicing the fingering drills. If you *do* complete the drill successfully, try the Proficiency Test on page 97.

1.	52,790	2.	1,453	3.	76,043
	23,776		37,009		55,901
	11		23,457		20,139
	15,362		830,954		1,622
	436,957 (23)		3,219 (74)		45,630 (124)
	40,115		176,347		33,619
	397,582		21,319		21,424
	597,635		9,001		32,651
	21,406		14,782		11,492
	78,026 (50)		243,753 (100)		450,928 (150)
	1,663,660		1,361,294		749,449

4.	5,601			5.	431,219			6.	432,190	
	31,492				32,472				124,709	
	74,298				1,856				893	
	38,309				219,911				51,653	(270)
	45,798	(174)			24,379	(226)			621,790	
	321,589				5,423				377,654	
	4,132				180,509				785,729	
	34,783				4,600				275	
	21,435				27,509				12,425	
	187,750	(200)			19,141	(250)			8,112	(300)
	765,187				947,019				2,415,430	
7.	154,721			8.	2,026			9.	30,009	
	185,268				4,867				8,356	
	35,411				297				245,793	
	1,278				77,430				6,433	
	3,302	(325)			5,743				943,567	(425)
	299				8,397	(374)			441,165	
	3,974				34,466,421				386	
	213,215				721,578				540,612	
	311,573				882,643				959,520	
	934,275	(350)			219,912	(400)			6,634	(450)
	1,843,316				36,389,314				3,182,475	

10.
    1,456
  27,540
141,357
    2,854
  10,812 (474)
142,699
    2,730
  34,851
  76,627
211,509 (500)
652,435

REVIEW QUIZ 1

Turn back to page 97 and try the Proficiency Test under timed conditions.

Unit 2

Electronic Calculator Basic Operations

TOUCH SYSTEM REVIEW

Be sure to keep your index finger, your middle finger, and your ring finger on the home row (4, 5, and 6) if you are using your right hand. Keep your ring finger, your middle finger, and your index finger on the 4, 5, and 6 if you are using your left hand.

444	454	464	454	646	455
555	445	556	556	665	644
666	456	456	654	654	456
666	445	554	665	556	464
555	465	454	655	465	456
444	444	666	555	444	555
666	666	444	555	666	666
444	456	456	654	654	456
555	666	555	444	555	666
666	464	565	646	565	656
5,661	4,961	5,170	5,838	5,870	5,474

Are you keeping your head turned toward your copy? Do not turn your head to look at your keys. If you must look, turn your eyes only. Keep your head turned toward your copy if you want to attain speed and accuracy.

123	123	123	123	123	123
222	111	333	333	111	333
333	222	111	111	333	111
233	233	322	322	122	122
311	311	311	112	112	113
123	132	132	123	133	231
111	222	333	333	222	111
123	321	123	132	123	321
223	332	122	322	133	211
123	123	321	321	123	123
1,925	2,130	2,231	2,232	1,535	1,799

Can you find the keys without looking? Are you getting the right answers?

789	789	789	789	789	789
777	888	999	888	777	888
999	888	777	888	999	888
778	887	778	887	778	887
998	997	998	997	998	997
788	799	788	799	889	998
789	798	987	789	879	798
777	999	888	999	777	888
789	789	987	987	978	879
788	887	977	998	889	977
8,272	8,721	8,968	9,021	8,753	8,989

For the right hand, use your thumb for the zero. For the left hand, use your little finger for the zero.

300	209	103	205	307	407
500	206	102	202	303	409
700	204	100	206	301	401
800	101	108	200	300	404
100	200	104	208	308	400
400	208	106	203	305	403
200	205	101	209	302	405
600	202	105	204	304	408
900	203	107	201	309	406
100	207	109	207	306	402
4,600	1,945	1,045	2,045	3,045	4,045

When adding dollars and cents, set your decimal for the Add Mode.

$ 8.08	$ 7.70	$ 3.09	$ 4.08	$ 5.05	$ 7.01
2.02	9.90	3.06	4.10	5.09	6.08
5.05	2.20	3.03	4.03	6.01	6.02
7.07	4.40	3.05	4.05	5.03	6.06
4.04	6.60	3.07	4.07	5.04	6.09
6.06	1.10	4.01	4.06	5.07	7.02
1.01	8.80	3.08	4.04	6.02	6.03
3.03	1.01	4.02	5.01	5.06	6.05
1.00	3.30	3.10	4.09	5.08	6.07
9.09	5.50	3.04	5.02	5.10	6.04
$46.45	$50.51	$32.55	$42.55	$52.55	$62.47

Keep your fingers hovering over the home row. Don't lift your hand away from the keyboard.

$ 7.10	$ 9.01	$ 1.13	$ 4.01	$ 1.10	$ 1.01
7.04	8.05	9.05	5.05	5.60	7.80
7.09	8.08	9.07	5.00	9.90	1.01
7.03	8.10	9.03	2.24	5.50	2.02
7.07	8.03	9.08	3.04	7.70	3.04
7.05	8.07	1.12	4.04	6.60	7.08
7.09	8.04	9.06	5.06	1.20	9.10
7.06	9.02	9.04	2.03	4.50	6.70
8.02	8.06	9.10	3.03	3.20	5.06
8.01	8.09	9.09	4.06	8.80	8.90
$72.56	$82.55	$74.77	$37.56	$54.10	$51.72

When you are using the Add Mode for problems with two decimals, you need not enter the decimal by hand.

DECIMAL SETTINGS AND ROUND-OFF

Electronic calculators, including the hand-held ones, may have fixed decimals, floating decimals, or both. With the fixed decimal system you set your calculator for the desired number of decimals before you begin your problem. Your answer will show only the number of decimals you fixed. For example, if you fix your decimal at 2 and multiply 3.41 X 2.62, your answer will show 8.93, dropping off the last two decimal places.

Some calculators always use a floating decimal. Other calculators may be set for a fixed or a floating decimal. With a floating decimal, the calculator will accept and print or display all the decimals entered on the keyboard up to the capacity of the calculator. With an answer containing many decimals, the number of decimals shown will depend on the number of whole digits in your answer and on the capacity of the calculator. The more whole numbers there are, the less room there is for decimal places.

Some calculators round off all your answers *automatically*. For example, if you divide 100 by 6 and set your decimal at 4, these calculators will show your answer as 16.6667. Since the fifth decimal to the right would be 6, the calculator automatically rounds up the fourth decimal from 6 to 7. If you had set your decimal at 3, the answer would have been shown as 16.667.

Rounding off is done on the 5/4 principle: If the digit to the right of the last desired decimal place is 5 or more, the last decimal is rounded up one number. If the digit to the right of the last desired decimal place is 4 or less, the last decimal is left as is. For example, 16.666 rounded to two decimal places becomes 16.67; .833 rounded to two decimals is .83.

With some calculators the operator has the choice of setting the calculator to round off or not to round off. The round-off levers are usually labeled *5/4* or *RO*. Rounding off usually occurs only in the answers. However, a few calculators also have a switch which can be set for truncation. With this setting, in multiplication and division any digits beyond the decimal setting are dropped and do not affect the calculations or the result.

Many electronic calculators have an *Add Mode* switch, sometimes marked (+). If you are adding or subtracting and *all* your numbers contain two decimal places (dollars and cents, for example), you can use the Add Mode to advantage. Your calculator will then automatically point off all entries to two decimals. You will not need to enter your decimals on the keyboard. For example, in the Add Mode you would enter 1.37 as 137. Your calculator will place the decimal correctly for you. If you have a number like 121.00, you must be *sure* to enter the two zeros. Otherwise your calculator will enter 121 as 1.21.

Addition

Turn your calculator on. Be *sure* to turn off the calculator when you are finished working. Set your decimal at 4.

The *Correction key* is used to correct a keyboard entry error *before* it is entered into the calculator. If you have already entered an error in adding or subtracting functions, you can correct your work by subtracting out the amount you have added in error, or by adding in the amount you have subtracted in error. Then continue with the problem.

Example.   18.714
                3.917
                ─────

1. Depress $\boxed{T}$ or $\boxed{*}$ to clear the machine.
2. Enter $\boxed{1}$ $\boxed{8}$ $\boxed{.}$ $\boxed{7}$ $\boxed{1}$ $\boxed{4}$ on the keyboard.
3. Depress $\boxed{+}$.
4. Enter $\boxed{3}$ $\boxed{.}$ $\boxed{9}$ $\boxed{1}$ $\boxed{7}$ on the keyboard.
5. Depress $\boxed{+}$.
6. Depress $\boxed{T}$ or $\boxed{*}$ if you are working on a tape machine. If you are working on an electronic display calculator, your answer will show in the display after Step 5.
7. Your answer, 22.631, will appear on the tape or the display.

Practice Problems 1. Perform the following additions:

	1.	2.	3.	4.	5.
	7.48	52.78	.672	782	7.682
	6.67	69.01	.421	342	.127
	30.24	67.38	.460	389	2.720
	7.22	61.11	.559	473	.489
	45.72	39.48	.946	125	3.709
	42.87	41.70	.638	654	16.509
	63.89	10.73	.185	741	4.702
	84.43	30.22	.499	678	.377
	15.55	53.42	.319	536	.97
	38.88	4.45	.139	456	.504
	70.55	.97	.678	507	3.709
	23.89	9.62	.589	686	4.709
	437.39				

	6.	7.	8.	9.	10.
	197.4	7.85	5.32	66.24	5.9
	98.5	37.12	63.28	313.16	7.1
	307.3	1.28	5.11	26.94	6.6
	307.4	37.22	5.42	38.52	3.3
	179.5	6.52	54.22	89.35	4.1

	11.	12.	13.	14.	15.
	5.26	30.56	.450	560	5.460
	4.45	47.81	.209	120	.905
	18.02	45.16	.248	167	9.508
	5.00	25.00	.338	251	.267
	23.50	17.26	.724	803	1.587
	20.65	29.58	.416	432	84.387
	41.67	8.51	.963	529	2.589
	62.21	18.00	.277	456	.155
	83.33	31.20	.917	304	.75
	16.66	2.25	.456	245	.387
	58.33	.75	.367	385	1.587
	91.67	7.40	.245	464	2.578

	16.	17.	18.	19.	20.
	875.2	4.63	3.19	44.02	3.7
	78.3	15.90	41.06	94.72	4.4
	185.1	8.06	3.88	101.94	5.8
	185.2	25.10	3.20	16.30	1.1
	857.3	4.39	32.09	87.42	2.9

DECIMAL SETTINGS AND ROUND-OFF   125

21.	22.	23.	24.	25.
6.37	41.67	.561	671	6.571
5.56	58.92	.310	231	.016
29.13	56.27	.359	278	1.619
6.11	50.00	.449	362	.378
34.61	28.37	.835	914	2.698
31.76	30.69	.527	543	95.498
52.78	9.62	.074	631	3.691
73.32	29.11	.388	567	.266
94.44	42.31	.028	415	.86
27.77	3.35	.567	356	.498
69.44	.86	.478	496	2.698
12.78	8.51	.356	575	3.698

26. 986.3 + 87.4 + 296.2 + 387.2 + 839.5 + 34.57 + 12.78 =

27. 5.74 + 26.01 + 8.17 + 26.11 + 5.41 + 65.90 + 8.75 =

28. 4.21 + 52.17 + 4.99 + 4.32 + 43.11 + 89.75 + 35.77 =

29. 55.13 + 15.83 + 202.05 + 27.41 + 98.53 + 3.77 + 38.86 =

30. 4.8 + 5.5 + 6.9 + 2.2 + 3.0 + 3.5 + 7.6 + 4.5 + 8.9 =

31. 8,764 + 291 + 3,987 + 67 + 7,700 + 3,992 + 505 + 2,900 =

32. 26,301 + 423 + 5,596 + 852 + 9,427 + 398 + 25 + 44 =

33. 294 + 341 + 826 + 391 + 557 + 747 + 582 + 916 + 583 =

34. 8.74 + 9.36 + 12.91 + 2.86 + 1.35 + 5.07 + 8.12 + 5.99 =

35. 1.4 + 12.6 + 5.7 + 7.5 + 8.2 + 9.4 + 14.6 + 5.4 + 21.1 =

Subtraction

Example. 719.2
             −3.1

1. Is your calculator clear?
2. Enter [7] [1] [9] [.] [2] on the keyboard.
3. Depress [+].
4. Enter [3] [.] [1] on the keyboard.
5. Depress [−].
6. If your calculator is a display, your answer will now appear on the display. If your calculator has a tape, depress [T].
7. Your answer, 716.1, will appear on the tape or on the display.

ELECTRONIC CALCULATOR BASIC OPERATIONS

Practice Problems 2. Perform the following subtractions:

1. 2,551
   -305
   2,246

2. 6,171
   -4,195

3. 5,822
   -4,286

4. 790.68
   -62.11

5. 1,944 - 4.9 =

6. 494 - .57 =

7. 49.4 - .287 =

8. 6,849.6 - 45.7 =

9. 2,365.67 - 24.99 =

10. 39,496 - 3,129 =

11. 1,140
    -294

12. 6,171
    -3,084

13. 4,711
    -3,175

14. 689.57
    -59.11

15. 1,944 - 3.8 =

16. 383 - .46 =

17. 38.3 - .176 =

18. 5,738.5 - 34.6 =

19. 1,254.56 - 13.888 =

20. 28,385 - 20,877 =

21. 2,339
    -183

22. 5,060
    -2,973

23. 3,600
    -2,064

24. 578.46
    -40.88

25. 2,033 - 2.7 =

26. 282 - .35 =

27. 27.2 - .065 =

28. 4,627.4 - 23.5 =

29. 143.45 - 12.777 =

30. 19,274 - 789 =

31. 3,662
    -416

32. 7,282
    -406

33. 6,933
    -5,397

34. 801.79
    -73.22

35. 2,055 - 5.1 =

CREDIT BALANCES

Example.   9.471
               -10.869

1. Is your calculator clear?
2. Enter $\boxed{9}$ $\boxed{.}$ $\boxed{4}$ $\boxed{7}$ $\boxed{1}$ on the keyboard.
3. Depress $\boxed{+}$.
4. Enter $\boxed{1}$ $\boxed{0}$ $\boxed{.}$ $\boxed{8}$ $\boxed{6}$ $\boxed{9}$ on the keyboard.
5. Depress $\boxed{-}$.
6. If your calculator is a display, your total will now show on the display. If you are using a tape, depress $\boxed{T}$.
7. Your answer, -1.398, will appear on the tape or on the display.
   NOTICE that the answer is a negative number. Your calculator will show you a minus sign, or a *Cr* (credit) so that you know you have reached a negative answer. Be sure to include the minus sign or *Cr* with your answer when you record it. Your answer will not be correct unless the negative is indicated.

CREDIT BALANCES

Practice Problems 3. Do the following problems. Be sure to show a minus sign or *Cr* with your answers.

	1.		2.		3.		4.		5.	
		84.67		72.77		-42.15		7.772		-5.35
		-2.69		-8.59		9.32		-9.9993		.82
		-11.99		-99.99		-99.89		9.04		46.56
		8.22		-4.63		17.99		-9.49		-91.04
		126.56		81.24		-74.43		-7.37		5.75
		-3,000.00		-97.77		-1.15		.79		-1.33
		-2,795.23								
6.		5.101	7.	54.26	8.	66.06	9.	-39.02	10.	-3.13
		-9.295		-7.49		-7.36		1.07		.06
		.084		-87.99		-77.77		-67.77		13.13
		-9.083		11.68		-1.42		-1.42		-28.78
		2.222		344.09		20.96		20.96		-3.35
		-.054		-2,000.00		-99.99		-99.99		-1.19
11.		1.555	12.	23,898	13.	65.37	14.	77.17	15.	-40.13
		-1.777		-34,888		-8.51		-8.47		2.18
		2.87		2,865		-98.00		-88.88		-78.88
		-3.88		-7,967		11.79		-2.53		88.60
		-1.55		1,111		455.10		31.07		-23.36
		.75		-23		-1,000.98		-99.99		-3.99
16.		-4.24	17.	1.666	18.	34,909	19.	76.48	20.	77.27
		.17		-2.888		-45,999		-9.62		-9.58
		24.24		3.98		3,976		-99.11		-99.99
		-39.89		-4.99		-8,978		22.80		-3.64
		-4.46		-2.66		1,111		566.21		42.18
		-2.20		.86		-34		-2,000.38		-77.77
21.		-51.24	22.	-5.35	23.	2.777	24.	45,101	25.	27.81
		3.29		.28		-3.999		-56,929		18.25
		-89.99		25.35		4.09		4,087		-57.66
		99.71		-40.91		-4.88		-9,089		-2.91
		-34.47		-5.57		-3.77		2,222		1.84
		-5.11		-3.31		.98		-45		-12.80
26.		176.39	27.	26.19	28.	3,964	29.	4.091	30.	67.84
		-28.04		-20.17		18,075		8.006		-6.92
		-207.55		-12.17		-40,043		2.041		-99.11
		11.14		2.86		1,291		-28.245		2.88
		-9.25		1.34		-461		5.577		561.65
		12.80		-10.04		919		-6.058		-998.32

ELECTRONIC CALCULATOR BASIC OPERATIONS

31.	77.27	32.	-15.24	33.	-5.35	34.	2.777	35.	1.105
	95.88		3.23		.28		-3.9999		-5.929
	-99.98		-99.99		65.64		4.08		.048
	-5.11		99.17		-40.19		-9.49		3.809
	-82.14		-34.47		-73.25		-7.37		2.222
	-352.75		3.46		3.11		.97		-7.46

ADDITION AND SUBTRACTION

Example. 25.76
9.48
-2.71
-8.85

1. Is your calculator clear?
2. Enter ☐2 ☐5 ☐. ☐7 ☐6 on the keyboard.
3. Depress ☐+ .
4. Enter ☐9 ☐. ☐4 ☐8 on the keyboard.
5. Depress ☐+ .
6. Enter ☐2 ☐. ☐7 ☐1 on the keyboard.
7. Depress ☐- .
8. Enter ☐8 ☐. ☐8 ☐5 on the keyboard.
9. Depress ☐- .
10. Display calculators will now show the answer. If you are using a tape calculator, depress ☐T .
11. Your answer, 23.68, will appear on the tape or on the display.

Practice Problems 4. Do the following problems. Set your decimal at 4 to accommodate problem 3. (Some of these may have a credit balance.)

1.	28.41	2.	327	3.	18.0076	4.	18.64
	-3.89		-214		-.2947		-1.75
	118.76		117		5.8875		9.24
	2.94		928		1.006		3.23
	-7.68		-907		-3.2987		-12.75
	-4.91		28		5.0055		-8.98
	21.01		-776		-12.9877		29.15
	-3.76		13		1.0741		9.12
	150.88						

5. 1,429 862 −941 491 1,769 −106 −27 133 1,443	**6.** 894,322 −8,604 −12,787 3,424 −98,300 7,676 −18,074 −29,709 873	**7.** 2.006 −.007 −.007 −.391 −.004 5.067 −.675 −1.043 −.297	**8.** 19,999 287 −555 −600 1,200 19 −10,937 5,056 4,345
9. $20.19 19.32 −15.05 38.26 −37.38 −5.35 7.63 −4.19	**10.** $18.08 19.32 −15.05 16.20 −7.55 −8.04 9.29 −1.24	**11.** $ 871.26 −1,901.35 56.57 −743.01 26.26 290.48 830.49 77.76	**12.** 86 34 78 −101 −76 −186 29 68
13. 49.49 −87.16 9.77 −50.50 10.86 4.19	**14.** 26.007 −119.321 40.775 28.076 −4.499 3.078	**15.** $ 8,888.19 −209.37 −10,041.87 388.65 1,111.23 −30.00	**16.** 202 −60 422 −77 38 85
17. 803 901 −66 −453 772 321 368 −77 −37	**18.** 199 −567 45 −7 90 788 −90 −34 6,894	**19.** 90.54 −77.77 50.55 −9.23 590.21 −5.55 80.12 −377.79 6.09	**20.** .1 −.8 .9 6.7 −.8 .3 .2 .67 −.4
21. 17,059 −5,079 7,059 5,098 −5,322	**22.** 50,192 −6,509 99,999 −9,598 −5,501	**23.** 5.9 −.7 6.7 6.7 −.9	**24.** 58.99 −44.59 51.62 −45.67 −2.88

25.	5.9	26.	879	27.	590	28.	788
	-5.2		-27		678		-234
	6.7		199		-33		12
	-3.3		-157		-130		-4
	-3.4		44		449		67
	.7		-138		198		455
	9.8		52		145		-67
	-7.2		8,765		-44		-77
	1.1		-99		-14		456
29.	67.21	30.	.7	31.	74,826	32.	27,689
	-44.44		-.5		-2,746		-3,276
	39.22		.8		4,726		77,777
	-6.90		3.4		2,746		-6,265
	367.98		-.5		-1,300		-7,287
33.	2.6	34.	25.66	35.	2.6		
	-.7		-11.26		-1.9		
	3.5		38.39		3.4		
	3.5		-12.34		-1.1		
	-.7		-.55		-1.2		

REPEATED ADDITION

Example. 19.87
4.31
4.31
4.31

1. Is your calculator clear?

2. Enter [1] [9] [.] [8] [7] on the keyboard.

3. Depress [+] .

4. Enter [4] [.] [3] [1] on the keyboard.

5. Depress [+] .

6. Depress [+] two more times.

Note: Most electronic calculators have the capability of re-entering amounts in this way. If your calculator does not have this feature, review the illustrations on pages 86–92 to see whether your calculator has a constant lever or "K" (constant) function to simplify working with constants.

7. If your calculator is a display, your answer will now show on the display. If you are using a tape, depress [T] .

8. Your answer, 32.80, will appear on the tape or on the display.

Practice Problems 5. Perform the following repeated additions. Set your decimal at 3.

	1.	916.33	2.	28.2	3.	222.22	4.	89	5.	301.88
		916.33		5.6		222.22		89		301.88
		916.33		5.6		222.22		89		301.88
		916.44		5.6		222.22		83.5		301.88
		60.8		5.6		53.35		24.8		301.88
		363.158		91.32		36.09		3.096		2.335
		4,089.388								
6.	683.22	7.	75.8	8.	888.88	9.	56	10.	177.55
	683.22		2.3		888.88		56		177.55
	683.22		2.3		888.88		56		177.55
	683.33		2.3		888.88		70.2		177.55
	27.5		2.3		20.02		81.5		177.55
	131.827		68.08		13.76		1.763		8.002
11.	794.11	12.	86.9	13.	999.99	14.	67	15.	188.66
	794.11		3.4		999.99		67		188.66
	794.11		3.4		999.99		67		188.66
	794.22		3.4		999.99		81.3		188.66
	28.6		3.4		31.13		92.6		188.66
	141.938		79.19		14.87		1.874		9.112
16.	805.22	17.	94.1	18.	111.11	19.	78	20.	299.77
	805.22		4.5		111.11		78		299.77
	805.22		4.5		111.11		78		299.77
	805.33		4.5		111.11		92.4		299.77
	49.7		4.5		42.24		13.7		299.77
	252.049		80.21		25.99		2.985		1.224
21.	234.56	22.	777.77	23.	567	24.	100.45	25.	86.03
	234.56		777.77		567		10.89		2.1
	234.56		777.77		567		10.89		2.1
	234.56		777.77		567		10.89		2.1
	6.89		777.77		567		10.89		2.1
	1.01		23.56		8		614.58		65.43
26.	43.789	27.	666.6	28.	48	29.	890.36	30.	17.45
	43.789		666.6		8.9		890.36		17.45
	43.789		666.6		8.9		390.36		17.45
	43.789		666.6		8.9		890.36		17.45
	.22		431.04		8.9		134.65		89.3
	.22		1.57		8.9		20.01		5.01

ELECTRONIC CALCULATOR BASIC OPERATIONS

31. 581	32. 100.57	33. 998.8	34. 750.4	35. 429.05
581	73.21	998.8	12.87	7.9
581	73.21	998.8	100.4	7.9
581	73.21	4	100.4	7.9
81	73.21	10	100.4	7.9
881	73.21	328.5	100.4	54.34

REPEATED SUBTRACTION

Example. 491.6
            -3.8
            -3.8
            -3.8
            -3.8

1. Is your calculator clear?
2. Enter ④ ⑨ ① . ⑥ on the keyboard.
3. Depress +.
4. Enter ③ . ⑧ on the keyboard.
5. Depress −.
6. Depress − three more times.

   Note: If you do not have the re-entry capability, you may be able to store −3.8 in memory and recall it from memory. If your calculator does not have memory or a constant function for subtraction, you will need to re-enter your amounts each time by keying them in.

7. If your calculator is a display, your answer will now show on the display. If you are using a tape, depress T.
8. Your answer, 476.4, will appear on the tape or on the display.

Practice Problems 6. Perform the following repeated subtractions:

1. 5,136.08	2. 8,813.638	3. 331.88	4. 2,888	5. 8.94
−31.13	−33.33	−5.42	−5	−.19
−31.13	−33.33	−5.42	−5	−.10
−31.13	−33.33	28.93	−5	−.10
−31.13	−33.33	−.87	−5	−.10
5.07	−50.186	−.87	−5	−.10
5,016.63				

ADDITION AND SUBTRACTION OF FRACTIONS 133

6.	2,803.75	7.	118.57	8.	7,580.417	9.	8,555	10.	7.61
	−18.81		−2.18		−11.1		−2		−.79
	−18.81		−2.18		−11.1		−2		−.79
	−18.81		76.65		−11.1		−2		−.79
	−18.81		−3.21		39.28		−2		−.79
	−2.74		−3.21		−17.853		−2		−.79
11.	2,914.86	12.	8,691.428	13.	119.68	14.	9,666	15.	8.72
	−19.91		−11.1		−3.29		−3		−.80
	−19.91		−11.1		−3.29		−3		−.80
	−19.91		−11.1		−3.29		−3		−.80
	−19.91		−11.1		87.76		−3		−.81
	−3.85		40.39		−4.32		−3		−.81
16.	4,025.97	17.	9,702.529	18.	220.79	19.	1,777	20.	9.83
	−20.02		−22.2		−4.31		−4		−.91
	−20.02		−22.2		−4.31		−4		−.91
	−20.02		−22.2		98.87		−4		−.91
	−20.02		51.41		−5.43		−4		−.91
	4.96		−29.075		−22.02		−4		−.91
21.	78,431.23	22.	6,422.003	23.	1,437.56	24.	555	25.	2.34
	1,287.3		−111.001		2,589.04		430		.80
	−333.45		−111.001		−76.2		−13		−.2
	−333.45		−111.001		−76.2		−13		−.2
	−333.45		287.376		−76.2		−13		−.2
	−333.45		57.092		543.33		−13		1.4
26.	4,817.75	27.	188.36	28.	4,604.61	29.	6,478.302	30.	3.33
	−20.81		−.02		−100		5.831		−.04
	−20.81		−.02		−100		−19.9		−.04
	−20.81		−.02		−100		−19.9		−.04
	−2.08		14.32		−100		−19.9		1.32
	−2.08		21.45		78.1		−19.9		3.49
31.	644	32.	1,123,034	33.	78.346	34.	9,098.43	35.	300.98
	−2		−123,034		−2.222		4,137.56		−19.32
	−2		−123,034		−2.222		−.38		17.3
	−2		1,334,897		−2.222		−23.86		−4
	−2		−343,876		2.145		−23.86		−4

ADDITION AND SUBTRACTION OF FRACTIONS

Before you work with addition or subtraction of fractions on the calculator, convert them to decimal form. A Table of Decimal Equivalents of Common Fractions is presented in Appendix A. For those not given, to convert any fraction to a decimal, divide the numerator by the denominator. Set your decimal at 5, and round your answers to four decimal places.

Example 1. 1/2 + 3/7 =

1. Is your calculator clear?
2. Convert 1/2 to decimal form:
   Enter 1 on the keyboard.
   Depress $\boxed{\div}$ or First Number key.
   Enter 2 on the keyboard.
   Depress $\boxed{=}$.
3. Convert 3/7 to decimal form:
   Enter 3 on the keyboard.
   Depress $\boxed{\div}$ or First Number key.
   Enter 7 on the keyboard.
   Depress $\boxed{=}$.
4. We now have .5 + .4286 (rounded to four decimals).
5. Enter $\boxed{.}$ $\boxed{5}$ on the keyboard.
6. Depress $\boxed{+}$.
7. Enter $\boxed{.}$ $\boxed{4}$ $\boxed{2}$ $\boxed{8}$ $\boxed{6}$ on the keyboard.
8. Depress $\boxed{+}$.
9. If you are using a display calculator, your answer will now appear on the display. If you are using a tape, depress $\boxed{T}$.
10. Your answer, .9286, will appear on the tape or on the display.

Example 2. 3/4 - 1/16 =

1. Convert both fractions to decimal form. (Round to four decimal places.)
2. We now have .75 - .0625 =
3. Subtract.
4. Your answer, .6875, will appear on the tape or on the display.

Practice Problems 7. Convert the following fractions to decimals and whole numbers. Then add or subtract as indicated. For those conversions you don't know by heart, look in the Table of Decimal Equivalents of Common Fractions in Appendix A. For those not shown, obtain the decimal equivalent by dividing the numerator by the denominator. Set your decimal at 5. (Round to four decimal places.)

ADDITION AND SUBTRACTION OF FRACTIONS

1.	19-5/8	2.	87-3/4	3.	2-1/3	4.	26-1/2	5.	18-11/12
	4-1/2		7-1/4		4-1/6		23-2/3		26-5/12
	20-1/3		5-1/3		9-5/6		19-1/6		45-2/3
	18-1/8		64-1/8		8-11/12		70-3/4		39-1/8
	2-1/4		12-3/8		3-7/12		8-5/8		8-1/2
	41-3/8		6-7/8		5-5/8		12-3/4		2-5/6
	3-1/6		8-5/8		1-1/4		1-5/12		4-1/12
	75-2/5		1-2/3		3-1/12		5-7/12		7-1/3
	184.7750								

6.	4-1/16	7.	83-1/4	8.	12-1/2	9.	6-1/12	10.	4-3/4
	7-15/16		4-1/2		89-3/4		8-9/16		1-12/16
	8-1/2		7-5/8		7-5/8		5-1/4		7-5/8
	1-9/16		19-11/16		5-1/6		4-3/4		9-1/3
	3-3/4		5-1/12		44-5/16		9-7/8		20-1/2
	6-2/3		15-2/3		6-1/4		1-1/2		1/8
	9-13/16		72-5/6		11/12		7-2/3		7/8
	10-5/8		24-5/12		9-7/8		2-11/12		8-1/4

11.	7-1/4	12.	18-2/3	13.	2/3	14.	1/2	15.	14-9/16
	3-1/3		9-5/8		1-5/16		3/4		10-1/16
	1-7/8		30-5/16		2-3/4		7/8		5-2/3
	2-1/2		4-3/4		7-1/4		2/3		7-5/8
	4-2/3		16-7/16		5/8		5/16		9-1/2
	8-5/8		15-1/12		1/12		5/12		11-7/8
	9-5/12		5-7/8		4-7/8		11/12		3-3/16
	15-11/16		7-3/16		8-1/2		1/4		2-1/12

16.	29-13/16	17.	4-2/3	18.	3-1/3	19.	89-3/8	20.	6-1/2
	18-1/12		7-5/8		4-2/3		94-1/2		4
	64-1/4		6-7/16		9-7/8		17-1/4		9-9/16
	35-5/8		9-1/12		15/16		56-2/3		3-5/12
	77-1/2		10-3/4		13/16		12-3/16		12-2/3
	92-1/4		7-1/2		1-5/8		39-11/12		5-5/8
	56-2/3		5-5/16		2-5/6		71-5/16		6-1/4
	8-3/4		1-7/8		8-1/4		82-5/12		7-3/8

21. 18/61 + 28/74 =

22. 29/84 + 3/9 =

23. 304/209 + 21/70 =

24. 14/71 + 1/2 =

25. 2/9 + 2/3 =

26. 3/8 − 3/8 =

27. 1/8 − 4/9 =

28. 11/12 − 14/16 =

29. 15/16 − 8/14 =

30. 3/5 − 2/5 =

31. 3/7 − 9/19 =

32. 1/4 − 3/7 =

33. 3/4 − 1/9 =

34. 1/8 − 6/8 =

35. 21/96 − 1/4 =

SUBTOTALS

Example.
　　39.7
　　14.81
　　190　　　
　　　　　Subtotal
　　46.19　
　　　　　Total

1. Is your calculator clear?
2. Enter [3] [9] [.] [7] on the keyboard.
3. Depress [+].
4. Enter [1] [4] [.] [8] [1] on the keyboard.
5. Depress [+].
6. Enter [1] [9] [0] on the keyboard. (It is not necessary to enter a decimal for a whole number.)
7. Depress [+].
8. If your calculator is a display, you always get a running subtotal. Your subtotal, 244.51, now shows on the display. Write it down in the space provided for the subtotal. If you are using a tape calculator, depress [S] or ◇.
9. Your subtotal for the problem thus far is 244.51, which will now show on the tape or on the display.
10. You may continue adding the problem without losing the total of the numbers entered so far.
11. Enter [4] [6] [.] [1] [9] on the keyboard.
12. Depress [+].
13. If your calculator is a display, your total will now show on the display. If you are using a tape, depress [T].
14. The grand total, 290.70, will appear on the tape or on the display.

Practice Problems 8. Add the following problems, showing subtotals and totals where indicated:

1.　18.49
　　2.87
　　113.02　
　　134.38　Subtotal
　　39.67
　　4.89　　
　　178.94　Total

2.　2.9
　　3.6　
　　　　　Subtotal
　　18.80
　　9.00
　　4.60　
　　　　　Total

3.　606.12
　　35.54
　　60.71　
　　　　　Subtotal
　　889.02
　　67.51　
　　　　　Total

SUBTOTALS 137

4. 94.61	5. 82.93	6. 3.8
22.35	3.98	4.3
65.70	204.31	Subtotal
82.90	Subtotal	8.9
Subtotal	48.76	6.0
129.04	2.19	4.2
Total	Total	Total
7. 343.91	8. 83.50	9. 88.78
46.73	11.24	7.04
50.82	54.89	609.07
Subtotal	Subtotal	2.13
977.30	228.19	Subtotal
26.72	Total	100.27
Total		Total
10. 2,319.40	11. 23,298	12. 94,090
1,806.21	4,367	5,776
Subtotal	18,909	2,344
890.77	Subtotal	Subtotal
600.41	3,000	5,766
3,029.66	55,559	39,724
Total	Total	Total
13. 18,900	14. 55,557	15. 29,000
2,345	1,090	839
7,726	Subtotal	1,285
Subtotal	385	Subtotal
6,728	83	8,888
29,396	122	920
Total	Total	Total
16. 13.85	17. 218.38	18. 53.87
381.88	301.01	87.35
36.75	98.78	6.60
Subtotal	Subtotal	Subtotal
899.44	1.23	8.55
20.09	.07	.04
Total	Total	Total
19. 564.99	20. 38.45	21. 2.3831
60.21	22.89	6.2098
35.98	Subtotal	17.9028
Subtotal	90.10	Subtotal
3.67	9.09	.8587
1,000.39	Total	.7999
Total		Total

ELECTRONIC CALCULATOR BASIC OPERATIONS

22. .085
    .308
            Subtotal
    .009
    .007
    .029
            Total

23. 23.678
    21.888
            Subtotal
    3.895
    0.093
    0.896
            Total

24. 1.78
    1.29
     .30
            Subtotal
    5.54
     .76
            Total

25. .4
    .5
            Subtotal
    .3
    .57
    .98
            Total

NON-ADD FUNCTION (for tape calculators only)

Example. Inventory #69433
                     19.50
                     18.72

1. It is possible to enter a reference number (such as an inventory number, a purchase order number, etc.) on your tape without having this number enter into your calculations.
2. Is your calculator clear?
3. Enter 69433 on the keyboard.
4. Depress [#] or [N/A] . The number will now print on the tape for identification purposes but will *not* add into the calculation.
5. Enter [1] [9] [.] [5] on the keyboard. (It is not necessary to enter an ending zero which occurs after a decimal unless you are in the add mode.)
6. Depress [+] .
7. Enter [1] [8] [.] [7] [2] on the keyboard.
8. Depress [+] .
9. Depress [T] .
10. Your answer, 38.22, will print on the tape.

Practice Problems 9. On your next set of problems, practice entering the number of your problem with the Non-add key.

MULTIPLICATION

Example. 12.3 × 15 =

1. Is your calculator clear?
2. Enter ☐1 ☐2 ☐. ☐3 on the keyboard.
3. Depress ☐× (or First Number key).
4. Enter ☐1 ☐5 on the keyboard.
5. Depress ☐= or ☐×= .
6. Your answer, 184.5, will now appear on the tape or on the display.

Practice Problems 9. Solve the following problems. (Round your answers to five decimal places.)

1. 558 × 30 = 16,740
2. 190 × 34 =
3. 965 × 85 =
4. 139 × 71 =
5. 713 × 15 =
6. .678 × .7 =
7. 75.6 × .98 =
8. 767.1 × .632 =
9. 78.19 × 94.93 =
10. 62.4 × 7.774 =
11. 225 × 87 =
12. 781 × 21 =
13. 347 × 77 =
14. 719 × 85 =
15. 195 × 39 =
16. .347 × .4 =
17. 43.5 × .67 =
18. 854.5 × .041 =
19. 79.65 × 27.27 =
20. 20.4 × 2.555 =
21. 336 × 98 =
22. 892 × 32 =
23. 458 × 88 =
24. 820 × 96 =
25. 206 × 40 =
26. .458 × .5 =
27. 54.6 × .78 =
28. 965.6 × .125 =
29. 80.76 × 38.38 =
30. 31.5 × 2.666 =
31. 447 × 19 =
32. 901 × 43 =
33. 569 × 99 =
34. 931 × 17 =
35. 317 × 51 =

THREE-FACTOR MULTIPLICATION

Example 1. 12.12 × 40 × 3.816 =
(Set your decimal at 5 and round the answer to four decimal places.)

1. Is your calculator clear?
2. Enter [1] [2] [.] [1] [2] on the keyboard.
3. Depress [X] or First Number key.
4. Enter [4] [0] on the keyboard.
5. Depress [=] or [X=].
6. Your intermediate product, 484.8, will appear on the display or tape.
7. Re-enter this product as your new multiplier by depressing [X] or First Number key.
8. Enter [3] [.] [8] [1] [6] on the keyboard.
9. Depress [=] or [X=].
10. Your final product, 1,849.9968, will appear on the display or tape.

Example 2. 3.1 × 47.891 × 100.98 =
(Round the answer to four decimal places.)

1. If you do not need to know the intermediate product, you can use the following short cut procedure with most electronic calculators:
   Is your calculator clear?
2. Enter [3] [.] [1] on the keyboard.
3. Depress [X].
4. Enter [4] [7] [.] [8] [9] [1] on the keyboard.
5. Depress [X].
6. Enter [1] [0] [0] [.] [9] [8] on the keyboard.
7. Depress [=].
8. Your final product, 14,991.7029 (rounded to four decimal places), will appear on the display or tape.

Practice Problems 10. Solve the following multiplication problems. (Round your answers to four decimal places.)

1. 27 × 89 × 14 = 33,642
2. 3.91 × 4.1 × 6 =

3. 3,801 × 4 × 3.7 =
4. 555 × 444 × 86.7 =
5. 909 × 12.61 × 3.091 =
6. 25 × 18.16 × 15.399 =
7. 18,001 × 12.1 × 20.6 =
8. 24,007 × 3,911 × 4.1 =
9. 19,755 × 106 × 25 =
10. .076 × 2.5 × 3.19 =
11. 178.3 × 29.14 × 806 =
12. 975 × 50.5 × 1.3976 =
13. 41.2 × 200.43 × 2.69 =
14. 7,950 × 30 × 1,309 =
15. .466 × .0743 × 4.011 =
16. 72 × 98 × 41 =
17. 4,071 × 2.3 × 101.777 =
18. 10,004 × 8.75 × 55.3 =
19. 273 × 507 × 8.943 =
20. 22.1 × 87.3 × 56.3 =
21. 98.1 × 443 × 27 =
22. 18,993 × 12.1 × 99.31 =
23. 3,108 × 5 × 7.33 =
24. 333 × 999 × 6.78 =
25. 444 × 43.56 × 907 =
26. .086 × 4.2 × 99.31 =
27. 19,433 × 52 × 103 =
28. 14.995 × 61.81 × 290 =
29. .4207 × 36.9 × 5,390 =
30. 3.2 × .096 × 1.8 =
31. 579 × 5.05 × 139.84 =
32. 9,570 × 3 × 9,301 =
33. .744 × .0437 × 5.021 =
34. 27 × 98 × 35 =
35. 9,268 × 5.6 × 101.894 =

DIVISION

Example. 19.11 ÷ 4.6 =

1. Is your calculator clear?
2. Enter $\boxed{1}$ $\boxed{9}$ $\boxed{.}$ $\boxed{1}$ $\boxed{1}$ on the keyboard.
3. Depress $\boxed{\div}$ or First Number key.
4. Enter $\boxed{4}$ $\boxed{.}$ $\boxed{6}$ on the keyboard.
5. Depress $\boxed{=}$ or $\boxed{\div}$.
6. Your answer, 4.1543, rounded to four decimals, will appear on the tape or on the display.

Practice Problems 11. Solve the following division problems. Set your decimal at 5, and round your answers to four decimal places.

1. 47,016 ÷ 235 = 200.0681
2. 86,949 ÷ 986 =

ELECTRONIC CALCULATOR BASIC OPERATIONS

3. 112,842 ÷ 94 =
4. 66,694 ÷ 894 =
5. 903.4 ÷ 42.3 =
6. 49,852 ÷ 310 =
7. 72,746 ÷ 467 =
8. 126,099 ÷ 27 =
9. 27,444 ÷ 286 =
10. 178.9 ÷ 12.1 =
11. 50,963 ÷ 421 =
12. 83,857 ÷ 578 =
13. 137,100 ÷ 38 =
14. 38,555 ÷ 387 =
15. 289.1 ÷ 13.2 =
16. 61,074 ÷ 532 =
17. 94,968 ÷ 49 =
18. 248,211 ÷ 689 =
19. 49,666 ÷ 498 =

20. 390.2 ÷ 24.3 =
21. 86.94 ÷ 8.5 =
22. 7.56 ÷ .67 =
23. 6.899 ÷ 2.12 =
24. 68.644 ÷ 7.79 =
25. 89,754.3 ÷ 80.88 =
26. 27.46 ÷ 7.7 =
27. 28.6 ÷ 8.77 =
28. 7.764 ÷ 8.77 =
29. 22.464 ÷ 7.55 =
30. 12,357.6 ÷ 88.86 =
31. 38.57 ÷ 8.8 =
32. 39.7 ÷ 9.88 =
33. 8.875 ÷ 8.01 =
34. 33.575 ÷ 8.66 =
35. 23.9 ÷ 9.88 =

MIXED PROBLEMS

Example 1. (13.4 + 2.8) ÷ 14.22 =

1. Is your calculator clear?
2. Always do the operations *within* the parentheses *first*.
3. Enter [1] [3] [.] [4] on the keyboard.
4. Depress [+].
5. Enter [2] [.] [8] on the keyboard.
6. Depress [+].
7. If your calculator is a display, make a note of this sum (16.2). If you are using a tape, depress [T].
8. Your sum, 16.2, will appear on the tape.
9. With most electronic calculators, you can depress [÷] and the sum will be

entered as your dividend. If your calculator does not have this chain function, you can re-enter the sum on the keyboard by hand and then depress $\boxed{\div}$.

10. Enter $\boxed{1}$ $\boxed{4}$ $\boxed{.}$ $\boxed{2}$ $\boxed{2}$ on the keyboard.
11. Depress $\boxed{=}$.
12. Your quotient, 1.1392 (rounded to four places), will appear on the tape or on the display.

Example 2. (41.93 × 3.3) ÷ 15.6 =

1. Is your calculator clear?
2. Always do the operations within the parentheses first.
3. Enter $\boxed{4}$ $\boxed{1}$ $\boxed{.}$ $\boxed{9}$ $\boxed{3}$ on the keyboard.
4. Depress $\boxed{\times}$.
5. Enter $\boxed{3}$ $\boxed{.}$ $\boxed{3}$ on the keyboard.
6. Depress $\boxed{=}$.
7. If your calculator has a re-entry feature, be *sure* to take advantage of it. Depress $\boxed{\div}$ to re-enter your product (138.369) as the dividend for the second part of the problem. With the re-entry feature, it is not necessary to key in the new dividend on the keyboard.
8. Enter $\boxed{1}$ $\boxed{5}$ $\boxed{.}$ $\boxed{6}$ on the keyboard.
9. Depress $\boxed{=}$.
10. Your quotient, 8.8698, rounded to four decimals, will now appear on the tape or on the display.

Example 3. (2,914 + 38.6 - 1,488) (8.5 - 3.2) =

1. Is your calculator clear?
2. Always do the operations within the parentheses first.
3. Enter $\boxed{2}$ $\boxed{9}$ $\boxed{1}$ $\boxed{4}$ on the keyboard.
4. Depress $\boxed{+}$.
5. Enter $\boxed{3}$ $\boxed{8}$ $\boxed{.}$ $\boxed{6}$ on the keyboard.
6. Depress $\boxed{+}$.
7. Enter $\boxed{1}$ $\boxed{4}$ $\boxed{8}$ $\boxed{8}$ on the keyboard.
8. Depress $\boxed{-}$.
9. If you are using a display calculator, make a note of your total. If you are

using a tape calculator, depress Total key, and make a note of your total (1,464.6), or store total in memory if your calculator has a memory function.

10. Enter $\boxed{8}\boxed{.}\boxed{5}$ on the keyboard.
11. Depress $\boxed{+}$.
12. Enter $\boxed{3}\boxed{.}\boxed{2}$ on the keyboard.
13. Depress $\boxed{-}$.
14. Total (5.3).
15. We want to multiply the total from the first set of parentheses by the total in the second set of parentheses. Depress $\boxed{X}$ to make 5.3 your multiplier.
16. Enter $\boxed{1}\boxed{4}\boxed{6}\boxed{4}\boxed{.}\boxed{6}$ on the keyboard.
17. Depress $\boxed{=}$.
18. Your answer is 7,762.38.

Example 4. (26.4 - 13.5) × 8 (3.4 + 2.7) =

1. Is your calculator clear?
2. Always do the operations within the parentheses first.
3. Enter $\boxed{2}\boxed{6}\boxed{.}\boxed{4}$ on the keyboard.
4. Depress $\boxed{+}$.
5. Enter $\boxed{1}\boxed{3}\boxed{.}\boxed{5}$ on the keyboard.
6. Depress $\boxed{-}$.
7. Total, and make a note of this amount (12.9).
8. Enter $\boxed{3}\boxed{.}\boxed{4}$ on the keyboard.
9. Depress $\boxed{+}$.
10. Enter $\boxed{2}\boxed{.}\boxed{7}$ on the keyboard.
11. Depress $\boxed{+}$.
12. Total (6.1).
13. Depress $\boxed{X}$ to make 6.1 your multiplier.
14. Enter $\boxed{8}$ on the keyboard.
15. Depress $\boxed{X}$.
16. Enter $\boxed{1}\boxed{2}\boxed{.}\boxed{9}$ on the keyboard.
17. Depress $\boxed{=}$.

18. Your answer is 629.52.

Example 5. $(18.3 \div 6.1) + (105.2 \div 4) =$

1. Is your calculator clear?
2. Always do the operations within the parentheses first.
3. Enter [1] [8] [.] [3] on the keyboard.
4. Depress [÷].
5. Enter [6] [.] [1] on the keyboard.
6. Depress [=].
7. Make a note of this quotient (3).
8. Enter [1] [0] [5] [.] [2] on the keyboard.
9. Depress [÷].
10. Enter [4] on the keyboard.
11. Depress [=].
12. Your quotient is 26.3.
13. Depress [+].
14. Enter [3] on the keyboard.
15. Depress [+].
16. Total.
17. Your answer is 29.3.

Practice Problems 12. Solve the following problems. Perform the operations within the parentheses first. (Round your answers to four decimal places.)

1. $(30 + 18 - 15.6) \times 39.8 = 1{,}289.52$
2. $(300 - 15.7 + 29) \div 15.3 =$
3. $(304 - 5.24) \times 34.4 \times 5.5 =$
4. $(29 + 45.4 - 32) \div 6.7 =$
5. $(19 + 27.4 - .5) \times (29.3 - 5.4) =$
6. $(30 + 18 - 14.5) \times 38.7 =$
7. $(299 - 14.6 + 18) \div 14.2 =$
8. $(293 + 413 - 23.3) \times 4.4 =$
9. $(18 + 34.3 - 21) \div 5.6 =$
10. $(19 + 16.3 - 2.2) \times (18.1 - 3) =$
11. $(29 + 7 - 3.4) \times 27.6 =$
12. $188 \div (999 - 42 + 17) =$
13. $(827 - 302 - 32.1) \times .4 =$
14. $(27 + 3.4 - 8) \div 6.5 =$
15. $(8 + 16.4 - .3)(1.1 - .9) =$
16. $(41 + 81 - 1.6) \times 93.4 =$
17. $(411 - 5.8 + 31) \div 22.3 =$
18. $(415 - 63 - 45.5) \times .5 =$

19. $(30 + 56.5 - 23) \div 7.6 =$
20. $(27 + 7.4 - 4.4) \times (301 - 5.4) =$
21. $23.3 \times (97 \div 34.2) =$
22. $(249 - 345 - 24)(97 - 5) =$
23. $(34 \times 26.6) \div 57 =$
24. $3.4 (34.4 - 5) =$
25. $(299 - 45) \div (35 - 8.2) =$
26. $12.2 \times (86 \div 23.2) =$
27. $(385 - 234 - 13)(86 - 4) =$
28. $(23 \times 15.5) \div 46 =$
29. $2.3 (23.3 \div 4) =$
30. $(18.8 - 34 + 99)(24 - 7.1) =$
31. $3.2 \times (75 \div 12.1) =$
32. $(274 - 123 - 6)(77 + 8) =$
33. $(12 \times 14.4) \div 64 =$
34. $1.2 (12.2 \div 3) =$
35. $(17.7 - 9 + 8)(13 - 8.1) =$

DECISION PROBLEM

To Rent an Apartment or Buy a Mobile Home

Jack and Jill are to be married in a few weeks. They plan to save their money for the next five years in order to make a down payment on a home. They are trying to decide whether it would be wiser to rent an apartment or to buy a mobile home to live in for the next five years.

They can rent a furnished apartment with a one-year lease for $225 per month. They anticipate that with inflation the monthly rental cost might increase about five percent a year for the remaining four years. The cost of heating the apartment is included in the rental price. They must pay for their own electricity, which averages about $14 a month. Using the laundry facilities will cost about $2 per week.

Jack and Jill can buy a used, furnished mobile home (including a washer and dryer) for $7,500, or $1,500 a year for five years, plus simple interest charges of 10 percent per year on the amount owed. The interest the first year will be (7,500 × .10 × 1). The interest for the second year will be (7,500 - 1,500) × .10 × 1. The interest for the third year will be (6,000 - 1,500) × .10 × 1, etc. Moving and hookup will cost $100. Their utilities would cost about $45 per month. Rental space in the mobile home park is $35 per month. Insurance will cost about $38 per year. At the end of the five years, the mobile home with furnishings could be sold for about $1,200. Jack and Jill could save about $150 per year on their federal income tax because of the interest charges.

Figure the cost for both situations for five years. What is the five-year cost for each arrangement?

REVIEW QUIZ 2

(In Quiz 2, round your answers to four decimal places.)

1.	461.80	2.	5.41	3.	174.22
	3.914		-5.87		80.61
	1.6181		.921		80.61
	31.42		-56.38		800.61
	51.09		-2.048		-9.32
	82.1		1.61		-9.32

Convert to decimal
form and add: (for tape calculators only)

4. 4-2/7   5. .61   6. Inventory # 19762
    1-1/2   3.28   18.50
    26-1/3   1.11   12.91
    2-3/8   Subtotal   3.76
    1-7/16   .39
                               4.67
                               2.09
                                   Total

7. 3.1 × 46.91 × 8.214 =

8. 714.92 ÷ 27.04 =

9. 191.4 ÷ (86.1 - 4.8 + 30.41) =

10. (29.6 × 3.01) ÷ (4.2 × .061) =

Sample Examination

You may want to be timed as you try the Unit 2 sample examination, which is presented in the Introduction.

Unit 3

Electronic Calculator Percent Applications

TOUCH SYSTEM REVIEW

Be sure to keep your index finger, your middle finger, and your ring finger on the home row (4, 5, and 6) if you are using your right hand. Keep your ring finger, your middle finger, and your index finger on the 4, 5, and 6 if you are using your left hand.

555	456	454	655	444	555	564	456	564	564
444	444	666	555	666	666	456	564	456	654
666	666	444	654	654	666	446	664	565	656
555	456	456	555	565	456	445	554	664	665
444	666	555	444	555	656	456	456	654	654
666	464	565	646	646	455	444	555	666	555
666	445	464	454	665	644	445	556	465	554
666	454	456	556	654	456	464	565	666	646
555	456	556	654	556	464	444	555	656	666
444	445	554	665	465	456	465	465	665	465
5,661	4,952	5,170	5,838	5,870	5,474	4,629	5,390	6,021	6,079

Remember: For the right hand, use your index finger for 1, 4, and 7, your middle finger for 2, 5, and 8, and your ring finger for 3, 6, and 9. Use your thumb for the zero and your little finger for the Add bar. For the left hand, use your ring finger for the 1, 4, and 7, your middle finger for 2, 5, and 8, and your index finger for 3, 6, and 9.

Are your fingers curved over the home row? Do not lift your hand away from the keyboard. Keep your fingers hovering over the home row.

654	654	111	132	333	123
565	554	123	222	123	333
556	656	233	321	122	123
666	555	321	322	133	211
666	444	131	332	221	231
456	654	333	321	112	221
546	654	123	331	321	133
555	444	113	331	221	132
465	465	312	123	213	112
564	564	333	222	123	321
5,693	5,644	2,133	2,657	1,922	1,940

TOUCH SYSTEM REVIEW

Are you keeping your head turned toward your copy? Do not turn your head to look at your keys. If you must look, turn your eyes only. Keep your head turned toward your copy if you want to attain speed and accuracy.

132	113	221	312	323	233
222	231	111	321	112	113
123	111	332	221	213	321
232	121	232	332	223	332
222	323	132	231	313	121
331	133	122	121	312	213
221	122	333	222	331	221
123	132	312	111	223	312
313	212	221	333	112	221
111	313	212	123	112	333
2,030	1,811	2,228	2,327	2,274	2,420

Can you find the keys without looking? Are you getting the right answers? Are you keeping your head turned toward your copy? Be sure you don't turn your head back and forth from the keys to the copy. You will lose valuable time and effort that way.

212	313	112	789	897	889
111	331	221	987	789	987
111	123	321	999	978	987
113	331	212	897	778	779
131	112	113	997	979	897
123	321	112	798	778	777
112	122	133	987	887	787
123	313	333	789	897	999
313	212	211	799	897	878
212	232	322	897	888	797
1,561	2,410	2,090	8,939	8,768	8,777

For the right hand, use your thumb for the zero. For the left, use your little finger.

100	101	109	201	301	401
200	202	108	202	302	402
300	203	107	203	303	403
400	204	106	204	304	403
500	205	105	205	305	405
600	206	104	206	306	406
700	207	103	207	307	407
800	208	102	208	308	408
900	209	101	209	309	409
100	200	100	200	300	400
4,600	1,945	1,045	2,045	3,045	4,044

ELECTRONIC CALCULATOR PERCENT APPLICATIONS

Keep your head turned toward your copy.

1.01	2.20	3.30	4.03	5.03	6.03
2.02	3.30	3.04	4.04	5.04	5.04
3.03	4.40	3.05	4.05	5.05	6.05
4.04	5.50	3.06	4.06	5.06	6.06
5.05	6.60	3.07	4.07	5.07	6.07
6.06	7.70	3.08	4.08	5.08	6.08
7.07	8.80	3.09	4.09	5.09	6.09
8.08	9.90	3.10	4.10	5.10	6.10
9.09	1.10	4.01	5.01	6.01	7.01
1.00	1.01	4.02	5.02	6.02	7.02
46.45	50.51	32.82	42.55	52.55	61.55

FINDING THE PERCENTAGE OF A NUMBER

Example. What is 18.6% of 971.84?

Set your decimal at 3. (Round your answer to two decimal places.)

1. Is your calculator clear?
2. Base × Rate = Percentage
3. Base = 971.84. Rate = 18.6% (or .186)
4. 971.84 × .186 = 180.762 (percentage)

   Note: If your calculator has a $\boxed{\%}$ key, enter 971.84, then $\boxed{\times}$, then 18.6, then $\boxed{\%}$. If your calculator does not have a $\boxed{\%}$ key, convert the percent to a decimal (18.6% = .186) and multiply by .186.

5. The percentage (rounded to two decimal places) is 180.76.

Practice Problems 1. Find the percentage in each of the following problems. (Round your answers to two decimal places.)

1. In a graduating class of 1,200, 30% of the students majored in business. What was the number of students majoring in business? (*Ans.* 360)
2. In a freshman class of 1,800, 12% of the students are majoring in food service management. How many are majoring in food service management?
3. The Anderson Corporation employs 3,850 people. Of this number, 28% live more than 20 miles away from the plant. How many employees live more than 20 miles away?
4. Thirty-six percent of the 3,850 Anderson employees received a bonus last year. How many employees received a bonus?
5. At Anderson, 46% of the employees are employed in manufacturing. How many employees are in manufacturing?

6. Fourteen percent of the Anderson employees work in the Data Processing Department. How many are in data processing?
7. Sixteen percent of the Anderson employees are in the Sales Division. How many employees work in sales?
8. Sixty-eight percent of Anderson employees are married. How many employees are married?
9. Forty-two percent of Anderson's employees participate in the stock purchase plan. How many employees participate?
10. Thirty-eight percent of Anderson's employees have more than ten years' service. How many employees have more than ten years' service?
11. A large tire should weigh 982 pounds after it is filled with foam. A 2% weight tolerance is allowed. What are the maximum and minimum weights allowed for this tire?
12. A large earth-mover tire should weigh 1,875 pounds when built. A weight tolerance of 2.5% is allowed. What are the maximum and minimum weights allowed for this tire?
13. Ray bought a new car for $4,750. He must pay a 5% sales tax on the purchase price. How much is the sales tax?
14. At Lorenzo Technical College, 36.5% of the students are part-time. If the student population is 870, how many students are part-time students? (Round to the unit.)
15. At Tallmadge University, 26% of the students live off campus. If the student body is 4,350, how many students live off campus? (Round to the unit.)
16. What is 95.84% of 4,192?
17. What is 55.20% of 534?
18. What is 313.55% of 50?
19. What is .71% of 4.4?
20. What is 9.27% of 313.1?
21. What is 29.2% of 33.3?
22. What is 4% of 88.8?
23. What is 202% of 999?
24. What is 5% of 9?
25. What is 7.7% of 98?
26. What is 18.1% of 22.2?
27. What is 3% of 99.9?
28. What is 100% of 999?
29. What is .4% of 8?
30. What is 6.6% of 87?
31. What is 17.9% of 11.1?

152 ELECTRONIC CALCULATOR PERCENT APPLICATIONS

32. What is 3% of 88.8?
33. What is 102% of 777?
34. What is 3% of 7?
35. What is 5.5% of 78?

FINDING THE NUMBER IF THE PERCENT IS KNOWN

Example. Seventy-two is 30% of what number?

1. Is your calculator clear?
2. Base = Percentage/Rate.
3. Base = 72 ÷ 30% if you have a $\boxed{\%}$ key, or Base = 72 ÷ .30 if you have no $\boxed{\%}$ key.
4. Base = 240
5. Therefore, 72 is 30% of 240.

Practice Problems 2. Solve the following problems. Set your decimal at 3 and round your answers to two decimal places.

1. Last month Paul Martin's home was damaged by fire. Paul's insurance company paid him $4,920, which represented 80% of the loss. How much was the loss? (*Ans.* $6,150)
2. Alice King pays 18% of her monthly salary for federal income tax. Her federal tax deduction this month is $145. What is her monthly salary?
3. Marilyn Smith received $78.50 in tips this week from her work as a waitress. Tips represent 60% of her weekly income. How much did she earn this week?
4. If you spend 28% of your monthly income, or $180, on rent, what is your monthly income?
5. George Akins uses his personal car for his job in technical sales. His employer reimburses him for 85% of the cost of his gasoline each month. How much did he spend on gasoline last month if he was reimbursed $74.80?
6. Donna Wilson has a new coat in layaway. She has paid the store $35.50, which is 40% of the price of the coat. What is the price of her new coat?
7. Andy received a dividend check for $21.30, which represents a 5% return on the price he paid for his stock. How much did he pay for his stock?
8. Last month a tool and die company had to scrap 6.5% of the metal used in their manufacturing process. They scrapped 120 pounds. How many pounds of metal did they use all together?
9. Your company had to pay $228 this week for goods lost or damaged in transit.

This $228 represented 2% of goods sold this week. How much did your company sell?

10. A cafeteria offered the following entrees yesterday: tuna casserole, fish and chips, beef and noodles, and cheese rarebit. If the cafeteria sold 221 servings of cheese rarebit, and if 23% of the customers ordered cheese rarebit, how many customers did they serve yesterday?

11. Jack Imes will receive a wage increase of $.35 per hour, or 6.5% of his present hourly rate. What is his present hourly rate? What is his new hourly rate?

12. Minnie's car repair bill included $29.50 for labor. The labor represented 45% of the total cost of the repair. What was Minnie's total bill?

13. The Johnstown Community and Technical College donated $181,400 to the United Appeal. This sum represented 104.5% of their goal. What was their goal?

14. Jamestown Electronics has hired 21 new employees. This number represents 62% of the number of new employees they plan to hire this year. What is the total number of employees to be hired this year?

15. The Phillips family purchased a new organ for their home. They paid a 5% sales tax, which amounted to $91. What was the cost of the organ?

16. 86 is 81% of what number?
17. 4,070 is 95.5% of what number?
18. 29 is 104% of what number?
19. 387 is 20% of what number?
20. 12 is 206% of what number?
21. 12 is 30% of what number?
22. 206 is 12% of what number?
23. 20 is 8% of what number?
24. 104 is 46% of what number?
25. 95.4 is 19% of what number?
26. 81 is 2% of what number?
27. 56 is 31% of what number?
28. 2 is 8% of what number?
29. 4 is 6% of what number?
30. 16 is 8.4% of what number?
31. 54 is 51% of what number?
32. 21.1 is 5.6% of what number?
33. 4.7 is 2% of what number?
34. 59 is 7.6% of what number?
35. 2.4 is 3% of what number?

FINDING WHAT PERCENT ONE NUMBER IS OF ANOTHER

Example. What percent is 29 of 32? (Round off your percent answers to two decimal places; e.g., 90.63%.)

1. Is your calculator clear?
2. Rate = Percentage/Base
3. The "is" number (29 in this problem) is *always* the dividend.
   The "of" number (32 in this problem) is *always* the divisor.
   The dividend always goes into the machine first.
4. 29/32 = 29 ÷ 32 = .90625 = 90.62$\underline{5}$%, which rounded to two decimal places, is 90.63%.

   If your calculator has a $\boxed{\%}$ key, enter 29, then $\boxed{\div}$, then 32, then $\boxed{\%}$. Your calculator will move the decimal over two places for you and give you 90.625%. If your calculator does not have a $\boxed{\%}$ key, you will need to convert the answer, .90625, to 90.63% by moving the decimal two places to the right and rounding off. If you have a round-off switch on your calculator, you can set it so that your answer is rounded for you.
5. Therefore, the Rate = 29/32 or 90.63%.

Practice Problems 3. Solve the following problems. (Round your answers to two decimal places.)

1. In January of this year your company had sales of $3.7 million. In January of last year your company had sales of $3.4 million. What percent is this year's January sales of last year's January sales? (*Ans.* 108.82%)
2. The Research Department's budget this year is $220,300. Last year's budget was $235,200. What percent is this year's budget of last year's budget?
3. On a recent mathematics test you correctly solved 69 of the 75 problems. What percent is 69 of 75?
4. You recently sent out 300 copies of a questionnaire. Two hundred sixty people responded. What percent of return did you have? (The total is always the base; the base is the divisor. Divide 260 by 300.)
5. The Jackson family spent $56 last week on food. If their weekly income is $254, what percent is their food cost of their income?
6. Manchester Cargo Company moved a total of 65 tons of freight last month. Twelve tons went by air freight. What percent of the total weight was sent by air freight?
7. Beth received $81.90 in interest on savings of $1,560. What interest rate did she receive?
8. At Summit College 321 students out of a student body of 1,529 are married. What percent of the students are married?

FINDING WHAT PERCENT ONE NUMBER IS OF ANOTHER 155

9. Jean Shelton received a monthly paycheck of $1,040. Of this amount, $250 was for commission on sales. What percent of her total pay was commission?
10. The total quarterly budget of Butler Engineering Company is $179,500. Of this total, $125,300 is for salaries and employee benefits. What percent of the budget is for salaries and employee benefits?
11. A $37.50 U.S. Savings Bond pays $12.50 in interest at maturity. What percent is the interest of the cost?
12. Michael O'Brien received a monthly paycheck of $975.00 gross pay. The following deductions were made for taxes: $9.75 city tax, $185.50 federal tax, and $15.50 state tax. What percent of his paycheck is the total deduction for taxes?
13. Your school's basketball team has played seven games so far this year and has won six of them. What percent of the games have they won?
14. A salaried employee earns $986 per month. He is scheduled to receive a raise of $78 per month. What percent of his present salary is the raise?
15. The Trenton Food Company has a voluntary additional pension plan. A participating employee who earns $15,500 a year contributes $1,123.75 to the plan. What percent of his salary is his contribution?
16. What percent of 142 is 111?
17. What percent of 293 is 56?
18. What percent of 23.3 is 4.7?
19. What percent is 87 of 37?
20. What percent is 97 of 378?
21. What percent of 931 is 777?
22. What percent of 182 is 45?
23. What percent of 12.2 is 3.6?
24. What percent is 8.3 of 50.36?
25. What percent is 96.1 of 310.22?
26. What percent is 11.34 of 11.85?
27. What percent is 59.16 of 104.01?
28. What percent is 322,225 of 98,801?
29. What percent is 599.4 of 55.45?
30. What percent is 89.34 of 92.49?
31. What percent is 867.43 of 680.3?
32. What percent of 33.54 is 6.84?
33. What percent is 79.9 of 83.41?
34. What percent is 63.7 of 187.99?
35. What percent is 87.21 of 87.36?

PERCENT OF THE WHOLE

Example. The quarterly budget for the Marketing Department of ABC Company is $196,300. The items budgeted include:

	Amount	Percent
Salaries and employee benefits	$117,000	59.6
Rent and electricity	20,000	10.2
Telecommunications and postage	18,000	9.2
Company automobiles (purchase and maintenance)	15,700	8.0
Brochures, advertising, customer entertainment	12,700	6.5
Charitable contributions	9,000	4.6
Office supplies, furniture, and equipment	3,900	2.0
Total Budget	$196,300	

Find what percent each amount is of the whole (the total).

1. To find what percent each item is of the total, divide the total into each part. (See pie graph.) Show your answers in percent form, rounded to one decimal place.
2. 117,000 ÷ 196,300 = 59.6%
3. 20,000 ÷ 196,300 = etc.

If your calculator has a $\boxed{\%}$ key, be sure to take advantage of it. If you do not have a $\boxed{\%}$ key, your answers will need to be converted to percent form by moving the decimal two places to the right.

Note: This problem has a constant divisor (the total). Many calculators have the capability of entering a constant divisor. (Refer to the illustrations on pages 86–92. Some calculators have a First Number–Second Number switch to use in entering constants. Since the dividend is entered first and the *divisor* is entered second, the switch would be placed in "Second Number." Other calculators use the Memory keys to hold a constant. If your calculator has a short-cut method for a constant divisor, take advantage of it on problems of this type.

Practice Problems 4. What percent of the total is spent on each item? Add all the expenses. Divide the total expenses into each part. Express your answers in percent form, rounded to one decimal place.

1. The monthly expense budget for the Martin family is:

PERCENT OF THE WHOLE

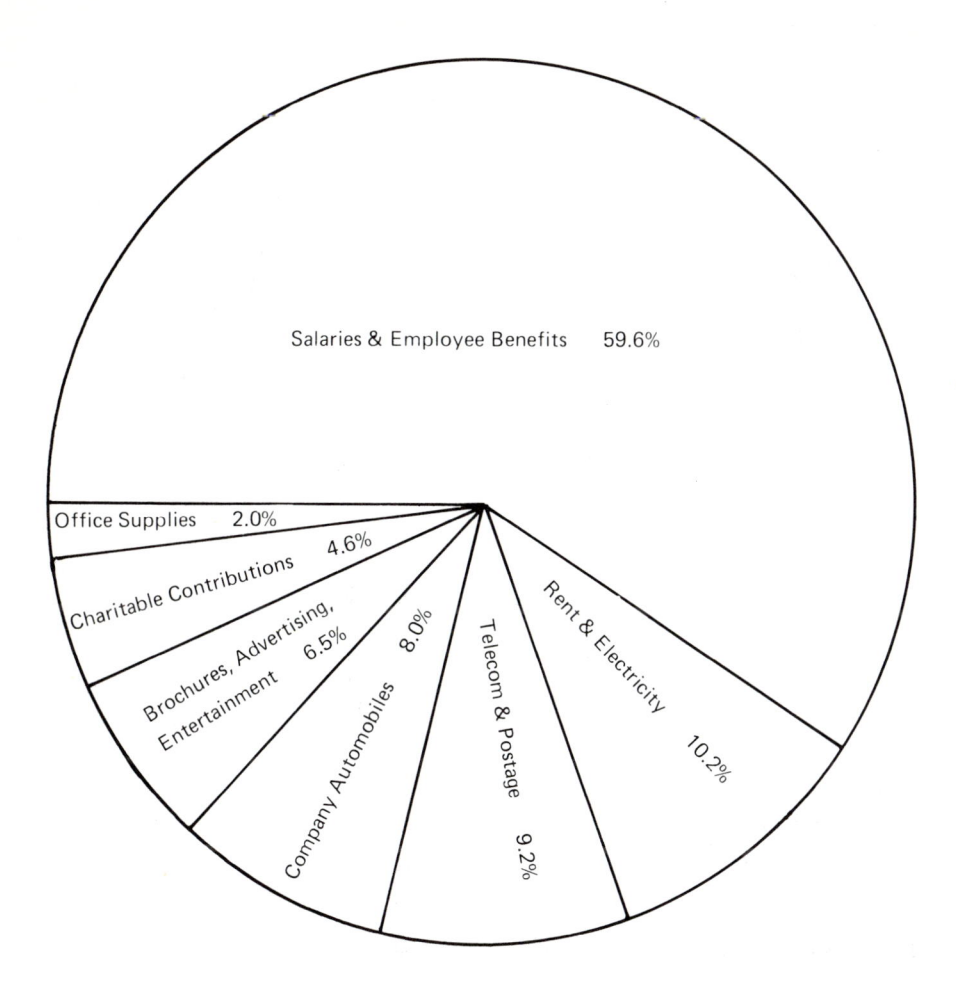

- Salaries & Employee Benefits 59.6%
- Office Supplies 2.0%
- Charitable Contributions 4.6%
- Brochures, Advertising, Entertainment 6.5%
- Company Automobiles 8.0%
- Telecom & Postage 9.2%
- Rent & Electricity 10.2%

Marketing Department Quarterly Budget Distribution

	Item	Amount ($)	Percent of the Whole
(a)	Mortgage payment	274.38	31.9
(b)	Transportation	105.33	12.3
(c)	Food	105.00	12.2
(d)	Medical and Insurance	75.00	8.7
(e)	Savings	110.00	12.8
(f)	Recreation	40.00	4.7
(g)	Clothing	50.00	5.8
(h)	Miscellaneous	100.00	11.6
	Total	$859.71	100.0

2. The monthly expense budget for the Smith family is:

Item	Amount ($)	Percent of the Whole
(a) Rent	155.00	_____
(b) Transportation	45.00	_____
(c) Food	65.20	_____
(d) Medical and Insurance	45.00	_____
(e) Savings	150.00	_____
(f) Recreation	25.00	_____
(g) Clothing	40.00	_____
(h) Miscellaneous	40.00	_____
Total		

3. The monthly expense budget for the Kallen family is:

Item	Amount ($)	Percent of the Whole
(a) Rent	225.00	_____
(b) Transportation	48.90	_____
(c) Food	90.00	_____
(d) Medical and Insurance	38.00	_____
(e) Savings	100.00	_____
(f) Recreation	30.00	_____
(g) Clothing	35.00	_____
(h) Utilities	39.30	_____
(i) Miscellaneous	30.00	_____
Total		

4. The monthly expense budget for the Jones family is:

Item	Amount ($)	Percent of the Whole
(a) Mortgage	280.27	_____
(b) Transportation	151.85	_____
(c) Food	160.00	_____
(d) Medical and Insurance	56.75	_____
(e) Savings	120.40	_____
(f) Recreation	40.00	_____
(g) Utilities	68.70	_____
(h) Clothing	60.00	_____
(i) Installment payment (washer)	37.50	_____
(j) Miscellaneous	75.00	_____
Total		

PRORATION

Example 1. Several departments use the company airplane for business trips. At the end of each month the departments are charged for their share of the expense of operating the plane for that month. Their respective shares are based on their percent of the total miles flown. In other words, a department which used 20% of the total miles flown would pay 20% of the total expenses. During June, use of the company plane by department was as follows:

Department	Miles Flown
Advertising	2,100
Technical Service	1,025
Marketing	3,900
Research and Development	1,500
Total	8,525

For June, the cost of operating the company plane (including pilots' salaries, fuel, insurance, maintenance, etc.) was $45,200. What percent of the total cost did each department incur? (Round the percent to two decimal places.) Also, what is the amount of prorated expense that will be charged against each department's budget?

1. Is your calculator clear?
2. Add the miles flown (total = 8,525).
3. Divide each department's mileage by the total mileage: 2,100 ÷ 8,525 = 24.63%, etc.
   Note: Use the constant divisor capability if your calculator has one.

Department	Percent of Total Mileage
Advertising	24.63
Technical Service	12.02
Marketing	45.75
Research and Development	17.60

4. Multiply each percent times the total cost ($45,200) to find the prorated expense to be charged to each department.

$$24.63\% \text{ (or .2463)} \times 45,200 = 11,132.76$$
$$12.02\% \text{ (or .1202)} \times 45,200 = 5,433.04, \text{ etc.}$$

(Use the % key if your calculator has one.)

Note: Some calculators have the capability of holding a constant multiplier (45,200 in this problem). If your calculator has a constant multiplier feature, use it for problems such as this one.

Department	Prorated Expense ($)
Advertising	11,132.76
Technical Service	5,433.04
Marketing	20,679.00
Research and Development	7,955.20
Total	45,200.00

Example 2. If you do not need to know the *percent* of the total cost, this type of proration problem can be done in fewer steps. For July, the departments used the company plane as follows:

Department	Miles Flown
Advertising	1,900
Technical Service	960
Marketing	5,800
Research and Development	750
Total	9,410

The total expense for operating the company plane for July was $43,150. If we divide the company plane expense for July by the total miles flown, we can find the constant ratio of each department's expense to its number of miles flown. Then we multiply this constant ratio by each department's miles flown.

1. Total operating expense for July = 43,150.
2. Total miles flown by all departments = 9,410.
3. Divide the total expense by the total miles flown. 43,150 ÷ 9,410 = 4.5855 (rounded to four decimals). For automatic round-off, set your decimal for 4 with the Round-off switch "on."
4. To determine each department's prorated plane expense, multiply each department's total miles flown by the ratio (4.5855):

$$1,900 \times 4.5855 = 8,712.45$$
$$960 \times 4.5855 = 4,402.08$$
$$5,800 \times 4.5855 = 26,595.90$$
$$750 \times 4.5855 = 3,439.125$$

Note: If your calculator has a constant multiplier feature, set 4.5855 as the constant.

5. Add the prorated expense for the four departments for July. The total expense should be close to $43,150. If your calculator has a memory, you may add each product in step 4 into memory as it is calculated, and then recall

total memory to check your expense total. If you do not have the memory function, add the four products as a regular addition problem.

Total prorated expense = $43,149.56*(rounded to the penny)

Practice Problems 5. Find the percent of the whole and the prorated expense in the following problems. (Round the percent to two decimal places. Round the prorated expense to the penny.)

1. The following departments of a branch location of a chemical company use a telephone tie line to the home office. The departments are charged according to the number of minutes per month that each spends making calls on the tie line. During June, the number of minutes by department were:

Department	Minutes Used	Percent of the Whole	Amount of Prorated Expense ($)
(a) Elastomers	2,030	23.12	208.08
(b) Polymers	939	10.69	96.21
(c) Marketing	508	5.78	52.02
(d) Data Processing	264	3.01	27.09
(e) Telecommunications	5,041	57.40	516.60
Total	8,782	100.00	900.00

What percent of the total number of minutes did each department use? (2,030 ÷ 8,782, etc.)
If the cost of the tie line is $900 per month, how much is each department's prorated share of this expense?

2. During July, the minutes used by department were:

Department	Minutes Used	Percent of the Whole	Amount of Prorated Expense ($)
(a) Elastomers	1,061	_____	_____
(b) Marketing	1,302	_____	_____
(c) Polymers	574	_____	_____
(d) Data Processing	190	_____	_____
(e) Telecommunications	4,976	_____	_____
Total			

What percent of the total number of minutes did each department use? How much is each department's prorated share of this expense? (Tie line costs $900 per month.)

---

*Your total may be slightly different from the actual expense (as this one is) because of rounding off. This total is close enough that we can assume correct work.

3. The Anderson Company has three offices located in Chicago. All three telephone systems are linked together through one switchboard. The three offices share the expense of the switchboard operator's salary and employee benefits. The cost is prorated according to the percent of calls each office placed or received. The data for August are as follows:

Office	Number of Calls Placed/Received	Percent of the Whole	Amount of Prorated Expense ($)
(a) Main Street	1,209	_____	_____
(b) Elm Street	840	_____	_____
(c) High Boulevard	567	_____	_____
Total			

What is each office's percent of the total number of calls? If the switchboard operator's salary is $675 per month and the cost of her employee benefits is $229 per month, how much is each office's prorated share of her monthly salary plus benefits?

4. Your company, a textile manufacturer, has decided to sponsor a television special, with commercials to advertise the products of your various divisions. The cost of this special is $985,300. Each division will be charged a portion of this cost, according to its percent of last year's sales. Last year's sales by division were as follows:

Division	Sales ($)	Percent of the Whole	Amount of Prorated Expense ($)
(a) Wearing Apparel Fabric	10,500,000	_____	_____
(b) Upholstery	12,300,000	_____	_____
(c) Carpeting	24,600,000	_____	_____
(d) Industrial Fabrics	18,400,000	_____	_____
Total			

What was the percent of the total sales for each division? What is each division's prorated share of the cost of the television special?

5. The Blandon Corporation charges the departments using the computer according to the percent of the total time used. The amount of time used, by department, for the last month is as follows:

Department	Time (hours)	Amount of Prorated Expense ($)
(a) Payroll	14.1	_____
(b) Research and Development	29.3	_____
(c) Marketing	7.6	_____
(d) Accounts Receivable	10.7	_____

	Department	Time (hours)	Amount of Prorated Expense ($)
(e)	Administrative Services	6.3	_____
(f)	Accounts Payable	8.3	_____
(g)	Manufacturing	19.5	_____
(h)	Employee Services	13.7	_____
(i)	Advertising	6.9	_____
	Total		

In this problem, find *only* the prorated expense for each department. Do *not* figure the percent of the total. Use the constant ratio method shown in Example 2. (Divide the total expense by the total number of hours.) If the computer charge to be prorated is $2,500, what is the charge to each department?

6. Your company has outgoing WATS service, which costs a flat fee of $1,500 per month. The users are charged for the number of minutes they use the WATS service. The cost is prorated by the percentage of the total minutes each department uses. The minutes used, by department, for last month are as follows:

	Department	Minutes Used	Amount of Prorated Expense ($)
(a)	Telecommunications	994	_____
(b)	Order Entry	1,871	_____
(c)	Marketing	2,509	_____
(d)	Research and Development	1,486	_____
(e)	Technical Service	307	_____
(f)	Manufacturing	402	_____
(g)	Shipping	311	_____
(h)	Accounting	107	_____
(i)	Credits and Collections	971	_____
(j)	Safety	295	_____
	Total		

How much is each department charged for last month's WATS line service? Use the constant ratio method. Do *not* figure the percent of the total.

7. At a recent home show, held at the convention hall, exhibitors rented space to display their products and services to the public. The cost to exhibitors was based on the number of square feet that their exhibit required. The exhibitors and the number of square feet each one used are given below:

	Exhibitors	Number of Square Feet Used	Amount of Prorated Expense ($)
(a)	Aladdin Roofing Co.	400	_____
(b)	Best-Ever Kitchen Appliances	155	_____
(c)	Joslyn and McIntyre, Architects	210	_____
(d)	Alboni & Sons, Contractors	190	_____
(e)	Lindon Water Softeners, Inc.	180	_____
(f)	Barbecue Specialists, Inc.	650	_____
(g)	Magic-Eye Garage Doors, Inc.	550	_____
(h)	American Home Heating Corp.	576	_____
(i)	Lenny's Pianos and Organs	560	_____
(j)	Econo-Carpet Company	560	_____
(k)	Susanne Interior Decorator	304	_____
(l)	Tildon's Furniture Store	2,600	_____
(m)	Ambrose Paint & Wallpaper Company	526	_____
(n)	Ruth Korman Art Gallery	750	_____
(o)	The Lamplight Shoppe	826	_____
	Total		

If the cost for renting space at the home show was $15,000, how much is each exhibitor's prorated cost? Use the constant ratio method.

PERCENT OF INCREASE OR DECREASE

Example 1. Our company's sales this year are $36,593; our sales last year were $30,219. Find the amount of change (in dollars). Did the sales increase or decrease? Also find the percent of change (increase +; or decrease, -). (Round off the percent to one decimal place.)

1. *Always* subtract the smaller amount from the larger amount. Since our sales this year are larger than those of last year, we have an *increase* (+).

$$36,593 - 30,219 = +6,374$$

2. *Always* divide the amount of change (the difference) by the *last year* amount.
3. $6,374 \div 30,219 = +21.1\%$ (rounded to one decimal place)
   If your calculator has no Percent key, convert your decimal answer (.2109) to a percent by moving the decimal two places to the right.
4. Round off your answer to one decimal place (21.1%). If your calculator has a Round-off switch, you can set your decimal at 1 and the Round-off switch to "on."

Example 2. The Broadhurst Company has sales this year of $355,090; their sales last year were $400,368. Find the amount of change (in dollars). Have their

PERCENT OF INCREASE OR DECREASE   165

sales increased or decreased? Also find the percent of change. Show (+) for an increase; show (-) for a decrease. (Round off the percent to one decimal place.)

1. 400,368 - 355,090 = 45,278 (decrease)
2. *Always* divide the difference by the *last year (earlier)* amount.

$$45{,}278 \div 400{,}368 = .11309 = -11.3\%$$

3. Be sure to mark your percent answer with a (+) or a (-) to indicate whether your change is an increase or a decrease.

Practice Problems 6. The first column in the following problems shows our sales to each of our customers for this year. The second column shows our sales to these same customers for last year. Calculate the amount of change (to the penny) and the percent of change (to the tenth of a percent). Be sure to indicate whether the change is an *increase* (+) or a *decrease* (-).

	Sales This Year By Customer ($)	Sales Last Year By Customer ($)	Amount of Change ($)	Percent of Change
1.	247,799.00	399,496.00	(-) 151,697.00	-38.0
2.	13,999.00	12,426.00		
3.	3,962,864.00	4,988,667.00		
4.	449,646.87	333,469.77		
5.	459,777.00	599,864.00		
6.	570,022.00	622,729.00		
7.	36,222.00	35,759.00		
8.	5,295,197.00	6,211,991.00		
9.	772,979.11	666,792.11		
10.	782,888.00	822,197.00		
11.	469,991.00	511,618.00		
12.	25,111.00	24,648.00		
13.	5,184,086.00	5,100,889.00		
14.	661,868.09	555,681.99		
15.	671,999.00	711,086.00		
16.	358,800.00	400,507.00		
17.	14,000.00	13,537.00		

ELECTRONIC CALCULATOR PERCENT APPLICATIONS

	Sales This Year By Customer ($)	Sales Last Year By Customer ($)	Amount of Change ($)	Percent of Change
18.	4,075,975.00	5,900,778.00		
19.	550,757.98	444,570.88		
20.	560,888.00	600,975.00		
21.	570,022.00	622,729.00		
22.	36,222.00	35,759.00		
23.	5,295,197.00	6,211,991.00		
24.	772,979.11	666,792.11		
25.	782,888.00	822,197.00		

CHAIN DISCOUNT

Example 1. What will Ruth's Fashion Boutique pay for a pants suit which is priced at $50, on which the manufacturer allows a chain discount of 10%, 10%, and 2-1/2%? (Method 1)

1. Is your calculator clear?
2. If we multiply $50.00 by 10% (or .1 if you have no $\boxed{\%}$ key), we find that the first discount is $5.00. That is, she will pay $50.00 - 5.00 or $45.00 for the suit after the first discount. A quicker way to do this would be to multiply by the complement of the percent (100 - 10 = 90); therefore, $50.00 × 90% (or .9) = $45.00 she will pay after the first discount. Multiplying by the complement takes one step instead of two.
3. Re-enter the $45.00 as our new multiplier by depressing $\boxed{\times}$
4. Enter 90% (or .9) on the keyboard (100 - 10 = 90).
5. Depress $\boxed{\%}$ (or $\boxed{=}$).
6. Re-enter this $40.50 as our new multiplier by depressing $\boxed{\times}$.
7. Enter 97.5% (or .975) on the keyboard (100.0 - 2.5% = 97.5%).
8. Depress $\boxed{\%}$ (or $\boxed{=}$).
9. Your answer, $39.49 (rounded to the penny) will appear on the display or tape. Ruth will pay $39.49 for a $50.00 item after it has been discounted 10%, 10% and 2-1/2%.

Example 2. What will Ruth's Fashion Boutique pay for a pants suit priced at $50, on which the manufacturer allows a chain discount of 10%, 10%, and 2-1/2%? (Method 2)

CHAIN DISCOUNT

1. A quicker way to figure the net cost after a series of discounts is to refer to the Table of Chain Discount Equivalents (Appendix D). To find the equivalent amount, look across the top of the table until you find the first discount (in this problem, 10). Then come down this column until you find the combination of 10 and 2-1/2 shown on the left-hand side. Where the column and the row intersect, you will find the decimal amount (.78975) by which to multiply the price ($50).
2. Multiply the equivalent (.78975) by the price.

    .78975 × 50 = $39.49 (rounded to the penny)

Note: The equivalent discount is found by determining the complements of the discounts in the chain and then multiplying them together. For example, the complement of 10% is 90% (100 - 10 = 90); the complement of 2-1/2% is 97.5% (100 - 2.5 = 97.5). *Convert* these percents to decimals; then multiply (.9 × .9 × .975 = .78975).

If you have several items to multiply by the same chain discount, it is worthwhile to take the time to find the equivalent by multiplying the complements of the chain. However, if you need to find only one or two discounts, it is not worthwhile to calculate the equivalents of chains not shown in the table.

Practice Problems 7. Solve the following chain discount problems. Use Appendix D for finding chain discount equivalents. (Round your answers to the penny.)

1. $423.67 less 10% - 8% - 20% = $280.64
2. $28.99 less 5% - 2-1/2% =
3. $3,278.33 less 20% - 5-1/2% - 2% =
4. $325.55 less 25% - 10% - 12-3/4% =
5. $69.69 less 50% - 2% - 7-1/2% =
6. $200.27 less 10% - 33% - 2% =
7. $22.43 less 66-1/2% - 2-1/2% =
8. $202.87 less 8-1/4% - 10% - 3% =
9. $8.97 less 12-3/4% - 9% - 3.3% =
10. $211.11 less 34% - 3.4% =
11. $312.56 less 10% - 8% - 20% =
12. $17.88 less 5% - 2-1/2% =
13. $2,167.22 less 20% - 5-1/2% - 2% =
14. $214.44 less 25% - 10% - 12-3/4% =
15. $68.58 less 50% - 2% - 2-1/2% =
16. $199.16 less 10% - 33% - 3% =
17. $11.32 less 66-1/2% - 2-1/2% =
18. $191.76 less 8-1/4% - 10% - 3% =
19. $7.86 less 12-2/3% - 9% - 3% =
20. $100.00 less 34% - 2% - 2-1/2% =
21. $201.45 less 9% - 7% - 10% =
22. $16.77 less 4% - 2-3/4% =
23. $1,056.11 less 20% - 5-1/2% - 1% =
24. $103.33 less 25% - 9% - 12-1/4% =
25. $78.47 less 40% - 2% - 6-1/2% =
26. $188.05 less 10% - 33% - 2% =
27. $11.21 less 66-1/2% - 2-3/4% =
28. $181.65 less 8-3/4% - 8% - 2% =
29. $6.75 less 11-3/4% - 8% - 3% =
30. $200.00 less 67% - 4% - 1-1/2% =

168   ELECTRONIC CALCULATOR PERCENT APPLICATIONS

31. $534.78 less 12% - 8% - 10% =
32. $29.11 less 5% - 2-1/2% =
33. $4,389.00 less 30% - 5-1/2% - 3% =
34. $536.66 less 15% - 20% - 12-3/4% =
35. $70.70 less 50% - 2% - 5% =

CASH DISCOUNTS

Many times companies grant buyers a discount for paying their invoice within a given time. Also, companies often give their buyers a discount for buying in quantity.

Example 1. The Xavier Paper Company grants its customers a 2% discount for paying the invoice within ten days. If the invoice is not paid within the ten-day period, the net amount of the invoice is due within 30 days (2/10, n/30). If the customer's invoice is for $23,400, how much will he pay if he sends his check within ten days?

1. 23,400 × 2% (or .02) = 468
2. 23,400 - 468 = $22,932 due within ten days
3. The net amount, $23,400, is due if the invoice is paid after the ten-day limit.

Example 2. The Xavier Paper Company charges $12.20 for a ream of document-quality 75% rag 20-lb. bond paper. If a customer buys 10 reams, he receives a 15% quantity discount. How much will a customer pay if he buys 10 reams of this bond paper and pays his invoice within ten days (terms 2/10, n/30)?

1. If we do not need to know the actual *amount* of the discounts, we can use a short-cut method to solve this problem: If the customer receives a 15% quantity discount, this means that he pays 85% of the original price (100% - 15% = 85%). Also, if he receives a 2% cash discount, he pays 98% of the invoice after the quantity discount (100% - 2% = 98%).
2. 10 × 12.20 × .85 × .98 = Customer payment
3. 10 × 12.20 × .85 × .98 = $101.626 = $101.63 (rounded to the penny)

Practice Problems 8. Figure the amount of the discount(s) and the amount due on the following invoices. All were paid within the time limit for the cash discount. Remember: take the quantity discount first; then take the cash discount on the amount due after the quantity discount is deducted. (Round your answers to the penny.)

	Amount of Invoice ($)	Quantity Discount (%)	Cash Discount Terms	Amount of Discount(s) ($)	Amount Due ($)
1.	139.40	10	2/10	16.45	122.95
2.	26.81	15	2/15	_____	_____
3.	3,942.55	20		_____	_____

CASH DISCOUNTS

	Amount of Invoice ($)	Quantity Discount (%)	Cash Discount Terms	Amount of Discount(s) ($)	Amount Due ($)
4.	764.19	18	3/30	_____	_____
5.	18.64	12	–	_____	_____
6.	306.18	5	–	_____	_____
7.	2,492.26	25	2/10	_____	_____
8.	804.77	10	1/10	_____	_____
9.	96.41	–	1-1/2/10	_____	_____
10.	100.07	–	2-1/2/15	_____	_____
11.	5,609.44	12-1/2	2/30	_____	_____
12.	378.98	3	5/5	_____	_____
13.	102.93	–	1/15	_____	_____
14.	4,857.56	18-1/4	–	_____	_____
15.	208.69	15	–	_____	_____
16.	215.40	10	10/30	_____	_____
17.	78.32	24	2/15	_____	_____
18.	15.06	21	3/10	_____	_____
19.	200,456.90	25	–	_____	_____
20.	35,317.96	10	1/30	_____	_____
21.	340.28	5	2/60	_____	_____
22.	110.02	8	1/15	_____	_____
23.	25.11	16-2/3	2/10	_____	_____
24.	125.50	8-1/2	–	_____	_____
25.	37.32	2	1/10	_____	_____

On the following invoices assume that we do not need to know the amount of discount(s). Find only the amount due on each invoice, using the short-cut method. All invoices are paid within the cash discount time limit.

Example. How much does Santa Dominion Co. owe on an invoice of $266.70 if they receive a 12% quantity discount and terms of 2/10? (266.70 × .88 × .98 = $230.00)

Practice Problems 9.

	Amount of Invoice ($)	Quantity Discount (%)	Cash Discount Terms	Amount Due ($)
26.	5,020.40	10	2/10	4,427.99
27.	651.70	5	1/10	_____
28.	13.58	–	2/5	_____
29.	2,506.50	7-1/2	1/30	_____
30.	15.75	–	2/15	_____
31.	300.18	8	2/30	_____
32.	160.25	4	4/15	_____
33.	23,959.74	12-1/2	2/10	_____
34.	384,600.24	12-1/2	2/90	_____
35.	50,120.62	10	1/10	_____
36.	381.21	20	2/10	_____
37.	21.80	–	2/10	_____
38.	36.18	5	–	_____
39.	721.12	7	3/10	_____
40.	9,981.19	18	2/30	_____
41.	204.42	40	1/30	_____
42.	17.05	–	1/15	_____
43.	6,205.48	10	1/10	_____
44.	1,111.01	8	–	_____
45.	600.60	6-1/2	2/15	_____
46.	2.59	5	3/30	_____
47.	306.14	10	2/45	_____
48.	5.05	–	2/60	_____
49.	390.60	2	–	_____
50.	79.85	–	1/15	_____

SALES TAXES

Example 1. If you buy a shirt for $14.98 and your state charges a 5% sales tax, how much will you pay for the shirt plus tax? (Round to the nearest penny.)

1. 14.98 × 5% (or .05) = .749 = $.75 rounded to the penny
2. Depress the Plus bar to re-enter .749 to be added.
3. Enter 14.98 and depress Plus bar.
4. Depress Total.
5. Your answer is $15.73 (rounded to the penny).

Note: Some electronic calculators have one or more memory registers, which enable you to accumulate, store, and recall products, quotients, or sums. If your calculator has the memory function, you can enter your product ($.75) in the memory, and enter the cost ($14.98) in the memory and recall the total.

1. Clear your calculator.
2. Clear the memory.
3. Enter 14.98 on the keyboard.
4. Depress |M+| or |I+|.
5. Depress |×|.
6. Enter 5% (or .05) on the keyboard.
7. Depress |%| or |=|.
8. Add this product ($.75) into the memory by depressing |M+| or |I+|.
9. Recall the total from memory by depressing |MT| or the appropriate key on your calculator.

Example 2. Another way to figure your cost for the shirt plus tax, if you do not need to know the actual amount of the tax, is to multiply the price by 105%. In other words, you will pay 105% of the price of the shirt for the shirt and the tax combined.

14.98 × 105% (or 1.05) = $15.73 rounded to the penny

Practice Problems 10. Find the amount of tax and the total price (amount of the sales tax plus the amount of the item) for the following sales. (Round your answers to the penny.)

ELECTRONIC CALCULATOR PERCENT APPLICATIONS

	Amount of the Sale ($)	Sales Tax (%)	Amount of Sales Tax ($)	Total Amount of Sale plus Tax ($)
1.	24.98	5	1.25	26.23
2.	640.28	4		
3.	320.20	6		
4.	19.64	6		
5.	1.00	4-1/2		
6.	4.48	5-1/2		
7.	22.50	7		
8.	123.60	5		
9.	153.22	4-1/2		
10.	4,815.20	6		
11.	3.99	8		
12.	7.88	3-1/2		
13.	857.96	3		
14.	115.24	6		
15.	6.80	5		
16.	21.41	6-1/2		
17.	24.98	7		
18.	80.15	5		
19.	4.14	5-3/4		
20.	24.32	5		
21.	4.00	4-3/4		
22.	48.79	4-1/2		
23.	10.48	4		
24.	12.42	6		
25.	5.18	3		

For the following problems, find only the total price (the amount of sale plus the sales tax). Since we do not need to know the amount of the sales tax in these problems, we can use the short-cut method. (Round your answers to the penny.)

SALES TAXES 173

Example. What is the total selling price of an item costing $3.28 if the sales tax rate is 5-1/2%? (3.28 × 105.5% = $3.46)

	Amount of the Sale ($)	Sales Tax Rate (%)	Total Amount of Sale plus Sales Tax ($)
26.	1.94	5	2.04
27.	26.87	4	
28.	151.70	5-1/2	
29.	7,323.00	4-1/2	
30.	8,252.82	6	
31.	40.35	2	
32.	3.25	2-1/2	
33.	2.40	5	
34.	20.12	4	
35.	462.10	3	
36.	60.09	3-1/2	
37.	5.50	3-3/4	
38.	160.60	4-1/2	
39.	29.16	4-3/4	
40.	908.91	5	
41.	8.86	5-1/2	
42.	99.99	6	
43.	.98	4	
44.	100.70	6-1/2	
45.	70.83	7	
46.	10.61	7-1/2	
47.	5.98	8	
48.	40.85	6	
49.	1,000.96	4	
50.	19.40	5	

CITY TAXES

Example. If your city charges 1.5% tax on your earnings, how much will you pay for city taxes if your monthly gross pay is $938? (Round to the nearest penny.)

$$938 \times 1.5\% \text{ (or .015)} = \$14.07$$

How much of your earnings will be left after deducting the 1.5% city tax?

$$938 \times 98.5\% \text{ (or .985)} = \$923.93$$

Practice Problems 11. The city of Newtown assesses a 3/4% income tax on earnings for all people in Newtown. How much city tax will each of the following residents pay out of his weekly paycheck? (Round your answers to the penny.) Use the constant multiplier feature if your calculator has one.

Name	Weekly Pay ($)	Amt. of Tax ($)
1. Allen Adams	125.36	.94
2. Sharon Cardarelli	124.91	_____
3. Anne Dennison	160.73	_____
4. John Falcone	180.94	_____
5. Jill Jackson	175.88	_____
6. Ralph Larsen	167.41	_____
7. Andrew Tatum	220.19	_____
8. Leslie Tucker	210.07	_____
9. Michael Vandervoor	182.06	_____
10. Rita Zelaski	189.34	_____

The city of Roxborough has an income tax as follows:

Annual Income ($)	Tax Rate (%)
0 - 8,000.00	1/2
8,000.01 - 10,500.00	1
10,500.01 - 14,000.00	1-1/2
14,000.01 - 18,000.00	2
over 18,000.00	3

What is the annual city tax for the following residents?

CITY TAXES 175

Name	Yearly Income ($)	Amt. of Annual Tax ($)
11. Theresa Andrick	18,040.20	541.21
12. William Gray	8,500.91	
13. Bertha Lowry	5,060.37	
14. Walter Olson	9,412.75	
15. Robert Rennie	12,866.01	
16. Jane Somerville	7,923.42	
17. David Thompson	30,021.18	
18. Susan Tipton	27,041.29	
19. Roy Yelin	16,200.12	
20. Albert Zabik	13,061.97	

The city of Baytown has a city income tax as follows:

Annual Income ($)	No. Dependents	Tax Rate (%)
0 - 10,000.00	5 or more	0
0 - 10,000.00	3 or 4	1/2
0 - 10,000.00	1 or 2	1
0 - 10,000.00	0	1-1/2
10,000.01 - 15,000.00	5 or more	1/2
10,000.01 - 15,000.00	3 or 4	1
10,000.01 - 15,000.00	1 or 2	1-1/2
10,000.01 - 15,000.00	0	2
Above 15,000.00	any number	2-1/2

What is the amount of the annual city tax for the following people? (Round your answers to the penny.)

Name	Annual Income ($)	No. Dependents	Amt. of Annual Tax ($)
21. Gregory Brook	9,200.24	1	92.00
22. Katherine Edwards	10,024.80	0	
23. Bruce Harper	8,600.41	3	
24. Kenneth Morris	18,906.80	2	
25. Anna Patrick	12,467.47	1	

ELECTRONIC CALCULATOR PERCENT APPLICATIONS

	Name	Annual Income ($)	No. Dependents	Amt. of Annual Tax ($)
26.	Priscilla Roush	14,000.00	1	_____
27.	Mary Snyder	15,861.34	2	_____
28.	Ina Stack	9,041.87	0	_____
29.	Eugene West	14,917.45	5	_____
30.	Arnold Yeager	13,646.11	4	_____

The city of Lester has the following tax structure for city income tax:

Code	Classification	Income Tax Rate (%)
1 A	Nonresidents employed in Lester	1/2
2 A	Residents not employed in Lester	1-1/2
1 B	Residents employed in Lester	2

What is the amount of the annual city income tax for each of the following people?

	Name	Code	Annual Income ($)	Amt. of Annual Tax ($)
31.	Arthur Bozak	1 A	9,308.16	46.54
32.	Enid Cooper	1 A	12,400.00	_____
33.	William Dembosky	2 A	18,291.00	_____
34.	Jack Hill	1 B	24,600.00	_____
35.	Lola Kirby	1 B	14,907.64	_____
36.	Louis Maloney	1 A	13,007.50	_____
37.	Wilma Miller	2 A	11,909.16	_____
38.	Georgia O'Conner	1 B	7,390.12	_____
39.	Rebecca Paton	1 A	15,000.00	_____
40.	Daniel Pemberton	1 B	16,914.00	_____
41.	Alex Rentz	2 A	13,800.65	_____
42.	Leo Salvadore	2 A	14,030.80	_____
43.	Gerald Shulman	1 A	11,806.04	_____
44.	Cleo Taska	1 A	9,341.20	_____

	Name	Code	Annual Income ($)	Amt. of Annual Tax ($)
45.	Victor Travis	2 A	45,860.00	_____
46.	Lisa Tucker	1 A	9,990.00	_____
47.	Maryanne Webb	2 A	8,611.09	_____
48.	Mark Webster	2 A	17,500.00	_____
49.	Art Wilde	1 A	21,306.48	_____
50.	Ho Yee	1 A	17,040.20	_____

SIMPLE INTEREST

Example. How much interest must you pay on a principal of $1,492, with an interest rate of 7.5%, borrowed for 169 days? (Round the answer to the penny.)

1. To find simple interest, multiply the principal times the rate times the time. The *principal* is the amount borrowed. The *rate* is the percent interest rate per year. The *time* is the length of time for which the money is borrowed. Time is shown as a fraction of a year—for example, half a year is 1/2; 169 days is 169/360. A year can be counted as 365 days (exact interest) or as 360 days (ordinary interest). Most offices use 360. We will use 360 days in our problems.

$$I = P \times R \times T \quad \text{(In this example, Time} = 169 \div 360.)$$

2. I = (1,492 × 7.5 × 169/360), or .075 if you don't have a $\boxed{\%}$ key.
3. I = (1,492 × 7.5 × 169) ÷ 360 = $52.53 (rounded to the penny)

Note: Most electronic calculators have a re-entry capability so that answers from one problem can be re-entered as the first part of a new problem by merely depressing the function key. If your calculator has this capability, be sure to take advantage of the short-cut, as follows:

1. Enter 1,492 on the keyboard.
2. Depress $\boxed{\times}$.
3. Enter 7.5 (or .075) on the keyboard.
4. Depress $\boxed{\times}$.
5. Enter 169 on the keyboard.
6. Depress $\boxed{\%}$ or $\boxed{=}$.
7. Re-enter this product as your new dividend by depressing the $\boxed{\div}$ key.
8. Enter 360 on the keyboard.

9. Depress $\boxed{=}$.

10. Your answer, $52.53, will appear on the tape or on the display. Use your Round-off switch if your calculator has one.

Practice Problems 12. Calculate the amount of simple interest for the following problems:

	Principal ($)	Rate (%)	Time (days)	Interest ($) (rounded to the penny)
1.	35,788.00	7.7	345	2,640.86
2.	459.12	6	340	
3.	50.00	8	30	
4.	3,450.00	6.7	23	
5.	90,000.32	8	90	
6.	5,086.01	7-3/4	46	
7.	214.41	7.6	214	
8.	72.00	10	52	
9.	4,975.99	7-3/4	35	
10.	103.30	6.5	103	
11.	345.21	9	75	
12.	239.30	5	98	
13.	35,000.00	9-1/4	360	
14.	456.32	6	86	
15.	46,111.00	9-1/4	720	
16.	5,672.00	8.9	720	
17.	30,889.31	8.8	45	
18.	560.23	7	240	
19.	61.00	9	41	
20.	4,561.00	7.8	34	
21.	91,111.43	9	94	
22.	340.41	6	89	
23.	57,991.39	9.9	247	

	Principal ($)	Rate (%)	Time (days)	Interest ($) (rounded to the penny)
24.	571,380.00	8	56	
25.	35,778.09	7.7	345	
26.	459.34	6	300	
27.	65.31	8	57	
28.	7,780.22	6	20	
29.	34,275.83	8	60	
30.	2,395,387.77	6-3/4	15	
31.	204.99	5.5	203	
32.	644.33	9	72	
33.	783.22	5.5	89	
34.	85,773.00	8-1/4	1,080	
35.	43,991.57	9	147	

DECISION PROBLEM

Ordering Raw Materials

Your company makes metal alloys to sell to industry. You now have the following customer orders:

Purchase Order Number	Alloy	Quantity
50102	Cast iron	1 ton (2,000 lb.)
50103	Wrought iron	500 lb.
50104	Medium steel	1.5 ton
50105	Hard steel	2 ton
50106	Steel alloy	5 ton
50107	Red brass	450 lb.
50108	Cartridge brass	600 lb.
50109	Gun-metal bronze	420 lb.
50110	Nickel bronze	365 lb.

The alloys contain the following metals (in the percents shown):

ELECTRONIC CALCULATOR PERCENT APPLICATIONS

Alloy	% Carbon	% Copper	% Iron	% Manganese	% Nickel	% Phosphorus	% Silicon	% Sulfur	% Tin	% Zinc
Cast iron	2.7		95.4				1.9			
Wrought iron	0.2		99.5				0.5			
Medium steel	0.6		99.1	.1		.1		.1		
Hard steel	1.5		98.2	.1		.1		.1		
Steel alloy	1.4		97.5	.05	1.01	.04				
Red brass		85								15
Cartridge brass		65.9								34.1
Gun-metal bronze		88							10	2
Nickel bronze		80			8				10	2

Calculate the quantity of each metal you need to buy in order to make the alloys for your customers. Add 5% to the total weight of each metal you buy to cover anticipated scrap and waste. (Round your answers to the pound.)

Metal	Quantity Needed (lb.)
(a) Carbon	_____
(b) Copper	_____
(c) Iron	_____
(d) Manganese	_____
(e) Nickel	_____
(f) Phosphorus	_____
(g) Silicon	_____
(h) Sulfur	_____
(i) Tin	_____
(j) Zinc	_____

REVIEW QUIZ 3

(Round your answers to two decimal places.)

1. What is 22.1% of 813.99?
2. Thirty-nine is 42.1% of what number?
3. You recently sent out 150 copies of an invitation. One hundred thirty people accepted. What percent of the people receiving invitations accepted?

4. The Johnsons have a monthly budget of $790. They spend $205 a month on rent. What percent of the total budget is the rent?

5. The five sales offices of the Bluebird Clothing chain share the cost of the sales order forms on a prorated basis. Last quarter the total cost of the forms was $407.50. The total number of forms used was 509. The New York sales office used 192 forms. What is the New York office's share of the expense of these forms? Use the constant ratio method (rounding the ratio to four decimal places). (Round your answer to the penny.)

6. Last month our department had $420,321 in sales. This month we had $431,677 in sales. What is our percent of increase or decrease in sales?

7. How much will Shirt Box, Inc., pay for a $16.50 shirt after taking a chain discount of 6% - 2-1/2%?

8. The Bentley Card Shop purchased 50 boxes of stationery for $1.90 per box. Bentley's received a 20% quantity discount and a 2% cash discount for paying the invoice within ten days. How much did Bentley's pay?

9. How much city tax is paid per month by an employee who earns $1,230 per month if the tax rate is 1-3/4%?

10. How much interest must you pay on a loan of $750, with an interest rate of 8-1/4%, borrowed for 86 days?

Sample Examination

You may want to be timed as you try the Unit 3 sample examination, which is presented in the Introduction.

Unit 4

Business Problems

TOUCH SYSTEM REVIEW

Be sure to keep your index finger, your middle finger, and your ring finger on the home row (4, 5, and 6) if you are using your right hand. Keep your ring finger, your middle finger, and your index finger on the 4, 5, and 6 if you are using your left hand.

555	456	556	556	656	654
444	454	464	454	646	455
666	445	456	654	654	644
555	464	554	665	556	456
666	666	666	555	465	654
444	456	454	654	464	555
666	454	565	444	555	465
444	465	555	464	565	666
666	464	456	545	666	656
555	454	444	645	444	645
5,661	4,778	5,170	5,636	5,671	5,850

Are your fingers curved over the home row? Don't lift your hand away from the keyboard.

544	564	565	445	654	456
646	555	656	646	456	654
444	465	666	656	454	455
654	646	565	464	565	656
465	456	654	554	664	556
446	564	645	564	456	654
446	464	565	654	456	555
646	465	645	665	445	464
456	646	446	556	665	445
444	666	555	456	456	645
5,191	5,491	5,962	5,660	5,271	5,540

TOUCH SYSTEM REVIEW

Are you getting the right answers? Keep your eyes on your copy. Don't lose valuable time.

333	232	212	212	122	133
111	123	321	222	111	333
123	321	231	132	122	311
112	133	113	121	112	221
212	121	313	131	123	321
111	222	333	323	232	131
212	131	322	311	122	133
133	231	123	132	121	333
233	111	333	222	232	323
123	322	223	113	133	211
1,703	1,947	2,524	1,919	1,430	2,450

Can you find the keys without looking? Are you getting the right answers?

789	877	987	897	879	998
778	887	979	797	789	987
788	899	879	998	889	977
777	999	888	887	778	977
779	799	999	998	789	798
998	997	998	997	999	998
789	798	987	789	879	978
787	887	779	899	989	997
789	789	978	789	987	997
778	879	887	799	899	879
8,052	8,811	9,361	8,850	8,877	9,586

Keep your fingers curved.

100	200	300	400	500	600
700	800	900	100	200	300
101	102	103	104	105	106
107	108	109	110	110	120
130	140	150	160	170	180
190	200	210	220	230	240
250	260	270	280	290	300
202	302	402	403	404	405
406	407	408	409	410	400
120	310	210	410	570	807
2,306	2,829	3,062	2,596	2,989	3,458

BUSINESS PROBLEMS

Don't lift your hand away from the keyboard. Keep your fingers hovering over the home row.

7.10	9.01	1.13	4.01	1.01	1.10
8.01	8.09	9.09	4.06	8.80	8.90
8.02	8.06	9.10	3.03	3.20	5.06
7.09	9.02	1.04	9.06	4.50	3.04
7.07	8.07	1.12	4.04	1.20	2.02
7.09	8.08	9.07	5.00	9.90	2.80
8.80	8.10	9.03	3.04	6.60	7.08
7.70	6.60	5.06	9.05	9.01	7.07
7.05	9.04	1.12	1.01	9.02	2.01
7.05	8.06	6.00	7.50	7.80	8.60
74.98	82.13	51.76	49.80	61.04	47.68

COST OF ITEMS

Example 1. What is the cost of 349 ballpoint pens if the pens cost 39 cents each? 349 X .39 = $136.11

Example 2. What is the cost of 530 notepads which sell for 13 cents each? 530 X .13 = $68.90

Practice Problems 1. Calculate the cost of the items in the following problems:

1. 5,611 @ $4.61 = $25,866.71
2. 408 @ .23 =
3. 4,624 @ 2.23 =
4. 789 @ 6.26 =
5. 4 @ .30 =
6. 7,811 @ 23.24 =
7. 986 @ .16 =
8. 35 @ .46 =
9. 4,500 @ 3.50 =
10. 397 @ .12 =
11. 3,513 @ 1.11 =
12. 678 @ 5.15 =
13. 3 @ .19 =
14. 6,700 @ 12.13 =
15. 875 @ .05 =
16. 34 @ .22 =
17. 24 @ .35 =
18. 3,000 @ 1.99 =
19. 12 @ 5.09 =
20. 30 @ 3,040.00 =
21. 3,499 @ $100.36 =
22. 3,807 @ 3.49 =
23. 2,402 @ 1.11 =
24. 567 @ 5.14 =
25. 2 @ 1.18 =
26. 20 @ .19 =
27. 5,699 @ 12.12 =
28. 864 @ .04 =
29. 23 @ .21 =
30. 22 @ .34 =

EXTENSIONS AND CROSSFOOTING   185

31. 6,722 @ 5.72 =   36. 8,922 @ 34.35 =
32. 519 @ .89 =   37. 997 @ .27 =
33. 4,735 @ 2.34 =   38. 46 @ .57 =
34. 891 @ 7.37 =   39. 200 @ 8.19 =
35. 5 @ .41 =   40. 36 @ 4.05 =

EXTENSIONS AND CROSSFOOTING

Example.

You will notice that the Travel Expense Report form requires that the columns be added vertically and the rows be added horizontally. Naturally, your grand total should be the same both ways. Adding the same figures both horizontally and vertically is referred to as crossfooting. The company then has a record of what each expense totaled; for example, the total cost for travel, the total cost for lodging, etc. It also has a per-diem cost. Often companies charge each type of expense to a separate charge code for their budget records. Travel expenses, entertainment of customers, and telephone charges would, for example, each be charged to a different budget code.

   Check the vertical addition for each column and the horizontal addition for each row. Make a note of any discrepancies you find.

Practice Problems 2. Complete the calculations on the following forms:

41. Complete the Long and Company invoice. Deduct 10% for the fall sale discount. Then add 5% for sales tax.
42. Complete the work copy of the Travel Expense Report form. Remember that the vertical total and the horizontal total must agree.
43. Complete the extensions and the total for the Departmental Requisition.
44. The Freight Bill shows a shipment which we are sending collect. We need not figure the cost. However, we do have to figure the total weight and the total value of the shipment.

Item	Quantity	Weight Each	Value Each	Total Value
Sealing rings	12	1 lb.	$ 2.415	_____
15-in. flange rings	6	6.25 lb.	25.50	_____
20-in. flange rings	18	8.75 lb.	104.40	_____
Metal inserts	20	.64 lb.	3.68	_____
Carbide cutting blades	16	2.33 lb.	15.60	_____
Tool holders	6	5.3 lb.	25.00	_____
Total		(a) _____		(b) _____

ADDITRON CORPORATION
TRAVEL EXPENSE REPORT
Form # 1

NAME Julia W. Smith
CHARGE DEPT./SPECIAL FUND: Advertising - 36-467
ADDRESS Advertising Department - Additron Bldg.
DATES-from June 12 **to** June 14
PURPOSE Customer Seminar

LIST EXPENSES BY DAYS IN SEPARATE COLUMNS - IF MORE THAN FIVE DAYS USE ADDITIONAL SHEETS WITH ONE TOTAL

DATES	June 12	J 13	J 14			TOTAL
COMMERCIAL TRANSPORTATION - Attach receipts						
Plane St. Louis to New York, NY	137.00					137.00
New York to St. Louis			137.00			137.00
Other Limo to Hotel & A.P.	8.25		8.25			16.50
taxi to 43rd St.	5.70	5.80				13.50
LOCAL TRANSPORTATION (MILEAGE) @ 10¢ (See Reverse)						
From St. Louis to air port miles 27	2.70		2.70			4.70
From S.L. a.p. to home miles 27						
From to miles						
LODGING - List and attach receipted bills						
Ambassador	32.86	32.86				65.62
MEALS - If for more than one person show (No.)						
Breakfast (5 customers) June 13		19.26	2.40			21.60
Lunch	2.75	1.50	3.17			7.37
Dinner (2 customers) June 12	24.36					24.36
Special - Banquet, etc., attach receipt or program		12.75				12.75
OTHER - Telephone, Tips, Registration, Etc. (Explain)						
bellhop	1.00					1.00
valet	2.50					2.50
Phone call - St. Louis	4.65					4.65
DAILY TOTALS	$221.77	$72.17	$153.52	$	$	$448.55

REMARKS OR EXPLANATIONS
receipts attached

ADVANCE $ -0-
AMT. CLAIMED $ 448.55
AMT. RETURNED $ -0-

I hereby certify that the expenses as detailed above have actually been incurred by me and are proper reimbursable items.

SIGNED *Julia W. Smith* **DATE** 6/16

APPROVED _____ Department Head and
APPROVED _____
APPROVED _____ Vice President

AMOUNT APPROVED $ 448.55

CHARGE ACCOUNTING CODE(S)
36 4670 02 71
0500 2839 01 1

Travel Expense Report Form Number 1

216 - 928 - 1166

Long and Company

FURNITURE   INTERIOR DESIGN

1700 State Road
CUYAHOGA FALLS, OHIO 44223

September 20, 19--

Mr. and Mrs. John Doe
2400 Elm Drive
Cuyahoga Falls, OH 44223

INVOICE

2	#7621	Wing-backed Early American Chairs - floral @	$189.00
1	#7020	Queen Anne Sofa - green	799.00
1	#5090	Floral print Hooked Rug	329.00
1	#6077	Maple Rocker	69.00
2	#2649	Gone with the Wind Lamps @	79.50
2	#1044	Room Divider Stands - cherry @	129.00
6	#4393	Cherry Dining room chairs @	72.50
1	#6603	Queen Size cherry bed	394.00

LESS   10% Fall Sale Discount

ADD   5% Sales Tax

- - - -   GOOD DESIGN: *The Key to Comfortable Living*   - - - -

Long and Company Invoice

BUSINESS PROBLEMS

work copy

A., B., & C. COMPANY
TRAVEL EXPENSE REPORT

Form #2

NAME John Doe
CHARGE DEPT./SPECIAL FUND: Marketing 2097
ADDRESS A., B., + C. Co. - Marketing
DATES from Dec. 1, 19— **to** Dec. 5, 19—
PURPOSE Customer Calls and Industrial Exhibit

LIST EXPENSES BY DAYS IN SEPARATE COLUMNS - IF MORE THAN FIVE DAYS USE ADDITIONAL SHEETS WITH ONE TOTAL

DATES	Dec. 1	Dec. 2	Dec. 3	Dec. 4	Dec. 5	TOTAL
COMMERCIAL TRANSPORTATION - Attach receipts						
Plane Chicago, IL to San Francisco, CA	153 00				~~153~~	
SF to Chicago					153 00	
Other Limo to Hotel	7 50					
Limo to A.P.					7 50	
LOCAL TRANSPORTATION (MILEAGE) @ 10¢ (See Reverse)						
From taxi in SF miles		8 65				
From " to " " miles			4 95			
From " to " " miles				5 90		
LODGING - List and attach receipted bills	30 15	30 15	30 15	30 15		
Sheraton - S.F.						
MEALS - If for more than one person show (No.)						
Breakfast	2 05	60	3 09	2 70	2 75	
Dec 1 Lunch (4 - customers)	12 85	2 75	4 00	3 05		
Dec 2 Dinner (2 customers)	5 90	24 07	5 95			
Special - Banquet, etc., attach receipt or program				14 00		
OTHER - Telephone, Tips, Registration, Etc. (Explain)						
bellhop	75			75		
Phone call - Chicago		5 45				
Ind. Exhibit Registration		25 00				
DAILY TOTALS	$	$	$	$	$	

REMARKS OR EXPLANATIONS
receipts attached

ADVANCE $ —
AMT. CLAIMED $
AMT. RETURNED $ —

I hereby certify that the expenses as detailed above have actually been incurred by me and are proper reimbursable items.

SIGNED John Doe   DATE Dec. 7

APPROVED _____ Department Head and
APPROVED _____
APPROVED _____ Vice President

AMOUNT APPROVED $

CHARGE ACCOUNTING CODE(S)
| 2 | 0 | 9 | 7 | 3 | 1 | 4 | 2 | 9 | 1 |
| 1 | 6 | 5 | 9 | 4 | 9 | 3 | 8 | 6 | 6 |

Travel Expense Report Number 2

EXTENSIONS AND CROSSFOOTING 189

		I, Z & Z COMPANY - **Departmental Requisition**	No. **13346**	
		TO: CENTRAL SUPPLY	DATE May 14, 19--	
			PURCHASE ORDER 4241C	

ITEM	QUANTITY	DESCRIPTION (Please give full description)	ESTIMATED UNIT PRICE	ESTIMATED TOTAL PRICE
1	4	1573 File box, metal business card size, gray	$ 4.99	
2	12 boxes	File folders, letter size, 1/3 cut, center post, 100/box - 1375	2.59	
3	3 pkg	Index cards, 3 X 5, plain, blue 100/pkg - 1285	.35	
4	5	5837 Staple Removers, Ace	.59	
5	6	3833 Desk Trays, black	1.39	
6	3	3859 Fluid Type Cleaner (bottle)	.63	
7	4	2837 Rulers, 12-inch size, wooden	.36	
8	6	21578 Stencils, legal size, green F2856 (quire)	5.20	
9	4 dz	3852 Pencils, #2, black lead (doz)	.40	
10	24	2977 Adding machine tape, 2 1/4" wide (roll)	.24	
11	1	2466 Dating Stamp 1 1/2" (ea.)	1.80	
12	6	985 Scotch recording tape, cartridge, C-90 cassette (roll)	2.45	
13	2	5500 Chairs, stacking, w/arms, 1275B, black frame (ea.)	36.00	
14	30	562 Index markers (ea.)	.70	
			TOTAL	

The office of the Director of Purchasing is vested with sole authority to order materials and contract for services

PLEASE ORDER THE ABOVE AND CHARGE TO:

Balance per last Requisition $ 1,075.08

DEPARTMENT (OR SPECIAL FUND) Accounting

Supplies and Expense ☐ $ _____
Permanent Equipment ☐ $ _____

DELIVER TO BUILDING Main Office ROOM # 2199

To be housed in (bldg & room) _____
Probable life in years _____
☐ Replacement ☐ Addition
Balance in Appropriation $ _____

CODE 7016-03210
REQUESTED BY M. L. Harrison EXT 387
APPROVED BY _____

THIS IS A	ORDER, DATED:	FOB	SHIPPING PROMISE	
PRICES PER		TERMS		**PURCHASING**

Departmental Requisition

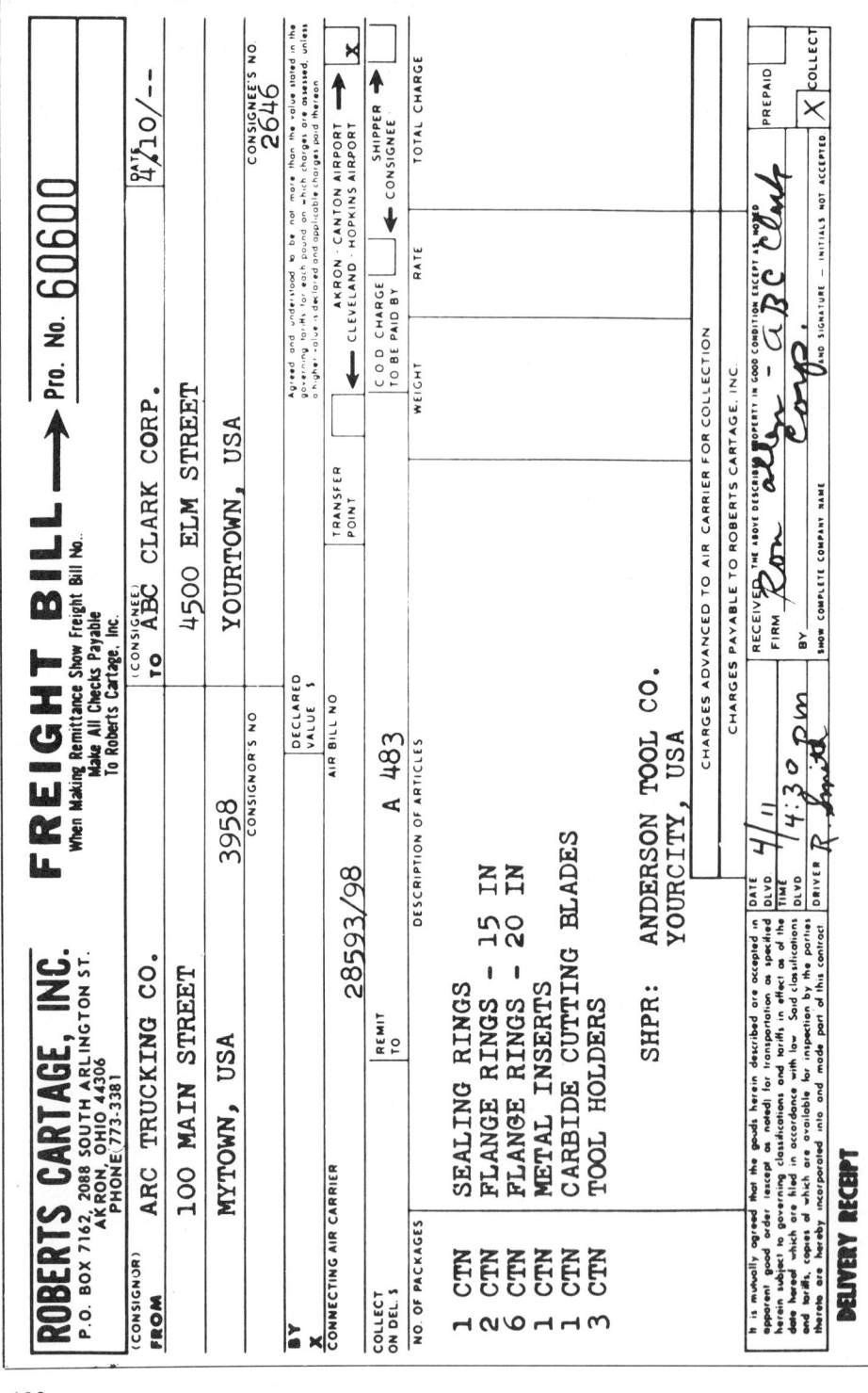

FREIGHT BILL

ROBERTS CARTAGE, INC.
P.O. BOX 7162, 2088 SOUTH ARLINGTON ST.
AKRON, OHIO 44306
PHONE 773-3381

When Making Remittance Show Freight Bill No.
Make All Checks Payable To Roberts Cartage, Inc.

Pro. No. 60600 DATE 4/10/--

(CONSIGNOR) FROM: ARC TRUCKING CO.
100 MAIN STREET
MYTOWN, USA

(CONSIGNEE) TO: ABC CLARK CORP.
4500 ELM STREET
YOURTOWN, USA

CONSIGNOR'S NO: 3958
CONSIGNEE'S NO: 2646
DECLARED VALUE $:
AIR BILL NO:
TRANSFER POINT:

REMIT TO: 28593/98 A 483

COLLECT ON DEL. $:
BY: X

CONNECTING AIR CARRIER:

AKRON - CANTON AIRPORT
CLEVELAND - HOPKINS AIRPORT

C.O.D. CHARGE TO BE PAID BY: SHIPPER → CONSIGNEE

NO. OF PACKAGES	DESCRIPTION OF ARTICLES	WEIGHT	RATE	TOTAL CHARGE
1 CTN	SEALING RINGS			
2 CTN	FLANGE RINGS - 15 IN			
6 CTN	FLANGE RINGS - 20 IN			
1 CTN	METAL INSERTS			
1 CTN	CARBIDE CUTTING BLADES			
3 CTN	TOOL HOLDERS			

SHPR: ANDERSON TOOL CO.
YOURCITY, USA

Agreed and understood to be not more than the value stated in the governing tariffs for each pound on which charges are assessed, unless a higher value is declared and applicable charges paid thereon.

DATE DLVD: 4/11
TIME DLVD: 4:30 PM
DRIVER: R. Smith

CHARGES ADVANCED TO AIR CARRIER FOR COLLECTION
CHARGES PAYABLE TO ROBERTS CARTAGE, INC.

RECEIVED THE ABOVE DESCRIBED PROPERTY IN GOOD CONDITION EXCEPT AS NOTED
FIRM: Ron ally - ABC Clark
BY: Corp.
SHOW COMPLETE COMPANY NAME
(HAND SIGNATURE — INITIALS NOT ACCEPTED)

PREPAID COLLECT X

DELIVERY RECEIPT

Freight Bill

FINDING THE AMOUNT OF SIMPLE INTEREST

Example. Donald Duck borrowed $800 from the credit union, to be repaid in 180 days. If the interest rate is 7-1/2%, how much total interest will he pay?

1. Interest = Principal × Rate × Time
2. Interest *rate* means rate per year. *Time* means the fraction of a year the loan is for—in this problem, 180/360 (360 is counted as one year).
3. I = (800 × .075 × 180) ÷ 360
   Note: Use 7.5% if your calculator has a Percent key.
4. I = $30

If your calculator has the re-entry feature, just depress ÷ after you obtain the answer to the three-factor multiplication; it is not necessary to re-enter the dividend by hand on the keyboard.

Practice Problems 3. Solve the following problems. (Round your answers to the penny.)

45. Mickey Mouse borrowed $525 from the bank, to be repaid after 60 days. If the in-interest rate is 8%, how much total interest will he pay? (*Ans.* $7)

46. Mr. Anderson, who owns a discount store, borrowed $10,500 from the bank at 8-1/2% interest in order to take advantage of a warehouse sale. The loan is to be repaid in 45 days. How much interest will he pay on the $10,500 principal?

47. Georgie Porgie borrowed $300 to pay his baker's bill. If the interest rate is 6-1/2% and he repays the loan in 120 days, how much interest will he pay?

48. Little Miss Muffet borrowed $125 to buy a new tuffet. If the interest rate is 7% and she repays the loan in 90 days, how much interest will she pay?

49. Miss Jackson borrowed $10,000 in order to begin a stenographic service. If the interest rate is 7-1/2% and she repays the loan in 360 days, how much interest will she pay?

50. Humpty Dumpty borrowed $15,000 to have a balcony built on his wall. If he pays an interest rate of 8-1/4% and repays the loan in 57 days, how much interest will he pay? What will be the total amount he must repay?

INTEREST—FINDING THE INTEREST PERIOD IN DAYS

Example. How many days are needed to produce $9 in interest at 6% on a principal of $3,000?

1. When we know the principal, the rate, and the interest, we can determine the time in days as follows:
   a) Find the interest for one year.
   b) Divide the known interest by the yearly interest.
   c) Convert to days by multiplying by the days in a year (use 360).

2. Interest for one year = 3,000 × .06 = 180
3. Known interest = $9
   Yearly interest = $180

   9 ÷ 180 = .05
4. Multiply by 360.

   .05 × 360 = 18
5. Number of days = 18

Practice Problems 4. Solve the following interest problems. (Round your answers to the day.)

51. How many days are needed to produce $8 in interest at 5% on a principal of $200? (*Ans.* 288 days)
52. How many days are needed to produce $15.50 in interest at 8% on a principal of $27,000?
53. Jason, Inc., borrowed $4,500 and paid interest at 6-1/2%. If the interest came to $10.10, for how many days was the loan?
54. Mr. Johnson borrowed $1,200 from the bank and paid interest at 8-1/4%. If the interest came to $75, for how many days was the loan?
55. Mr. and Mrs. Wallace borrowed $650 from the bank and paid interest at 7-1/2%. If the interest came to $22, for how many days was the loan?
56. Mr. Collins borrowed $18,400 from the bank and paid interest at 7%. If the interest came to $1,044, for how many days was the loan?

INTEREST—FINDING THE RATE OF INTEREST

Example. What is the rate of interest that produces $10 on a principal of $1,400 in 60 days?

1. The rate can be found as follows:
   (a) Find the interest at 1%.
   (b) Divide the total interest by the interest at 1%.
2. Interest = P × R × T
   Interest at 1% = (1,400 × .01 × 60) ÷ 360
   Interest at 1% = $2.33 (rounded to the penny)
3. Rate = Total interest ÷ Interest at 1%
   Rate = 10 ÷ 2.33 = 4.29
   Rate = 4.3% (rounded to the tenth of a percent)

COMPOUND INTEREST

Practice Problems 5. Solve the following interest problems. (Round your answers to the tenth of a percent.)

57. What is the rate of interest that produces $20 in 160 days on a principal of $450? (*Ans.* 10%)
58. What is the rate of interest that produces $2.25 in 45 days on a $300 principal?
59. What is the rate of interest that produces $1.40 in 5 days on a principal of $1,440?
60. What is the rate of interest that produces $100 in 180 days on a principal of $1,250?
61. What is the rate of interest that produces $35 in 25 days on a principal of $15,400?
62. What is the rate of interest that produces $4.56 in 60 days on a principal of $875?

COMPOUND INTEREST

Example. If you deposit $100 in a savings account on July 1 in a bank which pays 6% computed quarterly, how much would you have in your account on June 30 (one year)?

1. While simple interest is figured on the original principal, compound interest, on the other hand, is figured on the original principal *plus* the interest that has been added. Savings accounts in many banks earn compound interest, in some cases, computed quarterly.

2. Since the rate in the example problem is 6% per year and since the interest is computed quarterly, the interest rate per quarter is 6% ÷ 4 = 1.5%.

3. Interest for the first quarter:
   100 × .015 (or 1.5% if you have a % key) = 1.50
   Principal at the end of the first quarter = 100.00 + 1.50 = 101.50.

4. Interest for the second quarter:
   101.50 × .015 (or 1.5%) = 1.52
   Principal at the end of the second quarter:
   101.50 + 1.52 = 103.02

5. Interest for the third quarter:
   103.02 × .015 (or 1.5%) = 1.55
   Principal at the end of the third quarter:
   103.02 + 1.55 = 104.57

6. Interest for the fourth quarter:
   104.57 × .015 (or 1.5%) = 1.57
   Principal at the end of the fourth quarter:
   104.57 + 1.57 = $106.14

194 BUSINESS PROBLEMS

FIGURING COMPOUND INTEREST WITH THE TABLE

Example. Using the Compound Interest Table in Appendix C, determine the amount of interest on $300 at 4% compounded quarterly for 3 years.

1. Since the interest is paid quarterly, multiply the number of years by 4:

$$3 \times 4 = 12 \text{ periods}$$

2. Since the interest is paid quarterly, find the rate of quarterly interest by dividing the annual rate (4%) by 4 quarters:

$$4\% \div 4 \text{ quarters} = 1\% \text{ per quarter}$$

3. Find the number of periods (12) in the Periods column. Then find the 12-period payment in the 1% column.
4. The amount of $1 compounded quarterly for 3 years at 4% is 1.126825.
5. Multiply 1.126825 by $300 to find the amount of $300 compounded quarterly for 3 years at 4%.

$$1.126825 \times 300 = 338.0475$$

6. The amount of compound interest is the amount that $300 becomes after 3 years minus the original principal ($300).

338.0475 - 300 = 38.0475 or *$38.05* (rounded to the penny)

Practice Problems 6. Solve these compound interest problems without the Table. (Round your answers to the penny.)

63. If you invested $200 at 8% compounded semiannually, how much will you have at the end of one year? (Figure without the Table.) (*Ans.* $216.32)

64. If you invested $1,000 at 7% compounded quarterly, how much will you have at the end of two years? (Figure without the Table.)

FIGURING COMPOUND INTEREST WITH THE TABLE
(See Appendix C.)

Practice Problems 7. Calculate the compound interest for the following problems, using the Compound Interest Table in Appendix C.

65. If you invest $850 at 7% compounded semiannually, how much will you have at the end of two years? (Use the Table.) (*Ans.* $975.39)

66. If Jack Jones invests $15,000 at 8% compounded annually, how much will he have at the end of four years?

67. If Ann Star invests $925 at 6% compounded quarterly, how much interest will she have earned at the end of 18 months?

AMOUNT OF MARKON AND TOTAL COST

68. Ralph Randolph has an opportunity to invest $500 at 6% compounded quarterly for two years, or he can invest his $500 at 7% compounded semiannually for two years. Which investment plan would yield him the most interest? How much would the interest be for each plan?

AMOUNT OF MARKON AND TOTAL COST

Markon usually refers to the amount which the retailer adds to the price he paid for merchandise. The retailer decides what rate of markon he must use to take care of his operating expenses and to make a profit. The terms "markon" and "markup" are sometimes used interchangeably, although "markup" more correctly refers to adding to the selling price previously established.

Markon can be a percentage of the cost price or of the selling price. The cost price plus the amount of markon equals the selling price. The markon rate is usually expressed as a percent.

Example.1. A boutique shop owner paid $7.90 each for silk scarves. What must the owner charge for a scarf if he wants a 24% markon based on cost price?

1. 7.90 × .24 = 1.896 = $1.90 (rounded to the penny) amount of markon
2. 1.90 + 7.90 = $9.80 selling price
3. *Note:* Use 24% if you have a $\boxed{\%}$ key.
   Be sure to use the re-entry function if your calculator has this capability. That is, depress the $\boxed{+}$ key to re-enter the product as the addend, rather than to re-enter the figures on the keyboard by hand.
4. The owner must sell the scarves for $9.80 each to obtain a 24% markon based on cost.
5. (If you do not need to know the amount of markon and need to know only the selling price, multiply the cost by 124% or 1.24.)

Practice Problems 8. Figure the amount of markon (based on cost) and the selling price for the following items. (Round your answers to the penny.)

	Cost ($)	Percent Markon	Amount of Markon ($)	Selling Price ($)
69.	867.42	35	303.60	1,171.02
70.	2.14	15	_____	_____
71.	88.88	65	_____	_____
72.	1,395.75	20	_____	_____
73.	942.18	25	_____	_____

	Cost ($)	Percent Markon	Amount of Markon ($)	Selling Price ($)
74.	10,492.18	18	_____	_____
75.	.28	15	_____	_____
76.	68.74	30	_____	_____
77.	74.12	5	_____	_____
78.	9,875.66	40	_____	_____
79.	436.18	50	_____	_____
80.	54.20	17	_____	_____
81.	5,695.41	12	_____	_____
82.	.29	20	_____	_____
83.	1.45	23	_____	_____

84. A bookstore paid $9.86 each for dictionaries. What should the dictionaries sell for if the bookstore desires an 8% markon?

85. A furniture store paid $120 each for wing-backed chairs. What should the chairs sell for if the furniture store desires a 40% markon?

86. A jeweler paid $1,200 for a diamond pin. What should the pin sell for if the jeweler wants a 55% markon?

87. An appliance dealer paid $400 for a refrigerator. If he wants a 28% markon, what should he charge for the refrigerator?

88. Far Sounds, Inc., paid $625 each for stereo outfits. If Far Sounds desires a 35% markon, what should be the selling price for each stereo?

89. DiscoTapes, Inc., buys record albums for $4.50 each. If they want a 30% markon, at what price should they sell the albums?

Example 2. An appliance store sells a television set for $229.99. If the markon rate is 25% of the selling price, what was the cost price of the television set? (Round your answer to the penny.)

1. The selling price times the markon rate equals the amount of markon.

    229.99 × 25% (or .25) = 57.4975 = $57.50 (rounded to the penny)

2. The selling price less the amount of markon equals the cost price.

    229.99 - 57.50 = $172.49

3. If you don't need to know the amount of markon, you can find the cost price by multiplying the selling price by the complement of the markon rate.

AMOUNT OF MARKON AND TOTAL COST   197

$$100\% - 25\% = 75\% \text{ (complement)}$$
4. 229.99 × 75% (or .75) = $172.49

Practice Problems 9. Figure the amount of markon based on selling price, and the cost price, for the following items:

	Selling Price ($)	Percent Markon	Amount of Markon ($)	Cost Price ($)
90.	224.75	20	44.95	179.80
91.	39.98	24	_____	_____
92.	1,290.00	15	_____	_____
93.	575.25	37-1/2	_____	_____
94.	8.99	25	_____	_____
95.	70.00	33-1/3	_____	_____
96.	2.19	15	_____	_____
97.	61.98	30	_____	_____
98.	899.99	18	_____	_____
99.	95.00	24	_____	_____
100.	140.88	22	_____	_____

Figure *only* the cost price for the following items. Use the complement method.

	Selling Price ($)	Percent Markon	Cost Price ($)
101.	1.98	20	1.58
102.	136.56	18	_____
103.	28.79	25	_____
104.	2,381.99	14	_____
105.	684.39	32	_____
106.	78.99	22	_____
107.	789.55	30	_____
108.	52.78	15	_____
109.	3.98	38	_____
110.	50.00	40	_____

BUSINESS PROBLEMS

PERCENT OF MARKON

Example 1. A suit cost the Davis Men's Store $50, and the store sells the suit for $75. What is the amount of markon? What is the rate of markon based on the *cost*?

1. Sales price minus cost price equals markon amount.

$$75 - 50 = \$25 \text{ (amount of markon)}$$

2. Markon divided by *cost* equals the rate of markon on cost.

$$25 \div 50 = .50 \text{ or } 50\%$$

Note: Be sure to express the rate of markon in percent form. If you do not have a % key, move the decimal answer two places to the right to express the answer in percent.

Practice Problems 10. Solve the following markon problems. (Round your answers to the percent.)

111. The Alpine Shop's cost for a pair of skis was $95.12. If they sell the skis for $120.99, what is the markon and what is the rate of markon based on cost? (*Ans.* $25.87; 27%)

112. The Rose Red Florist Shop buys a dozen long-stemmed roses at a cost of $12.00. They sell the dozen roses for $18.75. What is the markon and what is the rate of markon based on cost?

113. Friendly Al's Used Car Lot buys a used Ford at a cost of $1,075. Friendly Al sells the Ford for $1,295. What is the markon? What is the rate of markon based on cost?

114. The Hide-a-Way buys blue jeans for $10.80 a pair. If they sell the jeans for $14.95, what is the markon and the rate of markon based on cost?

115. The Food Mart buys baked hams at $5.90. If they sell the hams for $7.95 each, what is the markon and the rate of markon based on cost?

116. The Needlepoint Shop buys yarn at $9.00 for a dozen skeins. If they sell each skein for $1.29, what is the markon per skein and the rate of markon per skein based on cost?

117. The International Shoppe imports Spanish lace tablecloths for $90.00 each. If they sell the tablecloths for $125.00, what is the amount of markon and the rate of markon based on cost?

118. The Gallery is selling a seascape for $400.00. If they paid the artist $325.00 for the painting, what is the amount of markon and the rate of markon based on cost?

119. Bartlett's Sport Shop sells a tennis racket for $26.75. If they paid $18.00 for the racket, what is the amount of markon and the rate of markon based on cost?

PERCENT OF MARKON 199

120. If you buy a used car for $2,475, what is the amount of markon and the rate of markon based on the dealer's cost of $2,100?

Example 2. A hand calculator is priced to sell for $14.98. If this calculator cost the seller $12.00, what is the percent of markon on the *sales price?*

1. Markon = 14.98 - 12.00 = 2.98
2. What percent is 2.98 of 14.98?
3. 2.98 ÷ 14.98 = 19.89% (rounded to two decimal places) Remember: Divide the "is" number by the "of" number. Give the answer in percent form. If your calculator has a $\boxed{\%}$ key, use it. If not, convert your answer to percent by moving the decimal two places to the right.
4. The percent of markon is 19.89 (rounded to two decimal places).

Practice Problems 11. In the following problems find the percent markon on the sales price. (Round your percent answers to two decimal places.)

121. If the Chic Dress Shoppe paid $21 each for satin blouses and is selling them for $30 each, what is the percent of markon on the sales price? (*Ans.* 30%)

122. The Fun and Games Store pays $3.20 for a deck of cards. They sell each deck of cards for $3.75. What is the amount of markon and the percent of markon on the sales price?

123. The Happy Home Company sold a cherry Early American canopy bed for $469. Their cost for the bed was $300. What was the amount of markon and the percent of markon on the sales price?

124. Harry's Home Appliance Store paid $197 for a lawnmower. The lawnmower is sold for $219. What is the amount of markon and the percent of markon on the sales price?

125. Shelly's Sport Shop buys mohair sweaters for $23 each. They sell the sweaters for $32.95. What is the amount of markon and the percent of markon on the sales price?

126. Dan's Auto Store buys tape decks for $92.50. The store sells these tape decks for $119.99. What is the amount of markon and the percent of markon on the sales price?

127. The Orient Salon paid $1,500 for a Persian rug and is selling it for $1,995. What is the percent of markon on the sales price?

128. Bob bought a bicycle for $189.00. If it cost the bicycle dealer $140.00, what is the percent of markon on the sales price?

129. If you pay $90 for a set of snow tires which cost the retailer $76, what is the percent of markon on the selling price?

130. Music Box, Inc., pays $4.80 for a record album and retails it for $5.98. What is the percent of markon based on the selling price?

PERCENT OF SELLING PRICE

Example. Mrs. Whistler sold one of her paintings to The Art Corner for $265. The Art Corner marked it up 58% over their cost. What was the dollar amount of markon? What percent of The Art Corner's selling price did Mrs. Whistler receive?

1. Markon = 265 × .58 (or 58%) = $153.70
2. Selling price = 265 + Markon amount (153.70) = $418.70
3. Mrs. Whistler's rate = 265 ÷ Selling price (418.70) = 63% (rounded to the percent)
4. (In steps 1 and 2, if you need to know only the selling price and do not need to know the markon amount, multiply $265 by 158% or 1.58.)

Practice Problems 12. Solve the following markon problems by finding the percent of the selling price. (Round your answers to the percent.)

131. The Olde Craft Shoppe bought a handmade quilt from Mrs. Jennings for $125. The Shoppe marked up the quilt 30% of the cost price. What percent of the Craft Shoppe's selling price did Mrs. Jennings receive? (*Ans.* 77%)

132. The Leather Shop buys handmade sandals from Larry Hansen for $8 a pair. The Leather Shop marks up these sandals 25% of the cost price. What percent of the Leather Shop's selling price does Mr. Hansen receive?

133. The Ivy Wholesale Greenhouse sells ferns to The Blossom Florist Shop for $6 each. The Blossom Florist Shop marks up the ferns 24-1/2% of the cost price. What percent of the selling price does the Greenhouse receive?

134. A rubber company sells tires to their retail outlets for $35.66 each. The retail outlet marks up the tires 30% of the cost price. What percent of the selling price does the rubber company receive?

135. The Lyons Import Store buys china for $135.22 a set. Lyons marks up the china by 40% of the cost price. What percent of the selling price does the china manufacturer receive?

136. A business machine manufacturer sells a retail office supply house a programmable electronic calculator for $1,500. The office supply house marks up the calculator by 20% of the cost price. What percent of the selling price does the manufacturer receive?

FINDING THE SELLING PRICE

Example. An antique dealer buys a spinning wheel for $95. How much must she sell it for if she desires a markon of 45% of the selling price?

1. The markon = 45% of the selling price.
2. The cost price, therefore, = 55% of the selling price (100% − 45% = 55%).

3. The selling price = 100%.
4. To find the *amount* of the selling price, divide the cost price by what percent the cost is of the selling price:
$$\$95 \div 55\% \text{ (or .55)} = \$172.727$$
5. The selling price is $172.73 (rounded to the penny).
6. Check: 45% of $172.73 = $77.73
   55% of $172.73 = $95.00
   $77.73 + 95.00 = $172.73

Practice Problems 13. Find the amount of the selling price for the following items. (Round your answers to the penny.)

	Cost Price ($)	Percent Markon on Selling Price	Selling Price ($)
137.	335.79	15	_____
138.	32.88	20	_____
139.	2.90	35	_____
140.	500.00	22	_____
141.	59.79	25	_____
142.	75.00	30	_____
143.	8.88	45	_____
144.	25.30	10	_____

MARKUP

Although the terms *markup* and *markon* are sometimes used synonymously, markup is usually defined as the amount *added* to the regular retail selling price to compensate for increased expenses.

Example. The regular selling price of an imported Delft lamp is $90. If the retailer marks up the lamp 25% of the present selling price, what is the amount of markup and the new selling price?

1. Markup amount = 90 × 25% (or .25) = *$22.50*
2. New selling price = 90 + 22.50 = *$112.50*
3. If you need to know *only* the new selling price, multiply the old selling price by 125% (or 1.25).
$$90 \times 125\% = \$112.50$$

BUSINESS PROBLEMS

Practice Problems 14. Find the amount of markup on selling price, and the new selling price, for the following items. (Round your answers to the penny.)

	Selling Price ($)	Percent Markup	Amount of Markup ($)	New Selling Price ($)
145.	256.00	20	51.20	307.20
146.	300.87	33		
147.	15.99	15		
148.	59.98	25		
149.	699.95	30		
150.	67.54	24-1/2		
151.	12.90	35		
152.	304.78	12-1/2		
153.	894.30	8		
154.	581.31	18		

Find *only* the new selling price by multiplying the regular selling price by 100% plus the percent of markup; e.g., 354.99 × 1.15.

	Regular Selling Price ($)	Percent Markup	New Selling Price ($)
155.	354.99	15	408.24
156.	20.76	23	
157.	54.88	50	
158.	587.84	20	
159.	56.43	25	
160.	22.88	33-1/3	
161.	493.67	40	
162.	783.29	5	
163.	470.20	18	

MARKDOWN

Markdown is usually defined as the amount deducted from the selling price when an item is placed on a special sale, such as an after-Christmas sale, moving sale, etc.

Example. Calculate the percent of markdown based on *selling price* for a swimsuit which originally sold for $13.99 and is now on sale for $9.99. (Round your answer to the percent.)

1. Subtract the sale price ($9.99) from the original selling price ($13.99).

    $$13.99 - 9.99 = 4.00$$

2. Divide the difference (4.00) by the original selling price (13.99).

    $$4.00 \div 13.99 = .2859 \text{ or } 29\% \text{ (rounded to the percent)}$$

3. The percent of markdown is 29.

Practice Problems 15. Find the percent of markdown based on original selling price for the following problems. (Round your answers to the percent.)

	Original Selling Price ($)	*Sale Price ($)*	*Percent of Markdown*
164.	82.88	74.99	10
165.	3.73	3.00	
166.	34.00	29.98	
167.	199.99	175.00	
168.	2,000.00	1,799.90	
169.	2,500.00	2,250.00	
170.	800.00	699.99	
171.	25.98	19.99	
172.	2.90	2.50	
173.	59.98	47.90	
174.	.99	.75	
175.	10.50	8.75	

SALES COMMISSION

Example 1. How much commission will Irma Smiley earn on sales of $100,000 if her commission rate is 3%?

$$100,000 \times 3\% \text{ (or .03)} = \$3,000$$

Example 2. How much commission will R.U. Pleasant earn on sales of $25,000 if his commission rate is 2% on the first $10,000 and 5-1/2% on sales over $10,000?

204 BUSINESS PROBLEMS

1. 10,000 × 2% (or .02) = 200
2. 25,000 - 10,000 = 15,000
3. 15,000 × 5.5% (or .055) = 825
4. 200 + 825 = $1,025

Example 3. How much will Jim Dandy earn this month on sales of $75,000 if he receives a flat salary of $900 a month for a sales quota of $50,000 and earns a 2% commission on sales over $50,000 for the month?

1. 75,000 - 50,000 = 25,000
2. 25,000 × 2% (or .02) = 500
3. 900 + 500 = $1,400 total monthly pay

Practice Problems 16. Solve the following commission problems. (Round your answers to the penny.)

176. Johnny Brown receives 7% commission on his sales of pencil boxes. He also receives 1% on the sales made by his employees, Jimmy and Donny. If Johnny's yearly sales are $300, and his salesmen's sales are $450 total, how much will Johnny earn? (*Ans.* $25.50)

177. Mr. Ross receives a 3% commission on his sales of house trailers for the first $10,000 in sales. He receives 5% commission on sales over $10,000. During this period, he had $14,500 in sales. What is his commission this period?

178. Jackie Winters works in a women's sportswear department. She receives 15% commission on the first $1,000 in sales. She receives 20% for sales over $1,000. What will her commission be if she sells $1,750 worth of goods?

179. Lee West sells organic vitamins. Her commission is 20% on the first $1,000 in sales; 25% for the second $1,000 in sales; and 30% for sales over $2,000. During the first quarter she sold $2,655 worth of vitamins. How much commission did she earn?

180. Robert Benson sells airline tickets, football and basketball tickets, and theater tickets. He receives 10% commission on the airline tickets, 15% on the football and basketball tickets, and 20% on theater tickets. In November he sold $1,500 in airline tickets, $250 in football and basketball tickets, and $175 in theater tickets. What is his total commission for November?

181. Robert Smedley sells business forms and stationery. He receives a commission of 12% on sales to new customers and 10% on sales to regular customers. If he sold $5,000 worth of forms to new customers in October and $2,500 worth of forms to regular customers, what is his October commission check?

PAYROLL—WAGES WITH OVERTIME

Example. Randy Day works in a factory. Last week he worked 7 days, 8 hours a day. His rate per hour is $5.47. Overtime is paid at time and a half for hours worked over 40 hours per week except for Sundays. If Randy works on Sunday, he is paid double time for hours worked that day. What was Randy's gross pay last week?

1. Monday through Friday he worked 40 hours (8 × 5 = 40) at regular pay.

   40 × 5.47 = 218.80

2. He worked 8 hours on Saturday at time-and-a-half.

   8 × 5.47 × 1.5 = 65.64

3. He worked 8 hours on Sunday at double time.

   8 × 5.47 × 2 = 87.52

4. 218.80 + 65.64 + 87.52 = $371.96

   Note: If your calculator has a memory, you can add each of these three amounts into memory as you go and recall the final sum from memory without re-entering the amounts on the keyboard.

Practice Problems 17. Calculate the gross pay in the following problems. (Round your answers to the penny.)

182. Allen Barbeto is a millman in a factory and is paid $5.687 per hour. Last week he worked 8 hours on Monday, 8 hours on Tuesday, 8 hours on Wednesday, 10 hours on Thursday, 8 hours on Friday, 4 hours on Saturday, and 6 hours on Sunday. He is paid time and a half for hours worked over 40, except hours worked on Sunday, which are paid at double time. What was his gross pay last week? (*Ans.* $346.91)

183. Pete Sully is a welder in a factory. He earns $7.04 per hour and is paid time and a half for hours worked over 40. Last week he worked Monday through Saturday for a total of 48 hours. Since he works the night shift, he also receives a night differential of 13.7 cents per hour additional wages. What were his earnings last week? *Note:* In this problem the 13.7 cents remains the same per hour; there is no additional differential for overtime hours.

184. The workers in the foam-filled tires department earn $5.426 per hour and are paid time and a half for hours worked over 40. Ed Bates worked 36 hours last week on the night shift, which means an additional 13.7 cents per hour for night shift differential. He also worked 8 hours on Saturday (day shift). What were his gross earnings last week?

185. George MacKenna builds V-belts at a rate of $5.13 per hour and is paid time and a half for hours worked over 40 (except Sunday). For hours worked on Sunday, he is paid double time. Last week he worked 36 hours Monday through Friday, 8 hours on Saturday, and 4 hours on Sunday. What was his gross pay last week?

186. Alicia Anderson worked in the plant cafeteria last week. She earned $3.75 per hour. She worked 8 hours each day Monday through Thursday, 12 hours on Friday, and 4 hours on Saturday. What were her gross wages last week? (Remember, these workers receive time and a half for hours over 40 and double time for hours worked on Sunday.)

206 BUSINESS PROBLEMS

187. Mary Sheridan, R.N., is a nurse in the factory hospital. She earns $5.85 per hour. Last week she worked 8 hours on Monday, 8 hours on Tuesday, 4 hours on Wednesday, 10 hours on Thursday, 8 hours on Friday, and 4 hours on Saturday. What was her gross pay last week? (She receives time and a half for hours over 40.)

PAYROLL–PIECEWORK RATES

Example. John Langdon builds passenger tires. He is paid 32.7 cents per tire. If he builds 803 tires in one week, what are his earnings?

$$803 \times .327 = \$262.581 = \$262.58 \text{ (rounded to the penny)}$$

Practice Problems 18. Determine the earnings for the following people. (Round your answers to the penny.)

188. Anthony Calan builds small industrial tires. He receives 9 cents per tire. Yesterday he built 750 tires. What did he earn yesterday? (*Ans.* $67.50)

189. James Riley is a production control supervisor. He earns $1,040 per month based on a 40-hour week. He receives a monthly bonus of $5 per day for each day that production rates meet the daily forecasted goals. Last month, his department met the forecasted goals on 18 days. What was his pay for last month?

190. Martha VanScott is an inspector on an assembly line. She earns 50 cents for every 100 coils she inspects. Yesterday she inspected 8,050 coils in an 8-hour shift. What did her earnings average per hour?
Note: She earns 1/2 cent per coil inspected; 1/2 cent should be expressed as $.005. Hourly rate = (.005 × 8,050) ÷ 8

191. Ernest Chandler earns $205 per 40-hour week for producing 100 rubber rings per day. For any number of rings over 100 per day, he is paid a bonus of $.265 per ring. If he produced 103 rings on Monday, 101 on Tuesday, 110 on Wednesday, 104 on Thursday, and 108 on Friday, what were his total earnings?

192. Jill Gibbons works in a box factory. Her job is to operate the box-folding machine. She is paid 3 cents for each box folded for the first 1,000. She is paid 4 cents each for the next 500 boxes, 5 cents each for the next 500 boxes, and 6 cents each for each box folded over 2,000. If she folded 3,020 boxes during the week, what will her gross pay be?

193. Janice Yarborough assembles dolls at the Magic Toy Company. She is paid 75 cents for each doll she assembles. On Monday she assembled 25 dolls; on Tuesday, 28 dolls; on Wednesday, 41 dolls; on Thursday, 39 dolls; and on Friday, 33 dolls. How much is her pay for this week?

SALARY AND HOURLY WAGES AFTER TAXES AND OTHER DEDUCTIONS

Example. J.P. O'Hara earned $287.65 in gross weekly wages. He had the following deductions:

Credit union $15.00

Federal tax	59.67
FICA	16.83
State tax	3.36
City tax	4.31

What were his net wages?

1. Enter 287.65 on the keyboard; depress $\boxed{+}$ key.
2. Enter 15 on the keyboard; depress $\boxed{-}$ key, etc.
3. Net wages = $188.48

Practice Problems 19. Solve the following payroll problems. (Round your answers to the penny.)

194. A.L. Lancaster receives a $1,050 monthly salary and has the following deductions: credit union, $20.00; federal tax, $40.59; FICA, $61.43; state tax, 1/2% of the monthly salary; city tax, 1% of the monthly salary; stock purchase plan, $16.00; savings bonds, $18.75. What is his take-home pay this month? (*Ans.* $877.48)

195. R.B. Bartlett receives a $925 monthly salary and has the following deductions: federal tax, $39.42; FICA, $54.11; state tax, 1% of the monthly salary; city tax, 1-1/2% of the monthly salary; stock purchase plan, $8.50; purchases at company store, $15.00. What is her take-home pay this month?

196. P.R. Bradley earned $200.28 in weekly wages. He had the following deductions: credit union, $10.00; federal tax, $35.59; FICA, $11.71; state tax, $1.61; city tax, $3.00; union dues, $9.04; supplementary accident and health insurance, $5.00. What were his net weekly wages?

197. Union dues are at present $9.04 per month. Dues are to be increased 2 cents per month for each one-cent-per-hour wage increase. If the union workers are scheduled to receive an 80-cent-per-hour wage increase, how much in dues will each worker pay when the wage increase takes effect?

198. T.C. MacArthur receives a monthly salary of $800 plus 1% commission on his sales. His sales last month totaled $12,400. He had the following deductions: credit union, $20.00; federal tax, $47.89; FICA, $54.05; state tax, 1% of salary plus commission; city tax, $6.33; supplementary life insurance, $4.35; stock purchase plan, $25.00. What was his net pay for last month?

199. B.W. Melvin receives a salary of $1,275 per month. In addition he was reimbursed for his month's travel expenses, which amounted to $375.16. He had the following deductions: federal tax, $120.15; FICA, $74.59; state tax, $12.75; county tax, $3.90; city tax, $6.33; supplemental accident and health insurance, $4.50; savings bond, $37.50. What was the amount of his check?

FICA

FICA (Social Security) deductions are 5.85% of the gross pay up to the annual limit of $16,500. After an employee has reached annual earnings of $16,500 no further deductions are made that year for FICA.

BUSINESS PROBLEMS

Example.

Calculate the FICA deduction for an employee whose weekly pay is $217.50.

$$217.50 \times 5.85\% \text{ (or .0585)} = \$12.72 \text{ (rounded to the penny)}$$

Practice Problems 20. Calculate FICA deductions for the following January payroll. Enter the constant multiplier as 5.85 (or .0585). (Round your answers to the penny.)

Employee	Gross January Pay ($)	FICA Deduction ($)
200. Antonio, J.	875	51.19
201. Burger, D.	927	
202. Dodge, E.	1,540	
203. Flint, A.	640	
204. Goodwin, P.	591	
205. Keller, R.	782	
206. McCaw, T.	520	
207. Milich, I.	980	
208. Ourner, P.	478	
209. Pedanti, A.	600	
210. Perez, B.	890	
211. Schlog, C.	955	
212. Snader, A.	865	
213. Stewart, F.	1,240	
214. Tippett, J.	686	
215. Wallace, H.	1,110	
216. Walters, R.	694	
217. Wilmott, L.	786	
218. Wonowski, P.	885	
219. Zappone, S.	584	

Subtract from the gross pay the deductions indicated and show the net January pay for the following payroll. Use the FICA deductions which you have already calculated for these employees.

JANUARY PAYROLL

	Employee Name	Gross Pay for Jan. ($)	Federal Income Tax ($)	FICA ($)	1.5% City Tax ($)	Savings Bonds ($)	A & H Ins. ($)	Company Store ($)	Stock Plan ($)	Net Pay ($)
220.	Antonio, J.	875	157.50	*51.19*	*13.13*	18.75	5.75	—	—	628.68
221.	Burger, D.	927	148.32			—	5.75	10.00	—	
222.	Dodge, E.	1,540	284.90			37.50	5.75	—	20.00	
223.	Flint, A.	640	102.46			—	—	10.00	10.00	
224.	Goodwin, P.	591	94.56			18.75	5.75	—	10.00	
225.	Keller, R.	782	136.85			—	—	10.00	20.00	
226.	McCaw, T.	520	78.05			18.75	5.75	—	—	
227.	Milich, I.	980	166.62			—	—	10.00	40.00	
228.	Ourner, P.	478	71.71			—	5.75	—	—	
229.	Pedanti, A.	600	87.02			18.75	5.75	—	10.00	
230.	Perez, B.	890	133.53			—	5.75	10.00	30.00	
231.	Schlog, C.	955	162.35			37.50	5.75	—	40.00	
232.	Snader, A.	865	138.41			75.00	5.75	—	—	
233.	Stewart, F.	1,240	210.81			—	5.75	—	50.00	
234.	Tippett, J.	686	96.04			18.75	5.75	—	—	
235.	Wallace, H.	1,110	192.54			—	5.75	10.00	40.00	
236.	Walters, R.	694	97.16			—	5.75	10.00	20.00	
237.	Wilmott, L.	786	106.11			18.75	5.75	10.00	—	
238.	Wonowski, P.	885	132.75			75.00	5.75	—	20.00	
239.	Zappone, S.	584	73.04			—	—	10.00	—	

SALARY INCREASES

Many companies and agencies give raises in the form of a percent of present salary. Types of increases include merit raises, adjustments, cost-of-living increases, and promotional increases. Sometimes more than one increase is given at one time. At times these combined raises include a flat sum plus a percentage of the present salary.

Example. Joanne Allen is scheduled to receive a promotion on June 1. The promotion will include a salary increase of $75 per month. On June 1 she will also receive a cost-of-living increase of 3.2% of her *present* salary, which is $690 per month. What will be her new monthly salary rounded to the dollar?

1. 690 × 3.2% (or .032) = 22.08
2. 690 + 22.08 + 75 = 787.08
3. 787.08 rounded to the dollar = $787 new monthly salary

Practice Problems 21. Calculate the new monthly salary for each of the following employees. (Round your answers to the *dollar.*)

	Employee	Present Monthly Salary ($)	Merit Raise ($)	Adjustment (%)	Cost of Living (%)	Promotion ($)	New Monthly Salary ($)
240.	Bennett, P.	503	50		4.1		574
241.	Csaszar, L.	940		3.8	4.1		
242.	DeWitt, M.	764			4.1		
243.	Freshwater, J.	690			4.1		
244.	Garcia, R.	825	60		4.1		
245.	Kowalski, A.	595			4.1	70	
246.	Leffler, T.	605		6.4	4.1		
247.	Myatt, S.	710	55		4.1		
248.	Smith, I.	1,040			4.1	90	
249.	Tenney, C.	1,124			4.1		
250.	Wilde, W.	841			4.1		

INSURANCE—PERCENT INSURED

Example. Your company has its office building insured for $350,600. Actually, your office building is worth $450,000. What percent of the office building is insured?

1. What percent is 350,600 of 450,000? The "is" number is the dividend; the "of" number is the divisor.
2. 350,600 ÷ 450,000 = 77.9% (rounded to the tenth of a percent)
   Express your answer in percent form. Use the % key if you have one. If not, be sure to convert your decimal answer to percent by moving the decimal two places to the right.

Practice Problems 22. In each of the following problems determine what percent of the property is insured. (Round your answers to the tenth of a percent.)

251. Your home is insured for $18,400 but has been valued at $26,800. What percent of your home is insured? (*Ans.* 68.7%)

252. The Holbrooks' farm is insured for $46,500. The farm, with stock and tools, is valued at $78,600. What percent of their farm is insured?

253. The Burnses' summer cottage is insured for $12,500. The cottage is valued at $15,250. What percent of their cottage is insured?

254. The Long & Co. Furniture insured its showroom building for $150,000. The showroom building was valued at $194,500. What percent of the building is insured?

255. The Brighton Laboratory is insured for $2,500,000; however, the property is valued at $3,100,000. What percent of the property is insured?

256. Mrs. Williams has her furniture and other household goods insured for $7,500. If these items are valued at $12,250, what percent of her furniture and household goods are insured?

INSURANCE–COST OF PREMIUM

Example. Mr. Jones's house is insured for $31,500. If he pays 40 cents a year per $100 of insurance, what does his yearly premium cost?

1. 31,500 × .4 = 12,600
2. To divide by 100, just move the decimal point two places to the left.
3. 12,600 ÷ 100 = $126 per year

Practice Problems 23. Find the amount of the insurance premium in the following problems. (Round your answers to the penny.)

257. Mr. Brown insured his home for $25,600. His annual premium is 42 cents per $100. What does he pay each year to insure his home? (*Ans.* $107.52)

258. Mr. Simon has his home insured for $35,000. If his insurance costs $1.25 per $100, what is his annual premium?

259. Mr. and Mrs. Farmer insured their home for $27,500. If their premium rate is $18.75 per $1,000 for a 5-year term, how much is the premium which they pay every 5 years? How much is this per year?

BUSINESS PROBLEMS

260. Mrs. Lancaster insures her home for $21,300. If she pays a rate of $12.40 per $1,000 every 3 years, how much is her premium?

261. Mr. Martin insures his home for $20,000. His rate is $4.32 per $1,000 for one year. What is his annual premium?

262. The Lawson home is insured for $35,000. The premium, which is paid every 2 years, is at a rate of $9.80 per $1,000. How much is the premium?

LONG-TERM PREMIUMS

Many fire insurance companies will offer lower rates when a policy is purchased for two or three years instead of one.

RATIOS PER $1 OF PREMIUM

Years	Ratio of Annual Premium
One	1.00
Two	1.85
Three	2.70

Example 1. The law firm of Smith, Smith, and Smith wants to insure its office furniture and equipment for $10,000 against fire. The annual premium is $.40 per $100. What is the firm's premium for one year?

1. Premium = Rate $\times$ Value (P = R $\times$ V)
2. Premium = (.40 $\times$ 10,000) $\div$ 100
3. Premium = 4,000 $\div$ 100 = $40

Example 2. What is the firm's premium if it prepays the policy for two years? (Refer to Ratios Per $1 of Premium.) How much will the firm save over the one-year rate?

1. P = 40 $\times$ 1.85
2. P = $74
3. Savings = (2 $\times$ 40) - 74
4. Savings = 80 - 74
5. Savings = $6

Example 3. What is the firm's premium if it prepays the policy for three years? How much will the firm save over the one-year rate?

1. P = 40 $\times$ 2.70
2. P = $108
3. Savings = (3 $\times$ 40) - 108

4. Savings = 120 - 108
5. Savings = $12

Practice Problems 24. Compute the premiums for the following insurance policies:

	Rate per $100 ($)	Value ($)	No. Years Prepaid	Amount of Premium ($)
263.	.39	15,000	1	58.50
264.	.45	25,000	1	_____
265.	.61	5,000	1	_____
266.	.33	18,600	2	_____
267.	.52	125,000	2	_____
268.	.80	64,300	2	_____
269.	.48	2,396,000	3	_____
270.	.55	426,400	3	_____
271.	.64	12,600	3	_____
272.	.85	4,200	3	_____

PROMISSORY NOTES—MATURITY DATE AND MATURITY VALUE

A *promissory note* is a written promise to repay a loan on a certain day in the future. For example, a 60-day note will be due 60 days from the date of issue. Notes may bear interest or not. The total amount of the note, including interest (if any), is called the *maturity value* and is due on the *maturity date*.

Example 1. Find the maturity date and the maturity value of an interest-bearing note for $600 plus interest at 8%, dated April 5, which is due 60 days from the date of issue.

1. Find the days remaining in April:

April 30
April 5
25 days remaining in April

2. Add the days in May:

25
+31
56

3. Find the number of days needed to complete 60 days:

$$\begin{array}{r} 60 \\ -56 \\ \hline 4 \end{array}$$

The date of maturity is June 4.

4. Maturity value is the face value plus the interest.
5. I = PRT
   I = (600 × .08 × 60) ÷ 360
   I = $8.00
6. Maturity value = 600 + 8.00 = $608.00

Practice Problems 25. Find the maturity date and the maturity value on the following interest-bearing notes. (Round your answers to the penny.)

273. Booming Business, Inc., signed a promissory note on March 16 for $250 plus interest at 7-1/2%. The note will mature 90 days after the date the note was signed. Determine the maturity date and the maturity value. (*Ans.* June 14; $254.69)

274. Mr. Anderson gave a creditor a promissory note for $5,200 plus interest at 7-1/4% on September 3. The note will mature in 60 days. When is the maturity date? What is the maturity value?

PROMISSORY NOTES—DISCOUNTING AND PROCEEDS

Sometimes a company needs cash and will want to collect on the note *before* the maturity date. Therefore, the company may sell a promissory note to a bank. The bank will give the company the maturity value of the note less the *bank discount*. A bank discount is actually the interest charged by the bank on the discounted note. The company is willing to give up a portion of the maturity value for the privilege of receiving the money early. The maturity value less the bank discount is called the company's *procceds* from the note.

Example. The OK Business Company sells to its bank John Smith's promissory note, which has a maturity value of $5,475, and which will mature in 60 days. The bank will pay the OK Company the maturity value of the note less a service charge called a *discount rate*. The bank's discount rate is 8%. How much money does the OK Business Company obtain from the bank for the note?

1. To find the bank discount, multiply the maturity value times the discount rate times the number of days; then divide by 360 (used as days in one year).

   (5,475 × .08 × 60) ÷ 360 = $73 bank discount

   Note: Use 8% if you have a Percent key.

2. OK will receive the maturity value of the note less the bank service charge (discount).

$$5{,}475 - 73 = \$5{,}402$$

Note: Use your re-entry feature if you have one. After you get 73 as the discount, enter it back by depressing the $\boxed{-}$ key. Then enter 5,475 and depress the $\boxed{+}$ key. This will save your having to re-enter the 73 on the keyboard by hand.

Practice Problems 26. Calculate the amount of proceeds in the following problems. (Round your answers to the penny.)

275. The Dyson Tool and Die Company gives its bank a promissory note worth $500 at maturity and which will mature in 82 days. If the bank discount rate is 7%, what proceeds will Dyson receive from the bank? (*Ans.* $492.03)

276. Mrs. Milton's Musical Kindergarten gives the bank a promissory note worth $750 at maturity and which will mature in 25 days. If the bank discount rate is 6-1/2%, what proceeds will Mrs. Milton's Musical Kindergarten receive from the bank?

277. Lauren, Little, and Smythe sells to its bank a promissory note worth $10,500 at maturity and which will mature in 180 days. If the bank discount rate is 8%, what proceeds will Lauren, Little, and Smythe receive from the bank?

278. Mr. Johansen sells to his bank a promissory note worth $4,375 at maturity and which will mature in 30 days. If the bank discount rate is 6-3/4%, what proceeds will Mr. Johansen receive from the bank?

BANKING–CHECKING ACCOUNTS

Example. You have just opened a checking account at your bank. There is no flat service charge for your account; however, you must pay 10 cents for each check you write and 5 cents for each deposit you make. You write about 8 checks a month and make 2 deposits each month. How much will it cost you to maintain your checking account for one year?

1. Multiply the number of months in a year times 8 checks per month times 10 cents a check.

$$12 \times 8 \times .1 = 9.60$$

2. Multiply the number of months in a year times 2 deposits per month times 5 cents a deposit.

$$12 \times 2 \times .05 = 1.20$$

3. $9.60 + 1.20 = \$10.80$

Note: If your calculator has a memory function, you can add the first and the second product into memory and then recall the memory total (10.80) without having to re-enter and add your two products.

Practice Problems 27. Solve the following checking account problems. (Round your answers to the penny.)

279. Mary opened a checking account at the Second National Bank. She pays a flat service charge of $1.75 per month. She can write 20 checks per month at no extra charge. However, beyond the first 20 checks, she pays 8 cents for each check she writes each month. She also pays 5 cents for each deposit. Mary writes 22 checks a month and makes 4 deposits each month. How much will her checking account cost per year? (*Ans.* $25.32)

280. At the Textron Bank you must keep a minimum balance of $200 in your checking account, or you must pay $1.00 service charge per month plus 8 cents per check that you write. You write about 21 checks a month. If you place the $200 in a savings account, you can earn 4% a year compounded quarterly. If you save the $200 instead of keeping a $200 minimum balance in your checking account, how much will your checking account cost for one year? (Deduct the interest you will earn from the total cost of maintaining the checking account.)

281. The Goodrich Bank offers two plans for opening a checking account: one, you pay $2.50 per month service charge regardless of how many checks you write; two, you pay 9 cents per check and no flat service charge. In January you wrote 12 checks, in February you wrote 18 checks, in March you wrote 8 checks, in April you wrote 15 checks, in May and June you wrote 16 checks each month. What would you be charged for checking account service for this six-month period if you had taken plan one? What would you be charged for checking account service if you had taken plan two?

282. In August the Jordon Company was charged 5 cents per check for writing 124 checks. It was also charged 25 cents for each of its 12 deposits. It was charged an additional $2.00 fee for a returned check. What was its total bank service charge for August?

283. In May, Mariott, Inc., paid 5 cents per check for writing 209 checks. It was charged 25 cents for each of its 25 deposits. It was charged an additional $3.25 by the bank for collection of a note due Mariott. What was its total bank service charge for May?

284. A.R. Park Corp. had deducted from its checking account a $4.75 service charge, $3.60 for collecting a note, $3.00 for a returned check, and 25 cents per $100 under the minimum balance of $1,500. A.R. Park's minimum balance during the month was $900. What was the total cost of maintaining its checking account for the month, based on the service charges and other fees deducted by the bank?

DEPOSIT SLIPS

Companies often need to use the long form deposit slip to make bank deposits. The amount of money in coins deposited and the amount of currency (paper money) deposited are shown separately. Each check is identified and listed separately.

DEPOSIT SLIPS 217

Example.

```
HOMEVILLE BANK AND TRUST COMPANY

            Homeville, USA

    Endorse all checks and list separately.
    Coin              $    17.83
    Currency               55.00
    Checks                  8.79
                          205.80
                          196.00
                            5.99
                           18.30
                          500.00
                           44.68
                           12.33
                          201.46
    TOTAL             $1,266.18

    No. of checks 9  Date 11-3

    Account Number    1234-05-6789
```

Check the total on this deposit slip.

Practice Problems 28. Total the following deposit slips:

```
        FIRST CENTRAL BANK

            Adrian, USA

    Endorse all checks and list separately.
    Coin              $  26.89
    Currency             48.00
    Checks              129.76
                          5.76
                        500.00
                        489.33
                          8.22
                          3.11
                         20.98
                        677.34
285.    TOTAL         _____

    No. of checks 8  Date 1-7

    Account Number   1380-00-2922
```

```
       TIFFANY CITIZENS BANK

            Tiffany, USA

    Endorse all checks and list separately.
    Coin              $300.65
    Currency            60.00
    Checks             124.33
                       505.50
                       787.56
                       100.40
                         3.29
                        63.38
                       502.35
                       211.01
286.    TOTAL         _____

    No. of checks 8  Date 6-7

    Account Number   1389-29-0030
```

```
┌─────────────────────────────────────────────┐
│          SECOND NATIONAL BANK               │
│             Marionville, USA                │
│                                             │
│   Endorse all checks and list separately.   │
│   Coin              $  234.89               │
│   Currency           1,120.00               │
│   Checks               529.39               │
│                        879.45               │
│                         67.55               │
│                        441.36               │
│                          9.00               │
│                          1.90               │
│                         56.76               │
│                        432.57               │
│ 287.  TOTAL           ────────              │
│                                             │
│   No. of checks 8  Date 3-14                │
│                                             │
│   Account Number  2830-09-2937              │
└─────────────────────────────────────────────┘

## RECONCILING BANK BALANCES

Most banks send a monthly statement to each of their checking account customers along with that customer's canceled checks. The statement shows the activity of the account for the month, including deposits, withdrawals, checks paid out of the account, service charge, loan charges, etc. The statement shows the balance in the customer's account at the end of that period.

Seldom does the bank statement show the same balance as the customer's check register balance. The customer may have written checks that have not yet cleared the bank. The customer may have made deposits after the bank statement cut-off date. The bank may have made a charge against the customer's account which he has not yet deducted from his balance. The customer or the bank may have made an error in the account.

Steps in Reconciling a Bank Balance:

*Note:* Most banks provide a useful reconciliation form on the back of the customer's statement.

1. Place the canceled checks in numerical order.
2. Compare these with your check register to be sure that the amount of each check agrees with the amount shown in the check register. Place a checkmark on the check register for each canceled check.
3. List the amounts and numbers of the checks you have written that the bank has not yet canceled and returned to you. These checks are called *outstanding checks*.
4. Check your deposits against those recorded on the bank statement.

Items to be *added* to the bank statement:
```

- deposits recorded in your check register but not shown on the bank statement

Items to be *deducted* from the bank statement:
- total of the outstanding checks (including any still outstanding from previous statements)

Items to be *added* to your check balance:
- any notes collected by the bank for your account

Items to be *deducted* from your check balance:
- bank service charge
- principal and interest payments on any loan you have with the bank
- charges for check printing
- any bad check you may have received from someone else and deposited in your account
- charge for any check you have written on your account which was returned for not sufficient funds (NSF)

After these adjustments, your corrected check register balance and the bank statement corrected balance should agree. If they don't agree, look back over your check register for transpositions and/or mathematical errors, or checks which you may have forgotten to record in your check register.

Example. The West Mark Company's check register shows a balance of $35,329.12. Their bank statement received today (June 15) from the Main Street Bank shows a balance of $37,054.00.

The following checks are outstanding:

#1001	$	86.29
#1005		41.13
#1007		109.15
#1011		1,299.33
Total		$1,535.90

A deposit of $105.00 was made on June 14 and was not shown on the bank statement. The bank's service charge was $6.02. The Main Street Bank collected a promissory note for $300.00 for the West Mark Company and added this amount to West Mark's account. The Reconciliation Statement is shown below:

RECONCILEMENT OF ACCOUNT
June 15, 19--

Bank Statement	$37,054.00	Check Register		$35,329.12
Add deposit not shown	105.00	Add proceeds of note		
	$37,159.00	collected		300.00
Less outstanding checks	−1,535.90			$35,629.12
Revised bank balance	$35,623.10	Less service charge		−6.02
		Revised check register		$35,623.10

Practice Problems 29. Prepare a reconcilement of account for the following checking accounts:

288. Lords, Inc., shows a check register balance of $150,390.14. Its bank statement shows a balance of $180,828.58.

    The following checks are outstanding:

#254		$30,314.18
#260		45.12
#271		192.04

    Lords, Inc., had deposited a check for $100.00, which was received from their customer, James Randolph. This check was returned NSF; therefore, Lords must deduct this amount from its check register balance. The bank service charge was $12.90. What is the adjusted check register balance? Does it agree with the adjusted bank statement balance? (*Ans.* $150,277.24; yes)

289. Lampart & Sons, Ltd., shows a check register balance of $25,609.21. Its bank account statement shows a balance of $26,667.49.

    The following checks are outstanding:

#2429		$ 101.43
#2861		29.50
#2870		1,300.42
#2871		860.18

    A recent deposit of $1,020.00 was not included on the bank statement. A loan payment of $203.00 and interest of $5.06 was deducted from Lampart's account by the bank. The bank service charge was $5.19. What is the adjusted balance?

DECISION PROBLEM

System for Processing Sales Orders

You work at your company's home office. The people at your location must communicate often with your plant, which is located in another state. At present, you are using U.S. mail service and long-distance telephone calls for these communications with your plant.

The home office sends an average of 85 ounces of first-class mail (at 13 cents per ounce) to your plant each work day (about 22 days a month).

The home office receives and processes sales orders from your customers. The sales orders are typed on multiple-copy forms at the home office and then mailed to the plant. These sales orders account for two-thirds of the mail the home office sends to the plant. The plant then fills these orders and ships your product to the customers.

In order to give quick service, it is often necessary to inform the plant immediately of a customer's order. In these instances, one of your order department staff telephones the information to the plant and confirms it by mailing the sales order. Fifty percent of the long-distance calls made to the plant concern sales orders. Your telephone bills for calls made to your plant average $1,905.50 a month.

You have been asked to investigate and compare the cost of your present system with the cost of sending the sales orders by teletypewriter. Your plant already has a teletype machine. If your home office acquires a teletype, you will be able to save two-thirds of the cost of your mail to the plant and one-half the cost of your long-distance telephone calls to the plant.

The cost of leasing a teletype is $88.50 a month, and the cost of the telephone access line is $18.75 a month. The maintenance contract is $24.00 a month. In addition you will have to pay $.55 per minute for each minute you are transmitting on line.

The teletype transmits at 100 words per minute. Your sales orders would be prepared on punched paper tape off line (there is no extra cost for using the teletype off line) and then transmitted on line by the prepunched paper tape at the rate of 100 words per minute. Prepared sales order forms contain about 55 words. You prepare about 100 sales orders per day.

The sales order forms would cost about the same as those which are presently being typed. However, additional supplies, such as paper tape, would cost about $10.00 a month. The typist who now prepares the sales orders would be trained on the teletype; therefore, no increase in your office staff would be necessary.

Calculate and give the cost of each system for a month. Would it save your company money to lease a teletype?

REVIEW QUIZ 4

(Round your answers to two decimal places.)

1. How much sales tax must you pay on a $41.95 suit if the sales tax is 5-1/2%?
2. The purchasing department's total annual budget is $156,395. Their salaries total $97,460. What percent of the total budget was allocated for salaries?
3. How many days are needed to produce $20 in interest at 8% on a principal of $500?
4. What is the rate of interest that produces $15 on a principal of $1,200 in 60 days?
5. How much interest will you earn in two years on $250 in a savings plan which pays 8% compounded semiannually?
6. What must a furniture dealer charge for a chair which cost $130, if he wants a 35% markon based on cost?
7. A pair of boots cost The Bootery $30. The Bootery sells the pair of boots for $44.95. What is the amount of markon? What is the percent of markon based on the cost?
8. A bookstore buys an atlas for $9.90 and sells it for $12.98. What is the amount of markon? What is the percent of markon based on the selling price?

9. A sports equipment store buys a football for $9.50. What must the football sell for if the store wants a markon of 25% of the selling price?

10. Rebecca Yost earns a commission of 22% of her first $1,000 in sales and 30% on sales over $1,000. Last month she made sales of $5,320. How much commission did she earn?

Sample Examination

You may want to be timed as you try the Unit 4 Sample Examination, which is presented in the Introduction.

Unit 5

Practical Problems

TOUCH SYSTEM REVIEW

Are your fingers curved over the home row? Do not lift your hand away from the keyboard. Keep your fingers hovering over the home row.

444	556	664	554	456	654
565	564	465	564	564	564
456	456	565	665	456	654
465	454	656	646	465	564
445	554	456	654	556	554
444	555	666	666	655	444
446	664	564	654	565	656
464	565	654	654	456	654
456	456	646	465	654	654
444	555	666	665	666	554
4,629	5,379	6,002	6,187	5,493	5,952

Are you getting the right answers? Don't turn your head back and forth between the keys and the copy. You will lose valuable time that way.

333	222	123	123	123	123
111	113	221	331	221	131
123	321	322	323	212	132
112	113	111	222	333	122
132	231	123	321	321	231
123	123	111	222	333	111
221	331	112	113	112	113
212	313	123	321	123	132
222	333	112	113	331	221
123	123	132	132	321	321
1,712	2,223	1,490	2,221	2,430	1,637

PRACTICAL PROBLEMS

Can you find the keys without looking? Are you getting the right answers?

777	888	999	888	777	888
778	887	778	887	778	887
788	799	788	799	889	998
777	999	888	999	777	888
788	887	977	998	889	977
789	789	789	789	789	789
999	888	777	888	999	888
998	997	998	998	798	997
789	798	987	789	879	798
789	789	879	987	978	879
8,272	8,721	8,860	9,022	8,553	8,989

Keep your eyes on your copy. Keep your fingers curved and hovering over the home row.

998	887	799	977	788	877
778	887	779	997	889	997
777	888	999	888	777	888
798	778	978	887	978	798
998	889	779	997	877	977
778	889	998	887	788	899
789	798	789	978	798	978
789	798	978	798	879	778
987	798	778	998	798	778
999	789	978	798	879	978
8,691	8,401	8,855	9,205	8,451	8,948

Use your right thumb for the zero. For the left hand, use your little finger for the zero.

200	202	108	202	302	402
400	204	106	204	304	404
600	206	104	206	306	406
800	208	102	208	308	408
100	200	100	200	300	400
100	101	109	201	301	401
300	203	107	203	303	403
500	205	105	205	305	405
700	207	103	207	307	407
900	209	101	209	309	409
4,600	1,945	1,045	2,045	3,045	4,045

Keep your head turned toward your copy.

2.02	3.30	3.04	4.04	5.04	6.04
4.04	5.50	3.06	4.06	5.06	6.06
6.06	7.70	3.08	4.09	5.08	6.08
8.08	9.90	3.10	4.10	5.10	6.10
1.00	1.01	4.02	5.02	6.02	7.02
1.01	2.20	3.03	4.03	5.03	6.03
3.03	4.40	3.05	4.05	5.05	6.05
5.05	6.60	3.07	4.07	5.07	6.07
7.07	8.80	3.09	4.08	5.09	6.09
9.09	1.10	4.01	5.01	6.01	7.01
46.45	50.51	32.55	42.55	52.55	62.55

INSTALLMENT BUYING

Example 1. Santa Claus bought a new color TV for $580. He paid $95 down and made 12 monthly payments of $48 each. How much more than the $580 price is Santa paying? What percent of the list price is interest (rounded to two decimal places)?

1. Interest = 95 + (48 × 12) - 580 = 91
2. Percent of interest = Interest ÷ List price
3. Percent of interest = 91 ÷ 580 = 15.6896% = 15.69% (rounded to two decimal places)

Practice Problems 1. In the following problems compute the installment charge (interest) and the percent the installment charge is of the list price. (Round your answers to two decimal places.)

1. Mrs. Claus bought a new stereo outfit for $600. She paid $100 down and made six monthly payments of $90 each. How much more than the $600 price is Mrs. Claus paying? What percent of the list price is interest? (*Ans.* $40; 6.67%)

2. A turntable is advertised at a list price of $99.99. If the customer wants to buy it on the installment plan, he must pay 10% down and make six monthly payments of $17.42. What is the amount of the down payment (.10 × 99.99)? What is the installment price [(6 × 17.42) + amount of down payment]? What is the installment charge (installment price - list price)? What percent is the installment charge of the list price (installment charge ÷ list price)?

3. The list price on an organ is $2,100. Alice buys the organ and pays 15% down and 10 monthly payments of $205 each. What is the down payment, the installment price, the installment charge, and the percent the installment charge is of the list price?

4. Lisa bought a used car for $1,800 with no down payment. She financed her car at her bank with 18 monthly payments of $110.60. What was the installment price

of the car? What was the installment charge? What percent of the cash price was the installment charge?

5. Don bought a tape player which was listed as $130 cash price. He paid $8.65 a month for 18 months. What was his total cost for the tape player? What was his installment charge? What percent of the cash price was the installment charge?

6. Sam bought a used car for $2,000. He paid $100 down and will pay 18 monthly payments of $120.28. What is the installment charge? What percent is the installment charge of the list price?

7. Tom borrowed $200 from his credit union to buy Christmas gifts. He paid back the credit union with 12 monthly payments of $17.75. What did it cost Tom to borrow the $200?

Example 2. Mother Goose bought a new $550 refrigerator. By paying cash, she received a 20% discount. If she paid 8% interest on the money she borrowed to pay for the refrigerator, how much did she save?

1. Amount saved on refrigerator = 550 × 20% (or .2) = 110
2. Cash price of refrigerator = 550 - 110 = 440
3. Cost of loan = 440 × 8% (or .08) = 35.20
4. Amount saved = 110.00 - 35.20 = $74.80

---

8. Mother Hubbard wants to buy a used Corvette which is priced at $4,000. If she pays cash, she can get the car for $3,600. If she borrows the money and pays 8-1/2% interest, how much can she save? (*Ans.* $94)

9. Mrs. Wilson wants to buy a new freezer. The cost of the freezer is $650, and the retailer will give her six months to pay for it. If she pays cash, the retailer will give her a 10% discount. She can borrow the amount needed for six months at 7% interest. Should she pay cash?

10. Mr. and Mrs. Everett want to buy carpeting for their downstairs. They can buy the carpeting (with free installation) at Lamb's Department Store for $185 a month for 12 months. They can buy the carpeting at a discount house for $1,600 if they pay cash. Installation will cost an additional $100. If they borrow the money to pay the discount store and pay 7-1/2% interest for one year, will they save any money?

11. Jack Belton wants to purchase a sofa for his living room. The sofa is priced at $700 for cash, or $60.15 a month for 12 months. If he pays cash, he will have to remove the $700 from his savings plan and will lose $42.10 in interest. Should he pay cash?

12. You would like to buy a filing cabinet for your home. You can buy the cabinet at Foster's Office Equipment Co. for $119.98. Delivery is free. You can buy a comparable filing cabinet at West's Office Supply at a 15% discount but would have to pay $20 to have the cabinet delivered. Where should you buy the filing cabinet?

13. Emerald, Inc., has a fleet of trucks. The company plans to purchase 100 truck tires. They can buy tires which are guaranteed for 25,000 miles for $240 each with a chain discount of 15%, 10%, and 2%; or they can buy tires which are guaranteed for 30,000 miles for $310 each with a discount of 20%, 2%. Which tires should they buy? (Find the cost per mile.)

INSTALLMENT LOANS

The American people spend great amounts of money for the privilege of buying on the installment plan. The Truth in Lending law, which became effective in 1968, makes it compulsory for the seller (or lender) to state the *exact cost* and *interest rate* the buyer (or borrower) is agreeing to pay.

Monthly interest rates charged by retailers and credit card agencies are usually 1% to 1-1/2% (or 12% to 18% a year). Interest rates often apply to the unpaid balance.

Example 3. If you buy, on the installment plan, a dryer selling for $150 and pay $25 down and six equal monthly payments of $21.90, what would be your total cost? The installment plan service charge? The interest rate?

1. Total cost = (6 × 21.90) + 25
2. Total cost = 131.40 + 25 = $156.40
3. Installment charge = Total cost − Cash price
4. Installment charge = 156.40 − 150 = $6.40
5. True Annual Interest Rate = $\dfrac{2 \times \text{Number of payments in a year} \times \text{Installment charge}}{\text{Amount of loan} \times (\text{Number of payments} + 1)}$
6. True Annual Interest Rate = $\dfrac{2 \times 12 \times 6.40}{(150 - 25) \times (6 + 1)}$ = 17.6% (rounded to the tenth of a percent)

Practice Problems 2. Find the installment charge rounded to the penny and the annual rate of interest rounded to the tenth of a percent in each of the following problems:

14. You decide to buy a chair which sells for $69 cash. If it is bought on the installment plan, the cost is $10.00 down and six monthly payments of $10.25. If you use the installment plan, what is the installment charge? What is the annual rate of interest you will pay? (*Ans.* $2.50; 14.5%)

15. Mrs. Anderson decided to buy an electric range which sells for $450 cash or $75 down and $18.60 a month for 24 months. What is the installment charge? What is the annual rate of interest?

16. Kim Yee purchased an oriental rug priced at $1,000. She paid $100 down and 12 monthly payments of $83.20. What did it cost her to buy on the installment plan? What annual rate of interest did she pay?

17. You buy a set of four new tires priced at $32.50 each, cash price. You will pay $11.75 per month for 12 months. What is the installment charge and the true annual rate of interest?

Example 4. Allison has a charge account at O'Hara's Department Store, which charges 1-1/2% per month on the unpaid balance of the account. If she pays off an account of $160 in six months, find the total interest. Determine her monthly payment if she makes six equal payments.

1. Total amount of interest = $\dfrac{\text{(Number of payments + 1)} \times \text{Amount of interest for first month}}{2}$

2. First find the amount of interest for one month:
   Interest = Principal × Rate × Time

3. P = 160
   R for one month = 1.5%
   T = one month

4. I = 160 × .015 × 1

5. I = $2.40 (interest for one month)

6. Total amount of interest = $\dfrac{(6+1)(2.40)}{2}$

7. Total amount of interest = $8.40

8. Monthly payments = (160 + 8.40) ÷ 6 = $28.07 (rounded to the penny)

Practice Problems 3. Solve the following installment problems. (Round your answers to the penny.)

18. How much total interest would Mr. Phillips pay if he borrowed $1,100 at 1% interest per month on the unpaid balance to be repaid in 12 equal monthly payments? What is his monthly payment? (*Ans.* $71.50; $97.63)

19. A tape deck may be purchased for $79.98 cash, or it may be purchased on the time plan at a monthly interest charge of 1-1/4% on the unpaid balance. If the tape deck is paid off in six equal monthly payments, what is the amount of the total interest? What is the monthly payment?

20. The Pied Piper borrowed $300 from the Ace Loan Company to buy a new flute. The loan company charged 2% interest per month on the unpaid balance. If the loan is paid off in nine equal monthly payments, how much is the total interest? What is the monthly payment?

21. Anne owed $220.20 on her credit card account. She is charged 1-1/2% interest on the unpaid balance. If Anne pays off her account in 10 equal monthly payments, how much total interest will she pay? What will be the amount of her monthly payment?

22. You purchase a diamond ring which costs $1,875 cash. If the ring is purchased on the time plan, monthly interest of 1-1/2% is charged on the unpaid balance. If the ring is paid off in 18 monthly payments, what is the total amount of interest that you will pay? What is your monthly payment?

REAL ESTATE—TAXES

Example 1. The Old Woman's shoe house has a real value of $32,000. Her property is assessed at 40% of its value, and her annual tax rate is $2.65 per C ($100). What is the amount of her real estate taxes?

1. To divide by 10, move the decimal one place to the left. To divide by 100, move the decimal two places to the left. 2.65 per C = .0265 per dollar
2. 32,000 × .0265 × 40% (or .4) = $339.20

Practice Problems 4. Calculate the following real estate taxes rounded to the penny:

23. The real value of Peter Rabbit's ranch house is $28,500. His property is assessed at 45% of its value, and his tax rate is $3.45 per C. How much real estate tax does Peter pay? (*Ans.* $442.46)

24. The Little Red Hen's chicken coop is assessed at $15,000. If she pays real estate taxes of $4.09 per C on the assessed value, what is the amount of her real estate tax?

25. Mr. Swanson's house has a real value of $38,500. His property is assessed at 50% of its value, and his tax rate is $4.00 per C. What is the amount of his real estate taxes?

26. Mr. and Mrs. Tompkins own a dry cleaning company. The building is assessed at $250,000, and their tax rate is $18.176 per $1,000. What is the amount of their tax?

27. The Brighton Local City School District has received a "yes" vote for 3.4 mills per one dollar of assessed valuation additional real estate tax. If Mr. Smith's home is assessed at $21,000, how much additional real estate tax will he pay for the school levy? *Note:* A mill equals a tenth of a cent. (21,000 × $.0034 = $71.40)

28. John Milligan's home has a real value of $42,500 and is assessed at 35% of the value for tax purposes. If the tax rate is $14.0554 per $100, how much does Mr. Milligan pay in taxes?

REAL ESTATE—TOTAL PRICE

Example 2. Joe Jackson wants to buy a new home and has $6,600 for the down payment. The bank will accept the down payment and will lend Joe the remaining 70% of the purchase price. What is the price of the house?

1. 30% of the purchase price = $6,600
2. 1% of the purchase price = $6,600 ÷ 30 = $220
3. $220 × 100 = $22,000

PRACTICAL PROBLEMS

29. John Jennings has the 35% down payment of $10,500 required to buy a condominium. What is the price of the condominium John wants to buy? (*Ans.* $30,000)

30. Ronald Lentz has the one-third down payment of $12,400 required to buy a duplex. What is the price of the duplex?

31. Leslie Hodges has the down payment of $7,150 required to buy a home. The $7,150 represents 20% of the total price. What is the price of the home Leslie wants to buy?

32. Kline, Inc., has $87,500 for the 25% down payment on an apartment house. What is the price of the apartment house?

PROFIT MARGIN ON SERVICES

Example. The Ace Contracting Company built a school building for $2.2 million. If the cost of building the school was $2.0 million, what rate of profit did Ace Contracting realize? Express your answer in percent form. (Round to the tenth of a percent.)

1. Price minus cost equals profit.
2. Profit divided by selling price equals rate of profit.
3. 2.2 M - 2.0 M = .2 M
4. .2 ÷ 2.2 = .0909 = 9.1% (rounded to the tenth of a percent)

Practice Problems 5.

33. The Forest Hills Contracting Co. built a new patio for Mr. and Mrs. Jamieson for $1,250. If the cost of building the patio was $975, what rate of profit did Forest Hills earn? Express the answer in percent form, rounded to the tenth of a percent. (*Ans.* 22.0%)

34. The Handy Plumbing Company repaired Mrs. Steiner's sink for $35.12. If the cost of the repair was $24.18, what was Handy's rate of profit?

35. Mrs. Watkins ordered a custom-made table pad from the Anson Table Pad Company and paid $104.13 for the pad. Anson's total cost for manufacturing and shipping the table pad and paying the salesman's commission was $80.10. What was the company's rate of profit?

36. The Home Siding Corporation charged Mr. O'Rourke $4,129.15 for installation of aluminum siding on his home. If the total cost to Home Siding for the manufacture and installation of the siding was $3,721.46, what was their rate of profit? Express your answer in percent form rounded to one decimal place.

37. Mr. and Mrs. Robertson paid $1,875.03 to have a new asphalt driveway put in by the Kantoski Construction Company. If the total cost to Kantoski Construction was $1,503.71, what was the rate of profit?

38. Miss McKinsey paid $2,495.17 to have her kitchen remodeled by Cozy Kitchen Decorators. If Cozy Kitchen's total cost for the remodeling was $2,206.31, what was the rate of profit?

STOCKS—DIVIDEND YIELD PER SHARE

The owners of a corporation may authorize the issuance of shares of stock. Each stockholder owns a share of the corporation. If a corporation has issued 100 shares of stock and you own one share, you have a 1% share of ownership in that corporation.

Example 1. The Cracking Cereal Company paid its stockholders an annual dividend per share of $1.45. Cracking's stock price per share is 23-1/4. What is the dividend yield per share? Express the answer in percent form, rounded to the tenth of a percent.

1. To find dividend yield per share, divide the annual dividend by the price per share of the stock. Usually, all other factors being equal, the higher the yield, the more desirable is the stock.
2. Stock prices are quoted with the cents shown as 1/8, 1/4, 3/8, 1/2, 5/8, 3/4, or 7/8.
3. 1/8 = $.125
   1/4 = .25
   3/8 = .375
   1/2 = .50
   5/8 = .625
   3/4 = .75
   7/8 = .875
4. 1.45 ÷ 23.25 = 6.2% rounded to the tenth of a percent

Practice Problems 6. Find the dividend yield per share on the following stocks (rounded to the tenth of a percent):

39. The Better Bottle Company paid an annual dividend of $3.25 per share. The stock sells for 31-1/8 per share. What is the dividend yield per share? (*Ans.* 10.4%)
40. Allen Company paid an annual dividend per share of $6.35. If the stock is selling for 90-1/8, what is the dividend yield per share?
41. The National Toy Company paid an annual dividend per share of $2.10. If the stock sells for 18-3/8, what is the dividend yield per share?
42. If Allied Chain, Inc., paid an annual dividend per share of $3.95 and the stock sells for 20-1/4 per share, what is the dividend yield per share?

STOCKS—PURCHASES

Example 2. You want to buy 25 shares of AB & C, Inc., stock for 51-1/2 per share. The broker's fee for this purchase is $34.25. How much will the stock and broker's fee cost you? Also, add one cent for every $300 for the SEC (Securities and Exchange Commission) fee.

1. (25 × 51.50) + 34.25 = $1,321.75
2. (1,321.75 ÷ 300) × .01 = $.04
3. 1,321.75 + .04 = $1,321.79

Practice Problems 7. Determine what you will pay for the stock, broker's fee, and SEC fee for the following stock purchases:

43. You wish to buy 50 shares of Chewy Chocolate Company stock which is selling for 15-1/8 (15.125) per share. The brokerage fee will be $30 (minimum charge). How much will you pay altogether? (*Ans.* $786.28)

44. Mr. Harper wants to buy 100 shares of Western Mining Company stock, which is selling at 40-1/2 per share. The broker's fee will be $71.60. What will be the cost of the stock, the broker's fee, and the SEC fee?

45. Mary Albertson plans to purchase 60 shares of Air Freight, Inc., stock at 17-3/4. The broker's commission will be 1-1/2% of the total stock price plus $15.50. How much will the stock, the broker's fee, and the SEC fee cost Mary?

46. The Willow City Investment Club plans to buy 300 shares of Fabric Mart, Inc., at 14-1/8 per share. The broker's fee is $44.50. What will the club pay for the stock purchase?

47. Mrs. McMillan is buying, for her grandson, 15 shares of Jackson Electronics stock at 67-1/2 per share. The broker's fee is 1.5% of the cost of the stock plus $15.50. How much will Mrs. McMillan pay for the stock plus the broker's fee and the SEC fee?

STOCKS—EARNINGS PER SHARE

The earnings per share of a company are the net income earned by the company for each share of stock. To find the earnings per share, divide the net income by the number of shares of stock.

Example 3. The net income of the Blue Bell Milk Company is $23,369,000. The company's stocks number 9,701,000. What are Blue Bell's earnings per share?

1. 23,369,000 ÷ 9,701,000 or, to simplify, divide first by 1,000.
2. 23,369 ÷ 9,701 = $2.41 (rounded to the penny).

48. The Apple Dumpling Corporation earned a net income of $16,274,000. The corporation has 9,443,000 shares of stock outstanding. What are Apple Dumpling's earnings per share? (*Ans.* $1.72)

49. The Jason Plastics Company earned a net income of $181,600,000. The company has 51,496,000 shares of stock outstanding. What are the earnings per share?

50. The American Industrial Company earned a net income of $31,914,000. The Company has 12,495,000 shares of stock outstanding. What are the earnings per share?
51. The Rest-Well Motel chain earned a net income of $13,255,000. Rest-Well has 9,041,000 shares of stock outstanding. What are the earnings per share?
52. The Lampert Seed Company earned a net income of $490,000 and has 761,340 shares of stock outstanding. What are the earnings per share?

STOCKS—CURRENT RATIO

Example 4. The current ratio of a company is its current assets (CA) divided by its current liabilities (CL) and indicates its ability to handle current debts. The Star Bright Company has current assets of $201,000,000. Its current liabilities amount to $81,000,000. What is the current ratio of Star Bright? (Round your answer to two decimal places. Since the answer will be a ratio, express your answer in relationship to 1.)

1. 201,000,000 ÷ 81,000,000 or to simplify, divide by 1,000,000 first.
2. 201 ÷ 81 = 2.48:1

53. What is the current ratio of the Everclean Detergent Company? Its current assets are $324,000,000, and its current liabilities are $198,000,000. (Express as a ratio in relationship to 1. Round the answer to two decimal places.) (*Ans.* 1.64:1)
54. Brandon, Inc., has current assets of $3,214,000 and has current liabilities of $2,115,000. What is the current ratio?
55. What is the current ratio of the Rockford Printing Corporation? Its current assets are $6,299,000 and its current liabilities are $3,577,000.
56. What is the current ratio of the Easton Housewares Corporation? Current assets amount to $25,391,000 and current liabilities are $5,914,000.
57. The Alton Steel Company has current assets of $961,478,000 and current liabilities of $325,731,000. What is the current ratio?

BONDS—MARKET VALUE

A bond is a certificate of indebtedness, issued by city, state, or federal governments, or by corporations, in exchange for needed funds. The bondholder is one who has lent such funds. The bond is for a specific amount of principal (face value) payable on the maturity date. The bond also states the amount or rate of interest. The face value is not necessarily the market value. Although bonds are issued in many denominations (such as $25, $1,000, $5,000, $100,000), market quotations are given on the basis of $100.

Example 1. The closing price of a corporate bond is quoted in the newspaper as 92-1/4. What is the market price of one of these bonds with a face value of $1,000?

1. $1,000 \div 100 = 10$
2. $92.25 \times 10 = \$922.50$
3. 92.25 per hundred = $922.50 per $1,000

---

58. What is the market value of a bond of $10,000 face value quoted at 102-1/8? (Remember that market quotations on bonds are given on a per-$100 basis.) (*Ans.* $10,212.50)

59. What is the market value of a bond of $5,000 face value quoted at 94-1/2?

60. What is the market value of two bonds of $1,000 face value each quoted at 97-5/8?

61. The Custom Corporation sold 100 bonds of $1,000 face value at 99-3/8. How much did the corporation receive?

62. Lemon Treet, Inc., sold five bonds of $100,000 face value at 95-7/8. How much did Lemon Treet, Inc., receive?

BONDS—INTEREST

Most bonds pay interest semiannually. The rate of the bond, however, is an *annual* rate. Therefore, the semiannual payment is for one-half the interest rate. There are two types of bonds: (1) negotiable bonds with the interest coupons attached, called *coupon bonds* or *bearer bonds;* (2) bonds without coupons, called *registered bonds*. These bonds are registered by the corporation or government which issued them. Interest payments are sent to the registered owner.

Example 2. Roger Peterson owns two coupon bonds, each of which has $1,000 face value with an interest rate of 5%. What is the amount of his semiannual interest?

$$(5\% \text{ or } .05 \div 2) \times 1,000 \times 2 = \$50.00$$

---

63. William Warren has 20 municipal bonds, each of which has a $5,000 face value with an interest rate of 7%. How much does he receive in interest at the end of six months? (*Ans.* $3,500)

64. The Jansen Corporation has $200,000 worth of bonds of $1,000 face value outstanding. The interest rate is 5-3/4% annually. How much interest must Jansen pay each six months?

65. The City of Anderson has $500,000 worth of bonds of $10,000 face value outstanding. The interest rate is 4-1/2% annually. How much interest does the city pay each six months?

66. Alicia Townsend has ten 6% corporate bonds of $1,000 face value each. How much semiannual interest does she receive?
67. Stanley Tompkins owns 32 bearer bonds, each of $1,000 face value and annual interest at 4-7/8%. How much interest does he receive *per year* on these bonds?

DEPRECIATION—STRAIGHT-LINE METHOD

To find annual depreciation by the straight-line method, subtract the salvage value of the item from the cost of the item. Then divide the difference by the estimated years of life of the item.

Example 1. The ABC Company's warehouse cost $251,290. The salvage value is $41,800. The estimated life of the warehouse is 40 years. What is the annual depreciation? (Round your answer to the dollar.)

1. Cost = $251,290
   Salvage value = $41,800
   Estimated life = 40 years
2. (251,290 - 41,800) ÷ 40 = $5,237.25

DEPRECIATION—SUM-OF-THE-DIGITS METHOD

Some assets, such as automobiles, depreciate very rapidly near the beginning of their useful life. The sum-of-the-digits method of depreciation provides for higher depreciation during the first years and lower depreciation in the later years of the life of the asset.

A series of fractions is formulated: the numerators are the useful years remaining in the life of the asset; the denominator is the total of these years.

Example 2. ABC Company purchased a company automobile for $6,200. It is estimated that the useful life will be four years and the salvage value will be $1,000. What is the amount of depreciation for each of the four years?

1. Cost - Salvage (resale value) = Amount to be depreciated
   6,200 - 1,000 = 5,200
2. The estimated life = 4 years. Therefore, the digit for the first year is the number of years to be depreciated: 4
3. The digit for the second year is the number of years remaining to be depreciated: 3
4. The digit for the third year is the number of years remaining to be depreciated: 2
5. The digit for the fourth year is the number of years remaining to be depreciated: 1
   Total 10

6. Form fractions using the total of the digits (10) as the denominator: 4/10, 3/10, 2/10, 1/10
7. To find the depreciation for each year, multiply the fraction times the amount to be depreciated (5,200).

   Depreciation first year = 4/10 × 5,200 = $2,080
   Depreciation second year = 3/10 × 5,200 = 1,560
   Depreciation third year = 2/10 × 5,200 = 1,040
   Depreciation fourth year = 1/10 × 5,200 =   520

8. Total depreciation = $5,200

DEPRECIATION—DECLINING BALANCE METHOD

The declining balance method offers the company using it the opportunity to take the largest amount of depreciation at the beginning years of life of the asset. Some assets, such as computers, lose much of their value early because of obsolescence.

In the declining balance method, only one fraction is formed, by using 1 as the numerator and the estimated number of years of life as the denominator. This fraction is then converted to a percent, or rate; e.g., if the estimated life is eight years, the rate would be 1/8, or 12.5% (or .125). The maximum rate that may be used is *twice* the rate of the straight-line method. Therefore, for each year of depreciation we will multiply by 2 × .125 for an asset with an estimated life of eight years. For an asset with an estimated life of five years, our rate would be 2 × 1/5, or 2 × 20% (or .20).

The amount to be multiplied for the first year is the *cost* of the asset (without deducting the salvage value). After the first amount of depreciation is calculated, this amount is subtracted from the *cost* of the asset. The second depreciation (2 × .125) is taken on the balance remaining after we subtract the year's depreciation from the cost of the asset. Each succeeding balance is multiplied by 2 × .125 until salvage value is reached as a remaining balance. Then no more depreciation may be taken.

In the sum-of-the-digits method we learned that a series of fractions is formed by using the sum of the years as the constant denominator, and the years remaining to be depreciated each time as the new numerator. The amount to be multiplied (the cost less the salvage value) remains the same for each year, but the fraction changes.

There are three differences between the sum-of-the-digits method and the declining balance method: (1) in the sum-of-the-digits method the amount to be depreciated remains the same in each calculation, while the fraction changes; in the declining balance method only one fraction is formed and the rate remains the same for each year's calculation, while the amount to be multiplied decreases after each year. (2) The sum-of-the-digits method multiplies the amount to be depreciated by only each succeeding fraction; in the declining balance method, we multiply by *twice* the constant rate each year. (3) In the sum-of-the-digits method, the amount we multiply by is the cost of the asset less its salvage value; in the declining balance method, we begin by

DEPRECIATION–DECLINING BALANCE METHOD

multiplying the *total cost* of the asset times twice the rate to find the amount of depreciation for the first year. Then we deduct this amount from the total cost of the asset and multiply twice the rate by the amount remaining to be depreciated, etc., until we reach the salvage value. After salvage value is reached, no further depreciation may be taken.

In the sum-of-the-digits method, the cost of the asset less the salvage value is depreciated totally, because the salvage value is deducted from the amount to be depreciated at the beginning; on the other hand, in the declining balance method, the salvage value is left at the end.

Example 3. Your company buys a forklift for $6,000 and expects it to have a useful life of eight years. The salvage value is estimated to be $900. Calculate the amount of depreciation for each year.

1. The maximum rate of depreciation will be 2 × (1 ÷ The expected years of life)

2. Rate of depreciation per year = 2 × (1/8) = 2 × 12.5%, down to the salvage value of $900

3. For the first year
   2 × .125 × 6,000 = 1,500
   6,000 - 1,500 = 4,500

4. For the second year
   2 × .125 × 4,500 = 1,125
   4,500 - 1,125 = 3,375

5. For the third year
   2 × .125 × 3,375 = 843.75
   3,375 - 843.75 = 2,531.25

6. For the fourth year
   2 × .125 × 2,531.25 = 632.81
   2,531.25 - 632.81 = 1,898.44

7. For the fifth year
   2 × .125 × 1,898.44 = 474.61
   1,898.44 - 474.61 = 1,423.83

8. For the sixth year
   2 × .125 × 1,423.83 = 355.96
   1,423.83 - 355.96 = 1,067.87

9. For the seventh year we have only $1,067.87 left. We can take depreciation down to $900 (salvage value).
   1,067.87 - 900 = 167.87 = the amount of depreciation for the seventh year

10. For the eighth year we can take no depreciation, since our balance is the salvage value of $900.

Year	Rate of Depreciation (%)	Remaining Cost ($)	Depreciation for Year ($)	Balance After Depreciation ($)
1	2 × 12.5 ×	6,000	1,500	4,500
2	2 × 12.5 ×	4,500	1,125	3,375
3	2 × 12.5 ×	3,375	843.75	2,531.25
4	2 × 12.5 ×	2,531.25	632.81	1,898.44
5	2 × 12.5 ×	1,898.44	474.61	1,423.83
6	2 × 12.5 ×	1,423.83	355.96	1,067.87
7	2 × 12.5 ×	1,067.87	167.87	900
	($1,067.87 less $900 salvage value leaves $167.87 for the seventh year depreciation and nothing for the eighth year)			
8		900	0	900

Practice Problems 8. Calculate the following depreciation problems using (a) the straight-line method, (b) the sum-of-the-digits method, and (c) the declining balance method (at two times the rate). (Round your answers to the penny.)

68. An automobile cost $5,325. The salvage value is $500, and the estimated life is six years. What is the depreciation?
    Ans. Straight-line method, $804.17 per year
    Sum-of-the-digits method:

    $1,378.57   First year
    1,148.81   Second year
    919.05   Third year
    689.29   Fourth year
    459.52   Fifth year
    229.76   Sixth year

    Declining balance method:
    (using the rate of .16667 rounded to five decimal places)

    $1,775.04   First year
    1,183.35   Second year
    788.89   Third year
    525.92   Fourth year
    350.61   Fifth year
    201.19   (leaving $500 balance) Sixth year

69. The ABC Company bought a truck for $6,500. The salvage value is estimated to be $1,000, and the estimated useful life is four years. What is the depreciation?

70. A rubber company purchased a new banbury for $130,000. The salvage value is $16,000, and the estimated useful life is 20 years. What is the depreciation?

71. The Caston Insurance Agency purchased a new IBM typewriter for $565. The salvage value is $105, and the estimated useful life is five years. What is the depreciation?

72. A rubber company purchased a new tire curing mold for $50,000. The expected useful life is 30 years, and the salvage value is $6,500. What is the depreciation?

73. A sales organization purchased several new office desks for $325 each. The salvage value is $40 and the expected life is 15 years. What is the depreciation?

UNIT PRICES

Example. The Sparkling Costume Shop wants to purchase 170 inches of metallic lace. The price is $2.98 per yard. How much will the lace cost?

1. 36 inches = 1 yard
2. (170 ÷ 36) × 2.98 = $14.07

Note: If your calculator has a re-entry feature, be sure to take advantage of it. Most electronic calculators make it possible to re-enter your last amount by depressing the next function key, thus making it unnecessary to re-enter an intermediate answer on the keyboard.

1. Enter 170 on the keyboard.
2. Depress ÷ .
3. Enter 36 on the keyboard.
4. Depress = .
5. Answer, 4.7222, will show on the tape or the display.
6. Depress × .
7. The 4.7222 will now be entered as your new multiplier for your second part of the problem.
8. Enter 2.98 on the keyboard.
9. Depress = .
10. Your answer is $14.07 (rounded to the penny).

74. The Apple Strudel Bakery orders 76 pints of apples. The apples cost $9.50 per bushel. How much will the apples cost? *Note:* There are 64 pints in a bushel.

$$(76 \div 64) \times 9.50 = \$11.28$$

75. You want to carpet the living room and the bedroom in your apartment with carpeting that costs $7.29 per square yard. If your living room is 21 × 16 feet and the bedroom is 19 × 15 feet, how much will the carpeting cost? *Note:* Nine square feet equals one square yard.

$$[(7.29 \times 21 \times 16) + (7.29 \times 19 \times 15)] \div 9 =$$

PRACTICAL PROBLEMS

76. Janet wants to have her foyer and kitchen tiled. The tile is $9.95 per square yard. Her foyer is 8 X 8 feet, and her kitchen is 12 X 9 feet. How much will the tile cost?

77. How many square feet are there in a rug which is 48 inches by 72 inches? *Note:* Divide by 144 to find *square* feet.

78. How much would it cost to buy 100,000 sheets of mimeograph paper which costs $1.51 per ream? *Note:* One ream is 500 sheets.

$$(100{,}000 \div 500) \times 1.51 =$$

79. How much would you have to pay for 168 stencils if they sell for $18.95 per quire? *Note:* There are 24 in a quire.

80. How much would 168 #2 pencils cost if they sell for $.49 per dozen?

81. How much would you pay for 720 pieces of chalk if the chalk costs $1.56 per gross? *Note:* A gross is 12 dozen (144).

82. How much will it cost to buy three bushels of tomatoes if they sell for $2.50 per peck? *Note:* There are four pecks in a bushel.

$$3 \times 4 \times 2.50 =$$

83. How much will the DeWitt Pickle Plant pay for 96 barrels of vinegar which sells for $1.19 per gallon? *Note:* There are 31-1/2 gallons to a barrel.

$$96 \times 31.5 \times 1.19 =$$

84. How much will the Fireside Restaurant pay for 168 pounds of potatoes if they cost $4.00 per Cwt (hundred pounds)?

85. An advertising firm will print a safety slogan on your company pencils for $18.00 per thousand. How much will it cost to print 3,610?

86. A box of fancy chocolates sells for $2.75 for a 12-ounce box. How much is this candy per pound? *Note:* There are 16 ounces in a pound.

$$(2.75 \div 12) \times 16 =$$

BASIC STATISTICS

Example 1. Arithmetic Mean

An arithmetic mean is one form of averaging. It is found by adding the individual values and dividing this sum by the number of values. If you earned grades of 88, 90, 85, 76, and 92 on your history tests, what is your mean score?

1. Mean score = Sum of the values ÷ Number of values
2. $(88 + 90 + 85 + 76 + 92) \div 5 = 86.2$

Example 2. Median

The median is another form of averaging. It is found by arranging a series of values in order from highest to lowest or from lowest to highest and then counting to find the middle value. The median is often a more meaningful statistic than the mean because one unusually high item can make the mean much higher than the median for the same array of values.

The following array is the annual salaries of employees in the Marketing Division given in *rank order*, from highest to lowest:

Manager	$40,000
Assistant Manager	25,100
Salesman A	18,000
Salesman B	17,500
Salesman C	17,000
Salesman D	16,800
Salesman E	16,400 ←
Order Analyst	14,000
Secretary A	8,200
Secretary B	8,000
Typist	6,200
Teletype Operator	6,150
Telephone Operator	6,000

What is the median salary (the one which is at the midpoint of the list which has been placed in rank order)?

1. The array has 13 items. The seventh one is the midpoint.
2. When we count down seven or count up seven, we are at $16,400.

Example 3. Median

The following array contains an even number of values. In order to find the midpoint of an even-numbered array, find the two items in the middle and average them.

Salesmen	Annual Sales ($)	
Coe	1,105,320	
Fisher	1,000,500	
Jesko	1,000,000	
Longshore	950,000	⟩ 925,000
Ponder	900,000	
Rucker	890,000	
Stewart	800,000	
Willis	754,800	

1. This array has eight values. The midpoint is between the fourth and the fifth value.
2. Average the fourth and the fifth value.

$$(950{,}000 + 900{,}000) \div 2 = 925{,}000$$

3. The midpoint (median) is $925,000.

GROUPED DATA

The methods of determining the mean and the median which you have just read work well for small groups of data. However, for a large number of items, the grouping of values is a more efficient method to use in analyzing data.

Example 4. For insurance purposes your company wants to analyze the ages of its employees. Group the following 30 employees into five classes and find the mean of the ages.

18	50	55	46	64	30
35	62	58	60	57	36
27	44	24	59	52	35
21	25	53	61	20	56
48	19	39	48	41	26

1. Find the oldest and the youngest employee (64 and 18).
2. Find the difference of these two numbers (the range):

$$64 - 18 = 46$$

3. Divide this difference by the number of classes you want. Five would be an appropriate choice for these data.

$$46 \div 5 = 9.2$$

4. Round to the next whole number (10).
5. Start at your lowest number and add 10 to find your first class interval.

$$18 + 10 = 28$$

Your lowest class interval will be 18 up to 28.

6. Therefore, 28 will be the beginning of your next class interval.

$$28 + 10 = 38$$

Your next class interval will be 28 up to 38.

7. Your third class interval will be 38 to 48.
8. Your fourth class interval will be 48 to 58.
9. Your fifth (highest) class interval will be 58 to 68.

Class Intervals	Tally
58 up to 68	||||	
48 up to 58	|||| |||
38 up to 48	||||
28 up to 38	||||
18 up to 28	|||| |||

10. Look at your raw data and tally the number of employees in each age group. We find that there are 6 employees in the first class, 8 employees in the second, 4 in the third, 4 in the fourth, and 8 in the fifth class.

11. Find the midpoint in each class by dividing by 2 the sum of the upper and the lower limit:

$$(58 + 68) \div 2 = 63$$
$$(48 + 58) \div 2 = 53$$
$$(38 + 48) \div 2 = 43$$
$$(28 + 38) \div 2 = 33$$
$$(18 + 28) \div 2 = 23$$

12. Then multiply the midpoint times the frequency in order to find the value of each class: (6 × 63 = 378, etc.)

Age Intervals	Frequency	Midpoint	Product
58 up to 68	6	63	378
48 up to 58	8	53	424
38 up to 48	4	43	172
28 up to 38	4	33	132
18 up to 28	8	23	184
			1,290

13. We can find the mean by dividing the total product by our number of values (30).

$$1,290 \div 30 = 43$$

The mean is 43.

Example 5. Mode

The mode is the value occurring most frequently in an array of values.

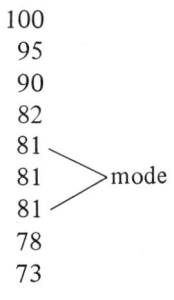

100
95
90
82
81
81 ⟩ mode
81
78
73

Practice Problems 9. Solve the following statistics problems. (Round your answers to two decimal places.)

87. The history scores of a class of 400 totaled 34,000. What was the mean score of this class? (*Ans.* 85)

88. The following array gives the monthly salaries of employees in the Tire Foam division:

Becker, Ralph	$892
Conti, Allen	870
Harmon, Peter	845
Jenkins, Samuel	839
Landers, Joseph	839
Miller, Michael	839
Satyshur, Leon	776
Schuck, Randolph	750
Trevillion, Henry	749

Determine the mean, the median, and the mode.

89. The following array gives the hourly wages for eight employees of El Bistro Restaurant:

Name	Hourly Rate ($)
Arrington, B.	7.84
Calhoun, A.	7.26
DiSalvo, C.	7.05
Gartner, P.	6.91
Haylett, J.	6.57
Leiby, E.	6.48
Strong, W.	6.10
Unger, R.	5.80

Find the mean and the median.

90. The following list shows the heights of the members of a basketball team.

Becker	6'8"
Kulscar	6'5"
Modari	6'4"
Zimmerman	6'3"
Azar	6'2"

What is the mean height? What is the median height?

91. The employees in the Data Processing department received the following monthly increases in salaries:

Lipps, Elsie	$85
Irven, Ronald	75
Imes, Dan	72
Woods, Nancy	69
Sliman, Fred	67
Castle, Alice	65
Harlin, Ray	65
Potter, Allen	60
Crenshaw, John	58
Lehrman, Walter	45
DiDonato, Sally	40

Determine the mean, the median, and the mode.

92. The Order department of Lanchester Tools, Inc., received the following total monthly orders (in dollars):

	Carbide Cutting Tools	Steel Cutting Tools	Grinding Tools	Throw-Away Inserts	Special Orders	Total
Jan.	25,010	23,929	15,904	18,929	7,500	_____
Feb.	23,049	19,677	16,544	12,867	10,900	_____
March	18,331	20,426	13,480	10,985	11,804	_____
April	27,656	22,223	14,807	15,784	11,065	_____
May	26,132	18,704	14,674	14,632	8,942	_____
June	26,090	18,702	14,050	16,390	9,370	_____
Total	_____	_____	_____	_____	_____	======

Find the mean for each month's orders:

Month	Mean Orders
(a) January	_____
(b) February	_____
(c) March	_____
(d) April	_____
(e) May	_____
(f) June	_____

Find the mean orders for each type of tool:

Tool	Mean Orders
(g) Carbide	_____
(h) Steel	_____
(i) Grinding	_____
(j) Throw-away	_____
(k) Special	_____

Find the mean of orders for *all* types of tools for the six-month period. _____ (ℓ)

93. Last year your monthly electric bills were as follows:

January	$14.81
February	13.92
March	13.86
April	13.07
May	12.99
June	10.54
July	14.86
August	15.97
September	13.28
October	12.88
November	13.75
December	14.60

What was the mean average of your monthly electric bills?

TRAVEL—MILES PER GALLON AND MILES PER HOUR

Example 1. On a round trip from Atlanta, Georgia, to Boston, Massachusetts (1,103 miles one way), 160 gallons of gasoline at 67.9 cents per gallon were consumed. How much did you spend for gasoline (rounded to the penny)? How many miles per gallon did you average (rounded to one decimal place)?

1. 160 × .679 = $108.64 spent for gasoline
2. (1,103 × 2) ÷ 160 = 13.78 or 13.8 (rounded to one decimal) miles per gallon

Practice Problems 10.

94. On a round trip from Cleveland to Detroit (170 miles one way), you bought 18.5 gallons of gasoline at 72.2 cents per gallon. How much did you spend for gasoline? How many miles per gallon did you average? (*Ans.* $13.36; 18.4)

95. On a one-way drive from New York, New York, to Dallas, Texas (1,632 miles one way), you bought 95.5 gallons of gasoline at 73.8 cents per gallon. How much did you spend for gasoline? How many miles per gallon did you average?

96. On a one-way trip from Chicago to New Orleans (957 miles one way), you purchased 55.5 gallons of gasoline at 68.9 cents per gallon. How much did you spend for gasoline? How many miles per gallon did you average?

97. On a round trip from Pittsburgh to St. Louis (602 miles one way), you purchased 41 gallons of gasoline at 72.9 cents per gallon. How much did you spend for gasoline? How many miles per gallon did you average?

98. On a round trip from Salt Lake City to Denver (518 miles one way), you purchased 49.5 gallons of gasoline at 75.9 cents per gallon. How much did you spend for gasoline? How many miles per gallon did you average?

Example 2. On a one-way trip from Philadelphia to Atlanta, you were on the road for a total of 17-1/2 hours. The distance is 797 miles. How many miles per hour did you average?

$$797 \div 17.5 = 45.5 \text{ miles per hour}$$

Practice Problems 11.

99. On a one-way trip from Dallas to Seattle (2,225 miles one way), you were on the road 9-1/2 hours the first day, 9-1/2 hours the second day, 13 hours the third day, and 12 hours the fourth day. How many miles per hour did you average?

100. On a one-way trip from Washington, D.C., to Tampa, Florida (1,186 miles one way), you drove for 10-1/2 hours the first day, 9-1/2 hours the second day, and 7-1/2 hours the third day. How many miles per hour did you average?

101. On a round trip from Detroit to Baltimore, Maryland (509 miles one way), you drove 8 hours the first day of travel and 5-1/4 hours the second day. On the third travel day you drove for 10 hours, and the fourth travel day you drove 2-1/2 hours. How many miles per hour did you average on the trip?

102. On a cross-country trip, your odometer reading was 23,109.1 when you left Chicago and was 25,321.4 when you arrived in San Francisco. Along the way you purchased the following gallons of gasoline: 20, 23.1, 17.4, 21.3, 22.2, 15, 16.1, and 14.9. How many miles per gallon did you average?

103. On a recent trip your odometer reading was 37,451.8 when you left Los Angeles and was 38,631.3 when you reached Seattle. You used the following gallons of gas: 20.2, 17.6, 13.4, 9.1. How many miles per gallon did you average?

TRAVEL–AIR

104. It is approximately 541 miles from St. Louis to Cleveland one way. If a round-trip coach-class airline ticket costs $124, how much per mile does this flight cost? (Round your answer to the penny.) (*Ans.* $124 ÷ (541 × 2) = 11 cents)

105. It is approximately 1,370 miles from Denver to Cleveland one way. If a round-trip first-class airline ticket costs $342, how much per mile does this flight cost?

106. It is approximately 346 miles from Cincinnati to St. Louis one way. If a round-trip coach-class airline ticket costs $72, how much per mile does this flight cost?

MONETARY EXCHANGE

Example 1. One British pound sterling will exchange for approximately $1.75. While you're in London, you see an antique grandfather clock that you like. The clock is priced at £240 (pounds). How much is this in U.S. currency? (Round your answer to the penny.)

$$240 \times 1.75 = \$420$$

248   PRACTICAL PROBLEMS

Example 2. Before leaving for England, you exchange $200 for British pounds. How many pounds will you receive? (Round your answer to the pound.)

200 ÷ 1.75 = £114 (rounded to the pound)

Practice Problems 12. Compute the following exchange problems, rounding your answers to the penny in U.S. currency, or to the unit in the foreign currencies.

107. Your lodging in Devonshire, England, is £10 per day. How much is this in U.S. dollars? (*Ans.* $17.50)

108. Your meals in Devonshire are averaging £4 a day. How much is this in U.S. dollars?

109. While in England, you spend £30 for transportation. How much is this in dollars?

110. When you are ready to leave England, you have £6 left. How much will you receive when you exchange this for U.S. dollars?

111. The Swiss franc will exchange for approximately 41-1/2 cents. While shopping in Switzerland, you see a watch that sells for 105 francs. How much is this in U.S. dollars?

112. In Switzerland you buy a ski sweater for 32 francs. How much is this in U.S. dollars?

113. You buy a ticket for a short train trip in Switzerland for 4 francs. How much is this in U.S. dollars?

114. When you leave Switzerland, you exchange 48 francs for U.S. currency. How much do you receive?

115. Before you go to West Germany, you purchase $150 worth of marks, which are worth approximately 43 cents each. How many marks do you receive?

116. You buy a cuckoo clock in the Black Forest for 51 marks. How much is this in U.S. currency?

117. You purchase a pair of binoculars in West Germany for 150 marks. How much is this in U.S. dollars?

118. When you are ready to leave Germany, you exchange 110 marks for dollars. How much do you receive?

119. Before your trip to Mexico, you buy $225 worth of pesos. A peso is worth approximately $.051. How many pesos do you receive?

120. In Mexico you buy a poncho for 300 pesos and a handmade leather belt for 120 pesos. How much did you spend in U.S. dollars?

121. When you leave Mexico, you exchange 990 pesos for U.S. currency. How much will you receive?

MEASURE AND COST

122. Mrs. Jackson wants to make a woolen pants suit. She needs 4-1/8 yd. of woolen fabric @ $9.59 per yd., 2-1/8 yd. of lining fabric @ $2.29 per yd., one zipper @

$.89, two spools of thread @ $.25, one package of seam binding @ $.59, and one card of buttons @ $1.30. How much will the fabric and other items cost her?

123. A Model 33 TWX can transmit messages at 100 words per minute. Your office transmits sales orders, which total about 18,500 words each day. It costs 38 cents per minute to transmit to your plant. How many minutes per day do you transmit? How much will it cost per month (20 working days per month)?

124. A real estate developer is planning to subdivide some lake-front property into lake-front lots. The property measures two miles of lake frontage. Each lot will measure 160 ft. of lake frontage and will sell for $8,200. How many lots will the developer have, and how much money will he receive from the sale of the lots? (A mile contains 5,280 feet.)

INVENTORY VALUATION

The following information is part of an inventory of the Tasty Supermarket. Figure the value of the inventory based on unit price. Multiply the number of cases times the number of items in a case times the price per unit.

125.

	Item	Cases in Stock	No. Items per Case	Price per Unit ($)	Inventory Valuation ($)
(a)	Asparagas, 14-1/2 oz. can	5	24	.67	80.40
(b)	French style green beans, 12 oz. can	10	24	.35	_____
(c)	Great Northern beans, 3 lb. jar	3	4	1.13	_____
(d)	Lima beans, 14 oz. can	9	24	.49	_____
(e)	Lima beans, 17 oz. can	6	12	.53	_____
(f)	Red kidney beans, 15-1/2 oz. can	11	24	.35	_____
(g)	Shelled beans, 16 oz. can	8	12	.37	_____
(h)	Whole green beans, 15-1/2 oz. can	6	24	.33	_____
(i)	Wax beans, 16 oz. can	4	12	.43	_____
(j)	Sliced beets, 14 oz. can	7	24	.35	_____
(k)	Whole beets, 16 oz. can	6	24	.49	_____
(l)	Mexican corn, 12 oz. can	8	24	.45	_____
(m)	White corn, 17 oz. can	12	12	.37	_____
(n)	Mushrooms, 4 oz. can	13	36	.69	_____
(o)	Peas, 14-1/2 oz. can	7	24	.45	_____
(p)	Peas, 17 oz. can	6	12	.33	_____
(q)	Spinach, 12-1/2 oz. can	5	24	.35	_____
(r)	Total				======

INCOME STATEMENTS

Professional people, such as physicians, dentists, and attorneys, as well as companies, often prepare income statements. An income statement deducts expenses from income and shows profit for a certain period of time, such as a month, a quarter, or a year.

Example 1. Alfred Morris, D.D.S., had the following income for the month of June: dental practice, $4,960; honorarium for a speech at a professional meeting, $100. His expenses for June were as follows: rent, $325; salaries and benefits—office staff, $1,732; utilities, $68; dental and office supplies, $251; miscellaneous expenses, $67. What was Dr. Morris's net profit for June?

1. For a service organization, use this formula:

   Income - Expenses = Net profit

2. Income $4,960
             100
           $5,060

3. Expenses $ 325
              1,732
                 68
                251
                 67
             $2,443

4. 5,060 - 2,443 = $2,617
5. Net profit = $2,617

Example 2. The Bristol Toy Company had sales of $1,526,800 for the year with sales returns of $2,500. Calculate its gross profit, its expenses, and its net profit for the year, using the following information: cost of goods sold, $703,400; salaries and employee benefits, $37,590; rent, $12,250; utilities, $5,750; insurance, $850; advertising, $2,500; other expense, $3,095.

1. For a manufacturing concern, use this formula:

   Sales - Cost of goods sold = Gross profit - Expenses = Net profit

2. Sales = 1,526,800 - 2,500 = 1,524,300
   Cost of goods sold = 703,400
   Gross profit = 1,524,300 - 703,400 = 820,900

3. Gross profit - Expenses = Net profit
   Expenses = 37,590 + 12,250 + 5,750 + 850 + 2,500 + 3,095 = 62,035

4. 820,900 - 62,035 = $758,865 Net profit

THE BRISTOL TOY COMPANY
INCOME STATEMENT
FOR THE YEAR ENDED DECEMBER 31, 19---

Sales		$1,526,800
Less sales returns		2,500
Net Sales		$1,524,300
Cost of goods sold		703,400
Gross profit		$ 820,900
Operating Expenses:		
Salaries and benefits	$37,590	
Rent	12,250	
Utilities	5,750	
Insurance	850	
Advertising	2,500	
Other expense	3,095	
Total operating expenses		62,035
Net profit for the year		$ 758,865

Practice Problems 13. Find the net profit for each of the following problems:

126. For the first quarter the Smith, Smith, and Smith law firm received $38,500 in fees. The firm had the following expenses: salaries and benefits, $3,900; rent, $1,850; utilities, $479; insurance, $65; office supplies, $350; other expense, $1,254.

127. James Bradshaw, C.P.A., had the following income for the month of March: income tax preparations, $2,540; clients' fees, $879. His expenses were as follows: rent, $460; utilities, $75; office supplies and postage, $124; secretary's salary and benefits, $890; miscellaneous expense, $205.

128. R.A. Winters, M.D., a radiologist, had income of $75,250 for the year. His expenses were as follows: salaries and employee benefits, $17,250; rent, $9,580; utilities, $1,950; insurance, $2,800; office and medical supplies, $1,950; other expense, $2,030.

129. Ethel's Dress Shop had sales of $5,859.25 last month. Cost of goods sold was $2,604.89. The expenses were rent, $225.00; utilities, $60.28; salaries and commissions, $1,280.40; supplies, $35.81; insurance, $28.52; advertising, $49.30; other expense, $79.44.

130. Cranston Chemicals, Inc., had sales of $1,250,429 for the year. Cost of goods sold was $691,566. Operating expenses were salaries and benefits, $65,691; real estate taxes, $4,200; utilities, $2,291; advertising, $3,490; property insurance, $324; other expense, $1,284.

131. English Imports, Ltd., had sales of $86,735 for last month. The cost of goods sold was $50,386. Expenses were as follows: salaries and benefits, $9,425; real

estate taxes, $360; utilities, $5,946; selling expense, $4,105; advertising, $1,525; other expense, $859.

DECISION PROBLEM

Quantity Pricing

Your company manufactures items such as tool holders, cutting blades, and inserts. It costs you more per piece to make a small quantity than to make several of the same pieces at one time. For example, set-up time is about the same whether you make 10, 50, or 100. Therefore, you charge less for quantity purchases. The following formula is used to establish your company's cost for producing one item:

$$\left[\left(\left(\frac{T}{Q}\right) + T_1\right) \times H\right] + (M \times 1.4) = \text{Cost Price}$$

T = the total set-up time—the time it takes to get the materials ready to run and to set up the machines

T_1 = total run time—the length of time it takes the machines to do such operations as squaring the metal, putting in the pockets, and drilling and tapping the tool

Q = quantity—number of tools being made on one run

H = hourly rate—including the machine operator, packing and shipping staff, and other factory personnel involved in manufacturing the pieces

M = material cost for one item—cost of metal and other raw materials

1.4 = overhead costs, utilities, sales people, order entry personnel, data processing, scrapped metal, etc.

Calculate the cost price for manufacturing an insert in quantities of 10, 25, 50, and 100. Add 10% of the cost price for profit. Give the selling price (cost price plus 10%) per tool for quantities of 10, 25, 50, and 100.

Tool	T (hours)	T_1 (hours)	Q	M ($)	H ($)
Insert	1.19	.131	10	1.94	18
Insert	1.19	.131	25	1.94	18
Insert	1.19	.131	50	1.94	18
Insert	1.19	.131	100	1.94	18

Using the formula will give you the cost price of one insert made in these four quantities. Add 10% of the cost price to each of your four cost answers. Your four final answers will give you the price for which you should sell the inserts in each of the four quantities.

(a) Price per insert in quantities of 10 = $_____

(b) Price per insert in quantities of 25 = $_____

(c) Price per insert in quantities of 50 = $_____

(d) Price per insert in quantities of 100 = $_____

REVIEW QUIZ 5

(Round your answers to two decimal places.)

1. Last week Thomas McKinley worked a total of 40 hours Monday through Friday. On Saturday he worked an additional 8 hours; and on Sunday he worked an additional 4 hours. His rate is $6.39 per hour. He receives time and a half for hours over 40 and double time for hours worked on Sunday. What were his gross wages?

2. Thomas McKinley had the following deductions from last week's gross pay: FICA, 5.85%; federal income tax, $21.00; city tax, 1/2%; state tax, 1-1/2%; union dues, $3; thrift plan, $20.00. What were his net wages? (You calculated his gross wages in problem 1.)

3. Mr. and Mrs. Robertson's home is insured for $38,500. They pay 45 cents a year per $100 of insurance. What is their annual premium?

4. Find the maturity date and the maturity value of a promissory note for $850 plus interest at 7-1/2%, dated June 1, which is due 30 days from the date of issue.

5. Find the proceeds of the note in problem 4, which was discounted 10 days before the maturity date at a discount rate of 6-1/2%.

6. Mrs. Temple bought a new range for $785. She paid $300 down and made 12 monthly payments of $50 each. How much more than the list price is she paying? What percent is the interest of the list price?

7. If you buy a vacuum cleaner for $149.95 and pay $26 down and six equal monthly payments of $21.20, what would be your total cost? What is the installment plan service charge? What is the true annual interest rate?

8. The Lancaster school district passed a school levy for 2.5 mills per one dollar of assessed valuation additional real estate tax. If the Morgans' house is assessed at $18,500, how much additional real estate tax will the Morgans pay?

9. The net income for Bartletts, Inc., is $21,911,000. The company's shares of stock number 8,651,000. What are Bartletts' earnings per share?

10. Randal Corporation sold 10 bonds of $5,000 face value at 98-5/8. How much did they receive?

Sample Examination

You may want to be timed as you try the Unit 5 Sample Examination, which is presented in the Introduction.

Unit 6

The International System of Units (SI)

TOUCH SYSTEM REVIEW

Be sure to keep your index finger, your middle finger, and your ring finger on the home row (4, 5, and 6). For the left hand, keep your ring finger, your middle finger and your index finger on the 4, 5, and 6.

555	445	556	556	665	644	464	565	656	646
666	445	554	665	556	464	465	465	465	465
444	444	666	555	444	555	456	456	456	654
444	456	456	654	654	456	445	554	664	665
666	464	565	646	565	656	444	555	666	555
444	454	464	454	646	455	445	556	665	554
666	455	456	654	654	456	444	555	666	666
555	465	454	655	465	456	465	564	564	564
666	666	444	555	666	666	456	664	565	656
555	666	555	444	555	666	445	456	654	654
5,661	4,960	5,170	5,838	5,870	5,474	4,529	5,390	6,021	6,079
456	654	222	111	333	222	111	333	333	222
465	444	233	233	322	322	122	122	132	132
654	564	123	132	132	123	132	231	113	131
556	656	123	132	123	132	123	321	221	331
666	654	123	321	321	321	123	123	321	121
456	444	133	123	123	123	333	123	212	313
555	654	333	123	111	222	113	111	311	121
465	444	311	222	311	113	222	113	322	333
565	654	111	311	333	333	133	111	132	231
456	554	223	222	122	322	213	211	123	132
5,294	5,722	1,935	1,930	2,231	2,233	1,625	1,799	2,220	2,067

Are your fingers curved over the home row? Do not lift your hand away from the keyboard. Keep your fingers hovering over the home row.

111	123	333	331	789	789	789	789	789	789
121	222	112	111	999	887	777	888	999	888
123	113	123	313	778	997	778	997	998	887
331	232	221	221	788	887	788	789	879	997
132	331	333	111	777	999	888	987	978	798
313	222	321	231	788	888	987	888	777	879
232	132	112	321	799	887	999	887	778	888
111	321	331	113	999	798	777	799	889	887
231	113	333	123	789	799	998	999	777	998
132	221	123	221	998	777	987	998	889	888
1,837	2,030	2,342	2,096	8,504	8,708	8,768	9,021	8,753	8,899

Are you keeping your head turned toward your copy? Do not turn your head to look at your keys. If you must look, turn your eyes only. Keep your head turned toward your copy if you want to attain speed and accuracy.

778	889	998	877	788	899	300	200	100	200
789	798	789	978	798	978	600	208	102	208
979	798	988	997	879	978	900	206	103	202
777	789	778	888	798	778	200	204	109	205
789	887	978	887	879	978	400	202	106	209
987	887	799	997	788	877	100	101	105	201
998	888	779	977	889	997	800	203	104	203
778	778	999	997	877	888	500	205	101	207
789	889	978	888	879	798	700	209	107	206
987	798	779	887	877	977	100	207	108	204
8,651	8,401	8,865	9,373	8,452	9,148	4,600	1,945	1,045	2,045

Don't lift your hand away from the keyboard! Are you getting the right answers? Are you keeping your head turned toward the copy? Can you find the keys without looking? Don't lose valuable time.

300	400	1.00	3.30	3.07	4.06	5.10	6.09	8.02	8.05
308	406	1.09	4.40	3.05	4.09	5.08	7.02	7.04	8.09
305	402	1.07	8.80	3.02	4.05	5.05	6.05	7.05	9.02
302	409	1.05	6.60	3.08	4.03	5.03	6.04	7.09	8.08
303	407	1.03	2.20	3.06	4.08	5.06	6.08	8.01	8.04
309	405	1.02	5.50	3.09	4.07	5.04	6.06	7.03	8.03
301	401	1.08	9.90	3.03	4.04	5.09	6.01	7.08	8.07
404	403	1.01	7.70	3.04	5.02	6.02	7.10	7.06	8.10
306	404	1.04	1.01	4.02	4.10	5.07	6.03	7.10	8.06
307	408	1.06	1.10	4.01	5.01	6.01	6.07	7.07	9.01
3,145	4,045	10.45	50.51	32.47	42.55	52.55	62.55	72.55	82.55

The forthcoming metric system will change many of the terms of measure which we are accustomed to using. For example, if Miss America's measurements in inches are 38-25-36, her approximate measurements in metric terms will be 95-62.5-90 centimeters. One inch is equal to approximately 2-1/2 centimeters. Multiply the number of inches times 2.5.

A man six feet tall (72 inches) will measure about 180 centimeters. What is your height in centimeters? (Multiply your height in inches times 2.5.)

A speed limit of 50 miles per hour will be approximately 80 kilometers per hour. A mile is about 1.6 kilometers. What are the kilometers per hour of a 35-mile speed zone? (Multiply 35 times 1.6.)

A pound is roughly 1/2 kilogram. A woman weighing 120 pounds weighs approximately 60 kilograms. How much do you weigh in kilograms?

An ounce is approximately 28 grams. How many grams does a quarter-pound hamburger weigh? (Multiply 4 ounces times 28.) How many grams are there in a one-pound box of chocolates?

A gallon is about 3.8 liters. How many liters does a 20-gallon gasoline tank hold? (Multiply 20 times 3.8.) How many liters does a 16-gallon gasoline tank hold?

The United States is the last major industrial country in the world to adopt the metric system as its standard of measurement. Americans will have to learn to use the metric system. It takes a while to get used to thinking in metrics, but actually metrics are far easier to work with than the English system of feet and inches, pounds and ounces, and gallons and pints. Every measure in metrics is in terms of 10s, 100s, or 1,000s, which means that mathematical calculations are far easier than calculations in the English measurement system. In the metric system, measurements can be made in tenths rather than in fractions, such as 1/4 and 5/8. A Metrics Conversion list is given in Appendix E.

PREFIXES

The three basic measurements are grams (weight), meters (length), and liters (volume). Learn by heart the following prefixes, which are most commonly used:

    centi- 1/100
    milli-   1/1,000
    kilo-   1,000

These prefixes mean the same for all three metric measurements; for example,

    a centigram is 1/100th of a gram
    a milligram is 1/1000th of a gram
    a kilogram is 1,000 grams

    a centimeter is 1/100th of a meter
    a millimeter is 1/1000th of a meter
    a kilometer is 1,000 meters

a centiliter is 1/100th of a liter
a milliliter is 1/1000th of a liter
a kiloliter is 1,000 liters.

To express this in another way,

there are 100 centigrams in a gram
there are 1,000 milligrams in a gram
there are 1,000 grams in a kilogram

there are 100 centimeters in a meter
there are 1,000 millimeters in a meter
there are 1,000 meters in a kilometer

there are 100 centiliters in a liter
there are 1,000 milliliters in a liter
there are 1,000 liters in a kiloliter.

ABBREVIATIONS

centigram (cg)   centimeter (cm)   centiliter (cl)
milligram (mg)   millimeter (mm)   milliliter (ml)
kilogram (kg)   kilometer (km)   kiloliter (kl)
gram (g)   meter (m)   liter (ℓ)

METRIC WEIGHT

The following comparisons will aid you in understanding the relative weights:

There are approximately 28 grams in an ounce.
There are about 2.2 pounds in a kilogram.
One short ton (2,000 pounds) is a little less than a metric ton.
Milligrams are very tiny amounts used to measure such quantities as those in vitamin capsules.

Converting Metric to Metric Weight

Since metric units of measurement are based on multiples of 10, it is not difficult to convert one metric weight to another.

We know that to multiply by 10, we merely move the decimal one place to the *right*.

$$3 \times 10 = 3.0 \ (30)$$

To multiply by 100, we move the decimal two places to the right.

$$3 \times 100 = 3.00 \ (300)$$

To multiply by 1,000, we move the decimal three places to the right.

$$3 \times 1,000 = 3.000 \ (3,000)$$

THE INTERNATIONAL SYSTEM OF UNITS (SI)

Also, to divide by 10, we move the decimal one place to the *left*.

$$3 \div 10 = 3. \ (.3)$$

To divide by 100, we move the decimal two places to the left.

$$3 \div 100 = 03. \ (.03)$$

To divide by 1,000, we move the decimal three places to the left.

$$3 \div 1,000 = 003. \ (.003)$$

The principle is the same when converting grams to kilograms, or kilograms to grams. When the conversion factor is 1,000, we move the decimal point three places. We know that a kilogram is 1,000 times as large as a gram. In other words, a gram is only 1/1000 of a kilogram. To convert a *smaller* measure (gram) to the larger measure (kilogram), move the decimal three places to the *left*.

$$525 \text{ grams} = 525. \ (.525) \text{ kilograms}$$

To convert a *larger* measure (kilogram) to a smaller measure (gram), move the decimal three places to the *right*.

$$314 \text{ kilograms} = 314.000. \ (314,000) \text{ grams}$$

Since there are 1,000 kilograms in a metric ton, we can convert in the same way by moving the decimal three places.

$$757 \text{ kilograms} = 757 \text{ metric tons}$$
$$1.946 \text{ metric tons} = 1,946. \text{ kilograms}$$

Make the following conversions:

Grams to Kilograms

(Remember: Move the decimal three places to the *left*.)

Practice Problems 1.

1. 397 g =	.397 kg	11. 26,895 g =		kg
2. 12 g =	kg	12. 42 g =		kg
3. 1,467 g =	kg	13. 775 g =		kg
4. 283.6 g =	kg	14. 3,046 g =		kg
5. 25.73 g =	kg	15. 1,000 g =		kg
6. 13 g =	kg	16. 259 g =		kg
7. 961 g =	kg	17. 104,096 g =		kg
8. 29 g =	kg	18. 12,704 g =		kg
9. 14,291 g =	kg	19. 30 g =		kg
10. 756 g =	kg	20. 300 g =		kg

Kilograms to Grams

(Remember: Move the decimal three places to the *right*.)

Practice Problems 2.

21.	1.4 kg =	1,400 g	31.	12 kg =	g
22.	30.96 kg =	g	32.	14.06 kg =	g
23.	1,041 kg =	g	33.	2.93 kg =	g
24.	.26 kg =	g	34.	.54 kg =	g
25.	1.479 kg =	g	35.	.054 kg =	g
26.	.06 kg =	g	36.	.0054 kg =	g
27.	.006 kg =	g	37.	1.72 kg =	g
28.	.0006 kg =	g	38.	526.97 kg =	g
29.	20,093 kg =	g	39.	74.1 kg =	g
30.	14.97 kg =	g	40.	18 kg =	g

Centigrams to Grams

Remember: There are 100 centigrams in a gram. To convert grams to centigrams, move the decimal two places to the right. To convert centigrams to grams, move the decimal two places to the left. 100 cg = 1 g

Practice Problems 3.

41.	100 cg =	1 g	51.	24,000 cg =	g
42.	10 cg =	g	52.	2,400 cg =	g
43.	1 cg =	g	53.	240 cg =	g
44.	1,000 cg =	g	54.	24 cg =	g
45.	50.6 cg =	g	55.	2.4 cg =	g
46.	61,934 cg =	g	56.	100,000 cg =	g
47.	.03 cg =	g	57.	7,306 cg =	g
48.	.3 cg =	g	58.	291 cg =	g
49.	3 cg =	g	59.	.23 cg =	g
50.	3.3 cg =	g	60.	.02 cg =	g

THE INTERNATIONAL SYSTEM OF UNITS (SI)

Grams to Centigrams

Remember: Move the decimal two places to the right. 1 g = 100 cg

Practice Problems 4.

61. .3 g = 30 cg
62. 3 g = ___ cg
63. 30 g = ___ cg
64. 300 g = ___ cg
65. 3,000 g = ___ cg
66. 2.1 g = ___ cg
67. 18.6 g = ___ cg
68. .497 g = ___ cg
69. 8.164 g = ___ cg
70. .07 g = ___ cg
71. .007 g = ___ cg
72. .0007 g = ___ cg
73. .364 g = ___ cg
74. 55 g = ___ cg
75. 5.5 g = ___ cg
76. 48.6 g = ___ cg
77. 6.911 g = ___ cg
78. .542 g = ___ cg
79. .061 g = ___ cg
80. .099 g = ___ cg

Milligrams to Centigrams and Grams

Remember: There are 1,000 milligrams in a gram. There are 100 centigrams in a gram. Therefore, there are 10 milligrams in a centigram. To convert milligrams to centigrams, move the decimal one place to the left. To convert centigrams to grams, move the decimal two places to the left. To convert milligrams to grams, move the decimal three places to the left.

Practice Problems 5.

81. 1,000 mg = 100 cg = 1 g
82. 22,130 mg = ___ cg = ___ g
83. 576 mg = ___ cg = ___ g
84. 38 mg = ___ cg = ___ g
85. 4 mg = ___ cg = ___ g
86. 2 mg = ___ cg = ___ g
87. 22 mg = ___ cg = ___ g
88. 222 mg = ___ cg = ___ g
89. 2,222 mg = ___ cg = ___ g
90. 22,222 mg = ___ cg = ___ g
91. 222,222 mg = ___ cg = ___ g
92. 2,222,222 mg = ___ cg = ___ g
93. 3,900 mg = ___ cg = ___ g
94. 476 mg = ___ cg = ___ g
95. 89,213 mg = ___ cg = ___ g
96. 16 mg = ___ cg = ___ g
97. 6 mg = ___ cg = ___ g
98. .6 mg = ___ cg = ___ g
99. .66 mg = ___ cg = ___ g
100. .666 mg = ___ cg = ___ g

Grams to Centigrams to Milligrams

Remember: Move the decimal two places to the right to convert grams to centigrams. Move the decimal one place to the right to convert centigrams to milligrams.

Practice Problems 6.

101. 1 g = 100 cg = 1,000 mg
102. 27 g = cg = mg
103. 270 g = cg = mg
104. 2,700 g = cg = mg
105. 2.7 g = cg = mg
106. .27 g = cg = mg
107. .027 g = cg = mg
108. .0027 g = cg = mg
109. 3,420 g = cg = mg
110. 967 g = cg = mg
111. 24 g = cg = mg
112. 5 g = cg = mg
113. 8.6 g = cg = mg
114. 8.76 g = cg = mg
115. .768 g = cg = mg
116. .0768 g = cg = mg
117. .00768 g = cg = mg
118. 19 g = cg = mg
119. 24 g = cg = mg
120. 2.9 g = cg = mg

Converting Kilograms to Metric Tons

Remember that 1,000 kg = 1 t. To convert a *smaller* measure (kg) to a larger measure (t), move your decimal to the left. To convert kg to t, move the decimal three places to the left. 1,000 kg = 1 t

Practice Problems 7.

121. 24,000 kg = 24 t
122. 2,400 kg = t
123. 240 kg = t
124. 24 kg = t
125. 2.4 kg = t
126. .24 kg = t
127. .02 kg = t
128. 674,000 kg = t
129. 1,296,311 kg = t
130. 359,707 kg = t
131. 27,396,000 kg = t
132. 83.1 kg = t
133. 961.8 kg = t
134. 31.55 kg = t
135. 86.1111 kg = t
136. 29 kg = t
137. 580 kg = t
138. 1,690 kg = t
139. 25,000 kg = t
140. 3,864 kg = t

THE INTERNATIONAL SYSTEM OF UNITS (SI)

Converting Metric Tons to Kilograms

Remember: Move the decimal three places to the right when converting t (larger measure) to kg (smaller measure). 1 t = 1,000 kg

Practice Problems 8.

141. 240 t =	240,000 kg	151. 6.45 t =		kg
142. 24 t =	kg	152. .82 t =		kg
143. 2.4 t =	kg	153. .961 t =		kg
144. .24 t =	kg	154. .0473 t =		kg
145. .025 t =	kg	155. .4062 t =		kg
146. .0025 t =	kg	156. .0041 t =		kg
147. 3,791 t =	kg	157. .00041 t =		kg
148. 26,897 t =	kg	158. 36.8 t =		kg
149. 841 t =	kg	159. 2.74 t =		kg
150. 43 t =	kg	160. 19.6 t =		kg

Below is a list of the metric measurements of weight. Grams, kilograms, and metric tons are the units of measure most often used.

Units smaller than a gram:

$$1,000 \text{ milligrams (mg)} = 1 \text{ gram (g)}$$
$$100 \text{ centigrams (cg)} = 1 \text{ gram (g)}$$
$$10 \text{ decigrams (dg)} = 1 \text{ gram (g)}$$

Units larger than a gram:

$$1 \text{ decagram (dkg)} = 10 \text{ grams (g)}$$
$$1 \text{ hectogram (hg)} = 100 \text{ grams (g)}$$
$$1 \text{ kilogram (kg)} = 1,000 \text{ grams (g)}$$
$$1,000 \text{ kilograms (kg)} = 1 \text{ metric ton (t)} = 1,000,000 \text{ grams (g)}$$

Metric Weight Problems

Example 1. 3.61 kg + 246 g =

Method one:
1. Convert grams to kilograms.
2. 246 g = .246 kg (Since kg are 1,000 times as large as a gram, we move the decimal three places to the left to go from the smaller measure to the larger measure.)

METRIC WEIGHT 263

3. 3.61 kg
    .246 kg

    3.856 kg

Method two:
1. Convert kilograms to grams.
2. 3.61 kg = 3,610 g (Since g are 1,000 times smaller than kg, we move the decimal three places to the right to go from the larger measure (kg) to the smaller measure (g).)
3. 3,610 g
     246 g

    3,856 g

Practice Problems 9. Do the following practice problems. Give the answer in both kg and g.

1. 2.93 kg + 54 g = 2.984 kg or 2,984 g   3. 34.1 kg + 879.6 g =
2. 16.83 kg + 28.4 g =   4. 906.32 kg + 306.4 g =
                    5. 18.9 kg + 12.3 g =

Example 2. Add 251 kg and 4.13 t. Give answers in both kg and t.

Method one:
1. Convert kg to t.
2. 251 kg = .251 t (Since 1 t = 1,000 kg, we move the decimal three places to the left to convert from the smaller measure (kg) to the larger measure (t).)
3. .251 t
    4.13 t

    4.381 t

Method two:
1. Convert t to kg.
2. 4.13 t = 4,130 kg (Since 1 t = 1,000 kg, we move the decimal three places to the right to convert from the larger measure (t) to the smaller measure (kg).)
3. 251 kg
    4,130 kg

    4,381 kg

Practice Problems 10. Do the following practice problems. Give answers in both kg and t.

6. 193.1 kg + 34.1 t =   8. 907.3 kg + 8.21 t =
7. 46 kg + 30.6 t =   9. 24.3 kg + 8.21 t =
                    10. 18 kg + 21.7 t =

Example 3. Add 3.81 g and 340 mg.

Method one:
1. Convert g to mg.
2. 3.81 g = 3,810 mg (Since 1 g = 1,000 mg, we move the decimal three places to the right to convert from the larger measure (g) to the smaller measure (mg).)
3. 3,810 mg
   <u> 340 mg</u>
   4,150 mg

Method two:
1. Convert mg to g.
2. 340 mg = .340 g (Since 1 g = 1,000 mg, we move the decimal three places to the left to convert from the smaller measure (mg) to the larger measure (g).)
3. 3.81 g
   <u> .34 g</u>
   4.15 g

Practice Problems 11. Do the following practice problems. Give answers in both g and mg.

11. 5.13 g + 187.2 mg =   13. 3.78 g + 26 mg =

12. .941 g + 604 mg =   14. .81 g + 397 mg =

15. 2.06 g + 1,485 mg =

Example 4. A box of currants weighs 312 grams and sells for 90 cents. A smaller box weighs 105 grams and sells for 36 cents. Which is the better buy?

1. 90 ÷ 312 = .288 cents per gram
2. 36 ÷ 105 = .342 cents per gram
3. The larger box is the more economical.

Practice Problems 12. Do the following practice problems:

16. A box of salt weighs 737 g and costs 11 cents. A package of six small boxes of salt, each weighing 33 g, costs 29 cents. How much does the large box cost per gram? How much does the package of six cost per gram?

17. A jar of grated cheese costs 88 cents and weighs 119 g. A larger jar weighs 302 g and costs $2.62. Which costs less per g?

18. A box of soda crackers weighs 454 g and costs 59 cents. A smaller box weighs 221 g and costs 29 cents. How much does each box cost per gram of soda crackers?

19. A can of salmon weighs 439 g and costs $1.95. A smaller can weighs 201 g and costs 99 cents. How much per g does each can of salmon cost?

20. A box of oatmeal weighs 540 g and costs 67 cents. A carton containing six packages of oatmeal, each weighing 36 g, costs 59 cents. How much does the box of oatmeal cost per gram? How much does the carton of six packages cost per gram?

Example 5. 2.81 kg - 261 g =

1. Convert kg to g.
2. 2.81 kg = 2,810 g
3. 2,810 g
   -261 g
   ―――――
   2,549 g or 2.549 kg

Practice Problems 13. Do the following practice problems. Give answers in both g and kg.

21. 13.94 kg - 871 g = 13.069 kg or 13,069 g   23. 1.5 kg - 29.4 g =
22. 1,329 g - .45 kg =   24. 141,629 g - 81.4 kg =
                  25. 2.49 kg - 18 g =

Example 6. 4.16 t - 248 kg =

1. Convert t to kg.
2. 4.16 t = 4,160 kg
   Since 1 t = 1,000 kg, we move three places to the right to convert from the larger measure (t) to the smaller measure (kg).
3. 4,160 kg
   -248 kg
   ―――――
   3,912 kg or 3.912 t

Practice Problems 14. Do the following practice problems. Give answers both in kg and in metric tons (t).

26. 4.16 t - 248 kg =   28. .875 t - 28.6 kg =
27. 29.17 t - 460 kg =   29. 28,600 kg - .97 t =
                  30. 13,742 kg - 1.86 t =

Example 7. 3.93 g - 151 mg =

1. Convert grams (g) to milligrams (mg).
2. 3.93 g = 3,930 mg
3. 3,930 mg
   -151 mg
   ―――――
   3,779 mg or 3.779 g

Practice Problems 15. Do the following practice problems. Give the answers in both g and mg.

31. 2.95 g - 158 mg =   33. 6.77 g - 18.54 mg =
32. 14.86 g - 219.4 mg =   34. 21,400 mg - 7.4 g =
              35. 18,605 mg - .648 g =

METRIC LENGTH

A unit of metric length is the meter, which is about 39.37 inches, or a little over a yard. A centimeter is 1/100 of a meter; a millimeter is 1/1000 of a meter; a kilometer is 1,000 meters. There are 100 centimeters in a meter, and there are 1,000 millimeters in a meter. A thousand meters equals one kilometer. A kilometer is about .6 mile. There are about 2-1/2 centimeters (cm) in an inch. A foot is about 30 centimeters.

Since there are 10 millimeters (mm) in a centimeter (cm), 2 cm 3 mm can be read as 2.3 cm. Each millimeter is a tenth of a centimeter. A meter stick, which is about 39.37 inches long, is divided into 100 parts, each of which is one cm long.

Converting Metric Length

Converting Centimeters to Meters

Remember: One meter equals 100 centimeters. In converting from a smaller unit of measure (cm) to a larger unit of measure (m), move the decimal to the left. 100 cm = 1.00. (1 m). To convert cm to m, move the decimal two places to the left.

Practice Problems 16. Make the following conversions:

1. 291 cm =   2.91 m   6. 600 cm =   m
2. 12.24 cm =   m   7. 6,000 cm =   m
3. 8,691 cm =   m   8. 60,000 cm =   m
4. 6 cm =   m   9. 109.46 cm =   m
5. 60 cm =   m   10. 8.6114 cm =   m

To convert m to cm, move the decimal two places to the right. Make the following conversions:

11. 2 m =   200 cm   16. .0203 m =   cm
12. 20 m =   cm   17. 4.6 m =   cm
13. 200 m =   cm   18. 37.55 m =   cm
14. .2 m =   cm   19. .8694 m =   cm
15. .220 m =   cm   20. .08694 m =   cm

METRIC LENGTH

Converting Millimeters to Centimeters

There are 10 mm in a cm. To convert mm to cm, move the decimal one place to the left.

Practice Problems 17.

21. 1,000 mm =   100 cm   26. 9,761 mm =   cm
22. 10,000 mm =   cm   27. 28,755 mm =   cm
23. 100,000 mm =   cm   28. 389.7 mm =   cm
24. 100 mm =   cm   29. 53,718 mm =   cm
25. 10 mm =   cm   30. .468 mm =   cm

Converting Centimeters to Millimeters

There are 10 mm in a cm. To convert cm to mm, move the decimal one place to the right.

31. 1 cm =   10 mm   36. 279.3 cm =   mm
32. 10 cm =   mm   37. 20,104 cm =   mm
33. 100 cm =   mm   38. .65 cm =   mm
34. 29.4 cm =   mm   39. .065 cm =   mm
35. 1.7 cm =   mm   40. 7.6 cm =   mm

Converting Meters to Millimeters

Remember: There are 1,000 mm in one m. To convert from a larger measure (m) to a smaller measure (mm), move the decimal to the right. To convert m to mm, move the decimal three places to the right.

Practice Problems 18.

41. 1 m =   1,000 mm   46. .0223 m =   mm
42. 10 m =   mm   47. .00223 m =   mm
43. 100 m =   mm   48. 46.8 m =   mm
44. .1 m =   mm   49. 9.84 m =   mm
45. .223 m =   mm   50. 5.5 m =   mm

Converting Millimeters to Meters

Move the decimal three places to the left. 1,000 mm = 1.000 (1 m)

51. 54,921 mm =   54.921 m   53. 10 mm =   m
52. 1,000 mm =   m   54. 100 mm =   m

55. 1 mm =	m	58. 4,201 mm =	m
56. 281,392 mm =	m	59. 376.4 mm =	m
57. 55,601 mm =	m	60. 77.945 mm =	m

Metric Length Problems

Example 1. 3 m 47 cm = 347 cm
            4 m 87 cm = 487 cm
                       834 cm or 8.34 m

Example 2. 3 m 47 cm = 3.47 m
            4 m 87 cm = 4.87 m
                       8.34 m or 834 cm

Example 3. 3 m   47 cm
            4 m   87 cm
            7 m 134 cm = 8.34 m or 834 cm or 8 m 34 cm
            Remember: 100 cm = 1 m

Practice Problems 19. Add the following problems and express the answer in m and cm; for example, 8 m 34 cm.

61. 7 m 21 cm + 3 m 38 cm =   66. 5 m 89 cm + 2.6 m 14 cm =
62. 14.1 m 18 cm + 2 m 96 cm =   67. 6.5 m 20 cm + 3.1 m 15 cm =
63. 2.1 m 12 cm + 4.6 m 56 cm =   68. .7 m 81 cm + .4964 cm =
64. 3.6 m 4.6 cm + 18 m 7.5 cm =   69. 1.4 m 91 cm + 2.1 m 17 cm =
65. 12.71 m 3.8 cm + 5 m 27 cm =   70. 2.6 m 35 cm + 4.2 m 91.4 cm =

Example 4. 4 m 12 cm - 2 m 47 cm =

1. Since we cannot subtract 47 from 12, we must borrow one from the meters and convert it to centimeters, then add it to the 12 cm.

2. 4 m 12 cm = 3 m 112 cm
              -2 m 47 cm
               1 m 65 cm

Practice Problems 20. Subtract the following and express the difference in m and cm; for example, 3.1 m 19.6 cm or 3 m 29.6 cm.

71. 12.6 m 14 cm - 8.1 m 26 cm = 4 m 38 cm
72. 184 m 90 cm - 89 m 46 cm =
73. 45.67 m 14.5 cm - 32.7 m 12.4 cm =
74. 4.68 m 18.3 cm - 3.4 m 12.7 cm =

75. 18.7 m 29.4 cm - 14.6 m 13.5 cm =

76. 2,901 m 86.4 cm - 1,040 m 29 cm =

77. 4.68 m 37.8 cm - 2.46 m 19.7 cm =

78. 27.36 m 71.4 cm - 13.4 m 81.7 cm =

79. 16 m 22 cm - 13 m 17 cm =

80. 6.7 m 18 cm - 1.4 m 3 cm =

Converting Meters to Kilometers

Remember 1,000 m equals 1 km. A kilometer is about .6 mile. To convert a smaller unit of measure (m) to a larger unit of measure (km), move the decimal to the left. 1,000 m = 1,000. (1 km)

Practice Problems 21.

81. 1,000 m =   km   86. 2,491 m =   km
82. 10,000 m =   km   87. 18,697 m =   km
83. 100,000 m =   km   88. 2,401.36 m =   km
84. 100 m =   km   89. 897.5 m =   km
85. 10 m =   km   90. 3,694.7 m =   km

Converting Kilometers to Meters

Remember: 1 km = 1,000 m. Move the decimal three places to the right. 1.000, km = 1,000 m

91. 1 km =   1,000 m   96. .29 km =   m
92. 10 km =   m   97. 3.6 km =   m
93. 100 km =   m   98. .064 km =   m
94. 1,000 km =   m   99. .007 km =   m
95. .1 km =   m   100. 99.4 km =   m

Problems with Kilometers and Meters

Express answers in km and m, then just in km, then just in m.

Example 1. 30 km 19 m + 18.6 km 94 m =

1. 30   km 19 m
   18.6 km 94 m
   ─────────────
   48.6 km 113 m = 48.6 km + .113 km = 48.713 km

2. 48.6 km 113 m = 48,600 m + 113 m = 48,713 m

Practice Problems 22.

101. 2 km 19 m + 4 km 21 m = 6 km 40 m; 6.040 km; 6,040 m
102. 18 km 205 m + 6 km 700 m =
103. 4.6 km 230 m + 2.5 km 107 m =
104. 8.04 km 104 m + 2.07 km 30 m =
105. 9 km 18.7 m + 8 km 20.7 m =
106. .9 km 309 m + .6 km 206 m =
107. 1.3 km 146.1 m + 2.8 km 397.7 m =
108. 26 km 904 m + 13 km 507 m =
109. 4.2 km 371 m + 6.1 km 309 m =
110. 6 km 22 m + 7.3 km 861 m =

Example 2. 4.2 km 206 m - 2.1 km 391 m =

1. Since we cannot subtract 391 from 206 m, convert 1 km to 1,000 m, or convert the .2 km to 200 m.

2. 3.2 km 1,206 m   or   4.0 km 406 m
    -2.1 km   391 m   -2.1 km 391 m
    ─────────────   ─────────────
    1.1 km   815 m   1.9 km 15 m or 1 km 915 m

Practice Problems 23. Do the following practice problems in subtraction. Show the answers in km and m, as shown in the example.

111. 8.1 km 407 m - 5.2 km 505 m =
112. 2.3 km 596 m - 1.2 km 87 m =
113. 1 km 886 m - 993 m =
114. 6.74 km 29 m - 4.6 km 18 m =
115. 18.9 km 555 m - 14.8 km 604 m =
116. 4.1 km 807 m - 2.1 km 309 m =
117. .86 km 20 m - .4 km 18.4 m =
118. 14.33 km 901 m - 2.3 km 806.1 m =
119. 3.09 km 207 m - 1.21 km 426 m =
120. 5 km 937 m - 4 km 786.4 m =

Example 3. 37 m 29 cm ÷ 3 =

1. Convert dividend to cm.

2. Remember that 1 m = 100 cm.
3. 37 m 29 cm = 3,729 cm
4. 3,729 cm ÷ 3 = 1,243 cm or 12 m 43 cm or 12.43 m

Practice Problems 24. Do the following division problems and express your answers in m. (Round your answers to four decimal places.)

121. 6 m 84 cm ÷ 4 =
122. 3 m 54 cm ÷ 2.5 =
123. 1 m 90 cm ÷ 3.6 =
124. 2.1 m 46 cm ÷ 6 =
125. 4.6 m 81 cm ÷ 2 =

126. .7 m 10 cm ÷ 2.1 =
127. 3.91 m 18 cm ÷ 5 =
128. 8.01 m 90.6 cm ÷ 13.1 =
129. 19 m 31 cm ÷ 4.7 =
130. 2.7 m 58.1 cm ÷ 2.2 =

Below is a list of the metric measurements of length. Meters, kilometers, centimeters, and millimeters are the units of measure most often used.

Units smaller than a meter:

$$1{,}000 \text{ millimeters (mm)} = 1 \text{ meter (m)}$$
$$100 \text{ centimeters (cm)} = 1 \text{ meter (m)}$$
$$10 \text{ decimeters (dm)} = 1 \text{ meter (m)}$$

Units larger than a meter:

$$1 \text{ decameter (dkm)} = 10 \text{ meters (m)}$$
$$1 \text{ hectometer (hm)} = 100 \text{ meters (m)}$$
$$1 \text{ kilometer (km)} = 1{,}000 \text{ meters (m)}$$

METRIC AREA

A square centimeter (cm^2) is a square that is one cm wide and one cm long. It takes a little more than 6 cm^2 to make one square inch. Amounts to be squared must be in the same metric unit.

Example 1. 2 cm × 3 cm = 6 cm^2

Practice Problems 25. Find the cm^2 for the following areas. (Round your answers to four decimal places.)

1. 34.1 cm × 19.6 cm =
2. 1.9 cm × 2.74 cm =
3. 26.3 cm × 4.1 cm =
4. .9 cm × .81 cm =
5. 2.04 cm × 3.86 cm =

6. 14.5 cm × 5 cm =
7. 9.4 cm × .6 cm =
8. 8.7 cm × .475 cm =
9. 1.054 cm × 2.074 cm =
10. 54 cm × 26.1 cm =

Example 2. 3.4 m × 8.1 m = 27.54 m²

A square meter is the length of an area in meters times the width in meters.

Practice Problems 26. Find the m² for the following. (Round your answers to four decimal places.)

11. 13.1 m × 4.6 m =
12. 29 m × 14.8 m =
13. 204 m × 609 m =
14. 19.6 m × 14.5 m =
15. 1,031 m × 598 m =

16. .9 m × .4 m =
17. 6.8 m × 4.3 m =
18. 15.14 m × 11.61 m =
19. 7.7 m × 5.4 m =
20. 20.4 m × 17.6 m =

Example 3. If mixed units are given, the units must be converted to the same unit of measure.

1. 20 m 88 cm × 15 m 19 cm =
2. Convert to meters.
   20 m 88 cm = 20.88 m
   15 m 19 cm = 15.19 m
3. 20.88 m × 15.19 m = 317.1672 m²

Practice Problems 27. Convert the following to meters; then determine the m². (Round to four decimal places.)

21. 18 m 29 cm × 14 m 13 cm =   m²
22. 2.1 m 80 cm × 1.4 m 29 cm =   m²
23. 4.6 m 15 cm × 2.1 m 40 cm =   m²
24. 209 m 90 cm × 106 m 13 cm =   m²
25. 5.7 m 40 cm × 4.7 m 51 cm =   m²
26. 10 m 81 cm × 8.8 m 12 cm =   m²
27. 15 m 24 cm × 13 m 18.6 cm =   m²
28. 30 m 91 cm × 21 m 56 cm =   m²
29. 4.1 m 29 cm × 3.8 m 76 cm =   m²
30. 3.6 m 50 cm × 2.6 m 50 cm =   m²

Determine the following in km². (Round your answers to four decimal places.)

31. 21 km × 18 km =   km²   33. 10.6 km × 8.4 km =   km²
32. 1.4 km × 1.1 km =   km²   34. 6.7 km × 4.91 km =   km²

METRIC AREA 273

35. 3.92 km × 2.86 km =   km²
36. 55.1 km × 46 km =   km²
37. 20.6 km × 17.75 km =   km²
38. 12.41 km × 9.64 km =   km²
39. 4.9 km × 3.8 km =   km²
40. 7.77 km × 5.68 km =   km²

Converting Square Centimeters to Square Meters

We know that a meter is 100 centimeters. A square meter is

$$100 \text{ cm} \times 100 \text{ cm} = 10,000 \text{ cm}^2$$
$$10,000 \text{ cm}^2 = 1 \text{ m}^2$$

To convert centimeters to meters, we move the decimal two places to the left. To convert *square* centimeters to *square* meters, we must move the decimal *four* places to the left.

Practice Problems 28. Convert the following cm² to m²:

41. 10,000 cm² = 1 m²
42. 25,000 cm² =   m²
43. 3,400,900 cm² =   m²
44. 126,942 cm² =   m²
45. 19,775 cm² =   m²
46. 407,583 cm² =   m²
47. 1,874 cm² =   m²
48. 91,765 cm² =   m²
49. 911,766 cm² =   m²
50. 4,007,601 cm² =   m²

Converting Square Meters to Square Centimeters

To convert a meter to centimeters, we move the decimal two places to the right. To convert a *square* meter to a *square* centimeter, move the decimal *four* places to the right.

$$1 \text{ m} = 1.00\text{\textasciicaron} \text{ cm}$$
$$1 \text{ m}^2 = 100 \text{ cm} \times 100 \text{ cm} = 10,000 \text{ cm}^2$$
$$(1.0000\text{\textasciicaron} \text{ cm}^2)$$

Practice Problems 29. Convert the following m² to cm²:

51. 1 m² = 10,000 cm²
52. 15 m² =   cm²
53. 3.9 m² =   cm²
54. 201 m² =   cm²
55. 804.7 m² =   cm²
56. 8,715 m² =   cm²
57. 204 m² =   cm²
58. 21 m² =   cm²
59. 8.6 m² =   cm²
60. .4 m² =   cm²

Converting Square Meters to Square Kilometers

We know that one km equals 1,000 m. To convert meters to kilometers, move the decimal three places to the left.

THE INTERNATIONAL SYSTEM OF UNITS (SI)

$$1{,}000 \text{ m} = 1{,}000\text{. km}$$

We also know that $1{,}000 \text{ m} \times 1{,}000 \text{ m} = 1 \text{ km}^2$

$$1{,}000{,}000 \text{ m}^2 = 1 \text{ km}^2$$

Move the decimal *six* places to the left to convert square meters to square kilometers.

$$1{,}000{,}000.$$

Practice Problems 30. Convert the following m² to km²:

61. $1{,}000{,}000 \text{ m}^2 = $ 1 km²
62. $2{,}500{,}000 \text{ m}^2 = $ _____ km²
63. $250{,}000 \text{ m}^2 = $ _____ km²
64. $25{,}000 \text{ m}^2 = $ _____ km²
65. $2{,}500 \text{ m}^2 = $ _____ km²
66. $109{,}643 \text{ m}^2 = $ _____ km²
67. $3{,}060{,}491 \text{ m}^2 = $ _____ km²
68. $64{,}197{,}555 \text{ m}^2 = $ _____ km²
69. $6{,}875{,}333 \text{ m}^2 = $ _____ km²
70. $907{,}544 \text{ m}^2 = $ _____ km²

Converting Square Kilometers to Square Meters

To convert square kilometers to square meters, move the decimal *six* places to the right.

$$1{,}000 \text{ m} \times 1{,}000 \text{ m} = 1 \text{ km}^2$$
$$1{,}000{,}000 \text{ m}^2 = 1 \text{ km}^2$$

Practice Problems 31. Convert the following km² to m²:

71. $1 \text{ km}^2 = $ 1,000,000 m²
72. $29 \text{ km}^2 = $ _____ m²
73. $.76 \text{ km}^2 = $ _____ m²
74. $.05 \text{ km}^2 = $ _____ m²
75. $4.6 \text{ km}^2 = $ _____ m²
76. $57.4 \text{ km}^2 = $ _____ m²
77. $675.3 \text{ km}^2 = $ _____ m²
78. $1{,}549.8 \text{ km}^2 = $ _____ m²
79. $26{,}778.3 \text{ km}^2 = $ _____ m²
80. $109{,}304 \text{ km}^2 = $ _____ m²

Ares and Hectares

An *are* (pronounced "air") is an area 10 meters wide by 10 meters long. The area of 1 *are* is 10 × 10 or 100 square meters. To convert square meters to ares, move the decimal two places to the left.

$$1 \text{ are} = 10 \text{ m} \times 10 \text{ m} = 100 \text{ m}^2$$
$$100 \text{ m}^2 = 1 \text{ are}$$

Practice Problems 32. Convert the following square meters to ares:

81. $100 \text{ m}^2 = $ 1 are(s)
82. $200 \text{ m}^2 = $ _____ are
83. $20 \text{ m}^2 = $ _____ are
84. $2 \text{ m}^2 = $ _____ are

85. 3,194 m² =   are   88. 4,709,821 m² =   are
86. 27,955 m² =   are   89. 694,810 m² =   are
87. 496,783 m² =   are   90. 26,517.66 m² =   are

To convert ares to square meters, move the decimal two places to the right.

$$1 \text{ are} = 100 \text{ m}^2$$
$$20.4 \text{ ares} = 2,040 \text{ m}^2$$

A *hectare* is an are 100 meters wide by 100 meters long.

$$1 \text{ hectare} = 100 \text{ m} \times 100 \text{ m} = 10,000 \text{ m}^2$$
$$1 \text{ hectare} = 100 \text{ ares}$$

To convert hectares to square meters, move the decimal four places to the right.

$$1 \text{ hectare} = 1.0000 \text{ m}^2$$

To convert square meters to hectares, move the decimal four places to the left.

Practice Problems 33. Convert the following square meters to hectares:

91. 10,000 m² =   1 hectare(s)   96. 209 m² =   hectare(s)
92. 100,000 m² =   hectare   97. 374,019.6 m² =   hectare
93. 1,000,000 m² = hectare   98. 875,329.7 m² =   hectare
94. 40,329 m² =   hectare   99. 1,865,403.2 m² =   hectare
95. 4,406 m² =   hectare   100. 39,603.1 m² =   hectare

Area Problems

101. A piece of land is 600 m × 1,200 m. Give the area in m², in km², in ares, in hectares. (*Ans.* 720,000 m²; .72 km²; 7,200 ares; 72 hectares)
102. A storage space measures 5 m 30 cm by 4 m 35 cm. Give the area in m², and in cm².
103. A bathroom floor measures 2 m 40 cm by 3 m 12 cm. What is the area in m²? How much will it cost for floor covering which costs $9 per m²?
104. You are making a rug that will measure 2 m 14 cm × 1.5 m 25 cm. What will be the area in m²? In cm²?
105. A window is 6.4 m 36 cm wide and 4 m 12 cm high. What is the area in m²? In cm²?

METRIC VOLUME

A common metric measurement for volume is the *liter*. A liter contains a volume of 1,000 cubic centimeters (cm³). A liter is a little larger than a quart, and four liters are a little more than one gallon. A *milliliter* (a cm³) equals 1/1000 of a liter. In other words, there are 1,000 milliliters (or cm³) in a liter. One fluid ounce is approximately 30 milliliters. A *kiloliter* is a cubic meter (m³) and contains 1,000 liters. It is often used to measure a large volume of liquid.

Conversions

Converting Milliliters to Liters

Remember that one liter (1 ℓ) = 1,000 milliliters (ml). To convert ml to ℓ, move the decimal three places to the left.

Practice Problems 34. Convert the following ml to ℓ:

1. 1,000 ml = 1 ℓ
2. 2,500 ml = ___ ℓ
3. 31,400 ml = ___ ℓ
4. 464,011 ml = ___ ℓ
5. 3,755,032 ml = ___ ℓ
6. 24,398,114 ml = ___ ℓ
7. 577.4 ml = ___ ℓ
8. 46 ml = ___ ℓ
9. 2 ml = ___ ℓ
10. 911.67 ml = ___ ℓ

Converting Liters to Milliliters

Remember that 1 ℓ = 1,000 ml. To convert liters to milliliters, move the decimal three places to the right.

11. 1 ℓ = 1,000 ml
12. 28 ℓ = ___ ml
13. 438 ℓ = ___ ml
14. 1,914 ℓ = ___ ml
15. 602.2 ℓ = ___ ml
16. 28.46 ℓ = ___ ml
17. 7.951 ℓ = ___ ml
18. 36.8 ℓ = ___ ml
19. 9.4 ℓ = ___ ml
20. .46 ℓ = ___ ml

Converting Kiloliters (Cubic Meters) to Liters

Remember that 1 kl (m³) = 1,000 ℓ. Therefore, to convert kl to ℓ, move the decimal three places to the right.

21. 1 kl = 1,000 ℓ
22. 2.6 kl = ___ ℓ
23. .54 kl = ___ ℓ
24. 18.4 kl = ___ ℓ
25. 129.8 kl = ___ ℓ
26. 3,046 kl = ___ ℓ
27. 89,046 kl = ___ ℓ
28. 306.4 kl = ___ ℓ
29. 14.1 kl = ___ ℓ
30. .06 kl = ___ ℓ

Converting Liters to Kiloliters (Cubic Meters)

Remember that 1 kl (m³) = 1,000 ℓ. To convert ℓ to kl, move the decimal three places to the left.

$$1{,}000. \, \ell = 1 \text{ k}\ell$$

Practice Problems 35. Convert the following ℓ to kl:

31. 1,000 ℓ =   1 kl
32. 460 ℓ =   kl
33. 74 ℓ =   kl
34. 6 ℓ =   kl
35. 5.3 ℓ =   kl
36. .45 ℓ =   kl
37. 21,687 ℓ =   kl
38. 307,557 ℓ =   kl
39. 4,291,865 ℓ =   kl
40. 8,009.6 ℓ =   kl

41. A container is 52 cm long, 14 cm wide, and 18 cm high. Find the volume in cm³. What is the volume in liters? (*Ans.* 13,104 cm³ or 13.104 ℓ)
42. A tub holds 4,600 ℓ. Give the volume in m³.
43. An aquarium is 65 cm long, 18 cm wide, and 24 cm high. What is the volume in cm³? In liters?
44. A barrel holds .55 m³. Give this volume in liters.
45. A large tank holds 92,402 ℓ. Give the volume in m³.

Metric units of measure for volume are shown below. The units most commonly used are liters, milliliters, and kiloliters.

milliliter—1/1000 of a liter (same as cm³)
centiliter—1/100 of a liter
deciliter—1/10 of a liter
liter—a little larger than a quart
decaliter—10 liters
hectoliter—100 liters
kiloliter—1,000 liters (same as m³)

ENGLISH–METRIC CONVERSIONS

WEIGHT

1 oz. = 28.3495 g
1 lb. = 453.5924 g or .4536 kg
1 short ton (tn.) = 0.9072 t
(2,000 lb.)

Example 1. A box of breakfast cereal weighs 15 ounces. How much does it weigh in grams?

$$15 \times 28.3495 = 425.2425 \text{ g}$$

THE INTERNATIONAL SYSTEM OF UNITS (SI)

Practice Problems 36. Convert the following English weights to metric (SI) weights (rounded to two decimal places):

1. 2.5 oz. = 70.87 g
2. 4.9 oz. = _____ g
3. 3-1/2 oz. = _____ g
4. 1 lb. 6 oz. = _____ g
5. 2-1/2 lb. = _____ g
6. 15.3 oz. = _____ g
7. 2 lb. 5 oz. = _____ g
8. 1/2 oz. = _____ g
9. .8 oz. = _____ g
10. 6-1/2 oz. = _____ g
11. 23 oz. = _____ g
12. 3-3/4 oz. = _____ g
13. 2 oz. = _____ g
14. 7 oz. = _____ g
15. 6 oz. = _____ g
16. 1 lb. 2 oz. = _____ g
17. 11 oz. = _____ g
18. 10.5 oz. = _____ g
19. 1 lb. 12 oz. = _____ g
20. 4 oz. = _____ g
21. 6-1/2 lb. = _____ kg
22. 14 lb. = _____ kg
23. 5-3/4 lb. = _____ kg
24. 17.8 lb. = _____ kg
25. 100 lb. = _____ kg
26. 150 lb. = _____ kg
27. 127-1/2 lb. = _____ kg
28. 4 lb. = _____ kg
29. 10 lb. = _____ kg
30. 1,000 lb. = _____ kg
31. .3 lb. = _____ kg
32. 3 lb. = _____ kg
33. 30 lb. = _____ kg
34. 300 lb. = _____ kg
35. 3,000 lb. = _____ kg
36. .74 lb. = _____ kg
37. 5-1/4 lb. = _____ kg
38. 5 lb. 8 oz = _____ kg
39. 50 lb. = _____ kg
40. 90.6 lb. = _____ kg
41. 2 tn. = _____ t
42. 14.6 tn. = _____ t
43. 7.1 tn. = _____ t
44. 35 tn. = _____ t
45. 3.56 tn. = _____ t
46. 1.5 tn. = _____ t
47. 60 tn. = _____ t
48. 45-1/2 tn. = _____ t
49. 5-3/4 tn. = _____ t
50. 16 tn. = _____ t

Most of our need is for converting English measurement units into metric measurement units. However, metric–English weight conversions are shown here so that we can convert metric–English when necessary.

METRIC-ENGLISH
WEIGHT

1 g = 0.0353 oz.
1 kg = 2.2046 lb.
1 t (1,000 kg) = 1.1023 tn. (short ton = 2,000 lb.)

Practice Problems 37. On the following problems, round your answers to three decimal places.

51. A box of salt is marked 737 g. What is its weight in oz.? (737 × .0353 = 26.016 oz.)
52. A box of cereal is marked 340 g. What is its weight in oz.?
53. A box of laundry detergent weighs 7.2 kg. What is its weight in lb.?
54. A turkey weighs 7.8 kg. What is its weight in lb.?
55. A coal company has just filled an order for 35.5 t (metric tons) of coal. How much is this order in short tons (English)?
56. One bag of apples weighs 5 lb., 4 oz. A second bag of apples weighs 2.3 kg. Which bag weighs more?
57. A jeweler ordered 3-1/2 oz. of gold. A week later he ordered 100 g of gold. Which order contained the larger quantity of gold?
58. A salvage company sells used paper at 10 cents a lb. The company sold 2-1/2 short tons (2,000 lb.) to one dealer and sold 2.25 t (metric tons) to another dealer. Which was the larger sale? How much money did he receive from each sale?
59. One manufacturer buys beams of nylon cord weighing 161 lb. per beam. Another manufacturer buys beams of nylon cord weighing 74.8 kg each. Which manufacturer uses the heavier beams?
60. One can of peaches weighs 2 lb., 2 oz. Another can of peaches weighs 926 g. Which can is heavier?

ENGLISH-METRIC CONVERSION
LENGTH

1 in. = 2.540 cm
1 ft. = 0.3048 m
1 yd.= 0.9144 m
1 mi.= 1.6093 km

Example 2. Three and one-fourth inches equals how many centimeters?

3.25 × 2.540 = 8.255 cm

THE INTERNATIONAL SYSTEM OF UNITS (SI)

Practice Problems 38. Convert the following English units of measurement to metric units of measurement. (Round your answers to three decimal places.)

61. 1/2 in. =   1.27 cm
62. 1/4 in. =   cm
63. 3-3/4 in. =   cm
64. 25-3/4 in. =   cm
65. 18-1/8 in. =   cm
66. 6 in. =   cm
67. 4-1/2 in. =   cm
68. 1/8 in. =   cm
69. 10-1/4 in. =   cm
70. 31 in. =   cm
71. 17-1/4 in. =   cm
72. 29 in. =   cm
73. 2-3/4 in. =   cm
74. 3/8 in. =   cm
75. 14 in. =   cm
76. 1-3/4 in. =   cm
77. 5-1/2 in. =   cm
78. 12-3/4 in. =   cm
79. 30 in. =   cm
80. 26-1/4 in. =   cm
81. 3 ft. 4 in. =   m
82. 1 ft. 6 in. =   m
83. 2 ft. =   m
84. 5 ft. 9 in. =   m
85. 4 ft. 7 in. =   m

86. 20 ft. =   m
87. 9 ft. 6-1/2 in. =   m
88. 18 ft. 4 in. =   m
89. 1/2 ft. =   m
90. 14 ft. 11 in. =   m
91. 2 ft. 9 in. =   m
92. 3-3/4 ft. =   m
93. 16 ft. =   m
94. 4 ft. 1 in. =   m
95. 5 ft. 7 in. =   m
96. 6 ft. 1 in. =   m
97. 35 ft. =   m
98. 50 ft. =   m
99. 100 ft. =   m
100. 200 ft. =   m
101. 1-1/2 yd. =   m
102. 2/3 yd. =   m
103. 3 yd. 14 in. =   m
104. 6 yd. =   m
105. 50 yd. =   m
106. 100 yd. =   m
107. 500 yd. =   m
108. 12-1/2 yd. =   m
109. 9 yd. 17 in. =   m
110. 1,000 yd. =   m

111. Give the measurements in centimeters of a sheet of paper 8-1/2 in. by 11 in. (*Ans.* 21.59 cm by 27.94 cm)
112. A flagpole is 120 ft. high. What is its height in meters?

ENGLISH–METRIC CONVERSIONS 281

113. You live 5-1/2 miles from your place of work. How far is this in meters?
114. Mr. Smith's house is on a lot 60 ft. wide by 180 ft. deep. What are these dimensions in meters?
115. A friend of yours lives in a city 250 mi. from your home. How far is this in kilometers?
116. You are thinking of buying a braided rug which is 12 ft. by 15 ft. What are the dimensions in meters?
117. You have a large conference-style desk, which measures 40 in. by 82 in. How many square meters are there in the desk top?
118. How many square meters are there in a rug 15 ft. by 18 ft.?
119. Your garage measures 20 ft. by 40 ft. How many square meters are there?
120. A swimming pool measures 30 ft. by 60 ft. Another swimming pool measures 25 ft. by 65 ft. Express these areas in m^2 and designate which pool is the larger.

Convert the following English measurements to metric (SI) measurements. (Round your answers to three decimal places.)

121.	3/4 mi. =	km	131.	150 mi. =	km
122.	4 mi. =	km	132.	175 mi. =	km
123.	5.5 mi. =	km	133.	200 mi. =	km
124.	5-3/4 mi. =	km	134.	500 mi. =	km
125.	10 mi. =	km	135.	1,000 mi. =	km
126.	14.6 mi. =	km	136.	1,476 mi. =	km
127.	54.3 mi. =	km	137.	3,000 mi. =	km
128.	60-1/4 mi. =	km	138.	1/4 mi. =	km
129.	75 mi. =	km	139.	1/2 mi. =	km
130.	100 mi. =	km	140.	.2 mi. =	km

ENGLISH–METRIC
VOLUME

1 fl. oz. = 29.57 ml
1 pt.   = .4732 ℓ
1 qt.   = .9464 ℓ (or 946.4 cm^3)
1 gal.   = 3.785 ℓ

Practice Problems 39. Convert the following English measurements to metric (SI) measurements. (Round your answers to three decimal places.)

141.	1 qt. =	.946 ℓ	143.	2-1/2 qt. =	ℓ
142.	1-1/2 qt. =	ℓ	144.	3 qt. =	ℓ

THE INTERNATIONAL SYSTEM OF UNITS (SI)

145. 4 qt. =	ℓ	163. 1-1/2 pt. =	ℓ
146. 7 qt. =	ℓ	164. 6 pt. =	ℓ
147. 8 qt. 1 pt. =	ℓ	165. 4.5 pt. =	ℓ
148. 2-1/2 fl. oz. =	ml	166. 4-3/4 pt. =	ℓ
149. 1/2 fl. oz. =	ml	167. 8 pt. =	ℓ
150. 4 fl. oz. =	ml	168. 1 gal. =	3.785 ℓ
151. 1.1 gal. =	ℓ	169. 1-1/2 gal. =	ℓ
152. 1-1/2 gal. =	ℓ	170. 1-3/4 gal. =	ℓ
153. 5.6 gal. =	ℓ	171. 2 gal. =	ℓ
154. 6-1/8 gal. =	ℓ	172. 4 gal. =	ℓ
155. 9 qt., 1 pt. =	ℓ	173. 5.6 gal. =	ℓ
156. 10 qt., 1/2 pt. =	ℓ	174. 6-1/2 gal. =	ℓ
157. 14 qt. =	ℓ	175. 7-1/8 gal. =	ℓ
158. 1 pt. =	ℓ	176. 10 gal. =	ℓ
159. 1/2 pt. =	ℓ	177. 11 gal., 1 qt. =	ℓ
160. 3 pt. =	ℓ	178. 5 gal., 3 qt. =	ℓ
161. 3-1/4 pt. =	ℓ	179. 2 gal., 1 qt. =	ℓ
162. 2-1/2 pt. =	ℓ	180. 1,000 gal. =	kℓ

THE CELSIUS THERMOMETER

The Celsius thermometer shows the freezing point of water at 0° C. instead of the 32° F. to which we have been accustomed. The Celsius thermometer shows the boiling point of water at 100° C., instead of 212° F. on the Fahrenheit scale.

On the Fahrenheit scale, there are 180° between freezing (32° F.) and boiling (212° F.). On the Celsius scale, there are only 100° between freezing (0° C.) and boiling (100° C.).

Converting Fahrenheit to Centigrade (or Celsius)

Example 1. Convert 49° F. to C. (Round to the tenth of a degree.)

1. Subtract 32; then multiply by 5/9.
   (The 5/9 is derived from the ratio of the 100° C. to the 180° F. range. 100/180 = 10/18 = 5/9)

$$49 - 32 = 17$$

2. Multiply by 5/9.

$$17 \times 5 = 85 \div 9 = 9.4° \text{ C.}$$

Practice Problems 40. Convert the following to C. rounded to one decimal place:

1. 212° F. =   100° C.
2. 200° F. =   _____ C.
3. 175° F. =   _____ C.
4. 120° F. =   _____ C.
5. 100° F. =   _____ C.
6. 98.6° F. = _____ C.
7. 86° F. =   _____ C.
8. 82° F. =   _____ C.
9. 79° F. =   _____ C.
10. 75° F. =   _____ C.
11. 70° F. =   _____ C.
12. 67° F. =   _____ C.
13. 64° F. =   _____ C.
14. 60° F. =   _____ C.
15. 55° F. =   _____ C.
16. 51° F. =   _____ C.
17. 46° F. =   _____ C.
18. 41° F. =   _____ C.
19. 38° F. =   _____ C.
20. 32°F. =   0° C.

Example 2. Convert 30° F. to C. (Round to the tenth of a degree.)

1. Subtract 32; then multiply by 5/9.
2. Enter 30 on the keyboard.
3. Depress $\boxed{+}$.
4. Enter 32 on the keyboard.
5. Depress $\boxed{-}$.
6. Total.
7. Your answer is -2 (like a credit balance).
8. Multiply -2 by 5/9.

$$(-2) \times 5 = -10$$

Note: When you multiply one negative number and one positive number, your product is *always* negative. Some electronic calculators will show you a negative product (in red, or with a (-) sign or with *Cr* (credit balance)). However, if your calculator does not show you a negative, you must remember that it *is* negative.

9. (-10) ÷ 9 = -1.1 (rounded to tenths)
Note: Again, in a division problem, if one number is positive and one number is negative, your quotient is *always* negative.
10. Your answer is:

30° F. = -1.1° C. (in other words, 1.1 degrees below 0)

284   THE INTERNATIONAL SYSTEM OF UNITS (SI)

Practice Problems 41.   Convert the following to C.:

21. 28° F. =   -2.2° C.
22. 25° F. =   C.
23. 20° F. =   C.
24. 17° F. =   C.
25. 14° F. =   C.
26. 10° F. =   C.
27. 8° F. =   C.
28. 5° F. =   C.
29. 2° F. =   C.
30. 0° F. = (-32) × 5/9 = -17.8° C. (or 17.8° below 0)

Example 3.   Convert -4° F. to C. (Round to the tenth of a degree.)

1. Subtract 32.
2. Enter 4 on the keyboard.
3. Depress $\boxed{-}$.
4. Enter 32 on the keyboard.
5. Depress $\boxed{-}$.
6. Total.
7. Your answer is -36.
8. Multiply by 5/9.
9. (-36) × 5 = -180
10. -180 ÷ 9 = -20
11. Your answer is -20° C. or 20° below 0.

Practice Problems 42.   Convert the following to C.:

31. -6° F. =   -21.1° C.   36. -28° F. =   C.
32. -10° F. =   C.   37. -39° F. =   C.
33. -15° F. =   C.   38. -35° F. =   C.
34. -18° F. =   C.   39. -40° F. =   C.
35. -21° F. =   C.   40. -50° F. =   C.

THE CELSIUS THERMOMETER

Converting Celsius to Fahrenheit

Example 4. Convert 30° C. to F. (Round to the tenth of a degree.)

1. Multiply by 9/5; then add 32.
2. 30 × 9 = 270
3. 270 ÷ 5 = 54
4. 54 + 32 = 86° F.

Practice Problems 43. Convert the following to F:

41. 100° C. =   212° F.
42. 91° C. =   F.
43. 86° C. =   F.
44. 80° C. =   F.
45. 78° C. =   F.
46. 73° C. =   F.
47. 65° C. =   F.
48. 59° C. =   F.
49. 50° C. =   F.
50. 46° C. =   F.

51. 42° C. =   F.
52. 39° C. =   F.
53. 31° C. =   F.
54. 27° C. =   F.
55. 20° C. =   F.
56. 15° C. =   F.
57. 11° C. =   F.
58. 8° C. =   F.
59. 5° C. =   F.
60. 0° C. =   32° F.

Example 5. Convert -10° C. to F. (Round to the tenth of a degree.)

1. Multiply by 9/5; then add 32.
2. (-10) × 9 = -90
3. *Note:* Remember if *one* multiplier is negative, the product is *always* negative.
4. (-90) ÷ 5 = -18
   Note: Remember that if *one* number in a division problem is negative and the other positive, the quotient is *always* negative.
5. Enter 18 on the keyboard.
6. Depress [-] .
7. Enter 32 on the keyboard.
8. Depress [+] .
9. Total.
10. Your answer is 14° F.

286   THE INTERNATIONAL SYSTEM OF UNITS (SI)

Example 6. Convert -28 C. to F. (Round to the tenth of a degree.)

1. Multiply by 9/5; then add 32.
2. (-28) × 9 = -252
3. (-252) ÷ 5 = -50.4
4. Enter 50.4 on the keyboard.
5. Depress $\boxed{-}$.
6. Enter 32 on the keyboard.
7. Depress $\boxed{+}$.
8. Your answer is -18.4° F. or 18.4° below 0.

Practice Problems 44. Convert the following to F. (Round to the tenth of a degree.)

61.	-3° C. =	26.6° F.	66.	-25° C. =	F.
62.	-8° C. =	F.	67.	-30° C. =	F.
63.	-10° C. =	F.	68.	-40° C. =	F.
64.	-15° C. =	F.	69.	-45° C. =	F.
65.	-19° C. =	F.	70.	-50° C. =	F.

REVIEW QUIZ 6

(Round your answers to two decimal places.)

1. The Green Thumb Florist's greenhouse cost $41,000. The salvage value is $2,000. The estimated life is 25 years. What is the annual depreciation? Use the straight-line method.
2. The Jamestown Hauling Company purchased a truck for $13,100. The estimated useful life is five years, and the salvage value will be $1,575. Determine the amount of depreciation for each of the five years, using the sum-of-the-digits method.
3. Find the midpoint in the following number of values. (Round your answer to the tenth of a mile.)

Company Car Serial Number	Mileage (as of May 31)
129764	50,321.8
129769	48,219.0
143218	46,228.9
116177	38,919.7
431920	37,927.8
370140	34,120.3

Company Car Serial Number	Mileage (as of May 31)
256997	30,981.6
254531	30,707.0
601897	27,785.4
991432	25,978.6

4. You exchange $259 for British pounds. How many pounds do you receive?
5. Johnston and Levine, dental surgeons, had the following income for the month of August: dental surgery, $41,900. Their expenses for August were as follows: rent, $1,325; salaries and benefits for office staff, $6,100; utilities, $191; dental supplies and drugs, $750; office supplies, $126; miscellaneous expense, $350. What was Johnston and Levine's net profit for August?
6. Make the following conversions. Show all decimal places.
   574.1 kg to g
   490 cg to g
   30,000 g to kg
   592 ℓ to kℓ
   35,000 mm to m
7. Subtract. Show answer in km.
   3.4 km 104 m
   -2.3 km 402 m
8. How much is 2,390,400 cm^2 in m^2?
9. Convert 7 lb., 8 oz. to kg.
10. Convert 55° F. to C. (Round your answer to the tenth of a degree.)

Sample Examination

You may want to be timed as you try the Unit 6 Sample Examination, which is presented in the Introduction.

Texas Instruments SR-52 Programmable Slide-Rule Calculator (Courtesy of Texas Instruments, Incorporated)

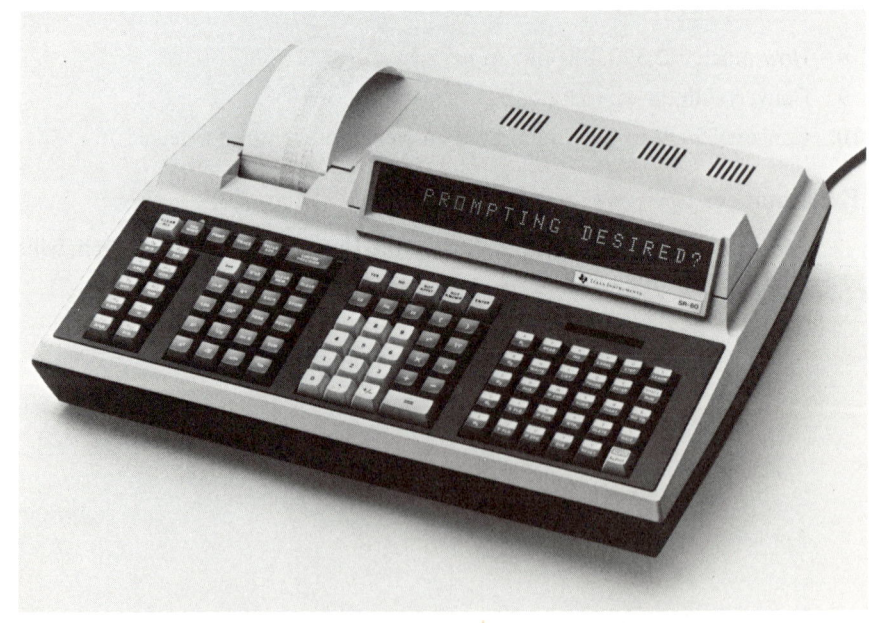

Texas Instruments SR-60 Programmable Prompting Calculator (Courtesy of Texas Instruments, Incorporated)

Unit 7

The Programmable Electronic Calculator

TOUCH SYSTEM REVIEW

Be sure to keep your index finger, your middle finger, and your ring finger on the home row (4, 5, and 6) if you are using your right hand. Keep your ring finger, your middle finger, and your index finger on the 4, 5, and 6 if you are using your left hand.

444	454	464	454	646	455
555	445	556	556	665	644
666	456	456	654	654	456
666	445	554	665	556	464
555	465	454	655	465	456
444	444	666	555	444	555
666	666	444	555	666	666
444	456	456	654	654	456
555	666	555	444	555	666
666	464	565	646	565	656
5,661	4,961	5,170	5,838	5,870	5,474

Are you keeping your head turned toward your copy? Do not turn your head to look at your keys. If you must look, turn your eyes only. Keep your head turned toward your copy if you want to attain speed and accuracy.

123	123	123	123	123	123
222	111	333	333	111	333
333	222	111	111	333	111
233	233	322	322	122	122
311	311	311	112	112	113
123	132	132	123	133	231
111	222	333	333	222	111
123	321	123	132	123	321
223	332	122	322	133	211
123	123	321	321	123	123
1,925	2,130	2,231	2,232	1,535	1,799

THE PROGRAMMABLE ELECTRONIC CALCULATOR

Can you find the keys without looking? Are you getting the right answers?

789	789	789	789	789	789
777	888	999	888	777	888
999	888	777	888	999	888
778	887	778	887	778	887
998	997	998	997	998	997
788	799	788	799	889	998
789	789	987	789	879	798
777	999	888	999	777	888
789	789	987	987	978	879
788	887	977	998	889	977
8,272	8,712	8,968	9,021	8,753	8,989

For the right hand, use your thumb for the zero. For the left hand, use your little finger for the zero.

300	209	103	205	307	407
500	206	102	202	303	409
700	204	100	206	301	401
800	101	108	200	300	404
100	200	104	208	308	400
400	208	106	203	305	403
200	205	101	209	302	405
600	202	105	204	304	408
900	203	107	201	309	406
100	207	109	207	306	402
4,600	1,945	1,045	2,045	3,045	4,045

Keep your head turned toward your copy.

8.08	7.70	3.09	4.08	5.05	7.01
2.02	9.90	3.06	4.10	5.09	6.08
5.05	2.20	3.03	4.03	6.01	6.02
7.07	4.40	3.05	4.05	5.03	6.06
4.04	6.60	3.07	4.07	5.04	6.09
6.06	1.10	4.01	4.06	5.07	7.02
1.01	8.80	3.08	4.04	6.02	6.03
3.03	1.01	4.02	5.01	5.06	6.05
1.00	3.30	3.10	4.09	5.08	6.07
9.09	5.50	3.04	5.02	5.10	6.04
46.45	50.51	32.55	42.55	52.55	62.47

The programmable calculator not only functions as a sophisticated electronic desktop calculator but also provides many of the functional benefits of a computer. The use of the Parentheses keys permits entry of a mixed problem in the same order in which the problem is normally written; for example,

$$\frac{(2.1 \times 46.98) + (6 \times 87.5)}{(3.1 \times 4) + (18.11 \times 8.3)} =$$

The Texas Instruments SR-60, which has both a display and a printer, can be programmed to prompt the user in making both entries and decisions about the problem on which he is working. Since the SR-60 can enter, display, and print both alphabetic and numeric data, the prompting is accomplished through printed words, phrases, symbols, and numbers which flash on the display screen.

The user can design and record his own program (for his payroll, for example) on a magnetic card, or he can buy magnetic cards which are already programmed and recorded to perform certain routines, such as figuring compound interest.

BASIC OPERATIONS

|CE| Clear Entry key (above the numerical keyboard)—Clears only the display when used after a numerical entry. It may be used to stop a flashing display and question mark.

|Clear| To the left of the numerical keyboard—Clears the display and clears calculations in progress.

|Clear All| Clear All key (to the extreme left of the keyboard)—Clears the display, the registers, and the memory. Results in displayed message PROMPTING DESIRED? If you are using a prerecorded program, you press YES. Pressing any other key returns the calculator to keyboard control.

How to Fix a Decimal Place

|Fix| With this key you can set the displayed number of decimals from 0 to 8.

Example 1. To round off to two places in the display.

1. |Clear| .
2. Depress |Fix| (above the numerical keyboard) and the 2.
3. Continue with your problem. The display will now show two decimal places rounded off.
   Note: This Fix key does *not* round off the number of digits the machine is using for calculations. You can call back the entire decimal reading by depressing |Fix| again and entering 9.

To round off the number of decimals used in the calculation and the number of decimals in the internal registers, use the |Limited Precision| key (upper left on the keyboard).

Example 2. To round off to the nearest penny in the display *and* in the calculations,

1. Depress $\boxed{\text{Clear}}$.
2. Depress $\boxed{\text{Limited Precision}}$
3. Depress $\boxed{\text{Fix}}$.
4. Enter 2.
5. Continue with the problem.

To cancel limited precision, depress the $\boxed{\text{Limited Precision}}$ key.

Printer

$\boxed{\text{Paper Adv}}$ This key (in the upper left of the keyboard) will advance the paper without printing.

$\boxed{\text{Print}}$ This key causes the current contents of the display to be printed.

$\boxed{\text{Trace}}$ This key causes the calculator to print every new function or result. A number key followed by a function will cause a line to be printed.

Note: Do *not* make entries while the printer is operating or you will damage the calculator.

Addition

Example. 12.4 + 36.57 =

1. When the display asks PROMPTING DESIRED?, press NO key above the numerical keyboard. This returns the control to the keyboard for manual operations.
2. Depress $\boxed{\text{Clear}}$.
3. Enter 12.4 on the keyboard.
4. Depress $\boxed{+}$.
5. Enter 36.57 on the keyboard.
6. Depress $\boxed{+}$.
7. Answer, 48.97, is displayed.

Practice Problems 1. Complete the following addition problems:

1. 48	2. 84	3. 34	4. 43	5. $26.76
61	16	62	26	38.34
24	42	11	10	62.11
26	62	37	73	49.59
76	67	48	84	25.12
38	83	25	52	93.36

6. $67.62	7. 6,783.72	8. 83,957.29	9. 12	10. 14
43.83	84,265.94	745.98	14	99
11.26	9,375.28	9,375.22	18	10
95.94	571.22	3.99	21	67
21.52	92.90	874.56	36	28
63.39	100.35	3,285.99	42	99

Subtraction

Example. 471.03 - 113.18 =

1. If your last entry was the $\boxed{=}$ sign, your calculator is clear. Otherwise, use the $\boxed{\text{Clear}}$ key.
2. Enter 471.03 on the keyboard.
3. Enter $\boxed{-}$.
4. Enter 113.18 on the keyboard.
5. Depress $\boxed{=}$.
6. Your answer, 357.85, will appear on the display.

Practice Problems 2. Complete the following subtraction problems:

1. 38.64	2. 93.50	3. 152.46	4. 56.87	5. 57.48
-24.68	-12.36	-69.12	-54.90	-36.69

6. 211.89	7. 842.06	8. 626.45	9. 1,000	10. 1,826
-48.07	-189.62	-418.96	-48	-63

Addition and Subtraction

Example. 29.7
   5.84
   -3.88
   -1.2
   26.4458

1. Enter 29.7 on the keyboard.
2. Depress $+$.
3. Enter 5.84 on the keyboard.
4. Depress $-$.
5. Enter 3.88 on the keyboard.
6. Depress $-$.
7. Enter 1.2 on the keyboard.
8. Depress $+$.
9. Enter 26.4458 on the keyboard.
10. Depress $=$.
11. Answer, 56.9058, will appear on the display.

Practice Problems 3. Do the following problems. Remember to enter your amounts *by touch*.

	1.	2.	3.	4.
	8.67	9,955	33,929	918.06
	-42.43	-1,396	-101	15.651
	67.29	-2,581	1,234	-4.22
	-.32	6,789	-60	.006
	-9.18	-349	-35	-.7834
	64.89	11,118	10,000	.65

	5.	6.	7.	8.
	18.4	505	12.84	80.74
	-9.2887	-449	-9.21	-6.42
	36.235	788	7.77	-.92
	110.2857	1,846	-.14	3.51
	-40.28	-129	-.12	-.14
	16.07	860	7.87	425.11

9.	1,306,428.37	10.	38,919.66
	201,471.86		89,628.75
	-11,692.17		85,811.41
	-235,785.01		-49,677.02
	-10,116.69		-29,160.08
	507,129.03		-3.73

Repeated Addition

Example. 99.114
2.768
2.768
2.768
1.432

1. Use [Clear Mem] key (Memory) at the upper right of the numeric keyboard.

2. Enter 99.114 on the keyboard.

3. Depress [+].

4. Enter 2.768 on the keyboard.

5. Depress [Store] key (to the immediate left of the numeric keyboard).

6. Depress [Recall] (to the immediate left of the keyboard) and [+]; depress [Recall] and [+]; depress [Recall] and [+].

7. Enter 1.432 on the keyboard.

8. Depress [=].

9. Answer, 108.85, will appear on the display.

Repeated Subtraction

Example. 13.6
-1.4
-1.4
-1.4
-2.1

1. Depress [Clear] and [Clear Mem].

2. Enter 13.6 on the keyboard.

3. Depress $\boxed{-}$.
4. Enter 1.4 on the keyboard.
5. Depress $\boxed{\text{Store}}$.
6. Depress $\boxed{\text{Recall}}$ and $\boxed{-}$ three times.
7. Enter 2.1 on the keyboard.
8. Depress $\boxed{=}$.
9. Your answer, 7.3, will appear on the display.

Practice Problems 4. Complete the following repeated addition problems:

	1.		2.		3.		4.		5.	
		80.905		18.66		24.701		94.211		65.56
		38.604		191.22		407.901		6.013		694.53
		2.001		191.22		1.155		6.013		694.53
		2.001		191.22		1.155		6.013		694.53
		2.001		191.22		1.155		6.013		32.19
		118.071		36.01		1.155		6.013		46.87

	6.		7.		8.		9.		10.	
		3.78		1,391.02		.455		46.87		22,129.32
		.09		2,046.27		.455		.33		22,129.32
		.09		132.33		.455		9.88		22,129.32
		.09		132.33		.455		11.93		22,129.32
		.09		132.33		.455		11.93		4,607.54
		.09		132.33		.889		11.93		18,809.05

Non-Add (with printed record)

Example. Inventory # 3364
26.91
557.85
33.46

1. Depress $\boxed{\text{Clear}}$.
2. Depress $\boxed{\text{Alpha}}$ key (at the extreme lower right of the keyboard).
3. Enter on the alphabetic keyboard (to the right of the numeric keyboard) INV (space) NO (space) then 3364 on the numeric keyboard.
4. Depress $\boxed{\text{Alpha}}$ key.
5. Depress $\boxed{\text{Print}}$ (upper left of the keyboard). This will print the inventory number on the tape for reference purposes but will *not* add into your total.

6. Depress [Clear].
7. Enter 26.91 on the keyboard.
8. Depress [+].
9. Depress [Print].
10. Enter 557.85 on the keyboard.
11. Depress [+].
12. Depress [Print].
13. Enter 33.46 on the keyboard.
14. Depress [Print].
15. Depress [=].
16. Depress [Print].
17. Your total, 618.22, will appear on the display. A complete record of the problem, including the inventory reference number, will print out on the tape.
    Be *sure* that you do *not* enter any digits or depress anything on the keyboard while the printer is printing.

Multiplication

Example. 2.113 × 6.75 =

1. Enter 2.113 on the keyboard.
2. Depress [×] (on the right side of the numeric keyboard).
3. Enter 6.75 on the keyboard.
4. Depress [=] (lower right of the numeric keyboard).
5. Your answer, 14.26275, will appear on the display.

Practice Problems 5. Complete the following multiplication problems. Do not round off.

1. 604 × 268 =
2. 64 × 6.08 =
3. 778 × 472 =
4. 691 × 603 =
5. 7.2 × 3.3 =
6. 43.2 × .78 =
7. 6.6 × 439 =
8. 8.7 × .89 =
9. 9,008 × 407 =
10. 18.41 × 36 =
11. 79.121 × 3.4 =
12. 4.03 × 90.6 =
13. 7.08 × 40.7 =
14. 6.6 × 3.84 =

15. 54.3 × .87 =

16. 68 × 386.8 =

17. 8.7 × 829.3 =

18. 870.9 × 47.20 =

19. 4.32 × 877.8 =

20. 745.1 × 89.9 =

Division

Example. 8,714.32 ÷ 201.6 =

1. Enter 8,714.32 on the keyboard.
2. Depress ÷ (right side of the numeric keyboard).
3. Enter 201.6 on the keyboard.
4. Depress = .
5. Answer, 43.22579365, will appear on the display.

Practice Problems 6. Complete these division problems. (Round your answers to four decimal places.)

1. 26,741 ÷ 23.1 =
2. 7,815.44 ÷ 2.09 =
3. 4,305.23 ÷ 234.22 =
4. 4,372.84 ÷ 37.9 =
5. 840.11 ÷ 1.44 =
6. 2,538 ÷ 109 =
7. 3,475 ÷ 101 =
8. 4.44 ÷ 1.7 =
9. 3.27 ÷ 9.11 =
10. 1,234 ÷ 6.54 =

Constants—Addition of a Constant

Example. Add 51 to *each* of these numbers: 2, -3.1, 5

1. Depress Clear .
2. Enter 2 on the keyboard.
3. Depress + .
4. Enter the constant, 51, on the keyboard.
5. Depress x▶k (upper left of the numeric keyboard).
6. Depress = .
7. Read answer, 53, on the display.
8. Enter 3.1 on the keyboard.
9. Depress +/- (to change the sign).
10. Depress = .

BASIC OPERATIONS   299

11. Read answer, 47.9, on the display.
12. Enter 5 on the keyboard.
13. Depress $\boxed{=}$.
14. Read answer, 56, on the display.

Subtraction of a Constant

Example. Subtract 8 from these numbers: 11, 20, 14.1

1. Depress $\boxed{\text{Clear}}$.
2. Enter 11 on the keyboard.
3. Depress $\boxed{-}$.
4. Enter 8 on the keyboard.
5. Depress $\boxed{x \rightleftarrows k}$.
6. Depress $\boxed{=}$.
7. Read first answer, 3, on the display.
8. Enter 20 on the keyboard.
9. Depress $\boxed{=}$.
10. Read second answer, 12, on the display.
11. Enter 14.1 on the keyboard.
12. Depress $\boxed{=}$. Read answer, 6.1, on the display.

Multiplication of a Constant

Example. Multiply 86, 19, 2.1 by 4.6.

1. $\boxed{\text{Clear}}$.
2. Enter 86 on the keyboard.
3. Depress $\boxed{\times}$.
4. Enter 4.6 on the keyboard.
5. Depress $\boxed{x \rightleftarrows k}$.
6. Depress $\boxed{=}$.
7. Read your first answer, 395.6, on the display.
8. Enter 19 on the keyboard.
9. Depress $\boxed{=}$.

10. Read your second answer, 87.4, on the display.
11. Enter 2.1 on the keyboard.
12. Depress [=] .
13. Read your third answer, 9.66, on the display.

Constant Divisor

Example. Divide 129, 13.6, 71.5 by 5.4.

1. [Clear] .
2. Enter 129 on the keyboard.
3. Depress [÷] .
4. Enter 5.4 on the keyboard.
5. Depress [x ⇆ k] .
6. Depress [=] .
7. Read your first answer, 23.88888889, on the display.
8. Enter 13.6 on the keyboard.
9. Depress [=] .
10. Read answer, 2.518518519, on the display.
11. Enter 71.5 on the keyboard.
12. Depress [=] .
13. Read your third answer, 13.24074074, on the display.

Addition, Subtraction, Multiplication, and Division with Constants 7.

1. 39.1 + .35 =
2. 12.8 + .35 =
3. 62 + .35 =
4. 87.14 + .35 =
5. 96.38 + .35 =
6. 556 + 11.2 =
7. .806 + 11.2 =
8. 5.97 + 11.2 =
9. 3,042 + 11.2 =
10. 28.9 + 11.2 =
11. 48.55 - 5.61 =
12. 11.268 - 5.61 =
13. 10.15 - 5.61 =
14. 39.2 - 5.61 =
15. 27.0391 - 5.61 =
16. 974.04 - .26 =
17. 918.86 - .26 =
18. 50.75 - .26 =
19. 101.15 - .26 =
20. 39.06 - .26 =

Round the following practice problems to four decimal places:

21. 62.26 × 186.8 =
22. 3.04 × 186.8 =
23. .12 × 186.8 =
24. 87.4 × 186.8 =
25. 65 × 186.8 =
26. 47.82 × 6.3 =
27. 40.23 × 6.3 =
28. 23,684 × 6.3 =
29. 31 × 6.3 =
30. 3.6 × 6.3 =
31. 116.04 ÷ 5.6 =
32. 137.097 ÷ 5.6 =
33. 729.64 ÷ 5.6 =
34. 57.06 ÷ 5.6 =
35. 78.93 ÷ 5.6 =
36. 48,555 ÷ 846.5 =
37. 8,450 ÷ 846.5 =
38. 6,937 ÷ 846.5 =
39. 6,114 ÷ 846.5 =
40. 31,249 ÷ 846.5 =

Percentage Problems

The Percent key $\boxed{\%}$ causes the calculator to convert the percent you have entered on the display to a decimal to be used in the calculator's computations. This saves you the trouble of converting the percent to a decimal (moving it two places to the left).

Example 1. Add 5% to the amount $60. (Round your answer to the penny.)

1. Depress $\boxed{\text{Clear}}$.
2. Depress $\boxed{\text{Fix}}$.
3. Enter 2 on the keyboard. Your decimal is now set for two decimals rounded to appear on the display.
4. Enter 60 on the keyboard.
5. Depress $\boxed{+}$.
6. Enter 5 on the keyboard.
7. Depress $\boxed{\%}$ (lower left of the numeric keyboard).
8. Depress $\boxed{=}$.
9. Your answer, $63.00, will appear on the display.

Practice Problems 8. Solve the following percentage problems. (Round your answers to two decimal places.)

1. Add 4% to the amount $55.50. (*Ans.* $57.72)
2. Add 3.5% to $480.

3. Add 6.1% to $2.40.
4. Add 26% to $67.
5. Add 9% to $860.30.
6. Add 17.4% to $102.91.

Example 2. What is the price of a $15.95 item that is discounted 20% and must include a sales tax of 5%? (Round to the penny.)

1. Depress [Clear].
2. Is the decimal still fixed at 2?
3. Enter 15.95 on the keyboard.
4. Depress [-].
5. Enter 20 on the keyboard.
6. Depress [%] key.
7. Depress [+].
8. Enter 5 on the keyboard.
9. Depress [%].
10. Depress [=].
11. Your answer, $13.40, will appear on the display.

Practice Problems 9. Complete the following percentage problems. (Round your answers to the penny.)

7. What is the price of a $15.50 item that is discounted at 15% and must include a sales tax of 4%? (*Ans.* $13.70)
8. What is the price of a $65.40 item that is discounted at 18% and must include a sales tax of 4.5%?
9. What is the price of a $60.60 item that is discounted at 10% and must include a sales tax of 6%?
10. What is the price of a $7.20 item that is discounted at 20% and must include a sales tax of 5%?
11. What is the price of a $1,059.33 item that is discounted at 40% and must include a sales tax of 5.5%?
12. What is the price of a $364.20 item that is discounted at 25% and must include a sales tax of 6%?

Example 3. What is 2.6% of $14?

1. Enter 14 on the keyboard.
2. Depress [X].

3. Enter 2.6 on the keyboard.
4. Depress $\boxed{\%}$.
5. Depress $\boxed{=}$.
6. Your answer, $.36, will appear on the display (rounded to two decimal places).

Practice Problems 10. Complete the following percentage problems. (Round your answers to two decimal places.)

13. What is 3.9% of 67.3? (*Ans.* 2.62)
14. What is 45% of $390.55?
15. What is 2.5% of $35?
16. What is 76% of 890.56?
17. What is 33.4% of 78?
18. What is 24.5% of 128.6?

Example 4. Eighteen dollars is 15% of what amount?

1. Enter 18 on the keyboard.
2. Depress $\boxed{\div}$.
3. Enter 15 on the keyboard.
4. Depress $\boxed{\%}$.
5. Depress $\boxed{=}$.
6. Your answer, $120, will appear on the display.

Practice Problems 11. Complete the following percentage problems. (Round your answers to two decimal places.)

19. Sixteen is 12% of what amount? (*Ans.* 133.33)
20. Twelve is 35% of what amount?
21. Thirty-seven is 49% of what amount?
22. Twenty is 88% of what amount?
23. One hundred three is 23% of what amount?
24. Four thousand is 28% of what amount?

Example 5. A $5 item is marked down to $3. What is the discount percent?

1. Enter 5 on the keyboard.
2. Depress $\boxed{\Delta\%}$ (lower left of the numeric keyboard).
3. Enter 3 on the keyboard.

4. Depress $\boxed{=}$.

5. Your answer, -40, will appear on the display. The *discount* (-) is 40%.

Practice Problems 12. Complete the following percent problems. (Round your answers to hundredths of the percent.)

25. A $23 item is marked down to $20. What is the discount percent? (*Ans.* 13.04%)
26. A $754 item is marked down to $650. What is the discount percent?
27. A $30 item is marked down to $28.50. What is the discount percent?
28. A $1,050.90 item is marked down to $898.98. What is the discount percent?
29. A $58.50 item is marked down to $45.99. What is the discount percent?
30. A $4 item is marked down to $3.25. What is the discount percent?

Example 6. A $3 item is marked up to $5. What is the percent of markup?

1. Enter 3 on the keyboard.
2. Depress $\boxed{\Delta\%}$.
3. Enter 5 on the keyboard.
4. Depress $\boxed{=}$.
5. Your answer, 66.67%, rounded to two decimal places, will appear on the display.

Practice Problems 13. Complete the following percent problems. (Round your answers to hundredths of the percent.)

31. A $4.50 item is marked up to $5.25. What is the percent of markup? (*Ans.* 16.67%)
32. A $900.20 item is marked up to $1,000. What is the percent of markup?
33. A $49.95 item is marked up to $60.95. What is the percent of markup?
34. A $37.50 item is marked up to $45.00. What is the percent of markup?
35. An $89.99 item is marked up to $99.99. What is the percent of markup?

Mixed Problems

Example. $\dfrac{(2+3) \times (4+5)}{(3+4) \times (5+6)} =$

$(2+3) \times (4+5)/((3+4) \times (5+6)) =$

1. Depress $\boxed{\text{Clear}}$.
2. Depress $\boxed{(}$ (left parentheses), which is located at the upper right on the numeric keyboard.

BASIC OPERATIONS   305

3. Enter 2 on the keyboard.
4. Depress $\boxed{+}$.
5. Enter 3 on the keyboard.
6. Depress $\boxed{)}$.
7. Depress $\boxed{\times}$.
8. Depress $\boxed{(}$.
9. Enter 4 on the keyboard.
10. Depress $\boxed{+}$.
11. Enter 5 on the keyboard.
12. Depress $\boxed{)}$.
13. Depress $\boxed{\div}$.
14. Depress $\boxed{(}$.
15. Depress $\boxed{(}$ again.
16. Enter 3 on the keyboard.
17. Depress $\boxed{+}$.
18. Enter 4 on the keyboard.
19. Depress $\boxed{)}$.
20. Depress $\boxed{\times}$.
21. Depress $\boxed{(}$.
22. Enter 5 on the keyboard.
23. Depress $\boxed{+}$.
24. Enter 6 on the keyboard.
25. Depress $\boxed{=}$. (The Equals key closes the parentheses automatically.)
26. Your answer, .5844155844, will appear on the display.

Practice Problems 14. Perform the following mixed problems. (Round your answers to three decimal places.)

36. $\dfrac{(35 + 4) \times (18.6 - 4.3)}{(85 + 34.7) \div (2.4 \times 6)} = 67.092$

37. $\dfrac{(32.1 - 4.8)(190 \times 3.7)}{(55.1 + 6) \div (6.3 \times 4)} =$

38. $\dfrac{(6.6 + 30) \times (23.9 - 4.6)}{(46 \div 3.1) + (8.2 - 4.3)} =$

39. $\dfrac{(77.9 + 1.95) \div (3.3 \times 1.8)}{(8.4 - 2.72) \times (18 \div 4)} =$

40. $\dfrac{(50.1 - 32.6) + (23.3 \times 2.2)}{(34 + 2.6) \times (19 \div 2.8)} =$

USING PRERECORDED PROGRAMS

Programs are recorded on magnetic cards. When a card is passed through the card-reading slot (upper right of the keyboard), the calculator reads and remembers the program.

The calculator will automatically run the program to solve the problem, stopping only for you to enter required quantities and to make decisions. The calculator remembers the program until:

1. the calculator is turned off, or
2. a new program is entered, or
3. the [Clear All] key is depressed.

Prompting

The calculator will prompt you on what to enter by displaying messages.

Be careful not to get dust, scratches, grease, or fingerprints on the magnetic card, or the program card cannot be read properly by the calculator.

Running the Prerecorded Program on Compound Interest

Assume that the problem you want to solve is:

Example. Find the future value of a $500 deposit in a savings account after five years if the interest rate is 6%, compounded annually.

1. Depress [Clear All] key.
2. The display shows "PROMPTING DESIRED?".
3. Depress [YES] key (upper left of the numeric keyboard).
4. The display shows "PRESS YES, LOAD CARD."
5. Depress [YES] key.
6. Carefully place the program card (with the arrow facing the slot and the white side up) into the slot.

Note: The card contains two programs; use the correct arrow.

7. The card-reader motor will guide the card through. Do *not* push or pull on the card once the machine grips the card.
8. The printer will print the title of the program preceded by **.
9. The display shows "ENTER PRESENT VALUE."
10. Enter the amount (for example, 500) on the keyboard.
11. Depress [Enter] key.
12. The calculator now displays "ENTER FUTURE VALUE."
13. Since this is the amount we don't know and are solving for, depress [Not Known] key (upper right of the numeric keyboard).
14. The display shows "ENTER INTEREST."
15. Enter the interest rate (for example, 6) on the keyboard.
16. Depress [Enter] key.
17. The display now shows "ENTER NO. PERIODS."
18. Enter the number of years (since this interest is compounded annually, or once a year; for this **Example**, enter 5 on the keyboard).
19. Depress [Enter].
20. The calculator automatically completes the problem and the printout. The future value, $669.11, is printed on the tape. Be *sure* you do *not* enter any amounts or depress any keys until the calculator stops printing.
21. You are now ready to enter a new set of data on compound interest.
    Note: The program will stay in the calculator's memory until (1) you enter a new program card, or (2) depress the [Clear All] key, or (3) turn off the power.

Practice Problems 15. Solve the following problems on compound interest, using the program card:

WITH FUTURE VALUE UNKNOWN

	Present Value ($)	Number of Periods	Future Value ($)	Interest Rate
1.	400	12	————	5
2.	400	12	————	6
3.	400	12	————	7
4.	6,000	2	————	5.5
5.	547	4	————	5

	Present Value ($)	Number of Periods	Future Value ($)	Interest Rate
6.	10,000	6	_____	5.25
7.	5,050	24	_____	6.5
8.	4,500	36	_____	7
9.	4,400	30	_____	8
10.	2,525	18	_____	7.5
11.	24,900	20	_____	7.25
12.	50	4	_____	5
13.	3,000	6	_____	5.75
14.	204	8	_____	4
15.	100,000	8	_____	6
16.	4,500	30	_____	5.5
17.	20,000	5	_____	18
18.	100	12	_____	4.25
19.	18,700	4	_____	5.5
20.	16,000	20	_____	6

WITH NUMBER OF PERIODS UNKNOWN

	Present Value ($)	Number of Periods	Future Value ($)	Interest Rate
21.	1,000	_____	1,500	6
22.	250	_____	300	5
23.	10,000	_____	20,000	4.5
24.	300	_____	400	5.5
25.	1,575	_____	1,775	4
26.	2,500	_____	3,100	6.25
27.	100	_____	150	5
28.	100	_____	200	5
29.	100	_____	300	5
30.	100	_____	400	5

WITH INTEREST RATE UNKNOWN

	Present Value ($)	Number of Periods	Future Value ($)	Interest Rate
31.	1,000	3	1,200	————
32.	8,050	3	10,025	————
33.	500	4	650	————
34.	200	8	300	————
35.	2,500	6	3,000	————
36.	1,000,000	3	1,250,000	————
37.	100,000	6	150,000	————
38.	35,100	5	40,500	————
39.	356	4	400	————
40.	619	8	1,000	————

WITH PRESENT VALUE UNKNOWN

	Present Value ($)	Number of Periods	Future Value ($)	Interest Rate
41.	————	12	1,200	6.5
42.	————	4	365	5.5
43.	————	10	100,000	5
44.	————	20	5,475	7.5
45.	————	6	50	5.25
46.	————	8	25,000	4.5
47.	————	12	38,000	5.75
48.	————	60	40,000	6
49.	————	4	1,000	18
50.	————	15	500	3.8

Running the Prerecorded Program on Add-On Rate Installment Loan

If you know the loan amount, the add-on rate of interest, the number of months, and the odd days the loan is for, the calculator is programmed to tell you the monthly installment rate, the total amount of interest, and the annual interest rate.

Example. What is the monthly installment payment, the total interest, and the annual rate of interest for a $1,000 loan for 10 months, in which the odd days are 10 and the add-on interest rate is 6%?

1. After loading the program card, the display reads, "ENTER NO. MONTHS."
2. Enter 10 on the keyboard.
3. Depress Enter .
4. The display now reads, "ENTER ODD DAYS," meaning the number of days left in the month in which you buy the item. For example, if the purchase of the item was on September 20, there are 10 days left in September (10 odd days).
5. Enter 10 on the keyboard.
6. Depress Enter key.
7. The display now reads, "ENTER ADD-ON RATE (%)."
8. Enter the amount of interest, 6.
9. Depress Enter key.
10. The display now reads, "ENTER LOAN AMOUNT."
11. Enter 1,000, as an example, on the keyboard.
12. Depress Enter .
13. The calculator now figures the monthly payment, $105.16; the total interest, $51.64; and the annual rate of interest, 10.48%. Because of the Truth in Lending law, the buyer must now be given this information at the time of purchase.
14. Do *not* enter any data into the calculator while the tape is printing, or the calculator will be damaged.
15. The complete transaction prints out on the tape for your record.

Practice Problems 16. Solve the following problems on add-on rate installment loans, using the program card:

	Number Months	Odd Days	Add-On Rate (%)	Loan Amount	Monthly Payment ($)	Total Int. ($)	Annual Rate (%)
1.	20	4	6.5	2,000	_____	_____	_____
2.	12	12	6	4,500	_____	_____	_____
3.	36	23	7	2,560	_____	_____	_____
4.	18	2	7.5	1,500	_____	_____	_____

	Number Months	Odd Days	Add-On Rate (%)	Loan Amount	Monthly Payment ($)	Total Int. ($)	Annual Rate (%)
5.	30	14	6.25	1,875			
6.	24	0	6.5	545			
7.	28	15	7.75	1,275			
8.	6	27	5	1,485			
9.	10	3	5.5	690			
10.	15	17	5.25	755			
11.	18	30	5	12,000			
12.	60	7	7.25	30,000			
13.	120	6	7	35,000			
14.	240	15	6.75	35,100			
15.	300	18	7	34,000			
16.	3	10	6.25	229			
17.	8	21	6.5	250.85			
18.	15	11	5.75	306.81			
19.	7	4	5	191.14			
20.	6	2	7.75	600			
21.	36	14	8.25	15,000			
22.	18	29	6.5	1,500			
23.	12	5	7.5	29,000			
24.	6	7	10.5	3,500			
25.	3	18	6.3	975			

Use the problems in Units 1 and 2 for additional practice.

Sample Examination

You may want to be timed as you try the Unit 7 Sample Examination, which is presented in the Introduction.

Unit 8

Ten-Key Adding and Listing Machines

Ten-key adding and listing machines are used in some smaller offices (such as service stations and doctors' offices) where the basic needs are addition and subtraction. As you will see in this unit, it is possible to multiply and divide (by multiplication) on these machines, but they are designed primarily for addition and subtraction.

These ten-keys (or eleven or twelve if they have double and triple zero keys) have the basic keyboard, which should be operated by touch. Other features include a column indicator, which lets the operator check how many digits he has entered into the keyboard. For example, after depressing 690, the column indicator will show 3. These machines also have a Clear key or Clear lever, which is used to clear a keyboard entry. It also clears the column indicator. Other keys include an $\boxed{X}$ or *Repeat* key, which is used for repeated addition, repeated subtraction, and multiplication.

DECIMALS

Some adding machines have no printed decimals. Others always print the decimal at two places automatically to accommodate dollars and cents problems. If you are adding or subtracting problems that do *not* contain two decimals, you will have to ignore the printed decimal and place your own decimals where needed. For example, in working with whole numbers there will be no decimals. If your adding machine prints one, ignore it.

Example 1. 39.14
  2.968
  .4703

1. Your decimal will need to be placed at *four* to accommodate the maximum number of decimal places in the problem.
2. Add zeros where needed in order to properly align your decimal at four places.

3. Your tape should look like this:

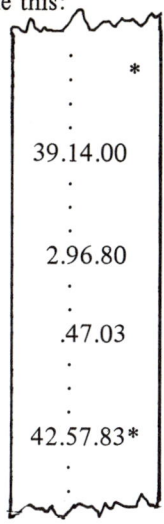

```
         *
     39.14.00

      2.96.80

       .47.03

     42.57.83*
```

4. If your machine prints a decimal between the 7 and the 8, ignore it.
5. Point off four places from right to left. Your *correct* answer is *42.5783*.

ADDITION

It is important that you operate all ten-key machines by touch. *Be sure to complete Unit 1 on the touch system to develop your skill in keying in figures by touch* (pages 93-119) before continuing with Unit 8.

Example 2. 32.49
                4.86

1. Depress Total key (T or *) to clear.
2. Enter 3 2 4 9 on the keyboard.
3. Depress Plus bar.
4. Enter 4 8 6 on the keyboard.
5. Depress Plus bar.
6. Depress Total key (T or *).
7. Your answer, 37.35, will print on the tape.

Practice Problems 1. Perform the following additions. Be sure to *align your decimal positions,* and place the correct decimal in your answers as they are completed.

TEN-KEY ADDING AND LISTING MACHINES

1.	5.18	2.	83.14	3.	245.1	4.	632	5.	4.590
	6.45		62.50		827.4		202		.259
	88.92		41.32		620.3		514		8.417
	83.03		88.30		611.9		34		.541
	10.51		4.50		62.7		186		5.736
	215.24		36.70		41.3		234		26.517

6.	63.05	7.	4.72	8.	.528	9.	814	10.	1.748
	11.15		49.17		.616		534		.404
	22.72		19.02		.068		932		.664
	51.55		4.12		.534		431		.72
	74.02		.86		.652		724		1.847
	800.65		3.76		.431		533		2.746

11. $839 + 337 + 2{,}174 + 26{,}819 + 23{,}017 + 512{,}390 =$

12. $67.0 + 2.86 + 1.5934 + 89 + 296.1 + .8678 =$

13. $99.0 + 2{,}980.75 + .9381 + 10.5 + 23.9 + 247.11 =$

14. $29 + .17 + 1{,}890.02 + .73 + 5.84 + 234.79 =$

15. $7.83 + 2.966 + 33{,}499 + .7953 + 34.111 + 2.9977 =$

Find the totals for each of the following deposit slips:

	Coin	$ 4.96
	Currency	9.00
	Checks	15.85
		105.00
		28.50
		36.90
		17.29
		48.00
16.	Total	$

	Coin	$ 48.29
	Currency	30.00
	Checks	205.37
		506.32
		800.00
		67.57
		15.89
		36.80
17.	Total	$

	Coin	$ 35.77
	Currency	120.00
	Checks	13.27
		960.30
		2.58
		84.38
		190.00
		201.33
18.	Total	$

	Coin	$ 18.34
	Currency	200.00
	Checks	18.48
		350.33
		34.60
		5.80
		56.20
		50.00
19.	Total	$

20. Find the total sales for the six-month period (in millions of $):

Jan.	Feb.	March	April	May	June	Total
3.8	2.5	4.4	5.4	3.9	3.9	_____

21.-30. Total the monthly budget expense by department (add horizontally) and the budget expense by item (add vertically) for the following:

Department	Salaries ($)	Benefits ($)	Office Supplies ($)	Telephone ($)	Total	
Purchasing	13,400	1,500	200	100	_____	21.
Sales	25,400	3,000	350	500	_____	22.
Technical Service	16,300	1,650	40	300	_____	23.
Research	4,500	430	35	50	_____	24.
Data Processing	5,000	500	45	60	_____	25.
Total	26. _____	27. _____	28. _____	29. _____	30. _____	

SUBTRACTION

Example.   817.63
              -802.14
              ───────
               15.49

1. Depress Total key to clear.
2. Enter ⑧ ① ⑦ ⑥ ③ on the keyboard.
3. Depress Plus bar.
4. Enter ⑧ ⓪ ② ① ④ on the keyboard.
5. Depress Minus bar.
6. Depress Total key (T or *).
7. Your answer, 15.49, will print on the tape.

Practice Problems 2. Perform the following subtractions. Be sure to *align your decimal positions,* and place the correct decimal in your answers as they are completed.

1. 79,728,164 - 37,186,928 =
2. 6,746,989 - 4,271,840 =
3. 2,995.75 - 1,826.87 =
4. 60,924.74 - 58,311.29 =
5. 102,378.45 - 88,186.43 =
6. 7,809 - 764 =

7. 347.8965 - 23.2756 =

8. 432.432 - 61.122 =

9. .8764 - .0786 =

10. 234.76 - 23.45 =

11. 6,947.24 - 896.70 =

12. 102,377.36 - 797.65 =

13. 654,382.98 - 544,898.02 =

14. 3,478,929 - 1,280,345 =

15. 184.63 - 75.20 =

16. 73.26 - 1.33 =

17. 30.260 - 1.39468 =

18. 2,272.99 - 885.25 =

19. 75.675 - 42.797 =

20. 29,172,282 - 19,426,947 =

21.-30. Perform the subtractions indicated, and complete the following check register:

	Balance
	$3,989.00
Check 103	-871.32
	_____ 21.
Check 104	-100.34
	_____ 22.
Check 105	-13.49
	_____ 23.
Check 106	-4.80
	_____ 24.
Check 107	-31.72
	_____ 25.
Check 108	-450.37
	_____ 26.
Check 109	-211.30
	_____ 27.
Check 110	-86.75
	_____ 28.
Check 111	-200.36
	_____ 29.
Check 112	-800.26
	_____ 30.

CREDIT BALANCES

When minus amounts are greater than plus amounts, most adding machines will print a negative answer (credit balance) for you. The answer will be shown with *Cr* (for credit balance) or with a minus sign (-), indicating that you have a credit or minus amount. Some calculators print credit balances in red.

Example.   3.39
               -4.06
               ─────
               - .67

1. Clear your machine.
2. Enter ③ ③ ⑨ on the keyboard.
3. Depress Plus bar.
4. Enter ④ ⓪ ⑥ on the keyboard.
5. Depress Minus bar.
6. Your answer, -.67, will print on the tape with a Cr or a (-) or a TC (for total credit).

Practice Problems 3. Complete the following credit balance problems. Remember to indicate *Cr* or (-) on your answers. Place your decimal point correctly as you complete each problem.

1. 788 - 3,951 =
2. 7.5 - 30.78 =
3. 71.2 - 81.62 =
4. 77.88 - 3,296.76 =
5. 360 - 390 =
6. 2,563.22 - 3,208.96 =
7. 787.56 - 1,961.35 =
8. 15.02 - 29.35 =
9. 187 - 563 =
10. 68.59 - 72.43 =
11. 2,369,478 - 3,476,898 =
12. 209.36 - 339.43 =
13. 248.59 - 432.76 =
14. .872 - 1.274 =
15. 121.33 - 203.67 =
16. 3,589.24 - 4,186.22 =
17. 23.32 - 304.77 =
18. 29,851.90678 - 30,256.768 =
19. 76.25 - 89.34 =
20. 202.32 - 304.77 =

NON-ADD FEATURE

When the Non-add (# or N) key is used, the figures entered in the keyboard are printed on the tape but are not calculated. This feature is helpful for coding on your tape such items as job or lot numbers, time clock numbers, inventory numbers, etc.

SUBTOTALS

The Subtotal key automatically prints the amount accumulated in the machine without clearing the amount from the machine and without adding the subtotal figure into the amount. Subtotals are usually printed with an *S* or a ◊ beside the amount, or *SC* (for subtotal credit balance) if your answer is a negative or credit balance.

Example. 29.10
40.23
───── Subtotal
.25
───── Total

1. Clear your machine.
2. Enter [2] [9] [1] [0] on the keyboard.
3. Depress Plus bar.
4. Enter [4] [0] [2] [3] on the keyboard.
5. Depress Plus bar.
6. We want to know what our subtotal is at this point, but we also want to continue adding the problem. Depress Subtotal key ([S]). Your subtotal, 69.33, will print on the tape but will not clear the amount from the machine, so that you may continue with the problem.
7. Enter [2] [5] on the keyboard.
8. Depress Plus bar.
9. Depress Total key ([T] or [*]).
10. Your final answer, 69.58, will print on the tape.

Practice Problems 4. Complete the following problems, taking a subtotal and a grand total where indicated. Be sure to align your decimals and point off the correct decimal in your answer as you complete each problem.

1. 80.35
    1.07
    ───── Subtotal
   18.38
    ───── Total
	2. 1,817.54
	      293.76
	    ───── Subtotal
	      219.02
	    ───── Total
		3. .04
		    1.06
		     .78
		    ───── Subtotal
		     .86
		    ───── Total

4. 5,546
    3,918
    ───── Subtotal
   29,155
    ───── Total
	5. 132,169
	        192
	    ───── Subtotal
	    123,755
	    ───── Total
		6. 109.07
		     12.65
		    ───── Subtotal
		      2.34
		    ───── Total

7. 4.87
    5.32
    4.48
    ___ Subtotal
    2.27
    ___ Total

8. 7,518.29
    1,285.34
    _____ Subtotal
    378.82
    _____ Total

9. 38.987
    172.762
    _____ Subtotal
    72.265
    _____ Total

10. 7.388
    1.564
    _____ Subtotal
    .176
    ____ Total

MULTIPLICATION

Multiplication on the ten-key adding machine is not automatic, but can be accomplished by repeated addition. Most adding machines have an $\boxed{X}$ key or a repeat mechanism, which makes it easy to repeat add a number. For example, to multiply 287 by 4, we can add 287 four times.

Example 1. 287 × 4 = 1,148

1. Clear your machine.
2. Enter $\boxed{2}$ $\boxed{8}$ $\boxed{7}$ on the keyboard.
3. Lock or depress the $\boxed{X}$ key or the Repeat key.
4. Repeat add four times.
5. Be sure that your column indicator is *clear*.
6. Depress the Total key.
7. Your tape will look like this:

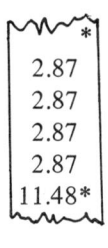

>   *
>   2.87
>   2.87
>   2.87
>   2.87
>   11.48*

8. Since we multiplied *whole numbers*, our answer is whole numbers. If your adding machine prints an automatic decimal, ignore it.
9. The correct answer is 1,148.

Example 2. 328 × 14 = 4,592

1. Clear your machine.

2. Enter ③ ② ⑧ on the keyboard.
3. Lock or depress the ⑧ key or the Repeat key.
4. Repeat add 328 four times (for the *4* in the units position of the multiplier).
5. Depress the zero key once. This will make our multiplicand 3,280 so that we can add it in the tens position. We can multiply any number by ten by merely adding a zero to that number.
    Note: Some models automatically "step over" (add the zero) for you.
6. Add one time (for the *1* in the tens position of the multiplier).
7. Be sure that your column indicator is *clear.*
8. Depress the Total key.
9. Your tape will look like this:

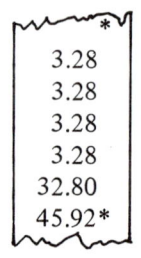

```
     *
 3.28
 3.28
 3.28
 3.28
32.80
45.92*
```

10. Since we multiplied *whole numbers,* our answer is whole numbers. If your adding machine prints an automatic decimal, ignore it.
11. The correct answer is 4,592.

Example 3. 876 × 432 = 378,432

1. Clear your machine.
2. Enter ⑧ ⑦ ⑥ on the keyboard.
3. Lock or depress the ⑧ key or the Repeat key.
4. Repeat add 876 two times (for the *2* in the units position of the multiplier).
5. Depress the zero key once. This will make our multiplicand 8,760 so that we can add it in the tens position.
6. Add three times (for the *3* in the tens position of the multiplier).
7. Depress the zero key once. This will make our multiplicand 87,600 so that we can add it in the hundreds position. We can multiply any number by 100 by merely adding two zeros to that number.
8. Add four times (for the *4* in the hundreds position of the multiplier).
9. Be sure your column indicator is *clear.*
10. Depress the Total key.

11. Your tape will look like this:

```
      *
   8.76
   8.76
  87.60
  87.60
  87.60
 876.00
 876.00
 876.00
 876.00
3784.32*
```

12. Since we multiplied *whole numbers,* our answer is whole numbers. If your adding machine prints an automatic decimal, ignore it.
13. The correct answer is 378,432.

MULTIPLICATION WITH ZEROS

Example 4. 421 × 304 = 127,984

1. Clear your machine.
2. Enter [4] [2] [1] on the keyboard.
3. Lock or depress the [X] key or the Repeat key.
4. Repeat add four times (for the *4* in the units position).
5. Add one zero.
6. Since the tens position in the multiplier (3<u>0</u>4) is a zero, there is nothing to add here. Therefore, add a second zero, which will place us in the hundreds position.
7. Repeat add three times (for the *3* in the hundreds position).
8. Clear your column indicator.
9. Depress the Total key.
10. Your answer, 127,984, will print on the tape. Your answer is *whole numbers.*

MULTIPLICATION WITH DECIMALS

Example 5. .65 × .25 = .1625

1. Clear your machine.
2. Enter [6] [5] on the keyboard.

3. Lock or depress the $\boxed{X}$ key or the Repeat key.
4. Repeat add five times.
5. Add one zero.
6. Repeat add two times.
7. Clear the column indicator.
8. Depress the Total key.
9. The number 16.25 will print on your tape. Obviously, the decimal point is incorrect. Most adding machines are set for printing two decimal places for use with adding and subtracting dollars and cents.
10. We will need to place our own decimal according to the usual rule of mathematics: add the number of decimal places in both factors of the problem (2 + 2 = 4 decimal places). Point off four places from right to left.
11. Our correct answer is .1625.

SHORT-CUT MULTIPLICATION

To multiply any number by ten on the adding machine, all we need to do is to enter the number on the keyboard, add a zero, and total.

Example 6. 286 × 10 = 2,860

1. Enter $\boxed{2}$ $\boxed{8}$ $\boxed{6}$ on the keyboard.
2. Add one zero.
3. Be sure the column indicator is clear.
4. Total.
5. Your answer is 2,860.

Example 7. 286 × 9 = 2,574

To multiply 286 by 9, it is much quicker to multiply 286 by 10 and subtract 286 once.

1. Clear your machine.
2. Enter $\boxed{2}$ $\boxed{8}$ $\boxed{6}$ on the keyboard.
3. Depress $\boxed{-}$ once.
4. Depress the Zero key once.
5. Add once.
6. Be sure your column indicator is clear.
7. Total.
8. Your answer is 2,574.

Notice the difference in the number of steps:

Short-Cut Method

```
      *
   2.86−
  28.60
  25.74*
```

Regular Method

```
      *
   2.86
   2.86
   2.86
   2.86
   2.86
   2.86
   2.86
   2.86
   2.86
  25.74*
```

Example 8. 453 × 287 = 130,011

Short-cut multiplication combines repeated addition and repeated subtraction for faster multiplication. Short-cut multiplication can be used to advantage when the multiplier contains digits of 7, 8, or 9 by the use of their complements. The complement of a number is the difference between that number and the next power of 10. For example, the complement of 7 is 3 (7 + 3 = 10); the complement of 80 is 20 (80 + 20 = 100); the complement of 200 is 800 (200 + 800 = 1,000), etc.

1. In the example, the complement of 287 is 13 (287 + 13 = 300).
2. It will take fewer steps to add 453 three times in the hundreds position and subtract it three times in the units position and once in the tens positions than to add 17 times (7 + 8 + 2 = 17).
3. Enter [4] [5] [3] on the keyboard.
4. Repeat subtract three times.
5. Add one zero.
6. Subtract once.
7. Add one zero.
8. Repeat add three times.
9. Be sure your column indicator is clear.
10. Total.
11. Your answer is 130,011 (whole numbers).

324 TEN-KEY ADDING AND LISTING MACHINES

Your tape will look like this:

```
        *
    4.53-
    4.53-
    4.53-
   45.30-
  453.00
  453.00
  453.00
 1300.11*
```

Practice Problems 5. Complete the following multiplication problems. Be sure to place your decimal correctly as you complete each problem.

1. 919 × 855 =
2. 56.5 × 22.3 =
3. 28.9 × 9.01 =
4. 348 × 302 =
5. 863 × 43 =
6. 58 × 4.3 =
7. 7,900 × .301 =
8. .487 × 2.901 =
9. 678 × 1.35 =
10. 284 × 209 =

AMOUNT OF MARKON

Markon usually refers to the amount which the retailer adds to the price he paid for merchandise. The retailer decides what rate of markon he must use to take care of his operating expenses and to make a profit. The terms "markon" and "markup" are sometimes used interchangeably, although "markup" more correctly refers to adding to the selling price previously established.

Markon can be a percentage of the cost price or of the selling price. The cost price plus the amount of markon equals the selling price. The markon rate is usually expressed as a percent.

Example. Sports Corner, Inc., paid $8.80 each for basketballs. What is the amount of markon if the rate of markon is 22% of the cost price?

1. 8.80 × .22 = 1.9360
2. Amount of markon = $1.94 (rounded to the penny)

11.–20. Calculate the amount of markon for the following items by multiplying the percent times the cost. Be sure to *convert* your percent to a decimal. (Round to the penny.)

	Cost of Item ($)	Percent of Markon (%)	Amount of Markon ($)
11.	43.80	22	9.64
12.	126.43	18	_____
13.	9.50	12	_____
14.	54.10	5	_____
15.	1,300.19	15	_____
16.	264.38	25	_____
17.	37.48	20	_____
18.	903.50	15	_____
19.	75.00	12.5	_____
20.	2.90	20	_____

DIVISION

On an adding machine, division is a multiplication process. We multiply the dividend by the reciprocal of the divisor. A reciprocal of any number is 1 divided by that number. For example, the reciprocal of 2 is 1 ÷ 2 or .5. A Table of Reciprocals from 1 to 1,000 is given in Appendix B. However, you can obtain the reciprocal of any number by merely dividing 1 by the number.

The answer we can obtain by using this reciprocal method is close to the real quotient but is not 100 percent accurate. For example, it will give us the quotient of 144 ÷ 12 as 11.999999, which is 12 when rounded off. For many types of problems, this degree of accuracy is sufficient.

Example. 124 ÷ 4 = 31

1. Clear your machine.
2. Look up the reciprocal of 4 in your Table of Reciprocals.
3. You find that the reciprocal of 4 is .25.
4. The problem now becomes 124 × .25.
5. Enter $\boxed{1}$ $\boxed{2}$ $\boxed{4}$ on the keyboard.
6. Lock or depress the $\boxed{X}$ key or the Repeat key.
7. Repeat add five times.
8. Add one zero.
9. Repeat add two times.
10. Clear your column indicator.

11. Depress the Total key.
12. Your tape will print 31.00.
13. Since 124 is a whole number and .25 has two decimals, we point off the answer two decimal places. Our correct answer is, then, 31.

Practice Problems 6. Do the following division problems by the multiplication of the reciprocal method. Place your decimal correctly in each answer as it is completed.

1. $3{,}365 \div 27 =$
2. $1{,}850.1 \div 36 =$
3. $726.2 \div 298 =$
4. $13.767 \div 44 =$
5. $16.5551 \div 23 =$
6. $171.58 \div 31 =$

Find the cost of individual items in the problems given below. A gross is 144; in these problems divide the cost by 144. A quire is 24; in these problems divide the cost by 24. (Round your answers to the penny.)

7. What is the cost of an individual stencil if a quire costs $7.50?
8. What is the cost of an individual offset mat if 100 mats cost $14.85?
9. What is the cost per pencil if a dozen pencils costs $1.39?
10. What is the cost for one piece of chalk if a gross costs $1.29?
11. What is the cost for one roll of adding machine tape if a dozen costs $2.50?
12. What is the cost per sheet of bond paper if a ream costs $13.50? (A ream is 500 sheets.)
13. What is the cost of a roll of Scotch tape if a dozen rolls costs $3.10?
14. What is the cost of one bottle of a soft drink if eight bottles cost $1.07?
15. A large urn holds 207 ounces of coffee. How many quarts does it hold? (There are 32 ounces in a quart.) (Round to the tenth.)
16. A rug measures 2,480 square inches. How much is this in square feet? (There are 144 square inches in a square foot.) (Round to the tenth.)

Use the problems in Units 1 and 2 for additional practice.

Sample Examination

You may want to be timed as you try the Unit 8 Sample Examination, presented in the Introduction.

Unit 9

Ten-Key Printing Calculators

ADDITION

Example. 123 + 456 = 579

1. Clear your calculator by depressing the Motor bar, $\boxed{T}$, or $\boxed{*}$.
   The appearance of the T or * on the tape indicates that your registers are clear for entering a new problem.

2. Enter $\boxed{1}$ $\boxed{2}$ $\boxed{3}$ on the keyboard.

3. Depress $\boxed{+}$ or Motor bar.

4. Enter $\boxed{4}$ $\boxed{5}$ $\boxed{6}$ on the keyboard.

5. Depress $\boxed{+}$ or Motor bar.

6. Depress $\boxed{T}$, $\boxed{*}$, or Motor bar.

7. Your answer, 579, will appear on the tape. This problem is *whole* numbers. If your tape shows an automatic decimal at two places, disregard it for problems of this type.

It is highly desirable to operate all ten-key calculators by touch. *Be sure to complete Unit 1 on the touch system to develop your skill in keying in figures by touch before continuing with Unit 9.*

Practice Problems 1. Perform the following additions. Be sure to align your decimal positions, and place the correct decimal in your answers as they are completed.

	1.	2.	3.	4.	5.
	4.14	94.25	.134	541	3.489
	5.34	73.60	.918	191	.148
	99.71	50.43	.731	615	9.528
	49.10	99.14	.722	125	.651
	21.57	15.61	.163	297	6.847
	106.35	47.81	.053	123	37.628

6.	65.03	7.	4.72	8.	.528	9.	814	10.	1.748
	11.15		49.17		.616		534		.404
	22.72		19.02		.068		932		.446
	51.55		4.12		.534		431		.72
	74.02		.86		.652		724		1.847
	800.65		3.76		.431		533		2.746

11. 176.4
    77.6
    841.3
    147.3
    647.5
    345.0

12.-25. Add the following sales figures for the six-month period. Add horizontally to find the sales by product, and add vertically to find the total sales by month. Your horizontal and vertical grand totals must agree.

PRODUCT SALES
JANUARY–JUNE
($)

Product	January	February	March	April	May	June	Total	
Passenger tires	135,400	141,600	129,650	138,500	149,650	150,320	_____	12.
Truck tires	128,600	130,500	131,600	125,300	150,500	138,700	_____	13.
Industrial tires	15,750	14,900	13,690	14,800	15,100	15,280	_____	14.
Foam tires	12,890	13,950	12,400	13,870	12,900	12,800	_____	15.
Rims	11,200	10,860	12,500	11,100	11,600	11,000	_____	16.
Fire hose	8,600	9,000	8,800	9,100	8,950	7,600	_____	17.
V-belts	7,450	6,950	7,800	7,600	7,900	7,800	_____	18.
								19.
	20.	21.	22.	23.	24.	25.		

SUBTOTALS

Example.
```
         .45
        4.56
        5.60
       10.61  Subtotal
         .89
       11.50  Total
```

1. Clear your calculator.
2. If necessary, place calculator in the subtotal mode.
3. Enter $\boxed{4}$ $\boxed{5}$ on the keyboard.
4. Depress $\boxed{+}$ or Motor bar.
5. Enter $\boxed{4}$ $\boxed{5}$ $\boxed{6}$ on the keyboard.
6. Depress $\boxed{+}$ or Motor bar.
7. Enter $\boxed{5}$ $\boxed{6}$ $\boxed{0}$ on the keyboard.
8. Depress $\boxed{S}$ (Subtotal key or Motor bar. Your subtotal, 10.61, will print on your tape.
9. Continue with the problem. Enter $\boxed{8}$ $\boxed{9}$ on the keyboard.
10. Depress $\boxed{+}$ or Motor bar.
11. If necessary, place your calculator in the total mode.
12. Depress $\boxed{T}$, $\boxed{*}$, or Motor bar.
13. Your total, 11.50, will print on your tape.

By using the Subtotal key, you can find the running total in your problem at any point, but the figures are retained in the calculator. The figures will not clear from your machine, and a running total will be retained until you depress the Total key.

Practice Problems 2. Complete the following problems, taking a subtotal and a grand total where indicated.

```
1.   91.46              2.  2,928.65             3.   .05
      2.18                    304.87                  .07
          Subtotal                   Subtotal         .89
                                                         Subtotal
     18.49                    230.11                  .97
          Total                      Total               Total
```

4. 6,667	5. 243,270	6. 111.18
4,029	203	23.76
Subtotal	Subtotal	Subtotal
30,266	234,866	3.45
Total	Total	Total
7. 5.98	8. 8,629.30	9. 149.098
6.43	2,396.45	283.873
5.59	Subtotal	Subtotal
Subtotal		
3.38	489.93	83.376
Total	Total	Total
10. 8.499		
2.675		
Subtotal		
.287		
Total		

SUBTRACTION

Example. 425
-98
327

1. Clear your calculator.
2. Enter [4] [2] [5] on the keyboard.
3. Depress [+] or Motor bar.
4. Enter [9] [8] on the keyboard.
5. Depress [-] .
6. Depress [T] , [*] , or Motor bar.
7. Your difference, 327, will print on the tape. The answer is *whole* numbers.

Practice Problems 3. Complete the following subtraction problems. Be sure to align your decimal position. Indicate the correct decimal as you complete each answer.

1. 80,839,275 - 48,297,039 =
2. 7,857,090 - 5,382,951 =
3. 3,006.86 - 2,937.98 =
4. 71,035.85 - 69,422.30 =
5. 213,489.56 - 99,297.54 =
6. 8,910 - 875 =
7. 458.9076 - 34.3867 =
8. 534.543 - 172.233 =
9. .9875 - .0897 =
10. 345.87 - 34.56 =
11. 7,058.35 - 907.81 =

12.-26. Perform the subtractions indicated and complete the following check register. Use the Subtotal key.

	Check No.	Date	To/For	Amount	Balance $2,978.00
12.	163	3/1	First National Bank	$110.40	_____
13.	164	3/1	Rent	210.00	_____
14.	165	3/6	Ajax Insurance Co.	65.30	_____
15.	166	3/7	Edison Electric	12.41	_____
16.	167	3/8	Telephone Company	14.76	_____
17.	–	3/8	Service Charge	2.60	_____
18.	168	3/15	Cash	30.00	_____
19.	169	3/21	A.R. Bradley, M.D.	15.00	_____
20.	170	3/26	The Fabric Shop	18.23	_____
21.	171	3/28	United Fund	50.00	_____
22.	172	3/30	Santoya Book Store	14.26	_____
23.	173	4/1	Rent	210.00	_____
24.	174	4/7	Allen Barton, D.D.S.	12.00	_____
25.	–	4/8	Service Charge	2.45	_____
26.	–	4/8	Check Printing	2.25	_____

CREDIT BALANCES

If you subtract a larger number from a smaller number, you will obtain a credit balance (negative total). A credit balance will be indicated on the tape by a *TC* (a total credit balance), an *SC* (a subtotal credit balance), a *Cr* (for credit balance), or a minus sign. On some calculators, the negative answer, or credit balance, is shown in red.

Example.   150
           -200
           ──────
            50   TC or -50 or 50-

1. Enter $\boxed{1}$ $\boxed{5}$ $\boxed{0}$ on the keyboard.
2. Depress $\boxed{+}$ or Motor bar.
3. Enter $\boxed{2}$ $\boxed{0}$ $\boxed{0}$ on the keyboard.
4. Depress $\boxed{-}$.

5. Depress $\boxed{T}$, $\boxed{*}$, or Motor bar.

6. Your answer, -50, will print on the tape with a minus sign, or Cr or TC.

Practice Problems 4. Complete the following credit balance problems. Remember to indicate *Cr* or (-) on your answers. Place your decimal point correctly as you complete each problem.

1. 98 - 4,062 = -3,964
2. 6.6 - 14.89 =
3. 82.3 - 97.3 =
4. 88.99 - 4,307.87 =
5. 471 - 489 =
6. 1,564.33 - 2,309.57 =

7. 898.67 - 3,072.46 =
8. 26.13 - 30.46 =
9. 117 - 674 =
10. 79.60 - 83.45 =
11. 3,470,589 - 3,568,909 =

Note: Be sure you have aligned your decimal places.

The following figures show deposits and check withdrawals from checking accounts. Add the deposits and subtract the withdrawals. Some of these accounts are overdrawn. Indicate a credit balance for the overdrawn accounts.

12. Beginning Balance $1,261.56
    Check #140   360.01
    Check #141   200.00
    Check #142   4.86
    Deposit   125.00
    Total

13. Beginning Balance $400.00
    Check #791   385.00
    Deposit   150.00
    Check #792   265.45
    Check #793   301.40
    Total

14. Beginning Balance $840.91
    Check #371   274.50
    Check #372   406.64
    Deposit   55.00
    Check #373   291.87
    Total

15. Beginning Balance $3,054.91
    Check #1004   2,918.66
    Check #1005   549.54
    Check #1006   10.81
    Check #1007   56.58
    Total

16. Beginning Balance $491.65
    Check #120   89.74
    Deposit   100.00
    Check #121   296.78
    Check #122   74.86
    Total

NON-ADD FEATURE

When the Non-add ($\boxed{\#}$ or $\boxed{N}$) key is used, the figures entered in the keyboard are printed on the tape but are not calculated. This feature is helpful for coding on your tape such items as job or lot numbers, time clock numbers, inventory numbers, etc.

MULTIPLICATION

Example 1. 12,345 × 12 = 148,140

1. If necessary, place your calculator in the multiply mode.
2. Enter $\boxed{1}$ $\boxed{2}$ $\boxed{3}$ $\boxed{4}$ $\boxed{5}$ on the keyboard.
3. Depress $\boxed{\times}$ or Motor bar.
4. Enter $\boxed{1}$ $\boxed{2}$ on the keyboard.
5. Depress $\boxed{=}$, $\boxed{\genfrac{}{}{0pt}{}{\times}{=}}$, or Motor bar.
6. Your product, 148,140, will print on the tape. This answer is *whole* numbers.

Example 2. .65 × .24 = .1560

1. Enter $\boxed{6}$ $\boxed{5}$ on the keyboard.
2. Depress $\boxed{\times}$ or Motor bar.
3. Enter $\boxed{2}$ $\boxed{4}$ on the keyboard.
4. Depress $\boxed{=}$, $\boxed{\genfrac{}{}{0pt}{}{\times}{=}}$, or Motor bar.
5. Place the decimal in your answer according to the usual rule of mathematics: add the number of decimals in the multiplier and the number of decimals in the multiplicand (2 + 2 = 4). Point off four places in the product from right to left.

Practice Problems 5. Perform the following multiplication problems. Be sure to place your decimal correctly in each product.

1. 121 × 966 =
2. 67.6 × 33.4 =
3. 39.1 × 1.12 =
4. 459 × 201 =
5. 974 × 54 =
6. 69 × 5.4 =
7. 8,011 × .412 =
8. .598 × 3.012 =
9. 789 × 2.46 =
10. 395 × 310 =
11. 864 × 34 =
12. 915 × .321 =
13. 36.8 × 5.2 =
14. 487.1 × .456 =
15. .689 × .321 =

DIVISION

Example. 1,914.6 ÷ 49.1 =

1. If necessary, place the calculator in the divide mode.
2. Enter [1] [9] [1] [4] [6] on the keyboard.
3. Depress the Dividend key or the Motor bar.
4. Enter [4] [9] [1] on the keyboard.
5. Depress [÷] or Motor bar.
6. A quotient of 38 (a whole number) with a remainder of 488 will print on the tape. This answer gives us very little accuracy.
7. We can obtain one additional decimal place for each zero that we add to our dividend. For example, if we add three zeros to the dividend (1,914.6000), we will obtain the quotient accurate to three decimal places. If we add six zeros to the dividend, we will obtain a quotient accurate to six decimal places.
8. Enter [1] [9] [1] [4] [6] and six zeros on the keyboard.
9. Depress the Dividend key or the Motor bar.
10. Enter [4] [9] [1] on the keyboard.
11. Depress [÷] or the Motor bar.
12. Your tape will print 38993890 with a remainder of 10.
13. The rule for placing the decimal in the quotient is as follows: subtract the number of decimals in the divisor from the number of decimals in the dividend (1,914.*6000000* ÷ 49.*1*). In this example, subtract *one* decimal from *seven* decimals. Point off *six* places from right to left in the quotient.
14. The correct answer is, then, 38.993890 with a remainder of 10.

Practice Problems 6. Perform the following divisions. For more accuracy, be sure to *add four zeros* to each dividend. Place the decimal correctly in each quotient according to the rule.

1. 4,476 ÷ 3.8 = 1,177.894
2. 2,961.2 ÷ .47 =
3. 837.3 ÷ 2.98 =
4. 24.878 ÷ 55 =
5. 17.6662 ÷ 33 =
6. 1,203 ÷ 31 =
7. 1,050 ÷ 1.99 =
8. 70 ÷ 84 =
9. 18,306 ÷ 3,444.39 =
10. 79,045 ÷ 980 =
11. 35.63 ÷ 93 =
12. 5,890 ÷ 789.2 =

13. 67.345 ÷ 2.92 =   15. 21 ÷ 68 =

14. .8376 ÷ .901 =

MULTIPLICATION OF A PERCENT

Example. What is 37.9% of 9,761.3?

1. Be sure your calculator is clear.
2. If necessary, place your calculator in the multiply mode.
3. Enter ③ ⑦ ⑨ on the keyboard.
4. Depress the Multiplier key ⓧ or the Motor bar.
5. Enter ⑨ ⑦ ⑥ ① ③ on the keyboard.
6. Depress ⌸, $\begin{array}{c}X\\=\end{array}$, or the Motor bar.
7. Your tape will show 36995327.
8. Count your decimals in the problem (percent must be converted to decimals by moving the decimal two places to the left). Your problem is, then, .379 × 9,761.3. You have a total of four decimals. Point off your product four places.
9. Your answer is 3,699.5327.

Practice Problems 7. Perform the following multiplications. Be sure to convert your percents to decimals.

1. What is 19.4% of 3,890? (*Ans.* 754.660)
2. What is 6% of 79.3?
3. What is 17.5% of 996?
4. What is 8% of 642.1?
5. What is 45% of 788.8?
6. What is 23.4% of 198.36?
7. What is 7.9% of 56.99?
8. What is 2.3% of 7,850.37?
9. What is 22% of 10,800?
10. What is 16.75% of 1,945.30?
11. What is .3% of 96? (Convert .3% to .003.)
12. What is 13.9% of 239.678?
13. What is 4.6% of 25?
14. What is 12% of 2,848.38?
15. What is 15% of 1,111.11?

FINDING WHAT PERCENT ONE NUMBER IS OF ANOTHER

Example. What percent is 29.41 of 38.7?

1. Remember that the "is" number (29.41) is the dividend. The "of" number (38.7) is the divisor. Alphabetically, "is" comes before "of."
2. The dividend *always* goes into the calculator first.
3. The problem can be thought of as a ratio:

$$\frac{29.41}{38.7} \text{ or roughly } \frac{30}{40} \text{ or } \frac{3}{4}$$

We know that 3 ÷ 4 or 3/4 will be 75%, our approximate answer.

4. Clear your calculator.
5. If necessary, place the calculator in the divide mode.
6. Enter the dividend, 29.410000, on the keyboard. (Four zeros will give your answer more decimal places and therefore more accuracy.)
7. Depress the Dividend key or the Motor bar.
8. Enter the divisor, 38.7, on the keyboard.
9. Depress the Divide key (÷) or the Motor bar.
10. Your tape will read 75994 with a remainder of 322.
11. By estimating your problem (29.41 ÷ 38.7) you can see that the answer will be less than one. (You are dividing a larger number into a smaller number; therefore, it will go less than one time.) When .75994 is converted to percent form, your answer will be 75.994%.
    You can achieve the correct decimal by using our decimal rule: Subtract the number of decimals in the divisor (1) from the number of decimals in the dividend (6). Point off five places in the quotient. Then convert to a percent answer by moving the decimal place two to the right.
12. Your final answer is 75.994%.

Practice Problems 8. Add four zeros to each dividend. Be sure to give your answers in *percent* form. Round to two decimal places after converting to percent. Remember: the "is" number is the dividend.

1. What percent is 24 of 29.3?
2. What percent is 21.6 of 87?
3. What percent is 8,899 of 90,395?
4. What percent of 13 is 60?
5. What percent of 2 is 1.45?
6. What percent of 91 is 88.9?

7. What percent is 540 of 651?
8. What percent is 18.2 of 94.6?
9. What percent is 78.06 of 69.7?
10. What percent is 64.3 of 85.4?
11. What percent is 7 of 15?
12. What percent is 45 of 41.2?
13. What percent of .864 is .789?
14. What percent of 16 is 77?
15. What percent of 33.3 is 66.7?

CONSTANT MULTIPLICATION

Example. $3 \times 6 = 18$
$3 \times 20 = 60$
$3 \times 4.8 = 14.4$

1. Clear your calculator.
2. If necessary, place your calculator in the multiply mode.
3. Enter the constant multiplier, 3, on the keyboard.
4. Depress $\boxed{X}$ or the Motor bar.
5. On some printing calculators it is necessary to place the Constant lever in the constant position to lock in the constant figure. Be sure to "unlock" the constant and clear when you have finished working with the constant.
6. Enter 6 on the keyboard.
7. Depress $\boxed{=}$, $\boxed{\overset{X}{=}}$, or the Motor bar.
8. Your product, 18, will print on the tape.
9. You can now continue entering the other multiplicands and multiplying without having to re-enter the constant, 3, on the keyboard. On some printing calculators it is necessary to depress the $\boxed{X}$ and the $\boxed{=}$ (or Motor bar) in order to recall the constant.
10. Your next two products are 60 and 14.4.
11. If necessary, unlock and clear the constant before proceeding to the next problem.

Practice Problems 9. FICA (Social Security) deductions are 5.85% of the gross pay up to the annual limit of $16,500. After an employee has reached $16,500 for the year, no further FICA deductions are made that year. Calculate the FICA deductions for the following payroll. Assume that none of these employees have yet reached their annual

TEN-KEY PRINTING CALCULATORS

maximum of $16,500. Enter the constant as .0585. (Round your answers to the penny.)

Employee Name	Gross Weekly Pay ($)	FICA Deduction ($)
1. Ayers, E.	197.60	11.56
2. Brewer, C.	206.75	_____
3. Cole, W.	125.00	_____
4. Duda, J.	285.34	_____
5. Frame, B.	198.33	_____
6. Goldberg, J.	225.00	_____
7. Griffa, D.	354.68	_____
8. Hairston, A.	329.80	_____
9. Horvath, J.	401.39	_____
10. Ingersoll, R.	265.45	_____
11. Jernigen, C.	175.00	_____
12. Kuss, R.	50.25	_____
13. Lehrman, S.	280.66	_____
14. McKay, B.	234.90	_____
15. Nauman, M.	197.56	_____
16. Ocepek, R.	210.80	_____
17. Paparone, L.	389.56	_____
18. Queen, E.	410.22	_____
19. Rowan, J.	75.00	_____
20. Savoy, L.	160.44	_____
21. Small, T.	155.39	_____
22. Timmis, W.	169.36	_____
23. Turner, U.	250.37	_____
24. Urdales, H.	248.37	_____
25. Weeks, D.	388.79	_____

PAYROLL

Subtract from the gross pay the deductions indicated and show the net pay. You have already calculated this week's FICA deduction for these employees. To find 1% city tax, merely move the gross pay decimal two places to the left. (Round to the penny.)

	Employee Name	Gross Weekly Pay ($)	Federal Inc. Tax ($)	FICA ($)	City Tax (1%)	Sav. Bonds ($)	A & H Ins. ($)	Net Pay ($)
1.	Ayers, E.	197.60	38.79	11.56	1.98	18.75	1.50	125.02
2.	Brewer, C.	206.75	41.82	___	___	—	1.50	___
3.	Cole, W.	125.00	12.50	___	___	9.37	—	___
4.	Duda, J.	285.34	51.32	___	___	18.75	1.50	___
5.	Frame, B.	198.33	28.63	___	___	—	1.50	___
6.	Goldberg, J.	225.00	54.00	___	___	37.50	—	___
7.	Griffa, D.	354.68	62.60	___	___	18.75	1.50	___
8.	Hairston, A.	329.80	49.37	___	___	—	1.50	___
9.	Horvath, J.	401.39	86.30	___	___	37.50	1.50	___
10.	Ingersoll, R.	265.45	41.76	___	___	18.75	1.50	___
11.	Jernigen, C.	175.00	30.47	___	___	—	—	___
12.	Kuss, R.	50.25	4.68	___	___	—	—	___
13.	Lehrman, S.	280.66	39.66	___	___	9.37	1.50	___
14.	McKay, B.	234.90	36.52	___	___	18.75	—	___
15.	Nauman, M.	197.56	36.29	___	___	9.37	1.50	___
16.	Ocepek, R.	210.80	41.87	___	___	18.75	—	___
17.	Paparone, L.	389.56	59.20	___	___	—	1.50	___
18.	Queen, E.	410.22	70.81	___	___	75.00	1.50	___
19.	Rowan, J.	75.00	13.76	___	___	—	—	___
20.	Savoy, L.	160.44	30.18	___	___	9.37	1.50	___
21.	Small, T.	155.39	19.42	___	___	—	1.50	___
22.	Timmis, W.	169.36	31.18	___	___	18.75	—	___
23.	Turner, U.	250.37	46.90	___	___	37.50	1.50	___

TEN-KEY PRINTING CALCULATORS

Employee Name	Gross Weekly Pay ($)	Federal Inc. Tax ($)	FICA ($)	City Tax (1%)	Sav. Bonds ($)	A & H Ins. ($)	Net Pay ($)
24. Urdales, H.	248.37	45.76	——	——	18.75	–	———
25. Weeks, D.	388.79	64.63	——	——	37.50	1.50	———

MARKON

Markon is usually defined as the amount added by the retailer to the cost price he paid for the item. It is, as a rule, a percentage of the *cost* price.

Example. Calculate the percent of markon for a sweater which cost $12 and which the store sells for $15.98. (Round to the percent.)

1. Subtract the cost price from the selling price (15.98 - 12.00 = 3.98).
2. Divide the difference (3.98) by the *cost* price (12.00).
3. 3.98 ÷ 12.00 = .33 = 33% (rounded to the percent)
4. The percent of markon is 33.

Practice Problems 10. Find the percent of markon for the following problems. (Round to the percent.)

	Cost Price ($)	Selling Price ($)	Percent of Markon
1.	85.04	100.00	18
2.	3.86	4.98	———
3.	20.00	25.00	———
4.	109.50	119.99	———
5.	2,300.06	2,750.00	———
6.	4,600.00	5,000.00	———
7.	899.40	999.99	———
8.	36.76	54.98	———
9.	2.80	3.50	———
10.	15.39	18.79	———
11.	5.85	7.50	———
12.	48.67	60.00	———
13.	500.76	700.00	———
14.	53.20	75.00	———
15.	3,800.00	4,500.00	———

MARKUP

Markup is usually defined as an amount added by the retailer to the selling price of an item to cover increased expenses. Markup is most often based on *selling price* rather than on cost price.

Example. Calculate the percent of markup based on selling price for an automobile floor mat which was marked up from $7.98 to $8.50. (Round to the percent.)

1. Subtract the old selling price (7.98) from the new selling price (8.50).

$$8.50 - 7.98 = .52$$

2. Divide the difference (.52) by the old selling price (7.98).

$$.52 \div 7.98 = .065 = 6.5\%$$

3. Rounded to the percent, 6.5% becomes 7%.
4. The percent of markup is 7%.

Practice Problems 11. Find the percent of markup for the following problems. (Round to the percent.)

	Old Selling Price ($)	New Selling Price ($)	Percent of Markup
1.	58.41	80.00	37
2.	8.63	9.99	____
3.	3.00	3.50	____
4.	901.49	1,000.00	____
5.	3,600.02	3,800.00	____
6.	6,400.00	7,200.00	____
7.	78.02	85.00	____
8.	64.29	70.20	____
9.	6.30	6.99	____
10.	25.83	29.99	____
11.	10.45	11.50	____
12.	67.84	69.98	____
13.	700.56	750.00	____
14.	25.33	27.50	____
15.	81.99	85.99	____

MARKDOWN

Markdown is usually defined as the amount deducted from the selling price when an item is placed on a special sale, such as a January white sale, a Founder's Day sale, etc.

Example. Calculate the percent of markdown based on *selling price* for a leather armchair, which originally sold for $229 and is now on sale for $199.99. (Round to the percent.)

1. Subtract the sale price (199.99) from the original selling price (229).

$$229 - 199.99 = 29.01$$

2. Divide the difference (29.01) by the original selling price (229).

$$29.01 \div 229 = .126 \text{ or } 12.6\%$$

3. Rounded to the percent, 12.6 becomes 13%.
4. The percent of markdown is 13%.

Practice Problems 12. Find the percent of markdown for the following problems. (Round to the percent.)

	Original Selling Price ($)	Sale Price ($)	Percent of Markdown
1.	75.99	69.99	8
2.	4.75	4.00	____
3.	24.00	19.98	____
4.	99.99	75.00	____
5.	1,000.00	799.00	____
6.	3,400.00	2,900.00	____
7.	750.00	687.00	____
8.	32.50	27.98	____
9.	1.50	.99	____
10.	14.99	10.00	____
11.	6.75	5.00	____
12.	49.50	24.99	____
13.	485.00	300.00	____

	Original Selling Price ($)	Sale Price ($)	Percent of Markdown
14.	59.99	40.00	_____
15.	2,800.00	2,100.00	_____

Use the problems in Units 1 and 2 for additional practice.

Sample Examination

You may want to be timed as you try the Unit 9 Sample Examination, which is presented in the Introduction.

Unit 10

Full-Bank Adding Machine

The full-bank adding machine has been popular in business for many years because of its simplicity of operation and its design, which shows the entire keyboard entry at a glance. The full-bank adding machine has a keyboard consisting of numerous columns (or banks) of keys from 1 to 9. Eight or ten banks of keys are commonly found, but some machines have more.

ENTERING AMOUNTS

There is no single method of fingering which should be used as there is on ten-key machines. The figures in an amount to be entered do *not* have to be entered one at a time, as we do on the ten-key machines. In fact, every figure in an amount can be depressed *simultaneously*. Figures should never be entered one at a time since this procedure is too time-consuming. Any comfortable combination of fingers can be used to enter an amount. For example, to enter 1123, it is easy to use the thumb to depress *both* ones while the index finger and the middle finger depress the 2 and the 3, *all at one time*. To enter 256, the thumb, the index finger, and the middle finger can make this depression at one time.

Zeros are not entered. A zero in a column is indicated by not depressing any key in that column. Also, you can use the little finger to depress the Plus bar (or Motor bar) *at the same time* that you depress the amount.

ERROR CORRECTION

If you depress 1397 (but have not yet operated the Add bar) and you meant to depress 1297, all you need to do is depress the 2 in the correct column. The 3 will be released as the 2 is depressed. If you wish to clear the entire keyboard entry, depress the Correction key, which will clear the keyboard.

If the incorrect amount has already been *added*, you can *subtract* the same amount and thereby leave your total unaffected. The error has been "canceled out."

DECIMALS

You will notice the color difference between the columns. Columns 1, 2, 3, 4, and 5 are usually used for decimal amounts, and columns 6, 7, 8, 9, and 10 (on ten-bank machines) are usually used for whole numbers. However, if you need more room for whole numbers, you can use any decimal placement that you wish, as long as you correctly line up your decimals around your predetermined decimal location.

The color setup on the full-bank machine is to aid you in lining up decimals and whole numbers and to differentiate by sight thousands from hundreds places. Always line up your amounts around your predetermined decimal position. For example, to add 3.97, .868, and 4.3, you can line up the numbers as follows:

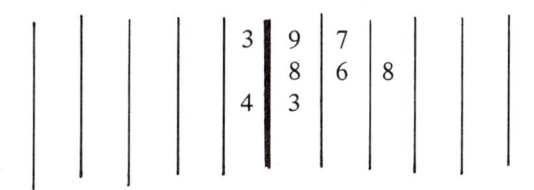

			3	9	7			
				8	6	8		
			4	3				

ADDITION

Example. 38.64
         19.29

         57.93

1. Depress the Total bar with your little finger to clear the machine.
2. Enter 38.64 on the keyboard (placing 38 in the sixth and seventh columns and 64 in the fourth and fifth columns) and depress the Plus bar.
3. Enter 19.29 on the keyboard and depress the Plus bar.
4. Depress the Total bar.
5. Your answer, 57.93, will print on the tape.

Practice Problems 1. Perform the following additions. Be sure to line up your decimal place correctly.

1.	8.25	2.	76.35	3.	.359	4.	892	5.	2.837
	8.46		63.90		.635		929		.356
	87.02		20.46		.148		1,155		8.834
	93.08		78.30		.336		258		.439
	19.82		42.17		.269		374		7.364
	207.38		81.47		.307		890		55.274

6. 348 + 258 + 5,973 + 56,392 + 78,298 + 364,290 =

7. 63.9 + 4.62 + 5.3967 + 34 + 200.7 + .0804 =

8. 34.9 + 75,013.23 + .8947 + 52.7 + 45.8 + 573.88 =

9. 60 + .47 + 9,210.33 + .64 + 8.32 + 114.76 =

10. 43.76 + 5.706 + 35,390 + .7089 + 74.111 + 7.20803 =

FULL-BANK ADDING MACHINE

11.	631.3	12.	3.78	13.	78.1	14.	73.54	15.	8.1
	33.7		31.76		19.3		72.10		4.4
	921.4		24.80		4.4		387.56		3.8
	358.2		94.03		35.7		51.37		2.9
	368.3		11.11		37.9		99.20		7.5
	909.9		36.56		21.2		84.21		9.3
16.	820	17.	82.11	18.	.897	19.	5.30	20.	8.11
	7,390		35.03		.802		85.67		98.52
	33,490		3.92		.026		1.47		.23
	252		.81		.308		.92		8.72
	320		56.76		.102		30.16		25.14
	39,920		39.05		.176		36.79		.02

21.–32. Add horizontally the number of tires produced by each tire builder for the week. Then add vertically the number of tires built each day. Your grand totals must agree.

Employee	M	T	W	Th	F	S	Total	
Bentz	21	20	22	19	23	22	_____	21.
Jackson	19	20	20	25	24	–	_____	22.
Smith	25	24	24	26	23	–	_____	23.
Thomas	24	22	22	24	25	24	_____	24.
Tokar	18	20	21	25	22	21	_____	25.
							_____	26.
	27.	28.	29.	30.	31.	32.		

Find the totals for the following deposit slips:

Currency	$340.00
Coin	25.47
Checks	103.50
	52.38
	504.19
	36.89
	87.50
	900.00
	436.40
	85.75
Total	_____ 33.
Date 12-2	

Currency	$850.00
Coin	92.11
Checks	24.60
	200.30
	36.79
	600.00
	65.80
	755.00
	17.11
	20.20
Total	_____ 34.
Date 12-4	

DOUBLE ADDITION

By using the extreme left and the extreme right columns of the full-bank adding machine, you can add two amounts at the same time.

Example. 4 lb., 3 oz.
6 lb., 7 oz.
2 lb., 4 oz.

1. Place the 4 on the left-hand side of the keyboard (one or two rows in from the left). Place the 3 at the right-hand side of the keyboard. Depress Plus bar.
2. Enter 6 under the 4 and enter 7 under the 3 on the keyboard. Depress Plus bar.
3. Enter the 2 under the 6 and the 4 under the 7 on the keyboard. Depress Plus bar.
4. Your total, 12 lb., 14 oz., will print on the tape.

Practice Problems 2. Complete the following double addition problems. In your answers, convert 16 oz. or over to lb.; convert 12 in. or over to ft.; convert 3 ft. or over to yd.

1. 5 lb., 6 oz.
9 lb., 14 oz.
10 lb., 20 oz.
9 lb., 1 oz.
14 lb., 12 oz.
3 lb., 9 oz.

2. 18 lb., 1 oz.
2 lb., 3.5 oz.
4 lb., 2.5 oz.
6 lb., .5 oz.
19 lb., 2 oz.
1 lb., 9 oz.

3. 7 lb., 3 oz.
1 lb., 15 oz.
22 lb., 6 oz.
3 lb., 9 oz.
12 lb., 13 oz.
4 lb., 6 oz.

4. 1 lb., 24 oz.
6 lb., 13 oz.
17 lb., 15 oz.
4 lb., 6 oz.
7 lb., 8 oz.
19 lb., 10 oz.

5. 3 lb., 3 oz.
4 lb., 6 oz.
1 lb., 12 oz.
22 lb., 6 oz.
9 lb., 1 oz.
1 lb., 2 oz.

6. 5 lb., 9 oz.
1 lb., 14 oz.
2 lb., 6 oz.
4.5 lb., 1 oz.
8 lb., 11 oz.
7 lb., 30 oz.

7. 9 lb., 15 oz.
1 lb., 9 oz.
14 oz.
3 oz.
6 lb., 12 oz.
3 oz.

8. 3 ft., 11 in.
1 ft., 4 in.
6 ft., 1 in.
17 ft., 2 in.
4 ft., 10 in.
9 in.

9. 1 ft., 1 in.
16 ft., 20 in.
8 ft.
6 ft.
3 ft.
5 in.

10. 2 ft., 10 in.
3 ft., 4 in.
6 ft., 5 in.
1 ft., 9 in.
15 ft., 3 in.
4 ft., 8 in.

SUBTRACTION

Example. 13.60
-2.58
11.02

1. Enter 13.60 on the keyboard with one depression and depress the Plus bar.
2. Enter 2.58 on the keyboard with one depression and depress the Minus bar.
3. Depress the Total key.
4. Your answer, 11.02, will print on the tape.

Practice Problems 3. Perform the following subtractions. Be careful to line up your decimal position correctly.

1. 76,372,163 - 31,972,093 =
2. 4,390,297 - 2,397,910 =
3. 1,937.28 - 1,900.10 =
4. 3,270.38 - 1,397.29 =
5. 125.60 - 34.39 =
6. 7,390 - 748 =
7. 80.2938 - 61.9370 =
8. 353.312 - 300.127 =
9. .79 - .34 =
10. 550.30 - 309.27 =

Perform the subtractions indicated and complete the following check register. Use the Subtotal key in order to keep your running balance throughout the problem.

	Balance
	$3,390.03
Check 1001	-36.21
	11.
Check 1002	-103.20
	12.
Check 1003	-36.75
	13.
Check 1004	-1,297.73
	14.
Check 1005	-600.39
	15.

Check 1006	−4.36	
		16.
Check 1007	−29.21	
		17.
Check 1008	−202.30	
		18.
Check 1009	−56.65	
		19.
Check 1010	−63.23	
		20.
Check 1011	−99.47	
		21.
Check 1012	−3.50	
		22.
Check 1013	−8.95	
		23.
Check 1014	−5.25	
		24.
Check 1015	−10.00	
		25.

CREDIT BALANCES

When minus amounts are greater than plus amounts, most full-bank adding machines will print a negative answer (credit balance) for you. The answer will be shown with *Cr* (for credit balance) or with a minus sign (−), indicating that you have a credit or minus amount.

For those machines which do not have the credit balance capability, the complement of the true answer (preceded by 9s) will print on the tape. To convert this complement to the true credit balance answer, depress the keys that are shown on the tape, including the 9s. Then subtract once and total. Your correct answer will now print on the tape. However, you must remember to mark your answer with a minus sign or with *Cr* to show that this is a negative or credit balance answer.

Example. 2.38
  −5.30
  −2.92

1. Clear your machine.
2. Enter 2.38 on the keyboard.
3. Depress the Plus bar.

FULL-BANK ADDING MACHINE

4. Enter 5.30 on the keyboard.
5. Depress the Minus bar.
6. Your answer, −2.92, will print on the tape.
7. If your machine prints the complement, 999997.08, copy the 999997.08 onto the keyboard by depressing each figure in the appropriate column. Subtract once. Total. You should now have 2.92 on the tape. *Be sure to indicate that this amount is a credit balance.*

Practice Problems 4. Complete the following credit balance problems. Remember to indicate *Cr* or (−) on your answers. Place your decimal point correctly as you complete each problem. The positive numbers represent deposits to a checking account, and the negative numbers represent checks drawn on that account. *Some* of these accounts are overdrawn.

	1.	2.	3.	4.
	$1,050.67	$500.00	$750.00	$643.20
	−271.00	−490.00	−529.36	−285.00
	−100.00	100.00	−2.76	−100.00
	−15.97	−165.35	−50.00	−110.68
	−25.43	−203.56	−5.32	−104.00
	−100.68	100.00	−10.00	−6.79
	$ 537.59			

	5.	6.	7.	8.
	$3,029.30	$400.60	$209.66	$2,000.00
	−296.00	−75.35	−180.20	−1,395.99
	−1,487.39	−86.20	50.00	−100.56
	−2,900.37	−83.67	−278.39	−379.24
	100.00	−200.35	50.00	−107.50
	−99.99	−18.26	−94.36	−231.00

	9.	10.	11.
	$45,000.37	$3,200.37	$9,356.29
	−8,037.26	−390.00	−803.45
	−9,456.28	−1,379.99	−837.27
	−1,391.11	−1,379.45	−8,375.28
	−28,390.27	100.00	−5.27
	−35.00	−56.37	50.20

	12.	13.	14.
	$3,789.38	$309.45	$100,397.00
	−2,387.28	−68.76	−90,375.88
	−47.28	−79.00	−312.00
	−55.65	−23.46	−356.37
	−30.00	−89.90	−121.11
	−26.33	−95.00	−10,400.66

15. $750.00	16. $639.27	17. $534.20
−630.90	−403.11	−491.16
200.00	−8.50	−100.12
−396.43	−17.50	50.50
50.00	−8.75	−78.63
−9.30	−5.00	−5.21

18. 379.35 − 490.38 =

19. 5,493.27 − 6,370.29 =

20. 105.30 − 148.66 =

NON-ADD FEATURE

When the Non-add (# or N) key is used, the figures entered in the keyboard are printed on the tape but are not calculated. This feature is helpful for coding on your tape such items as customer number, job or lot numbers, time clock numbers, inventory numbers, etc.

SUBTOTALS

The Subtotal key automatically prints the amount accumulated in the machine without clearing the amount from the machine and without adding the subtotal figure into the amount. Subtotals are usually printed with an *S* (for subtotal) beside the amount or *SC* (for subtotal credit balance) if your answer is a negative or credit balance.

Example. 30.23
  20.56
  ──── Subtotal
  1.49
  ──── Total

1. Clear your machine.
2. Enter 30.23 on the keyboard.
3. Depress the Plus bar.
4. Enter 20.56 on the keyboard.
5. Depress the Plus bar.
6. We wish to find out what our subtotal is, but we also want to continue adding the problem without losing the running total. Depress the Subtotal key (S). Your subtotal, 50.79, will print on the tape but will not clear the amount from the machine, so that you may continue with the problem.
7. Enter 1.49 on the keyboard.
8. Depress the Plus bar.

9. Depress the Total key.

10. Your final answer, 52.28, will print on the tape.

Practice Problems 5. The following amounts represent customer orders for the month. Use the Subtotal key to find the running total purchased by customers; use the Total key to find the total amount purchased by all customers. Use the Non-add key to indicate the customer number on your tape.

Customer #	Amount Purchased ($)	
103	20,349.10	
	6,347.12	
	8,297.34	
	Subtotal	1.
104	539.14	
	283.11	
	765.00	
	873.29	
	Subtotal	2.
105	329.45	
	100.76	
	232.22	
	Subtotal	3.
106	1,394.90	
	871.39	
	200.36	
	Subtotal	4.
	Total	5.

The following numbers indicate the number of calls made on customers by the salesmen. We want to know the running total of calls, plus the total calls made by all salesmen for the month.

Salesman #	No. of Customer Calls	
36	5	
	7	
	8	
	2	
	1	
	Subtotal	6.

Salesman #	No. of Customer Calls	
42	7	
	3	
	9	
	12	
	Subtotal	7.
51	8	
	7	
	10	
	3	
	5	
	Subtotal	8.
58	4	
	12	
	6	
	7	
	Subtotal	9.
60	4	
	7	
	7	
	5	
	6	
	Subtotal	10.
	Total	11.

MULTIPLICATION

Multiplication on the full-bank adding machine can be accomplished by repeated addition. For example, to multiply 2.53 by 241, we can add 2.53 one time (for the units position in the multiplier 24<u>1</u>), then add 25.30 four times (for the tens position in 2<u>4</u>1), then add 253.00 two times (for the hundreds position in <u>2</u>41).

Most full-bank adding machines have a Repeat key ($\boxed{R}$), which makes it easy to repeat add or repeat subtract a number.

Example 1. 2.53 × 241 = 609.73

1. Clear your machine.
2. Enter 2.53 on the keyboard and depress Plus bar.
3. Enter 25.30 on the keyboard and repeat add four times.
4. Enter 253.00 on the keyboard and repeat add two times.
5. Clear the keyboard.

FULL-BANK ADDING MACHINE

6. Total.
7. Your answer, 609.73, will print on the tape. Notice that your answer will have two decimal places, since there is a total of two decimals in the multiplication factors. You will have to place your own decimals in your products.

Your tape will look like this:

```
         T
   2.53
  25.30
  25.30
  25.30
  25.30
 253.00
 253.00
 609.73 T
```

Example 2. 203 × 4.5 = 913.5

1. Enter 203 on the keyboard and repeat add five times.
2. Enter 2030 on the keyboard and repeat add four times.
3. Be sure keyboard is clear.
4. Depress Total bar.
5. Your answer, 913.5, will print on the tape. Notice that your correct answer has one decimal place, since there was only one decimal in the multiplication factors.

Practice Problems 6. Perform the following multiplications. Be sure to place your decimal correctly as you complete each problem. Remember that you point off as many places as there are decimals in your multiplication factors.

1. 821 × 743 =
2. 34.2 × 43.1 =
3. 16.7 × 10.25 =
4. 732 × 104 =
5. 128 × 740 =
6. 43 × 6.7 =
7. 9,200 × .505 =
8. .567 × 5.201 =
9. 643 × 4.76 =
10. 940 × 372 =
11. 831 × 56 =
12. 602 × .308 =
13. 83.7 × 5.1 =
14. 529.3 × .372 =
15. .293 × .530 =
16. 506 × 802 =
17. 8.49 × .56 =
18. 358 × 5.6 =
19. 781 × .562 =
20. 469.3 × 8.95 =

Calculate the amount of markdown for the following items. Be sure to convert your percent to a decimal. (Round to the penny.)

	Regular Selling Price ($)	Percent of Markdown (%)	Amount of Markdown ($)
21.	98.73	12	11.85
22.	235.88	20	
23.	10.43	22	
24.	66.30	7	
25.	2,309.90	10	
26.	173.44	15	
27.	25.50	25	
28.	999.99	40	
29.	74.98	30	
30.	3.50	12.5	

DIVISION

On a full-bank adding machine, division is a multiplication process. We multiply the dividend by the reciprocal of the divisor. A reciprocal of any number is 1 divided by that number. For example, the reciprocal of 5 is $1 \div 5$ or .2. A Table of Reciprocals from 1 to 1,000 is given in Appendix B. However, you can obtain the reciprocal of any number by merely dividing 1 by the number.

The answer we can obtain by using this reciprocal method is close to the real quotient. In some cases, it is exactly the quotient, but in other cases, it is not 100 percent accurate. For example, it will give us the quotient of $144 \div 12$ as 11.999999, which is 12 when rounded off. For many types of problems, this degree of accuracy is sufficient.

Example. $950 \div 8 = 118.75$

1. Clear your machine.
2. If you don't know the reciprocal of 8 by heart, look it up in your Table of Reciprocals.
3. The reciprocal of 8 is .125.
4. The problem now becomes $950 \times .125$.
5. Enter 950 on the keyboard and repeat add five times.
6. Enter 9500 on the keyboard and repeat add two times.
7. Enter 95000 on the keyboard and add one time.
8. Be sure your keyboard is clear.

9. Depress the Total key.
10. Your tape will print 118750.
11. Point off three places. Your answer is 118.75.

Practice Problems 7. Do the following division problems by the reciprocal method. Place your decimal correctly in each answer as it is completed.

1. 5.470 ÷ 5 =
2. 4,630 ÷ 36 =
3. 453.1 ÷ 475 =
4. 14.463 ÷ 66 =
5. 18.434 ÷ 46 =
6. 463.32 ÷ 29 =
7. 54,836 ÷ 560 =
8. 356 ÷ 94 =
9. 542.37 ÷ 66 =
10. 5,326 ÷ 484 =
11. How many pounds are in 47 ounces? (Divide by 16 ounces. Round to the tenth.)
12. How many yards are there in 17 feet?
13. What is the cost per pen if a dozen pens costs $2.25?
14. What is the cost of one bottle of fruit punch if eight bottles cost $1.75?
15. What is the cost of an individual stencil if a quire costs $8.75? (A quire is 24.)
16. What is the cost for one roll of adding machine tape if a dozen costs $2.25?
17. A room measures 204 square feet. How much is this in square yards? (There are 9 square feet in a square yard.)
18. An aquarium holds 1,600 ounces of water. How much is this in gallons? (There are 128 ounces in a gallon.)
19. What is the cost of a sheet of copy paper if a ream costs $6.00? (There are 500 sheets in a ream.)
20. What is the cost of one marking pencil if a gross costs $90.00? (There are 144 in a gross.)

Sample Examination

You may want to be timed as you try the Unit 10 Sample Examination, which is presented in the Introduction.

Appendix A

Decimal Equivalents of Common Fractions

Fraction	Decimal Equivalent (rounded to 4 places)
1/2	.5
1/3	.3333
2/3	.6667
1/4	.25
2/4 = 1/2	.5
3/4	.75
1/5	.2
2/5	.4
3/5	.6
4/5	.8
1/6	.1667
2/6 = 1/3	.3333
3/6 = 1/2	.5
4/6 = 2/3	.6667
5/6 =	.8333
1/7	.1429
2/7	.2857
3/7	.4286
4/7	.5714
5/7	.7143
6/7	.8571

Fraction	Decimal Equivalent (rounded to 4 places)
1/8	.125
2/8 = 1/4	.25
3/8	.375
4/8 = 1/2	.5
5/8	.625
6/8 = 3/4	.75
7/8	.875
1/9	.1111
2/9	.2222
3/9 = 1/3	.3333
4/9	.4444
5/9	.5556
6/9 = 2/3	.6667
7/9	.7778
8/9	.8889
1/12	.0833
2/12 = 1/6	.1667
3/12 = 1/4	.25
4/12 = 1/3	.3333
5/12	.4167
6/12 = 1/2	.5
7/12	.5833
8/12 = 2/3	.6667
9/12 = 3/4	.75

DECIMAL EQUIVALENTS OF COMMON FRACTIONS

Fraction	Decimal Equivalent (rounded to 4 places)	Fraction	Decimal Equivalent (rounded to 4 places)
10/12 = 5/6	.8333	8/16 = 1/2	.5
11/12	.9167	9/16	.5625
		10/16 = 5/8	.625
1/16	.0625	11/16	.6875
2/16 = 1/8	.125	12/16 = 3/4	.75
3/16	.1875	13/16	.8125
4/16 = 1/4	.25	14/16 = 7/8	.875
5/16	.3125	15/16	.9375
6/16 = 3/8	.375		
7/16	.4375		

Appendix B

Table of Reciprocals

◤VICTOR 4-PLACE RECIPROCAL CHART

How to Find the Reciprocal:
Look up divisor in bold type column. The figure opposite in light type is the reciprocal for that number.

How to Divide
Multiply the dividend by the reciprocal to get quotient or answer.

How To Point Off Decimal Place Using 4-Place Reciprocal:
(a) For **percentage division**, count the number of whole digits in the divisor and add 1.
(b) For **straight division**, count the number of whole digits in the divisor and add 3.
(c) Point off from right to left.

How to Find "Adjusted" Reciprocals
In Reciprocal Division, most businesses find it practical to use only the first three digits of the divisor, dropping the fourth and subsequent digits.

However, the fourth digit can be used to "adjust" the reciprocal of the divisor. The procedure to find the adjusted reciprocal of 2245 is outlined below:
1. Find the reciprocal for 224. It is — — — — .4464
2. Find the reciprocal for 225
   (the next higher divisor) and subtract — — — 4444
   The difference between these reciprocals is   20
3. The fourth figure, considered as a tenth-fraction, determines what part of the difference is used to make up the adjusted reciprocal. The "5" in the divisor 2245 equals 5/10.   Note: 1 is 1/10; 2 is 2/10; 3 is 3/10, etc.
4. Multiply the fraction (5/10) times the difference (20)
   .5 X 20 = 10
5. **Subtract** the 10 from the largest reciprocal to get an adjusted reciprocal
   4464 — 10 = 4454 (Adjusted Reciprocal)

TABLE OF RECIPROCALS

1	1.0000	50	2000	100	1.0000	150	6667	200	5000	250	4000	300	3333	350	2857	400	2500	450	2222
2	5000	1	1961	1	9901	51	6623	1	4975	51	3984	1	3322	51	2849	1	2494	51	2217
3	3333	2	1923	2	9804	52	6579	2	4950	52	3968	2	3311	52	2841	2	2488	52	2212
4	2500	3	1887	3	9709	53	6536	3	4926	53	3953	3	3300	53	2833	3	2481	53	2208
5	2000	4	1852	4	9615	54	6494	4	4902	54	3937	4	3289	54	2825	4	2475	54	2203
6	1667	5	1818	5	9524	55	6452	5	4878	55	3922	5	3279	55	2817	5	2469	55	2198
7	1429	6	1786	6	9434	56	6410	6	4854	56	3906	6	3268	56	2809	6	2463	56	2193
8	1250	7	1754	7	9346	57	6369	7	4831	57	3891	7	3257	57	2801	7	2457	57	2188
9	1111	8	1724	8	9259	58	6329	8	4808	58	3876	8	3247	58	2793	8	2451	58	2183
		9	1695	9	9174	59	6289	9	4785	59	3861	9	3236	59	2786	9	2445	59	2179
10	1.0000	60	1667	110	9091	160	6250	210	4762	260	3846	310	3226	360	2778	410	2439	460	2174
11	9091	1	1639	11	9009	61	6211	11	4739	61	3831	11	3215	61	2770	11	2433	61	2169
12	8333	2	1613	12	8929	62	6173	12	4717	62	3817	12	3205	62	2762	12	2427	62	2165
13	7692	3	1587	13	8850	63	6135	13	4695	63	3802	13	3195	63	2755	13	2421	63	2160
14	7143	4	1563	14	8772	64	6098	14	4673	64	3788	14	3185	64	2747	14	2415	64	2155
15	6667	5	1538	15	8696	65	6061	15	4651	65	3774	15	3175	65	2740	15	2410	65	2151
16	6250	6	1515	16	8621	66	6024	16	4630	66	3759	16	3165	66	2732	16	2404	66	2146
17	5882	7	1493	17	8547	67	5988	17	4608	67	3745	17	3155	67	2725	17	2398	67	2141
18	5556	8	1471	18	8475	68	5952	18	4587	68	3731	18	3145	68	2717	18	2392	68	2137
19	5263	9	1449	19	8403	69	5917	19	4566	69	3717	19	3135	69	2710	19	2387	69	2132
20	5000	70	1429	120	8333	170	5882	220	4545	270	3704	320	3125	370	2703	420	2381	470	2128
21	4762	1	1408	21	8264	71	5848	21	4525	71	3690	21	3115	71	2695	21	2375	71	2123
22	4545	2	1389	22	8197	72	5814	22	4505	72	3676	22	3106	72	2688	22	2370	72	2119
23	4348	3	1370	23	8130	73	5780	23	4484	73	3663	23	3096	73	2681	23	2364	73	2114
24	4167	4	1351	24	8065	74	5747	24	4464	74	3650	24	3086	74	2674	24	2358	74	2110
25	4000	5	1333	25	8000	75	5714	25	4444	75	3636	25	3077	75	2667	25	2353	75	2105
26	3846	6	1316	26	7937	76	5682	26	4425	76	3623	26	3067	76	2660	26	2347	76	2101
27	3704	7	1299	27	7874	77	5650	27	4405	77	3610	27	3058	77	2653	27	2342	77	2096
28	3571	8	1282	28	7813	78	5618	28	4386	78	3597	28	3049	78	2646	28	2336	78	2092
29	3448	9	1266	29	7752	79	5587	29	4367	79	3584	29	3040	79	2639	29	2331	79	2088
30	3333	80	1250	130	7692	180	5556	230	4348	280	3571	330	3030	380	2632	430	2326	480	2083
31	3226	1	1235	31	7634	81	5525	31	4329	81	3559	31	3021	81	2625	31	2320	81	2079
32	3125	2	1220	32	7576	82	5495	32	4310	82	3546	32	3012	82	2618	32	2315	82	2075
33	3030	3	1205	33	7519	83	5464	33	4292	83	3534	33	3003	83	2611	33	2309	83	2070
34	2941	4	1190	34	7463	84	5435	34	4274	84	3521	34	2994	84	2604	34	2304	84	2066
35	2857	5	1176	35	7407	85	5405	35	4255	85	3509	35	2985	85	2597	35	2299	85	2062
36	2778	6	1163	36	7353	86	5376	36	4237	86	3497	36	2976	86	2591	36	2294	86	2058
37	2703	7	1149	37	7299	87	5348	37	4219	87	3484	37	2967	87	2584	37	2288	87	2053
38	2632	8	1136	38	7246	88	5319	38	4202	88	3472	38	2959	88	2577	38	2283	88	2049
39	2564	9	1124	39	7194	89	5291	39	4184	89	3460	39	2950	89	2571	39	2278	89	2045
40	2500	90	1111	140	7143	190	5263	240	4167	290	3448	340	2941	390	2564	440	2273	490	2041
41	2439	1	1099	41	7092	91	5236	41	4149	91	3436	41	2933	91	2558	41	2268	91	2037
42	2381	2	1087	42	7042	92	5208	42	4132	92	3425	42	2924	92	2551	42	2262	92	2033
43	2326	3	1075	43	6993	93	5181	43	4115	93	3413	43	2915	93	2545	43	2257	93	2028
44	2273	4	1064	44	6944	94	5155	44	4098	94	3401	44	2907	94	2538	44	2252	94	2024
45	2222	5	1053	45	6897	95	5128	45	4082	95	3390	45	2899	95	2532	45	2247	95	2020
46	2174	6	1042	46	6849	96	5102	46	4065	96	3378	46	2890	96	2525	46	2242	96	2016
47	2128	7	1031	47	6803	97	5076	47	4049	97	3367	47	2882	97	2519	47	2237	97	2012
48	2083	8	1020	48	6757	98	5051	48	4032	98	3356	48	2874	98	2513	48	2232	98	2008
49	2041	9	1010	49	6711	99	5025	49	4016	99	3344	49	2865	99	2506	49	2227	99	2004

TABLE OF RECIPROCALS

500	2000	550	1818	600	1667	650	1538	700	1429	750	1333	800	1250	850	1176	900	1111	950	1053
1	1996	51	1815	1	1664	51	1536	1	1427	51	1332	1	1248	51	1175	1	1110	51	1052
2	1992	52	1812	2	1661	52	1534	2	1425	52	1330	2	1247	52	1174	2	1109	52	1050
3	1988	53	1808	3	1658	53	1531	3	1422	53	1328	3	1245	53	1172	3	1107	53	1049
4	1984	54	1805	4	1656	54	1529	4	1420	54	1326	4	1244	54	1171	4	1106	54	1048
5	1980	55	1802	5	1653	55	1527	5	1418	55	1325	5	1242	55	1170	5	1105	55	1047
6	1976	56	1799	6	1650	56	1524	6	1416	56	1323	6	1241	56	1168	6	1104	56	1046
7	1972	57	1795	7	1647	57	1522	7	1414	57	1321	7	1239	57	1167	7	1103	57	1045
8	1969	58	1792	8	1645	58	1520	8	1412	58	1319	8	1238	58	1166	8	1101	58	1044
9	1965	59	1789	9	1642	59	1517	9	1410	59	1318	9	1236	59	1164	9	1100	59	1043
510	1961	560	1786	610	1639	660	1515	710	1408	760	1316	810	1235	860	1163	910	1099	960	1042
11	1957	61	1783	11	1637	61	1513	11	1406	61	1314	11	1233	61	1161	11	1098	61	1041
12	1953	62	1779	12	1634	62	1511	12	1404	62	1312	12	1232	62	1160	12	1096	62	1040
13	1949	63	1776	13	1631	63	1508	13	1403	63	1311	13	1230	63	1159	13	1095	63	1038
14	1946	64	1773	14	1629	64	1506	14	1401	64	1309	14	1229	64	1157	14	1094	64	1037
15	1942	65	1770	15	1626	65	1504	15	1399	65	1307	15	1227	65	1156	15	1093	65	1036
16	1938	66	1767	16	1623	66	1502	16	1397	66	1305	16	1225	66	1155	16	1092	66	1035
17	1934	67	1764	17	1621	67	1499	17	1395	67	1304	17	1224	67	1153	17	1091	67	1034
18	1931	68	1761	18	1618	68	1497	18	1393	68	1302	18	1222	68	1152	18	1089	68	1033
19	1927	69	1757	19	1616	69	1495	19	1391	69	1300	19	1221	69	1151	19	1088	69	1032
520	1923	570	1754	620	1613	670	1493	720	1389	770	1299	820	1220	870	1149	920	1087	970	1031
21	1919	71	1751	21	1610	71	1490	21	1387	71	1297	21	1218	71	1148	21	1086	71	1030
22	1916	72	1748	22	1608	72	1488	22	1385	72	1295	22	1217	72	1147	22	1085	72	1029
23	1912	73	1745	23	1605	73	1486	23	1383	73	1294	23	1215	73	1145	23	1083	73	1028
24	1908	74	1742	24	1603	74	1484	24	1381	74	1292	24	1214	74	1144	24	1082	74	1027
25	1905	75	1739	25	1600	75	1481	25	1379	75	1290	25	1212	75	1143	25	1081	75	1026
26	1901	76	1736	26	1597	76	1479	26	1377	76	1289	26	1211	76	1142	26	1080	76	1025
27	1898	77	1733	27	1595	77	1477	27	1376	77	1287	27	1209	77	1140	27	1079	77	1024
28	1894	78	1730	28	1592	78	1475	28	1374	78	1285	28	1208	78	1139	28	1078	78	1022
29	1890	79	1727	29	1590	79	1473	29	1372	79	1284	29	1206	79	1138	29	1076	79	1021
530	1887	580	1724	630	1587	680	1471	730	1370	780	1282	830	1205	880	1136	930	1075	980	1020
31	1883	81	1721	31	1585	81	1468	31	1368	81	1280	31	1203	81	1135	31	1074	81	1019
32	1880	82	1718	32	1582	82	1466	32	1366	82	1279	32	1202	82	1134	32	1073	82	1018
33	1876	83	1715	33	1580	83	1464	33	1364	83	1277	33	1200	83	1133	33	1072	83	1017
34	1873	84	1712	34	1577	84	1462	34	1362	84	1276	34	1199	84	1131	34	1071	84	1016
35	1869	85	1709	35	1575	85	1460	35	1361	85	1274	35	1198	85	1130	35	1070	85	1015
36	1866	86	1706	36	1572	86	1458	36	1359	86	1272	36	1196	86	1129	36	1068	86	1014
37	1862	87	1704	37	1570	87	1456	37	1357	87	1271	37	1195	87	1127	37	1067	87	1013
38	1859	88	1701	38	1567	88	1453	38	1355	88	1269	38	1193	88	1126	38	1066	88	1012
39	1855	89	1698	39	1565	89	1451	39	1353	89	1267	39	1192	89	1125	39	1065	89	1011
540	1852	590	1695	640	1563	690	1449	740	1351	790	1266	840	1190	890	1124	940	1064	990	1010
41	1848	91	1692	41	1560	91	1447	41	1350	91	1264	41	1189	91	1122	41	1063	91	1009
42	1845	92	1689	42	1558	92	1445	42	1348	92	1263	42	1188	92	1121	42	1062	92	1008
43	1842	93	1686	43	1555	93	1443	43	1346	93	1261	43	1186	93	1120	43	1060	93	1007
44	1838	94	1684	44	1553	94	1441	44	1344	94	1259	44	1185	94	1119	44	1059	94	1006
45	1835	95	1681	45	1550	95	1439	45	1342	95	1258	45	1183	95	1117	45	1058	95	1005
46	1832	96	1678	46	1548	96	1437	46	1340	96	1256	46	1182	96	1116	46	1057	96	1004
47	1828	97	1675	47	1546	97	1435	47	1339	97	1255	47	1181	97	1115	47	1056	97	1003
48	1825	98	1672	48	1543	98	1433	48	1337	98	1253	48	1179	98	1114	48	1055	98	1002
49	1821	99	1669	49	1541	99	1431	49	1335	99	1252	49	1178	99	1112	49	1054	999	1001

Appendix C

Compound Interest Table

AMOUNT OF $1.00 AT COMPOUND INTEREST

Periods	1/2%	1%	1-1/2%	2%	2-1/2%
1	1.005000	1.010000	1.015000	1.020000	1.025000
2	1.010025	1.020100	1.030225	1.040400	1.050625
3	1.015075	1.030301	1.045678	1.061208	1.076891
4	1.020151	1.040604	1.061364	1.082432	1.103813
5	1.025251	1.051010	1.077284	1.104081	1.131408
6	1.030378	1.061520	1.093443	1.126162	1.159693
7	1.035529	1.072135	1.109845	1.148686	1.188686
8	1.040707	1.082857	1.126493	1.171659	1.218403
9	1.045911	1.093685	1.143390	1.195093	1.248863
10	1.051140	1.104622	1.160441	1.218994	1.280085
11	1.056396	1.115668	1.177949	1.243374	1.312087
12	1.061678	1.126825	1.195618	1.268242	1.344889
13	1.066986	1.138093	1.213552	1.293607	1.378511
14	1.072321	1.149474	1.231756	1.319479	1.412974
15	1.077683	1.160969	1.250232	1.345868	1.448298
16	1.083071	1.172579	1.268986	1.372786	1.484506
17	1.088487	1.184304	1.288020	1.400241	1.521618
18	1.093929	1.196147	1.307341	1.428246	1.559659
19	1.099399	1.208109	1.326951	1.456811	1.598650
20	1.104896	1.220190	1.346855	1.485947	1.638616
21	1.110420	1.232392	1.367058	1.515666	1.679582
22	1.115972	1.244716	1.387564	1.545980	1.721571
23	1.121552	1.257163	1.408377	1.576899	1.764611
24	1.127160	1.269735	1.429503	1.608437	1.808726
25	1.132796	1.282432	1.450945	1.640606	1.853944

AMOUNT OF $1.00 AT COMPOUND INTEREST

3%	3-1/2%	4%	4-1/2%	5%	5-1/2%
1.030000	1.035000	1.040000	1.045000	1.050000	1.055000
1.060900	1.071225	1.081600	1.092025	1.102500	1.113025
1.092727	1.108718	1.124864	1.141166	1.157625	1.174241
1.125509	1.147523	1.169859	1.192519	1.215506	1.238825
1.159274	1.187686	1.216653	1.246182	1.276282	1.306960
1.194052	1.229255	1.265319	1.302260	1.340096	1.378843
1.229874	1.272279	1.315932	1.360862	1.407100	1.454679
1.266770	1.316809	1.368569	1.422101	1.477455	1.534687
1.304773	1.362897	1.423312	1.486095	1.551328	1.619094
1.343916	1.410599	1.480244	1.552969	1.628895	1.708144
1.384234	1.459970	1.539454	1.622853	1.710339	1.802092
1.424561	1.511069	1.601032	1.695881	1.795856	1.901207
1.468534	1.563956	1.665074	1.772196	1.885649	2.005774
1.512590	1.618695	1.731676	1.851945	1.979932	2.116091
1.557967	1.675349	1.800944	1.935282	2.078928	2.232476
1.604706	1.733986	1.872981	2.022370	2.182875	2.355263
1.652848	1.794676	1.947901	2.113377	2.292018	2.484802
1.702433	1.857489	2.025817	2.208479	2.406619	2.621466
1.753506	1.922501	2.106849	2.307860	2.526950	2.765647
1.806111	1.989789	2.191123	2.411714	2.653298	2.917757
1.860295	2.059431	2.278768	2.520241	2.785963	3.078234
1.916103	2.131512	2.369919	2.633652	2.925261	3.247537
1.973587	2.206114	2.464716	2.752166	3.071524	3.426152
2.032794	2.283328	2.563304	2.876014	3.225100	3.614590
2.093778	2.363245	2.665836	3.005434	3.386355	3.813392

AMOUNT OF $1.00 AT COMPOUND INTEREST

Periods	6%	6-1/2%	7%	7-1/2%	8%
1	1.060000	1.065000	1.070000	1.075000	1.080000
2	1.123600	1.134225	1.144900	1.155625	1.166400
3	1.191016	1.207949	1.225043	1.242296	1.259712
4	1.262477	1.286466	1.310796	1.335469	1.360488
5	1.338226	1.370086	1.402551	1.435629	1.469328
6	1.418519	1.459142	1.500730	1.543301	1.586874
7	1.503630	1.553986	1.605781	1.659049	1.713824
8	1.593848	1.654995	1.718186	1.783477	1.850930
9	1.689479	1.762570	1.838459	1.917238	1.999004
10	1.790848	1.877137	1.967151	2.061031	2.158925
11	1.898299	1.999151	2.104851	2.215608	2.331639
12	2.012196	2.129096	2.252191	2.381780	2.518170
13	2.132928	2.267487	2.409845	2.560413	2.719623
14	2.260904	2.414874	2.578534	2.752444	2.937193
15	2.396558	2.571841	2.759031	2.958877	3.172169
16	2.540352	2.739010	2.952163	3.180793	3.425942
17	2.692773	2.917046	3.158815	3.419352	3.700018
18	2.854339	3.106654	3.379932	3.675804	3.996019
19	3.025600	3.308586	3.616527	3.951489	4.315701
20	3.207135	3.523645	3.869684	4.247851	4.660957
21	3.399564	3.752681	4.140562	4.566439	5.033833
22	3.603537	3.996606	4.430401	4.908922	5.436540
23	3.819750	4.256385	4.740529	5.277092	5.871463
24	4.048935	4.533050	5.072366	5.672874	6.341180
25	4.291871	4.827699	5.427432	6.098339	6.848475

Appendix D

Chain Discount Equivalents

Rate %	5	7-1/2	10	12-1/2	15	16-2/3	20
Net	.95	.925	.90	.875	.85	.83333	.80
2-1/2	.92625	.90188	.8775	.85313	.82875	.8125	.78
5	.9025	.87875	.855	.83125	.8075	.79167	.76
5 2-1/2	.87994	.85678	.83363	.81047	.78731	.77187	.741
5 5	.85738	.83481	.81225	.78969	.76713	.75208	.722
5 5 2-1/2	.83594	.81394	.79194	.76995	.74795	.73328	.70395
7-1/2	.87875	.85563	.8325	.80938	.78625	.77083	.74
7-1/2 2-1/2	.85678	.83423	.81169	.78914	.76659	.75156	.7215
7-1/2 5	.83481	.81284	.79088	.76891	.74694	.73229	.703
10	.855	.8325	.81	.7875	.765	.75	.72
10 2-1/2	.83363	.81169	.78975	.76781	.74588	.73125	.702
10 5	.81225	.79088	.7695	.74813	.72675	.7125	.684
10 5 2-1/2	.79194	.7711	.75026	.72942	.70858	.69469	.6669
10 7-1/2	.79088	.77006	.74925	.72844	.70763	.69375	.666
10 10	.7695	.74925	.729	.70875	.6885	.675	.648
10 10 5	.73103	.71179	.69255	.67331	.65408	.64125	.6156
10 10 5 2-1/2	.71275	.69399	.67524	.65648	.63772	.62522	.60021

CHAIN DISCOUNT EQUIVALENTS

Rate%	25	30	33-1/3	35	37-1/2	40	50
Net	.75	.70	.66667	.65	.625	.60	.50
2-1/2	.73125	.6825	.65	.63375	.60938	.585	.4875
5	.7125	.665	.63333	.6175	.59375	.57	.475
5 2-1/2	.69469	.64838	.6175	.60206	.57891	.55575	.46313
5 5	.67688	.63175	.60167	.58663	.56406	.5415	.45125
5 5 2-1/2	.65995	.61596	.58663	.57196	.54996	.52796	.43997
7-1/2	.69375	.6475	.61667	.60125	.57813	.555	.4625
7-1/2 2-1/2	.67641	.63131	.60125	.58622	.56367	.54113	.45094
7-1/2 5	.65906	.61513	.58583	.57119	.54922	.52725	.43938
10	.675	.63	.6	.585	.5625	.54	.45
10 2-1/2	.65813	.61425	.585	.57038	.54844	.5265	.43875
10 5	.64125	.5985	.57	.55575	.53438	.513	.4275
10 5 2-1/2	.62522	.58354	.55575	.54186	.52102	.50018	.41681
10 7-1/2	.62438	.58275	.555	.54113	.52031	.4995	.41625
10 10	.6075	.567	.54	.5265	.50625	.486	.405
10 10 5	.57713	.53865	.513	.50018	.48094	.4617	.38475
10 10 5 2-1/2	.5627	.52518	.50018	.48767	.46891	.45016	.37513

Rate %	60	62-1/2	65	66-2/3	70	75	80
Net	.40	.375	.35	.33333	.30	.25	.20
2-1/2	.39	.36563	.34125	.325	.2925	.24375	.195
5	.38	.35625	.3325	.31667	.285	.2375	.19
5 2-1/2	.3705	.34734	.32419	.30875	.27788	.23156	.18525
5 5	.361	.33844	.31588	.30083	.27075	.22563	.1805
5 5 2-1/2	.35198	.32998	.30798	.29331	.26398	.21998	.17599
7-1/2	.37	.34688	.32375	.30833	.2775	.23125	.185
7-1/2 2-1/2	.36075	.3382	.31566	.30062	.27056	.22547	.18038
7-1/2 5	.3515	.32953	.30756	.29292	.26363	.21969	.17575
10	.36	.3375	.315	.3	.27	.225	.18
10 2-1/2	.351	.32906	.30713	2925	.26325	.21938	.1755
10 5	.342	.32063	.29925	.285	.2565	.21375	.171
10 5 2-1/2	.33345	.31261	.29177	.27788	.25009	.20841	.16673
10 7-1/2	.333	.31219	.29138	.2775	.24975	.20813	.1665
10 10	.324	.30375	.2835	.27	.243	.2025	.162
10 10 5	.3078	.28856	.26933	.2565	.23085	.19238	.1539
10 10 5 2-1/2	.30011	.28135	.26259	.25009	.22508	.18757	.15005

Appendix E

Metric Conversions

METRIC MEASURES AND WEIGHTS

LINEAR MEASURE

10 millimeters = 1 centimeter

10 centimeters = 1 decimeter

10 decimeters = 1 meter

10 meters = 1 dekameter

10 dekameters = 1 hectometer

10 hectometers = 1 kilometer

AREA MEASURE

100 square millimeters = 1 square centimeter

100 square centimeters = 1 square decimeter

100 square decimeters = 1 square meter

100 square meters = 1 are

100 ares = 1 hectare

100 hectares = 1 square kilometer

1,000,000 square meters = 1 square kilometer

CUBIC MEASURE

1,000 cubic millimeters = 1 cubic centimeter

1,000 cubic centimeters = 1 cubic decimeter

1,000 cubic decimeters = 1 stere (cubic meter)

VOLUME MEASURE

10 milliliters = 1 centiliter
10 centiliters = 1 deciliter
10 deciliters = 1 liter
10 liters = 1 dekaliter
10 dekaliters = 1 hectoliter
10 hectoliters = 1 kiloliter
1,000 liters = 1 kiloliter

WEIGHT

10 milligrams = 1 centigram
10 centigrams = 1 decigram
10 decigrams = 1 gram
10 grams = 1 dekagram
10 dekagrams = 1 hectogram
10 hectograms = 1 kilogram
1,000 grams = 1 kilogram
1,000 kilograms = 1 metric ton

METRIC CONVERSIONS

LINEAR MEASURE

1 millimeter = 0.03937 inch   1 inch = 2.54 centimeters
1 centimeter = 0.3937 inch   1 foot = 30.48 centimeters
1 decimeter = 3.937 inches   1 yard = 91.44 centimeters
1 meter = 39.37 inches   1 yard = 0.9144 meter
1 kilometer = 1,093.6 yards   1 mile = 1,609 meters
1 kilometer = 0.621 mile   1 mile = 1.609 kilometers

SQUARE MEASURE

1 square meter = 1.196 square yards   1 square yard = 0.836 square meter
1 are = 0.02471 acre   1 acre = 40.5 ares

1 hectare = 2.471 acres 1 acre = 0.405 hectare
1 square kilometer = 0.386 square mile 1 square mile = 2.59 square kilometers

CUBIC MEASURE

1 liter = 1.0567 quarts or 2.114 pints 1 gallon = 3.7853 liters

1 stere = 1.308 cubic yards 1 cubic yard = 0.765 stere

WEIGHTS

1 gram = 0.03527 ounce 1 ounce avoirdupois = 28.3495 grams

1 kilogram = 2.2046 pounds 1 pound avoirdupois = 453.5924 grams

1 metric ton = 1.1023 short tons 1 short ton = 0.907 metric ton or 907.185 kilograms

1 metric ton = 2,204.6 pounds

Appendix F

Answers to Even-Numbered Problems

INTRODUCTION

Basic Mathematics Pretest

Addition

    2. 459.52   4. 20-11/12

Subtraction

    6. $7.67   8. 30-1/2

Credit Balances

    10. −92.82

Multiplication

    12. 3,674.3   14. 86,945

    16. 39-19/28

Division

    18. 172.7046   20. 2-2/99

    22. 9,734.708   24. .0014

Complements

    26. 6   28. 349/1000

    30. 81/100

Fraction to Decimal

    32. .875

Rounding Off

    34. 97.9

Percent

   36. 138.4%

   38. 85.71%

Thought Problems

   40. $31.24

Mathematics Review

Addition

   2. 39,104

   4. 195,577

   6. 49.343

   8. 980.681

   10. 23.805

   12. 477,979

   14. 990,559

   16. a) 6,278   e) 7,887
           b) 4,642   f) 1,679
           c) 5,552   g) 1,620
           d) 16,472 h) 5,286

Subtraction

   2. 66,319

   4. 174,763

   6. 10,868

   8. 2,774

   10. 78,105

   12. 1,316.87

   14. 2,331.06

   16. 19.297

   18. .01446

   20. .4472

Multiplication

   2. 7,087,810

   4. 377,125

   6. 37.4986

   8. 40.45212

   10. 103.5683175

   12. 270,400

   14. 4.76

   16. .314

   18. 480,000

   20. 8,600

Division

   2. 36.55952

   4. 519.67592

   6. 29.88038

   8. .10340

   10. .49450

   12. 300

   14. .20242

   16. .2971

18. .00246
20. .00937

Complements

2. 3
4. 69
6. 691
8. 97.75%
10. 60%
12. 91.5%
14. 88%
16. 87.25%
18. 66-2/3 or 66.7%
20. 94.5%

Decimal to Fraction

2. 57/100
4. 598/625
6. 1-16/25
8. 5-21/25
10. 4-1/25

Fraction to Decimal

2. 1.1975
4. .375
6. .4
8. .4606
10. .8333
12. .9444
14. .4444
16. .4166
18. 1.619
20. .6666

Rounding Off Numbers

2. 29.4
4. 104.2
6. 11.5
8. 7.2
10. 50,914.7
12. 109.84
14. 39.87
16. 1.87
18. 77.33
20. .10
22. 27.004
24. 3.649
26. 1,698.049
28. 1.006
30. .327
32. 78
34. 1
36. 240
38. 58
40. 805
42. 6,000
44. 18,000
46. 40,000
48. 501,000
50. 869,000
52. 17.7 million

INTRODUCTION 373

54. 5.7 million
58. 1,000 million
56. 75.2 million
60. 2.6 million

Reducing Fractions

2. 49/75
6. 289/415
10. 13/81
4. 18/47
8. 1/5

Addition of Fractions

2. 1-39/98
6. 9
10. 20-49/80
14. 19-13/24
18. 24-31/45
4. 2-1/8
8. 7-1/3
12. 49-23/120
16. 18-257/630
20. 5-41/60

Subtraction of Fractions

2. 1-11/12
6. 1-8/15
10. 2-5/9
14. 5/72
18. 4-71/80
4. 3-118/135
8. 3-31/42
12. 2-1/15
16. 2-11/24
20. 1-5/12

Multiplication of Fractions

2. 12/73
6. 132-1/7
10. 65-67/72
14. 65-5/8
18. 26-3/5
4. 3-1/5
8. 8-2/3
12. 173-19/20
16. 147-1/35
20. 15-27/64

Division of Fractions

2. 1-3/32
6. 3/4
10. 1-1/7
14. 18
18. 50
4. 1-1/4
8. 2-97/104
12. 11/15
16. 29/39
20. 1-31/50

Aliquot Parts

2. Mrs. Jamieson's interest—$30,000 total value—$45,000
4. $126,000
6. 110-14/15
8. 148-11/16
10. 116

Converting Decimals to Percent

2. 50%
4. 145%
6. 35%
8. 90%
10. 63%
12. 40%
14. 83.2%
16. .32%
18. .037%
20. 55.55%
22. 8.57%
24. 26.79%
26. 38.56%
28. 30%
30. 3,038.5%

Converting Fractions to Percent

32. 20%
34. 33.33%
36. 12.5%
38. 62.5%
40. 8.33%
42. 125%
44. 366.67%
46. 197.06%
48. 3.06%
50. 5.24%
52. 16.46%
54. 88.89%
56. 81.4%
58. 90.48%
60. 18.75%

Converting Percents to Decimals

62. .284
64. 1.607
66. .9
68. .3828
70. .14378
72. .0008
74. .02
76. .00888
78. .00055
80. .00025

Rounding Off Percents (to hundredths)

- **82.** 103.46%
- **84.** 2.01%
- **86.** 75.61%

(to tenths)

- **88.** 47.0%
- **90.** 15.3%

(to units)

- **92.** 100%
- **94.** 86%
- **96.** 67%
- **98.** 39%
- **100.** 40%

Unit 2 Sample Examination
Basic Operations

Addition

- **2.** 3.56
- **4.** 5,137
- **6.** 11,917.81
- **8.** 4.2534
- **10.** $224

Subtraction

- **12.** 975.96
- **14.** .16021
- **16.** $29
- **18.** 920.9
- **20.** 1,992.31

Credit Balances

- **22.** −1.5246
- **24.** −11.8905
- **26.** −23,038
- **28.** −16.59
- **30.** −46.58

Addition and Subtraction

- **32.** 71.6295
- **34.** 17.29
- **36.** 1,141
- **38.** 20,318.95
- **40.** 2,448,816.62

Repeated Addition and Subtraction

- **42.** 111.42
- **44.** 5,018.78
- **46.** 6,316.463
- **48.** $63.96
- **50.** 418.84

Addition and Subtraction of Fractions

52. 26.6042 **54.** 22.0833
56. 4.0357 **58.** .6875
60. 9.2833

Subtotals

62. S 3.76 T 12.308 **64.** S 16,530.26 S 16,893.24
  T 17,024.46

Multiplication

66. 148.9418 **68.** 3,960.0284
70. 270,781 **72.** 14.2215
74. 388,206 **76.** 382,761.72
78. 172.416 **80.** 379.5825

Three-Factor Multiplication

82. 18.3524 **84.** 161,040
86. 41.4508 **88.** 15,497.1999
90. 1,662.4823

Division

92. 1.3420 **94.** 1.3676
96. .8148 **98.** 5.0321
100. .0125

Mixed Problems

102. 4.2920 **104.** 17.7552
106. 2.2 **108.** 3,131.31
110. 31.4438 **112.** 38.3457
114. 12.7577 **116.** 342.1217
118. 2.0005 **120.** 85.8864

Unit 3 Sample Examination
Percent Applications

Finding the Percentage of a Number

2. 1,311 **4.** 19

6. 5   **8.** 28

10. 229

Finding the Number if the Percent is Known

12. $114.29   **14.** 224

16. 170.48   **18.** 195.15

20. 56.18

Finding What Percent One Number is of Another

22. 82.86%   **24.** 89.75%

26. 68.81%   **28.** 112%

30. 81.30%

Percent of the Whole

32. 21.3%   **34.** 2.0%

36. 3.9%   **38.** 3.8%

40. 2.4%

Proration

42. $10,900   **44.** $7,150

46. $16,300   **48.** $8,800

50. $6,800

Percent of Increase or Decrease

52. −3.2%   **54.** +3.0%

56. +5.6%   **58.** +1.2%

60. −3.7%

Chain Discount

62. $10.40   **64.** $12.18

66. $23.69   **68.** $25.33

70. $6.33

Cash and Quantity Discounts

72. $22.28   **74.** $4,597.72

76. $1,554.56   **78.** $685.52

80. $1,785.66

Sales Taxes

82. $34.53
84. $464.08
86. $1,624.99
88. $132.78
90. $76.13

City Taxes

92. $.97
94. $1.26
96. $1.16
98. $.93
100. $1.45

Simple Interest

102. $10.28
104. $53.68
106. $1,363.40
108. $12.49
110. $24.51

Unit 4 Sample Examination Business Problems

Extensions

2. $6.75
4. $60.25
6. $59.04
8. $61.99

Simple Interest Problems

10. $21
12. 237
14. 425
16. 88
18. 181
20. 82
22. 9.1%
24. 12.0%
26. 12.0%
28. 5.0%
30. 7.5%

Compound Interest (without the table)

32. $205.03
34. $210.18
36. $215.47
38. $220.89

Compound Interest (with the table)

40. $450.60

Markon (on cost)

42. $1,680
44. $58.20
46. $168.75
48. $1,201.85
50. $129.83

Markon (on selling price)

52. $5.66
54. $7.16
56. $59.48
58. $50.99
60. $96.75

Markon Rate Based on Cost

62. 16.85%
64. 15.09%
66. 25.40%

Markon Rate Based on Selling Price

68. 21.47%
70. 53.61%
72. 17.11%

Percent of Selling Price

74. $56.25 68.97%
76. $52.00 71.43%

Markup Based on Selling Price

78. $4.20
80. $0.76
82. $0.65

Markdown

84. 10%

Sales Commission

86. $1,000
88. $860
90. $725

Payroll

92. $264.79

Salary Increases

94. $897

Insurance

96. $369.68

Banking

98. $22.80

100. $24,214.54

Unit 5 Sample Examination
Practical Problems

Installment Buying

2. 13.27%

4. cash $1,612.50; on time $2,184.00

6. 19.4%

8. 14.2%

10. 12.3%

12. $44.38

14. $42.10

16. $34.24

Real Estate

18. $7,350

20. $23,237.50

22. $23,750

Profit Margin

24. 20.8%

26. 9.8%

Stocks

28. 7.5%

30. 7.1%

32. $732.02

34. $2.36

36. 4.34:1

38. 1.61:1

Bonds

40. $241,250

42. $486,250

44. $3,281.25

46. $1,500

Depreciation

48. $850

50. $650

52. $1,740

54. $580

56. $455.76

58. $164.07

Unit Prices

60. $270.56

62. $6.65

Basic Statistics

64. $15,933.33

66. $18,200

68. $880.40

70. $6,011

72. $5,130
76. $6,329.50
74. $5,512.50
78. $4,598.33

Travel and Monetary Problems

80. 13.2
84. $159.25
88. $365.50
82. 15.0
86. $29.47
90. $10.71

Measure and Cost

92. $47.71

Inventory

94. $96.12
98. $28.44
102. $324
106. $61.92
110. $254.88
96. $42.84
100. $99.36
104. $144
108. $82.80
112. $54

Net Profit

114. $32,125

Unit 6 Sample Examination SI (Metrics)

Prefixes

2. 1,000
4. 1,000

Metric Weight

6. .384 kg
10. 25.2 kg
14. 64,700 g
18. 1.89 g
22. 4,100 cg
26. 2 g
30. 24,000.5 g
34. 1.4 cg
38. 37 t
8. .904 kg
12. 2,810 g
16. .97 g
20. .25 g
24. 5.2 cg
28. .42 g
32. 57.2 cg
36. 14.5 t
40. .0891 t

382 ANSWERS TO EVEN-NUMBERED PROBLEMS

42. 51,000 kg
44. 56 kg
46. 3,214 g
48. 904,780 g
50. 21,333.1 g
52. 36.9 t
54. 81.89 t
56. $0.0036 $0.0038
58. 14.131 kg
60. 2.3816 kg
62. 1.5426 kg
64. .144 m
66. 2,300 cm
68. 580 cm
70. 2.197 cm
72. 11.18 m
74. 1.444814 m
76. 102.32 m
78. 2.15 m
80. 11.024 m
82. 14.871 km
84. .0576 km
86. 8.15 km
88. 243.516 km
90. 8,704.2194 km
92. .904 km
94. .506 km
96. 1,627.6190 cm
98. 18.8889 cm
100. 417.6213 cm
102. 842.4 cm^2
104. 3.1946 cm^2
106. 259.982 m^2
108. 15.1119 m^2
110. 729.3008 m^2
112. 3.4 m^2
114. 40.1299 m^2
116. 1 hectare
118. 139.1465 hectares
120. 47.16539 hectares

Area Problems

122. 249.75 m^2

Volume

124. 31.561 ℓ
126. .0291 kl
128. 4,211.04 kl
130. .00061 kl
132. 82.75 m^3

English–Metric–English

134. 170.10 g
136. 340.19 g
138. 1,360.78 g or 1.36 kg
140. 2,540.12 g or 2.54 kg
142. 16.87 t
144. 33.2 oz. or 2.07 lb.
146. 45.72 cm
148. 7.32 m

150. 45.72 m
154. 5.95 km
158. 59.42 ℓ
162. 1.12 ℓ

152. 80.47 km
156. 1.42 ℓ
160. 1.89 ℓ
164. 3.55 ℓ

Temperatures

166. 3.9° C.
170. -7.2° C.
174. 50° F.

168. 93.3° C.
172. 102.2° F.

Unit 7 Sample Examination
Programmable Calculator

Addition
2. $425.32
4. 360.15186

Subtraction
6. 8.819
8. 33,884
10. 1,629.71

Addition and Subtraction
12. 116.20
14. 2.11

Repeated Addition and Subtraction
16. 171.678
18. 4.81
20. 113.4

Multiplication
22. 174,087
24. 1,470.3977

Division
26. 2,799.2363
28. .8571
30. 3.6975

Addition of Constants
32. 254.4
34. 64.477

Subtraction of Constants
36. 6.7
38. 173.5
40. 18,669.3

Multiplication of Constants

42. 12,070.279

44. 2,005,339.2

Constant Divisors

46. 28.4783

48. .8457

50. .0095

Percentage Problems

52. $21.66

54. $51.51

Discount and Sales Tax

56. $11.69

58. $13.36

60. $55.58

Finding the Percentage of a Number

62. $20.99

64. $61.08

Finding the Whole if the Percent is Given

66. $57.14

68. 103.7

70. 80.2

Markdown

72. 10.5%

74. 10.7%

Markup

76. 22.2%

78. 9.8%

80. 4.7%

Mixed Problems

82. 244.367

84. .611

Program—Compound Interest

86. $6,678.15

88. $13,593.54

90. $804.88

92. 8

94. 15.75

Program—Add-On Rate

96. $92.74; $169.37; 13.72%

98. $53.92; $234.62; 13.95%

100. $72.19; $31.94; 9.8%

Unit 8 Sample Examination
Ten-Key Adding Machine

Addition

2. 789.0052
4. 286,742
6. 62,054
8. 30.3
10. 12,346.31
12. $15,224.02
14. $68,630
16. $18,767
18. $164,110
20. $85,654

Subtraction

22. $187.46
24. $173.47
26. $155.74
28. $148.08
30. $143.69

Credit Balances

32. −.205
34. −4,556.42
36. −16.77
38. −10.62
40. −53,446

Non-Add

42. $49.42
44. $3.51

Multiplication

46. 183.77
48. 392.6064
50. 3,588
52. 5.4491
54. 5,597.28
56. 869.86
58. 2.1342
60. 382.6464

Markon

62. $41.69
64. $122.45
66. $0.40
68. $224.14
70. $12.25
72. $1.74
74. $396.57
76. $0.45
78. $15
80. $26

Division

82. 2	84. 1
86. 137	88. 11
90. 16	

Cost of Individual Items

92. $2.99	94. 8 cents
96. 5 cents	98. 14 cents
100. 2 cents	

Unit 9 Sample Examination
Ten-Key Printing Calculators

Addition

2. 3.466	4. 72.753
6. 43,525.842	8. 195.45

Subtotals

10. 201	12. 310

Subtraction

14. $1,247.24	16. $1,036.84
18. $995.89	20. $820.89
22. $750.63	

Credit Balances

24. -$421.58

Multiplication

26. 198,360	28. 88.621
30. .5446	32. 22.632
34. 3.4928	

Division

36. 1,584.4615	38. 194.2659
40. .4543	42. 3.9477
44. .8694	

Multiplication of a Percent

46.	1,575.97	48.	2,054
50.	5.6	52.	1,094.86

Finding What Percent One Number is of Another

54.	86.3%	56.	69.5%
58.	93.26%	60.	88.86%
62.	85.71%	64.	34.35%

Constant Multiplication

66.	$17.58	68.	$15.88
70.	$12.60	72.	$22.98
74.	$9.98	76.	$13.11

Markon

78.	12.1%	80.	18.5%
82.	11.1%	84.	16.7%
86.	9.8%	88.	2.7%

Markup

90.	18.5%	92.	23.8%
94.	10.3%	96.	16.7%
98.	7.5%	100.	12.0%

Markdown

102.	12.5%	104.	11.1%
106.	36.7%	108.	29.5%
110.	28.6%		

Unit 10 Sample Examination
Full-Bank Adding Machine

Addition

2.	6,056	4.	72,734
6.	343,322	8.	8,183.07
10.	102,349	12.	692
14.	773	16.	713

ANSWERS TO EVEN-NUMBERED PROBLEMS

18. 738
20. 771
22. 332
24. $1,008.03

Double Addition

26. 61 lb., 12 oz.
28. 17 yd., 7 in.
30. 67 yd.
32. 30 yd., 1 ft., 1/2 in.
34. 48 yd., 10 in.

Subtraction and Subtotals

36. $14,555.32
38. $12,092.06
40. $11,041.38
42. $9,430.08
44. $9,391.90

Credit Balances

46. $210.01
48. $615.17
50. -$26.71
52. -$15.92

Non-Add and Subtotals

54. $8,024
56. $14,316
58. $20,532
60. $31,314
62. $42,670

Multiplication

64. 214,176
66. 25.1638
68. 1,691.64
70. .3734
72. 231.5509
74. 423.156

Markdown

76. $79.15
78. $2.76
80. $27.49
82. $84.06
84. $16.31
86. $3.25

Division

88. 1.2
90. 6.1
92. .7
94. 43.1
96. 62 cents
98. 7.8; 166.7
100. 1.4

UNIT 1

(Answers given with problems)

UNIT 2
BASIC OPERATIONS

Addition

2.	440.87	4.	6,369
6.	1,090.1	8.	133.35
10.	27	12.	263.48
14.	4,716	16.	2,181.1
18.	83.42	20.	17.9
22.	359.68	24.	6,039
26.	2,643.95	28.	234.32
30.	46.9	32.	43,066
34.	54.40		

Subtraction

2.	1,976	4.	728.57
6.	493.43	8.	6,803.9
10.	36,367	12.	3,087
14.	630.46	16.	382.54
18.	5,703.9	20.	7,508
22.	2,087	24.	537.58
26.	281.65	28.	4,603.9
30.	18,485	32.	6,876
34.	728.57		

Credit Balances

2.	−56.97	4.	−9.2573
6.	−11.025	8.	−99.52
10.	−23.26	12.	−15,004
14.	−91.63	16.	−26.38

18. −15,015
20. −71.53
22. −29.51
24. −14,653
26. −44.51
28. −16,255
30. −471.98
32. −43.84
34. −13.0329

Addition and Subtraction

2. −484
4. 45.90
6. 738,821
8. 18,814
10. 31.01
12. −68
14. −25.884
16. 610
18. 7,318
20. 6.87
22. 128,583
24. 17.47
26. 9,518
28. 1,396
30. 3.9
32. 88,638
34. 39.9

Repeated Addition

2. 141.92
4. 378.396
6. 2,892.317
8. 3,589.30
10. 895.752
12. 179.69
14. 376.774
16. 3,522.739
18. 512.67
20. 1,500.074
22. 3,912.41
24. 758.59
26. 175.596
28. 92.5
30. 164.11
32. 466.62
34. 1,164.87

Repeated Subtraction

2. 8,630.132
4. 2,863
6. 2,725.77
8. 7,568.544
10. 3.66
12. 8,687.418
14. 9,651
16. 3,950.85

BASIC OPERATIONS 391

18. 283.59
22. 6,433.468
26. 4,751.16
30. 8.02
34. 13,187.89

20. 5.28
24. 933
28. 4,282.71
32. 1,867,987

Addition and Subtraction of Fractions

2. 194
6. 52.9167
10. 53.2083
14. 4.6876
18. 32.3333
22. .6785
26. 0
30. .2
34. −.625

4. 168.4584
8. 176.3959
12. 107.9375
16. 382.9375
20. 55.3959
24. .6972
28. .0417
32. −.1786

Subtotals

2. 6.5; 38.90
6. 8.1; 27.2
10. 4,125.61; 8,646.45
14. 56,647; 57,237
18. 147.82; 156.41
22. .393; .438

4. 265.56; 394.60
8. 149.63; 377.82
12. 102,210; 147,700
16. 432.48; 1,352.01
20. 61.34; 160.53
24. 3.37; 9.67

Multiplication

2. 6,460
6. .4746
10. 485.0976
14. 61,115
18. 35.0345
22. 28,544
26. .229

4. 9,869
8. 484.8072
12. 16,401
16. .1388
20. 52.1220
24. 78,720
28. 120.7

30. 83.979
32. 38,743
34. 15,827

Three-Factor Multiplication

2. 96.186
4. 21,364,614
6. 6,991.146
8. 384,954,645.7
10. .6061
12. 68,814.33
14. 312,196,500
16. 289,296
18. 4,840,685.5
20. 108,621.279
22. 22,822,957.443
24. 2,255,482.26
26. 35.8708
28. 268,783.8755
30. .5530
32. 267,031,710
34. 92,610

Division

2. 88.1836
4. 74.6018
6. 160.8129
8. 4,670.3333
10. 14.7851
12. 145.0813
14. 99.6253
16. 114.8008
18. 360.2482
20. 16.0576
22. 11.2836
24. 8.8118
26. 3.5662
28. .8853
30. 139.0682
32. 4.0182
34. 3.8770

Mixed Problems

2. 20.4771
4. 6.3284
6. 1,296.45
8. 3,003.88
10. 499.81
12. .1930
14. 3.4462
16. 11,245.36
18. 153.25
20. 8,868
22. −11,040
24. 99.96
26. 45.2241
28. 7.75

PERCENT APPLICATIONS

30. 1,416.22 **32.** 12,325
34. 4.88

UNIT 3
PERCENT APPLICATIONS

Finding the Percentage of a Number

2. 216   **4.** 1,386
6. 539   **8.** 2,618
10. 1,463   **12.** 1,828.13 1,921.88
14. 318   **16.** 4,017.61
18. 156.78   **20.** 29.02
22. 3.55   **24.** .45
26. 4.02   **28.** 999
30. 5.74   **32.** 2.66
34. .21

Finding the Number if the Percent is Known

2. $805.56   **4.** $642.86
6. $88.75   **8.** 1,846.15
10. 961   **12.** $65.56
14. 34   **16.** 106.17
18. 27.88   **20.** 5.83
22. 1,716.67   **24.** 226.09
26. 4,050   **28.** 25
30. 190.48   **32.** 376.79
34. 776.32

Finding What Percent One Number is of Another

2. 93.66%   **4.** 86.67%
6. 18.46%   **8.** 20.99%
10. 69.81%   **12.** 21.62%
14. 7.91%   **16.** 78.17%
18. 20.17%   **20.** 25.66%

22. 24.73%
24. 16.48%
26. 95.70%
28. 326.14%
30. 96.59%
32. 20.39%
34. 33.88%

Percent of the Whole

2. Total $565.20
   (a) 27.4%
   (b) 8.0%
   (c) 11.5%
   (d) 8.0%
   (e) 26.5%
   (f) 4.4%
   (g) 7.1%
   (h) 7.1%

4. Total $1,050.47
   (a) 26.7%
   (b) 14.5%
   (c) 15.2%
   (d) 5.4%
   (e) 11.5%
   (f) 3.8%
   (g) 6.5%
   (h) 5.7%
   (i) 3.6%
   (j) 7.1%

Proration

2. Total 8,103
   (a) 13.09% $117.81
   (b) 16.07% $144.63
   (c) 7.08% $63.72
   (d) 2.34% $21.06
   (e) 61.41% $552.69

4. Total $65,800,000
   (a) 15.96% $157,253.88
   (b) 18.69% $184,152.57
   (c) 37.39% $368,403.67
   (d) 27.96% $275,489.88

6. Total 9,253 (.1621)
   (a) $161.13
   (b) $303.29
   (c) $406.71
   (d) $240.88
   (e) $49.76
   (f) $65.16
   (g) $50.41
   (h) $17.34
   (i) $157.40
   (j) $47.82

Percentage of Increase or Decrease

2. $1,573 +12.7%
4. $116,177.10 +34.8%
6. $52,707 -8.5%
8. $916,794 -14.8%
10. $39,309 -4.8%
12. $463 +1.9%

PERCENT APPLICATIONS   395

14. $106,186.10 +19.1%
16. $41,707 -10.4%
18. $1,824,803 -30.9%
20. $40,087 -6.7%
22. $463 +1.3%
24. $106,187 +15.9%

Chain Discounts

2. $26.85
4. $191.73
6. $118.35
8. $162.49
10. $134.60
12. $16.56
14. $126.29
16. $116.49
18. $153.60
20. $63.06
22. $15.66
24. $61.88
26. $111.13
28. $149.45
30. $62.41
32. $26.96
34. $318.40

Cash Discounts

2. $4.48 $22.33
4. $156.35 $607.84
6. $15.31 $290.87
8. $87.72 $717.05
10. $2.50 $97.57
12. $29.75 $349.23
14. $886.50 $3,971.06
16. $40.93 $174.47
18. $3.52 $11.54
20. $3,849.66 $31,468.30
22. $9.81 $100.21
24. $10.67 $114.83
26. $4,427.99
28. $13.31
30. $15.44
32. $147.69
34. $329,794.71
36. $298.87
38. $34.37
40. $8,020.88
42. $16.88
44. $1,022.13
46. $2.39
48. $4.95
50. $79.05

Sales Taxes

2. $25.61 $665.89
4. $1.18 $20.82
6. $.25 $4.73
8. $6.18 $129.78

ANSWERS TO EVEN-NUMBERED PROBLEMS

10. $288.91 $5,104.11
12. $.28 $8.16
14. $6.91 $122.15
16. $1.39 $22.80
18. $4.01 $84.16
20. $1.22 $25.54
22. $2.20 $50.99
24. $.75 $13.17
26. $2.04
28. $160.04
30. $8,747.99
32. $3.33
34. $20.92
36. $62.19
38. $167.83
40. $954.36
42. $105.99
44. $107.25
46. $11.41
48. $43.30
50. $20.37

City Taxes

2. $.94
4. $1.36
6. $1.26
8. $1.58
10. $1.42
12. $85.01
14. $94.13
16. $39.62
18. $811.24
20. $195.93
22. $200.50
24. $472.67
26. $210.00
28. $135.63
30. $136.46
32. $62.00
34. $492.00
36. $65.04
38. $147.80
40. $338.28
42. $210.46
44. $46.71
46. $49.95
48. $262.50
50. $85.20

Simple Interest

2. $26.02
4. $14.77
6. $50.37
8. $1.04
10. $1.92
12. $3.26

14. $6.54
18. $26.14
22. $5.05
26. $22.97
30. $6,737.03
34. $21,228.82

16. $1,009.62
20. $33.60
24. $7,110.51
28. $25.93
32. $11.60

UNIT 4
BUSINESS PROBLEMS

Cost of Items

2. $93.84
6. $181,527.64
10. $47.64
14. $81,271
18. $5,970
22. $13,286.43
26. $3.80
30. $7.48
34. $6,566.67
38. $26.22

4. $4,939.14
8. $16.10
12. $3,491.70
16. $7.48
20. $91,200
24. $2,914.38
28. $34.56
32. $461.91
36. $306,470.70
40. $145.80

Extensions and Crossfooting

Example Travel Expense Report
    errors—horizontal:
    Taxi fare should be $11.50
    Local transportation should be $5.40
    Ambassador Hotel should be $65.72
    Breakfast should be $21.66
    Lunch should be $7.42
    Grand Total should be $447.46

42.

Horizontal	Vertical
$153.00	$212.20
153.00	96.67
7.50	48.14
7.50	56.55
8.65	163.25
4.95	
5.90	
120.60	
11.19	
22.65	
35.92	
14.00	
1.50	
5.45	
25.00	
$576.81	$576.81

44. (a) 288.88
(b) $2,534.38

Finding the Amount of Simple Interest

46. $111.56
48. $2.19
50. $195.94
52. 3 days
54. 273 days
56. 292 days

Interest—Finding the Rate

58. 6.0%
60. 16.0%
62. 3.1%

Compound Interest

64. $1,148.90
(rounded to penny each quarter)
66. $20,407.32
68. 7% yields most
$63.25; $73.76

Amount of Markon and Total Cost

70. $.32 $2.46
72. $279.15 $1,674.90
74. $1,888.59 $12,380.77
76. $20.62 $89.36
78. $3,950.26 $13,825.92
80. $9.21 $63.41
82. $.06 $.35
84. $10.65 $.79

BUSINESS PROBLEMS   399

86. $1,860.00 $660.00
88. $843.75 $218.75
90. $44.95 $179.80
92. $193.50 $1,096.50
94. $2.25 $6.74
96. $.33 $1.86
98. $162.00 $737.99
100. $30.99 $109.89
102. $111.98
104. $2,048.51
106. $61.61
108. $44.86
110. $30

Percent of Markon

112. $6.75;   56%
114. $4.15;   38%
116. $.54;   72%
118. $75;   23%
120. $375;   18%
122. $.55;   14.67%
124. $22;   10.05%
126. $27.49;   22.91%
128. $49;   25.93%
130. $1.18;   19.73%

Percent of Selling Price

132. 80%
134. 77%
136. 83%

Finding the Selling Price

138. $41.10
140. $641.03
142. $107.14
144. $28.11

Markup

146. $99.29 $400.16
148. $15.00 $74.98
150. $16.55 $84.09
152. $38.10 $342.88
154. $104.64 $685.95
156. $25.53
158. $705.41
160. $30.51
162. $822.45

Markdown

164. 10%
166. 12%
168. 10%
170. 13%
172. 14%
174. 24%

Sales Commission

176. $25.50
178. $300
180. $222.50

Payroll—Wages

182. $346.91
184. $254.53
186. $195
188. $67.50
190. $5.03
192. $136.20

Salary and Hourly Wages

194. $877.48
196. $124.33
198. $757.14

FICA

200. $51.19
202. $90.09
204. $34.57
206. $30.42
208. $27.96
210. $52.07
212. $50.60
214. $40.13
216. $40.60
218. $51.77

Payroll—Net Pay

220. $628.68
222. $1,078.66
224. $418.50
226. $379.23
228. $365.41
230. $645.30
232. $582.26
234. $515.04
236. $510.08
238. $586.45

Salary Increases

240. $574
242. $795
244. $919
246. $669
248. $1,173
250. $875

Insurance

252. 59.2%
254. 77.1%
256. 61.2%
258. $437.50
260. $264.12
262. $343

Long-Term Premiums

264. $112.50   **266.** $113.55

268. $951.64   **270.** $6,332.04

272. $96.39

Discounting Promissory Notes

274. November 2 $5,262.83   **276.** $746.61

278. $4,350.39

Checking Accounts

280. $24.04   **282.** $11.20

284. $12.85

Deposit Slips

Sample is correct.

286. $2,658.47

Reconciling Bank Balances

288. $150,277.24; yes.

UNIT 5
PRACTICAL PROBLEMS

Installment Buying

2. $10; $114.52; $14.53; 14.53%   **4.** $1,990.80; $190.80; 10.6%

6. $265.04 13.25%   **8.** $94

10. Yes–$392.50   **12.** Fosters is $2 less

Installment Loans

14. $2.50 14.5%   **16.** $98.40 20.2%

18. $71.50 $97.63   **20.** $30 $36.67

22. $267.19 $119.01

Real Estate

24. $613.50   **26.** $4,544

28. $2,090.74   **30.** $37,200

32. $350,000

Profit Margin

34. 31.2%

36. 9.9%

38. 11.6%

Stocks

40. 7.0%

42. 19.5%

44. $4,121.74

46. $4,282.14

48. $1.72

50. $2.55

52. $0.64

54. 1.52:1

56. 4.29:1

Bonds

58. $10,212.50

60. $1,952.50

62. $479,375

64. $5,750

66. $300

Depreciation

68. (a) $804.17
 (b) First year $1,378.57
  Second year 1,148.81
  Third year 919.05
  Fourth year 689.29
  Fifth year 459.52
  Sixth year 229.76
 (c) Leave decimal set at 5 with round off. Use .16667 as the rate.
  First year $1,775.04
  Second year 1,183.35
  Third year 788.89
  Fourth year 525.92
  Fifth year 350.61
  Sixth year 201.20

72. (a) $1,450
 (b) First year $2,806.45
  Second year 2,712.90
  Third year 2,619.35
  Fourth year 2,525.81
  Fifth year 2,432.26
  Sixth year 2,338.71

70. (a) $5,700
 (b) First year $10,857.14
  Second year 10,314.29
  Third year 9,771.43
  Fourth year 9,228.57
  Fifth year 8,685.71
  Sixth year 8,142.86
  Seventh year 7,600.00
  Eighth year 7,057.14
  Ninth year 6,514.29
  Tenth year 5,971.43
  Eleventh year 5,428.57
  Twelfth year 4,885.71
  Thirteenth year 4,342.86
  Fourteenth year 3,800.00
  Fifteenth year 3,257.14
  Sixteenth year 2,714.29
  Seventeenth year 2,171.43
  Eighteenth year 1,628.57
  Nineteenth year 1,085.71
  Twentieth year 542.86
 (c) First year $13,000
  Second year 11,700
  Third year 10,530

Seventh year	2,245.16	Fourth year	9,477
Eighth year	2,151.61	Fifth year	8,529.30
Ninth year	2,058.06	Sixth year	7,676.37
Tenth year	1,964.52	Seventh year	6,908.73
Eleventh year	1,870.97	Eighth year	6,217.86
Twelfth year	1,777.42	Ninth year	5,596.07
Thirteenth year	1,683.87	Tenth year	5,036.47
Fourteenth year	1,590.32	Eleventh year	4,532.82
Fifteenth year	1,496.77	Twelfth year	4,079.54
Sixteenth year	1,403.23	Thirteenth year	3,671.58
Seventeenth year	1,309.68	Fourteenth year	3,304.43
Eighteenth year	1,216.13	Fifteenth year	2,973.98
Nineteenth year	1,122.58	Sixteenth year	2,676.58
Twentieth year	1,029.03	Seventeenth year	2,408.93
Twenty-first year	935.48	Eighteenth year	2,168.03
Twenty-second year	841.94	Nineteenth year	1,951.23
Twenty-third year	748.39	Twentieth year	1,561.07
Twenty-fourth year	654.84		
Twenty-fifth year	561.29		
Twenty-sixth year	467.74		
Twenty-seventh year	374.19		
Twenty-eighth year	280.65		
Twenty-ninth year	187.10		
Thirtieth year	93.55		

(c) Use .03333.

First year	$3,333
Second year	3,110.82
Third year	2,903.45
Fourth year	2,709.91
Fifth year	2,529.27
Sixth year	2,360.67
Seventh year	2,203.30
Eighth year	2,056.43
Ninth year	1,919.35
Tenth year	1,791.41
Eleventh year	1,671.99

Twelfth year	1,560.54
Thirteenth year	1,456.51
Fourteenth year	1,359.42
Fifteenth year	1,268.80
Sixteenth year	1,184.22
Seventeenth year	1,105.28
Eighteenth year	1,031.60
Nineteenth year	962.84
Twentieth year	898.66
Twenty-first year	838.75
Twenty-second year	782.84
Twenty-third year	730.66
Twenty-fourth year	681.95
Twenty-fifth year	636.49
Twenty-sixth year	594.06
Twenty-seventh year	554.46
Twenty-eighth year	517.50
Twenty-ninth year	483.01
Thirtieth year	262.80 leaving scrap value of $6,500

Unit Prices

74. $11.28

76. $190.16

78. $302

80. $6.86

82. $30

84. $6.72

86. $3.67

Basic Statistics

88. $822.11; $839; $839

90. 6 ft., 4.4 in.; 6 ft., 4 in.

92. (a) $18,254.40
    (b) 16,607.40
    (c) 15,005.20

(d) 18,307
(e) 16,616.80
(f) 16,920.40
(g) 24,378
(h) 20,610.17
(i) 14,909.83
(j) 14,931.17
(k) 9,930.17
(l) 101,711.20

Travel

94. $13.36; 18.4
96. $38.24; 17.2
98. $37.57; 20.9
100. 43.1
102. 14.7
104. 11 cents
106. 10 cents

Monetary Exchange

108. $7
110. $10.50
112. $13.28
114. $19.92
116. $21.93
118. $47.30
120. $21.42

Measure and Cost

122. $47.71
124. 66; $541,200

Income Statements

126. $30,602
128. $39,690
130. $481,583

UNIT 6
INTERNATIONAL SYSTEM OF UNITS

Grams to Kilograms

2. .012 kg
4. .2836 kg
6. .013 kg
8. .029 kg
10. .756 kg
12. .042 kg
14. 3.046 kg
16. .259 kg
18. 12.704 kg
20. .3 kg

Kilograms to Grams

22. 30,960 g
24. 260 g
26. 60 g
28. .6 g
30. 14,970 g
32. 14,060 g
34. 540 g
36. 5.4 g
38. 526,970 g
40. 18,000 g

Centigrams to Grams

42. .1 g
44. 10 g
46. 619.34 g
48. .003 g
50. .033 g
52. 24 g
54. .24 g
56. 1,000 g
58. 2.91 g
60. .0002 g

Grams to Centigrams

62. 300 cg
64. 30,000 cg
66. 210 cg
68. 49.7 cg
70. 7 cg
72. .07 cg
74. 5,500 cg
76. 4,860 cg
78. 54.2 cg
80. 9.9 cg

Milligrams to Centigrams and Grams

82. 2,213 cg   22.13 g
84. 3.8 cg   .038 g
86. .2 cg   .002 g
88. 22.2 cg   .222 g
90. 2,222.2 cg   22.222 g
92. 222,222.2 cg   2,222.222 g
94. 47.6 cg   .476 g
96. 1.6 cg   .016 g
98. .06 cg   .0006 g
100. .0666 cg   .000666 g

Grams to Centigrams and Milligrams

102. 2,700 cg   27,000 mg
104. 270,000 cg   2,700,000 mg
106. 27 cg   270 mg
108. .27 cg   2.7 mg
110. 96,700 cg   967,000 mg
112. 500 cg   5,000 mg
114. 876 cg   8,760 mg
116. 7.68 cg   76.8 mg
118. 1,900 cg   19,000 mg
120. 290 cg   2,900 mg

Converting Kilograms to Metric Tons

122. 2.4 t
124. .024 t
126. .00024 t
128. 674 t
130. 359.707 t
132. .0831 t
134. .03155 t
136. .029 t
138. 1.69 t
140. 3.864 t

Converting Metric Tons to Kilograms

142. 24,000 kg
144. 240 kg
146. 2.5 kg
148. 26,897,000 kg
150. 43,000 kg
152. 820 kg
154. 47.3 kg
156. 4.1 kg
158. 36,800 kg
160. 19,600 kg

Metric Weight Problems

2. 16.8584 kg   16,858.4 g
4. 906.6264 kg   906,626.4 g
6. 34,293.1 kg   34.2931 t
8. 9,117.3 kg   9.1173 t
10. 21,718 kg   21.718 t
12. 1.545 g   1,545 mg
14. 1.207 g   1,207 mg
16. .01492 cents   .146 cents
18. .129 cents   .131 cents
20. .124 cents   .273 cents
22. 879 g   .879 kg
24. 60,229 g   60.229 kg
26. 3,912 kg   3.912 t
28. 846.4 kg   .8464 t
30. 11,882 kg   11.882 t
32. 14.6406 g   14,640.6 mg
34. 14 g   14,000 mg

Centimeters to Meters

2. .1224 m
4. .06 m
6. 6 m
8. 600 m
10. .086114 m

Meters to Centimeters

12. 2,000 cm
14. 20 cm
16. 2.03 cm
18. 3,755 cm
20. 8.694 cm

Millimeters to Centimeters

22. 1,000 cm
24. 10 cm
26. 976.1 cm
28. 38.97 cm
30. .0468 cm

Centimeters to Millimeters

32. 100 mm
34. 294 mm
36. 2,793 mm
38. 6.5 mm
40. 76 mm

Meters to Millimeters

42. 10,000 mm
44. 100 mm
46. 22.3 mm
48. 46,800 mm
50. 5,500 mm

Millimeters to Meters

52. 1 m
54. .1 m
56. 281.392 m
58. 4.201 m
60. .077945 m

Metric Length Problems

62. 17 m 24 cm
64. 21 m 72.1 cm
66. 8 m 63 cm
68. 1 m 51.4964 cm
70. 8 m 6.4 cm
72. 95 m 44 cm
74. 1 m 33.6 cm
76. 1,861 m 57.4 cm
78. 13 m 85.7 cm
80. 5 m 45 cm

Meters to Kilometers

82. 10 km
84. .1 km
86. 2.491 km
88. 2.40136 km
90. 3.6947 km

Kilometers to Meters

92. 10,000 m
94. 1,000,000 m
96. 290 m
98. 64 m
100. 99,400 m

Problems with Kilometers and Meters

102. 24 km 905 m or 24.905 km or 24,905 m
104. 10 km 244 m or 10.244 km or 10,244 m
106. 2 km 15 m or 2.015 km or 2,015 m
108. 40 km 411 m or 40.411 km or 40,411 m
110. 14 km 183 m or 14.183 km or 14,183 m
112. 1 km 609 m
114. 2 km 151 m
116. 2 km 498 m
118. 12 km 124.9 m
120. 1 km 150.6 m
122. 1.416 m
124. .4267 m
126. .3810 m
128. .6806 m
130. 1.4914 m

Area

2. 5.206 cm^2
4. .729 cm^2
6. 72.5 cm^2
8. 4.1325 cm^2
10. 1,409.4 cm^2
12. 429.2 m^2
14. 284.2 m^2
16. .36 m^2
18. 175.7754 m^2
20. 359.04 m^2
22. 4.901 m^2
24. 22,276.687 m^2
26. 96.4252 m^2
28. 666.4196 m^2
30. 12.71 m^2
32. 1.54 km^2
34. 32.897 km^2
36. 2,534.6 km^2
38. 119.6324 km^2
40. 44.1336 km^2
42. 2.5 m^2
44. 12.6942 m^2
46. 40.7583 m^2
48. 9.1765 m^2
50. 400.7601 m^2
52. 150,000 cm^2
54. 2,010,000 cm^2
56. 87,150,000 cm^2
58. 210,000 cm^2
60. 4,000 cm^2
62. 2.5 km^2
64. .025 km^2
66. .109643 km^2
68. 64.197555 km^2
70. .907544 km^2
72. 29,000,000 m^2

74. 50,000 m²
76. 57,400,000 m²
78. 1,549,800,000 m²
80. 109,304,000,000 m²

Ares and Hectares

82. 2 ares
84. .02
86. 279.55
88. 47,098.21
90. 265.1766
92. 10 hectares
94. 4.0329
96. .0209
98. 87.53297
100. 3.96031

Area Problems

102. 23.055 m² or 230,550 cm²
104. 3.745 m² or 37,450 cm²

Metric Volume

2. 2.5 ℓ
4. 464.011 ℓ
6. 24,398.114 ℓ
8. .046 ℓ
10. .91167 ℓ
12. 28,000 ml
14. 1,914,000 ml
16. 28,460 ml
18. 36,800 ml
20. 460 ml

Kiloliters to Liters

22. 2,600 ℓ
24. 18,400 ℓ
26. 3,046,000 ℓ
28. 306,400 ℓ
30. 60 ℓ

Liters to Kiloliters

32. .46 kl
34. .006 kl
36. .00045 kl
38. 307.557 kl
40. 8.0096 kl

Problems

42. 4.6 m³
44. 550 ℓ

English–Metric Conversions–Weight

2. 138.91 g
4. 623.69 g
6. 433.75 g
8. 14.17 g
10. 184.27 g
12. 106.31 g

14.	198.45 g	16.	510.29 g
18.	297.67 g	20.	113.40 g
22.	6.35 kg	24.	8.07 kg
26.	68.04 kg	28.	1.81 kg
30.	453.6 kg	32.	1.36 kg
34.	136.08 kg	36.	.34 kg
38.	2.5 kg	40.	41.1 kg
42.	13.25 t	44.	31.75 t
46.	1.36 t	48.	41.28 t
50.	14.52 t		

Metric–English Conversions—Weight

52.	12.002 oz.	54.	17.196 lb.
56.	5 lb., 4 oz. (2.381 kg)	58.	short tons $500 metric tons $496.04
60.	2 lb., 2 oz. (963 g)		

English–Metric Conversion—Length

62.	.635 cm	64.	65.405 cm
66.	15.24 cm	68.	.318 cm
70.	78.74 cm	72.	73.66 cm
74.	.953 cm	76.	4.445 cm
78.	32.385 cm	80.	66.675 cm
82.	.457 m	84.	1.753 m
86.	6.096 m	88.	5.588 m
90.	4.547 m	92.	1.143 m
94.	1.245 m	96.	1.854 m
98.	15.24 m	100.	60.96 m
102.	.610 m	104.	5.486 m
106.	91.44 m	108.	11.43 m
110.	914.4 m	112.	36.576 m
114.	18.288 by 54.864 m	116.	3.658 by 4.572 m

118.	25.084 m²	**120.**	167.225 m² 150.967 m²
			30 × 60 is larger
122.	6.437 km	**124.**	9.253 km
126.	23.496 km	**128.**	96.960 km
130.	160.930 km	**132.**	281.628 km
134.	804.650 km	**136.**	2,375.327 km
138.	.402 km	**140.**	.322 km

English–Metric Conversions—Volume

142.	1.42 ℓ	**144.**	2.839 ℓ
146.	6.625 ℓ	**148.**	73.925 ml
150.	118.280 ml	**152.**	5.678 ℓ
154.	23.183 ℓ	**156.**	9.701 ℓ
158.	.473 ℓ	**160.**	1.420 ℓ
162.	1.183 ℓ	**164.**	2.839 ℓ
166.	2.248 ℓ	**168.**	3.785 ℓ
170.	6.624 ℓ	**172.**	15.14 ℓ
174.	24.603 ℓ	**176.**	37.85 ℓ
178.	21.764 ℓ	**180.**	3.785 kℓ

The Celsius Thermometer

2.	93.3° C.	**4.**	48.9° C.
6.	37° C.	**8.**	27.8° C.
10.	23.9° C.	**12.**	19.4° C.
14.	15.6° C.	**16.**	10.6° C.
18.	5° C.	**20.**	0° C.
22.	−3.9° C.	**24.**	−8.3° C.
26.	−12.2° C.	**28.**	−15° C.
30.	−17.8° C.	**32.**	−23.3° C.
34.	−27.8° C.	**36.**	−33.3° C.
38.	−37.2° C.	**40.**	−45.6° C.

Celsius to Fahrenheit

42. 195.8° F.
44. 176° F.
46. 163.4° F.
48. 138.2° F.
50. 114.8° F.
52. 102.2° F.
54. 80.6° F.
56. 59° F.
58. 46.4° F.
60. 32° F.
62. 17.6° F.
64. 5° F.
66. –13° F.
68. –40° F.
70. –58° F.

UNIT 7
THE PROGRAMMABLE ELECTRONIC CALCULATOR

Addition

2. 354
4. 288
6. 303.56
8. 98,243.03
10. 317

Subtraction

2. 81.14
4. 1.97
6. 163.82
8. 207.49
10. 1,763

Addition and Subtraction

2. 23,536
4. 929.3636
6. 3,421
8. 501.88
10. 135,518.99

Repeated Addition and Subtraction

2. 819.55
4. 124.276
6. 4.23
8. 3.164
10. 111,933.87

Multiplication

2. 389.12
4. 416,673
6. 33.696
8. 7.743

ANSWERS TO EVEN-NUMBERED PROBLEMS

10. 662.76
12. 365.118
14. 25.344
16. 26,302.4
18. 41,106.48
20. 66,984.49

Division

2. 3,739.4450
4. 115.3784
6. 23.2844
8. 2.6118
10. 188.6850

Addition, Subtraction, Multiplication, and Division with Constants

2. 13.15
4. 87.49
6. 567.2
8. 17.17
10. 40.1
12. 5.658
14. 33.59
16. 973.78
18. 50.49
20. 38.80
22. 567.872
24. 16,326.32
26. 301.266
28. 149,209.2
30. 22.68
32. 24.4816
34. 10.1893
36. 57.3597
38. 8.1949
40. 36.9155

Percentage Problems

2. $496.80
4. $84.42
6. $120.82
8. $56.04
10. $6.05
12. $289.54
14. $175.75
16. 676.83
18. 31.51
20. 34.29
22. 22.73
24. 14,285.71
26. 13.79%
28. 14.46%
30. 18.75%
32. 11.09%
34. 20%

Mixed Problems

36. 67.092
38. 37.696
40. .277

Prerecorded Program – Compound Interest

With Future Value Unknown

2. $804.88
4. $6,678.15
6. $13,593.54
8. $51,407.74
10. $9,281.41
12. $60.78
14. $279.19
16. $22,427.78
18. $164.78
20. $51,314.17

With Number of Periods Unknown

22. 3.74
24. 5.37
26. 3.55
28. 14.21
30. 28.41

With Interest Rate Unknown

32. 7.5878%
34. 5.1990%
36. 7.7217%
38. 2.9034%
40. 6.1790%

With Present Value Unknown

42. $294.63
44. $1,288.89
46. $17,579.63
48. $1,212.57
50. $285.77

Add-On Rate Installment Loans

2. Monthly payment $398.24
   Total interest $278.88
   Annual int. rate 10.59%

4. Monthly payment $92.74
   Total interest $169.37
   Annual int. rate 13.72%

6. Monthly payment $25.66
   Total interest $70.85
   Annual int. rate 12.02%

8. Monthly payment $254.60
   Total interest $42.62
   Annual int. rate 7.78%

10. Monthly payment $53.76
    Total interest $51.39
    Annual int. rate 9.35%

12. Monthly payment $681.95
    Total interest $10,916.71
    Annual int. rate 12.85%

14. Monthly payment $344.09
    Total interest $47,482.37
    Annual int. rate 10.17%

16. Monthly payment $77.66
    Total interest $3.97
    Annual int. rate 8.90%

18. Monthly payment $21.96
    Total interest $22.58
    Annual int. rate 10.34%

20. Monthly payment $103.92
    Total interest $23.50
    Annual int. rate 13.06%

22. Monthly payment $91.89
    Total interest $154.00
    Annual int. rate 11.41%

24. Monthly payment $615.13
    Total interest $190.80
    Annual int. rate 17.30%

UNIT 8
TEN-KEY ADDING AND LISTING MACHINE

Addition

2. 316.46
4. 1,802
6. 1,023.14
8. 2.829
10. 8.129
12. 457.4212
14. 2,160.55
16. $265.50
18. $1,607.63
20. $23.9 million
22. $29,250
24. $5,015
26. $64,600
28. $670
30. $73,360

Subtraction

2. 2,475,149
4. 2,613.45
6. 7,045
8. 371.31
10. 211.31
12. 101,579.71
14. 2,198,584
16. 71.93
18. 1,387.74
20. 9,745,335
22. $3,017.34
24 $2,999.05
26. $2,516.96
28. $2,218.91
30. $1,218.29

Credit Balances

2. −23.28
4. −3,218.88
6. −645.74
8. −14.33
10. −3.84
12. −130.07
14. −.402
16. −596.98
18. −404.86122
20. −102.45

Subtotals

2. 2,111.30
   2,330.32

4. 9,464
   38,619

6. 121.72
   124.06

8. 8,803.63
   9,182.45

10. 8.952
    9.128

Multiplication

2. 1,259.95

4. 105,096

6. 249.40

8. 1.412787

10. 59,356

Markon

12. $22.76

14. $2.71

16. $66.10

18. $135.53

20. $.58

Division Problems

2. 51.395778

4. .31292391

6. 5.5351708

8. 14.85 cents (15 cents)

10. .8957 cents (.9 cent)

12. 2.7 cents (3 cents)

14. 13.375 cents (13 cents)

16. 17.22112 (17.2 square feet)

UNIT 9
TEN-KEY PRINTING CALCULATOR

Addition

2. 380.84

4. 1,892

6. 1,025.12

8. 2.829

10. 7.911

12. 845,120

14. 89,520

16. 68,260

18. 45,500

20. 319,890

22. 316,440

24. 356,600

Subtotals

2. 3,233.52
   3,463.63

4. 10,696
   40,962

ANSWERS TO EVEN-NUMBERED PROBLEMS

   6. 134.94
       138.39

  10. 11.174
      11.461

   8. 11,025.75
      11,515.68

Subtraction

   2. 2,474,139
   6. 8,035
  10. 311.31
  14. $2,592.30
  18. $2,532.53
  22. $2,435.04
  26. $2,208.34

   4. 1,613.55
   8. 362.31
  12. $2,867.60
  16. $2,565.13
  20. $2,499.30
  24. $2,213.04

Credit Balances

   2. −8.29
   6. −745.24
  10. −3.85
  14. −$77.10

   4. −4,218.88
   8. −4.33
  12. $821.69
  16. $130.27

Multiplication

   2. 2,257.84
   6. 372.6
  10. 122,450
  14. 222.1176

   4. 92,259
   8. 1.801176
  12. 293.715

Division

   2. 6,300.425
   6. 38.8064
  10. 80.6581
  14. .92963

   4. .4523272
   8. .8333
  12. 7.463

Multiplication of a Percent

   2. 4.758
   6. 46.41624

   4. 51.368
   8. 180.55851

10. 325.83775
12. 33.315242
14. 341.8056

Finding What Percent One Number is of Another

2. 24.83%
4. 461.53%
6. 97.69%
8. 19.23%
10. 75.29%
12. 109.2%
14. 481.25%

Constant Multiplication

2. $12.09
4. $16.69
6. $13.16
8. $19.29
10. $15.53
12. $2.94
14. $13.74
16. $12.33
18. $24.00
20. $9.39
22. $9.91
24. $14.53

Payroll

2. $149.27
4. $194.23
6. $118.09
8. $256.34
10. $185.26
12. $42.13
14. $163.54
16. $135.74
18. $234.81
20. $108.40
22. $107.83
24. $166.85

Markon

2. 29%
4. 10%
6. 9%
8. 50%
10. 22%
12. 23%
14. 41%

Markup

2. 16%
4. 11%
6. 13%
8. 9%

ANSWERS TO EVEN-NUMBERED PROBLEMS

10. 16%
12. 3%
14. 9%

Markdown

2. 16%
4. 25%
6. 15%
8. 14%
10. 33%
12. 50%
14. 33%

UNIT 10
FULL-BANK ADDING MACHINE

Addition

2. 362.65
4. 4,498
6. 505,559
8. 75,721.4047
10. 35,521.49393
12. 202.04
14. 767.98
16. 82,192
18. 2.311
20. 140.74
22. 108
24. 141
26. 625
28. 106
30. 119
32. 67
34. $2,661.91

Double Addition

2. 51 lb., 2.5 oz.
4. 58 lb., 12 oz.
6. 31 lb., 15 oz.
8. 34 ft., 1 in.
10. 34 ft., 3 in.

Subtraction

2. 1,992,387
4. 1,873.09
6. 6,642
8. 53.185
10. 241.03
12. $3,250.62
14. $1,916.14
16. $1,311.39
18. $1,079.88
20. $960.00
22. $857.03
24. $842.83

Credit Balances

2.	-$158.91	4.	$36.73
6.	-$63.23	8.	-$214.29
10.	$94.56	12.	$1,242.84
14.	-$1,169.02	16.	$196.41
18.	-111.03	20.	-43.36

Subtotals

2.	$37,454.10	4.	$40,583.18
6.	23	8.	87
10.	145		

Multiplication

2.	1,474.02	4.	76,128
6.	288.1	8.	2.948967
10.	349,680	12.	185.416
14.	196.8996	16.	405,812
18.	2,004.8	20.	4,200.235
22.	$47.18	24.	$4.64
26.	$26.02	28.	$400.00
30.	$.44		

Division

2.	128.6214	4.	.21911445
6.	15.9752736	8.	3.78784
10.	11.003516	12.	5.6661
14.	22 cents	16.	18.7 cents
18.	12.5	20.	62.5 cents

Glossary

Addend A number to be added.

Aliquot part Any number that can be divided evenly into another number; e.g., 5 is an aliquot part of 100.

Are An area 10 meters wide by 10 meters long (pronounced "air").

Bond A certificate of indebtedness.

C Per hundred.

Cancel To divide a number into a numerator and a denominator in a group of fractions that are to be multiplied.

Celsius thermometer Shows the freezing point of water at $0°$ C. and the boiling point of water at $100°$ C.

Centigram One-hundredth of a gram.

Centiliter One-hundredth of a liter.

Centimeter One-hundredth of a meter.

Chain discount A series of discounts, one to be applied on the net balance resulting from the previous discount.

Check register A record of checks written on an account, and showing a running balance.

Complement The difference between a number and the next power of ten. The complement of 7 is 3; the complement of 80 is 20.

Constant A value that remains the same in a series of problems.

Credit balance The balance which results when minus amounts are greater than plus amounts.

Denominator Shows the number of parts into which the whole is divided; e.g., in 2/3, the whole is divided into three parts.

Deposit slip A record of money deposited in a bank account.

Depreciation Allocating the cost of an asset over its period of life.

Difference The answer in a subtraction problem; the difference between the minuend and the subtrahend. Sometimes called the remainder.

Digit A single number from 0 to 9.

Dividend (a) In a division problem, the number that is to be divided. (b) Money or other value paid to stockholders.

Divisor In a division problem the number that is to be divided into the dividend.

FICA The Social Security tax paid by the employer and the employee to provide for benefits.

Fraction One or more parts of a whole number; e.g., 1/4, 3/8.

Gram .0353 ounce.

Gross One hundred and forty-four.

Gross pay Pay earned before deductions.

Hectare An area 100 meters wide by 100 meters long.

Improper fraction One in which the numerator is larger than the denominator; e.g., 8/5.

Installment loan A loan which is repaid in partial payments over a period of time.

Interest, compound Interest which is paid on both the principal and the accumulated interest.

Interest, simple The amount that is paid or charged for the use of money.

Kilogram One thousand grams.

Kiloliter One thousand liters.

Kilometer One thousand meters.

Liter 1.0567 liquid quarts.

Lowest common denominator (LCD) The smallest denominator into which all the denominators in a problem can be divided evenly.

Markdown Lowering the regular selling price of an item for a special sale, for damaged goods, etc.

Markon The amount added by retailers to the cost price.

Markup Usually defined as the amount added to the selling price of an item; sometimes used to mean the amount added to the cost price.

Mean An average; the mean is found by adding the individual values and dividing the sum by the number of values.

Median An average; the midpoint in an array of values.

Memory An additional register or registers on some models of electronic calculators and other business machines, used to accumulate, store, and recall products, quotients, or sums.

Meter 39.37 inches.

Metric ton One thousand kilograms or 2,204.6 pounds.

Milligram One-thousandth of a gram.

Milliliter One-thousandth of a liter.

Millimeter One-thousandth of a meter.

Minuend The number to be subtracted from.

Mixed number Contains a whole number and a fraction; e.g., 4-3/7.

Mode The value occurring most frequently in an array of values.

Multiplicand The number to be multiplied.

Multiplier The number by which the multiplicand is multiplied.

Net pay Pay after deductions.

Non-add feature The capability of many office machines to print a reference number on the tape without that number being included in the calculations.

Numerator Shows the number of parts; e.g., in 2/3, the number of parts is 2.

Percent A part of the whole based on 100.

Premium Payments on insurance policies.

Prime number One that can be divided evenly only by itself or by 1; e.g., 7.

Principal The amount of money borrowed or lent.

Product The answer in a multiplication problem.

Promissory note A promise to pay a certain amount of money.

Proper fraction One in which the numerator is smaller than the denominator; e.g., 2/3.

Proration The proportional division of an amount.

Quire Twenty-four.

Quotient The answer in a division problem.

Ream Five hundred sheets of paper.

Reciprocal The number 1 divided by the number. For example, the reciprocal of 4 is $1 \div 4$ or 1/4 or .25.

SI The International System of Units (metrics).

Stock A certificate that shows ownership in a company.

Subtotal The amount accumulated thus far in the computation. Printing or displaying a subtotal does not clear the machine of the amounts entered.

Subtrahend The number to be subtracted from the minuend.

Sum The answer in an addition problem.

Touch method Using correct fingering to enter figures on the ten-key keyboard by touch without looking at the keyboard.

Transposition The accidental reversing of digits; e.g., copying 427 instead of 472.